HOW TO READ
BETTER
AND
FASTER

BY THE AUTHOR

30 Days To a More Powerful Vocabulary
(In collaboration with Wilfred Funk)

How To Read Better and Faster

Word Power Made Easy

Rapid Vocabulary Builder

How To Get More Out of Your Reading

20 Days To Better Spelling

Better English

HOW TO READ
BETTER
AND
FASTER

NORMAN LEWIS

Third Edition
Completely Revised

Thomas Y. Crowell Company   •   *New York*

TO

Mary,
Margie,
and
Debbie

Prefaces are often cavalierly ignored.
Since this one contains important infor-
mation on a time schedule for your train-
ing, it should be read before you turn to
Chapter 1.

PREFACE

TO THE THIRD EDITION

How to Read Better and Faster is a step-by-step, day-by-day training manual in the techniques of rapid and skillful reading. As such,
it is intended for careful study, intensive and exciting learning, and
immediate, practical application.

It is a manual designed for the person who wishes to become a
faster and much more efficient reader than he is today and who is
willing to spend time and creative effort toward attaining his goal;
it is planned for anyone who has a good capacity for learning and
can work enthusiastically on an immensely rewarding project. For
such a person, the training offered in these pages can produce remarkable results—not because this book pretends in any way to be
remarkable, but because sound training in the techniques of efficient
reading is a remarkable and dynamic process, a process that actually
works, a process that unfailingly shows remarkable results in a
comparatively short period of time. With sound training it really
is possible to increase your general reading rate by 25 to 100 per
cent and simultaneously sharpen your comprehension. It is possible
because few people, without some degree of training or self-training,
ever read at the high level of skill and speed that their innate
capacities make easily attainable.

Because this is a training manual, it will be calculatedly repetitious, in the same way that any good classroom or clinic teacher
is repetitious—like such a teacher, it will pound and pound and
pound at the important principles, hammer and hammer at the
significant points, offer specimen after specimen for study, review

vii

and review and re-review, until it is certain that you have *over-learned*, i.e., have learned so completely that the correct reactions come reflexively, almost automatically; it will call for practice and more practice and still more practice, until it is assured that your learning has been driven deep into the lower levels of consciousness and has caused an actual and measurable change in your patterns of thinking and response.

Such learning requires time as well as calculated frequency of repetition. How much time? You can, of course, read through the *information* in this book in a few evenings—but to get the maximum degree of *training*, you should plan to cover the material in a number of successive periods of spaced learning.

How you space this learning will depend on your personal circumstances, and on the amount of free time you have, or can make, during your typical week. An ideal and most effective schedule, and one that I hope you will find it possible to follow, is to devote about an hour every day, or almost every day, to your work. I have divided the twelve chapters of the book into thirty sessions, each of which will require anywhere from 45–60 minutes of study and practice. This is a reasonable and realistic program that will not unduly interfere with your other activities or with your professional, required, or leisure-time reading. Operating under such a schedule, if you cover five sessions of material a week, you will finish your training in about a month and a half.

Perhaps you will prefer to cover more ground each time, or you may feel so stimulated at the indicated end of a session that you will want to go right on with the next session. By staying with your training for as much as two hours at a time, five days a week, you can complete the course in well under a month.

On the other hand, if you find it possible to work on your training only two or three days a week, one session each day, it will be about three to four months before you turn the last page. This, too, is a good schedule and one that will produce excellent results.

In any event, bear in mind that your total training should take *no more than four months;* that short, *frequent* sessions, especially when you feel fresh, result in the best learning; and that the important thing is to decide on a reasonable and convenient schedule and then to follow that schedule methodically, even religiously.

Now, before you turn to chapter 1, glance at the table of contents in order to get a feeling for what the broad outlines of your training will be, for what this book has to offer you in the way of improved reading habits. Note the emphasis on comprehension, on efficient techniques, on retention and recall, on perception training, and on vocabulary study. Glance, too, at the tables of reading selections in order to get an idea of the type of instructional materials with which you will be working for the next few weeks or months. And, finally, flip through the pages and notice the abundance of drills, practice devices, comprehension exercises, summaries, and reviews, all aimed at assuring you of a successful and productive learning experience, all devised for effecting a permanent increase in the efficiency, skill, and speed of your reading performance.

This third edition represents a thorough revision, for the second time, of a book originally published in 1944, and which has sold over 175,000 copies. The general approach of the first two editions has of course been retained, as has everything else that has proved valuable. Some material, however, has been eliminated, and a great deal of new material has been added, including fresh techniques and teaching devices, and a considerable amount of comprehension training. As a result, the present work is, I believe, vastly improved over the previous editions.

NORMAN LEWIS

CONTENTS

Chapter 7   How to Read with Aggressive Comprehension

(Sessions 14–19, in which you become more adept at recognizing an author's pattern of thinking, continue your practice in speeding up your comprehension, and learn a new technique for increasing the usability of your peripheral vision)

Chapter 8   How to Skim

(Sessions 20–22, in which you get intensive instruction in skimming, learning how, when, and why to use the technique; and are challenged to read a complete issue of your favorite magazine in a single evening)

xv

Table of Rapid Comprehension Exercises

Table of Rapid Perception Selections

Table of Selections for Skimming

HOW TO READ FASTER
THAN YOU NOW DO

Preview

If you are the average untrained reader, there is one central fact you must face at the outset.

And that is—*you read altogether too slowly.*

At this very moment, on this very page, you are reading more slowly than you should read—more slowly than you need to read for good comprehension—and, most important of all, *much more slowly than you are actually capable of reading.*

Your lack of speed—still assuming that you are the average untrained reader—results chiefly from three factors:

1. *bad habits* that you have built up through years of the wrong kind of practice;

2. *unaggressive techniques of comprehension* that interfere with total concentration and stand in the way of your responding to a page of print as rapidly and as actively as your potential ability makes possible; and

3. *poor techniques of perception* that cause an unnecessary time-lag between the *act of seeing* and the *mental interpretation* of what you see.

You read slowly, in short, not because you're a poor reader, but because you're an inefficient reader.

In this chapter you will learn:

- What a short period of intensive training in efficient reading techniques can do for your speed and comprehension.

1

- How similar training in adult and college reading clinics has increased the speed of thousands of students.
- What your *present* reading rate is on material of average difficulty.
- What your *potential* rate is on such material.
- How to apply six important rules for making your *potential* rate comfortable and habitual.

Chapter 1 will demonstrate that you are capable of reading 20 to 50 per cent faster than you now do.

★ SESSION 1

WHAT TRAINING CAN DO FOR YOU

Look at it this way:

If, within a short period of time, you could boost your general reading rate by at least 20 per cent, very likely by up to 50 or 60 per cent—

If, with continued and earnest application, you could eventually almost double your permanent speed—

If you could learn to strip a page down to its essentials without wasted time or effort—

If you could build up efficient habits of knifing cleanly and quickly through the words and details of material, straight to the main ideas and important points—

If you could accomplish all this after only a few months of stimulating practice—

Would it be worth trying?

Or look at it this way:

2

You now read, let us say for the sake of argument, ten books a year—

If you could finish twenty or more without spending one extra minute on your reading—

If, through more aggressive comprehension and greater perception skill, you could learn to cover an average-length book in an evening or two of solid concentration—

If, through the same means, you could learn to whip through your daily newspaper or favorite magazine in half the time you now take without missing anything of importance—

If you could develop the power of responding more actively to *everything* you read—

And if, as a result, you discovered such new or heightened pleasures in the printed page that you found yourself turning more and more frequently to reading as a rewarding leisure-time activity—

Would all that be worth a few months of serious effort?

Or take some other possibilities:

You are a business executive, and scores of papers come to your desk each day: reports, trade journals, minutes of meetings, clippings pertinent to the affairs of your firm. Each must be read, quickly but accurately; it is important, perhaps crucial, that you be able to glance through a page for a few seconds and pull out the essential points, the main ideas. You can't go slowly; in a busy day there simply isn't time to examine every word, to ponder every detail. You know that you must develop the ability to push through material at top speed.

Or you are a lawyer, an accountant, a tax expert, an engineer, a scientist, an editor, a proofreader. During your professional day you must read slowly, carefully, word by word in some instances, because every syllable, every punctuation mark, every subtle implication has to be studied and examined. And so you have built up habits of careful, minutely analytical, snail-paced reading, with infinite attention to minor details. The result? Your reading at the office or plant is efficient enough—efficient for the type of reading you are required to do professionally. But when you try to do reading of another sort, light, general reading purely for enjoyment and relaxation, you find (naturally enough) that your office habits have spread over into your personal life, and it takes you an hour to cover a long magazine article, a month or more to finish a novel. You note this phenomenon first with surprise, then with increasing annoyance, for you are getting practically no reading done after working hours.

Or you are a high school or college student, and in the time it takes you to absorb a few pages in a textbook your classmates are able to cover a whole chapter. Despite the hours of study you devote to your subjects, you're falling behind. And you begin to suspect the reason: your reading is too slow, too poky, too time-consuming, too inefficient.

Now—

Whether the circumstances of your life—because you are an executive, a professional person, or a student—require you to get *more* reading done in *less* time—

Or whether you have become aware that many of your friends or associates read much faster than you do, and with equally good— or often better—comprehension and retention—

Or whether you have simply begun to feel an uneasy sense of inadequacy in your day-to-day performance, and are disturbed by a growing realization that you are reading less than you used to, or less than you would like to, or less than you ought to—

If you were convinced that a few months of systematic and intensive training could materially increase the efficiency and speed of your reading, would you consider it time well spent?

You are now holding in your hands a book that aims to help you achieve all the goals catalogued above—a book that offers you the step-by-step training and practice which can make you a far better, far more efficient, far more rapid reader than you are today.

But merely *reading* this book is not enough.

You must *use* it, you must *work* with it—intensively, faithfully, honestly.

You must not skip one single page.

You must not let anything stop you from enthusiastically and methodically completing your job from beginning to end.

And most important, you must be willing to devote time and effort.

If you go through this book conscientiously, you have weeks and months of hard work ahead of you. Hard, but stimulating and encouraging from the start—for every small skill you master will

4

effect a noticeable change in your reading performance. *And when you have completed the last session of your training you will find that you have learned to cruise through print at a rate of speed, and with an effortless efficiency, that you might once have thought hardly possible.*

WHAT TRAINING HAS DONE FOR OTHERS

Is there any reason for feeling confident that efficiency, skill, and speed can be increased in a comparatively short time?

There are many reasons—and all of them are backed up by scientific findings, by laboratory results. That a person of normal intelligence can learn to read better and faster is not a theory; it is a fact.

It is a fact which has been established in the reading clinics of hundreds of colleges and adult education centers throughout the country. Here are a few random but representative examples:

At the University of Florida, as reported by John A. Broxson in the *Peabody Journal of Education*, 175 adults took a three-month reading course, meeting once a week for a four-hour session. The group was composed of business men and women, teachers, lawyers, ministers, a newspaperman, housewives, clubwomen, and two superintendents of schools. At the start of the course, 111 students were reading at the rate of 115 to 210 words per minute, or no better than seventh-grade primary-school level. Twelve weeks later almost all had shown spectacular improvement, 52 out of these 111 slowest readers sailing along at a rate of 295 to 325 words per minute—high school and college level. While only 20 per cent of the 175 adults had been able to read at college speed before training, over 40 per cent could do so before the course was over.

Another example: Dr. Robert M. Bear, director of the reading clinic at Dartmouth College, reports:

> In the ten years that we have been helping Dartmouth students improve their reading, I have seen few freshmen who read nearly as rapidly and efficiently as they should—and could after a little training. Year after year, our reading classes start off at an average of around 230 words per minute, and finish up a few weeks later at around 500 words per minute.

A third and fourth example: at Purdue University, a pilot training program was offered to 307 entering freshmen, and by the fifteenth week, as reported by Professors Russell Cosper and Barriss Mills in the *Journal of Higher Education*, members of this group had increased their speed by 62 per cent. Another group of 282 freshmen, similar in general and reading abilities to those enrolled in training, but pursuing only the regular course of study, made a gain of but 9 per cent over the same period. Professors Cosper and Mills draw these very significant conclusions from a comparison of training and nontraining:

> In general, results seemed to show that reading ability improves very slowly, if at all, in the conventional course of study. . . . By working directly on reading skill, it is possible to increase decidedly the rate at which a student can grasp the content of the printed page.

Through its Extension Center, Purdue offered a training course to industrial executives whose plants were located in the area. One group, ranging in age from 31–41, increased in average speed from 245 to 470 words per minute—a gain of over 90 per cent. A class of older executives, in the 46–58 age group, started at 256 words per minute and completed training with a speed of 414 words per minute—a gain of approximately 60 per cent. Age may play some part in slowing down the *rate* of improvement after the middle years are reached, but is apparently no bar to healthy gains—notice that the adults well beyond their prime came within 2 per cent of the achievement made by the Purdue freshmen.

Professor Ernest W. Kinne, to whose article in *College English* I am indebted for the above statistics, remarks:

> . . . one may conclude that the older adults responded somewhat more slowly in gains in speed, but had a slight advantage in comprehension. . . . On the whole, the adults compare very favorably with the average performance of the younger students, belying the old saw about teaching an old dog new tricks.

And a final example: at the Adult Reading Laboratory of the City College of New York, a group of fourteen students, at the end of a twelve-week training period in faster reading, recorded an average arithmetic gain in speed of 69.1 per cent. Notice some of the radical improvements in rate in the chart below.

6

	START OF COURSE		END OF COURSE	
STUDENT	Rate (Words per Minute)	Compre- hension (%)	Rate (Words per Minute)	Compre- hension (%)
A	237	100	360	100
B	400	100	675	100
C	325	100	540	100
D	289	85	540	100
E	237	92	540	90
F	217	95	337	95
G	260	100	386	100
H	237	95	540	100
I	217	80	337	90
J	434	100	600	100
K	325	100	514	100
L	237	90	416	100
M	237	60	360	80
N	306	100	540	100

Reports from college and adult reading clinics underline two facts:

1. The average person reads unnecessarily slowly and inefficiently.

2. After a comparatively short period of intensive training, such a reader can sharpen his comprehension skill, can increase his over-all efficiency, and can, as a result, add considerably to his speed.

HOW FAST DO YOU NOW READ?

Day by day, as your training progresses, we shall be on the alert to detect the changes in your reading performance. Individually, these changes may be slight, but they will be perceptible; they may be gradual, but they will be cumulative. And eventually they will add up to broad and sweeping alterations in basic habits, approach, and methods.

You will be in unending competition, as you move through your work, not with others, but with yourself, with your previous self as a reader. In what ways are you reading better today than you did yesterday? How much faster do you now cruise through print than you did last week? With how much more skill and assurance do you attack your twentieth reading selection than you did your first, or fifth, or tenth, or fifteenth? How many more books did you read this month than last?

In order to make these comparisons, we will keep continuous statistics on the rate of your reading and the efficiency of your comprehension. We will set up, one after another, specific goals for you to reach, and measure how successfully you have reached them. And throughout, as you gradually perfect your technique, increase your skill, and build up speed, you will set new personal records of performance—and then immediately attempt to beat them.

A Test of Your Present Reading Speed

Our first step, then, is to test your present performance so that we may establish a yardstick with which to measure your improvement, a criterion by which to judge your progress.

In taking this test, function as you normally do, reading for the kind of comprehension you are accustomed to, and in the same manner in which you generally cover any material of similar type *—avoid, as much as possible, any consciousness of a test situation.*

Start your timing at the first black arrow; when you reach the second arrow, note, in the appropriate blank, the exact number of minutes and seconds you required to finish the selection. The table for computing your present rate will be found on page 11, directly after the comprehension test.

Selection 1

SPEAKING OF BOOKS
by J. Donald Adams

Start timing→ One of this depart-ment's readers has a theory about the appeal of mystery stories which seems to me worthy of a little

From *The New York Times* Book Review. Reprinted with permission of the author.

thought. As I turned it over in my mind it occurred to me that possibly my correspondent's suggestion might apply equally well to Westerns, to spy stories and to tales of adventure in general. Her idea is that the popularity of the mystery story may in part be accounted for by the simple fact that in such tales, "justice inevitably triumphs, the wicked are punished, the character with whom the reader is usually bound up is on the side of the angels—all in terms, actually, of the fairy tales most of us absorbed in earliest childhood, as well as in terms of what many of us have come to believe ultimately happens, although not in external circumstance, to 'actual living beings.'"

Do I hear a snort of impatience from the inveterate addicts of the "whodunit"? Do I hear them loudly insist that the sport of reading mysteries lies wholly in matching your wits against those of the author, that the appeal of the detective story is solely that of solving a jigsaw puzzle, plus a few hours' blessed release from tomorrow's problems? I'm not so sure that such protestations are entirely correct.

My correspondent would not argue, I feel sure, and neither shall I, that her theory constitutes anything like a full explanation. But there seems to me little doubt that the characteristics to which she calls attention do play a part in swelling the ranks of mystery story readers. That the appeal of these characteristics is not peculiar to the mystery story is amply proved by the fact that many, if not most, of its addicts will not touch a Western or an adventure story with a ten-foot pole. They would rather, if matters came to a show-down, be caught reading "How to Win Friends and Influence People," or the Elsie books.

Well and good; the fact remains that, as any case-hardened devotee of books beginning with the figure slumped in a library chair will confess, if the author succeeds in enlisting his sympathy or his admiration for a character whom he is led mistakenly to suspect as the guilty person, our addict feels himself outraged and betrayed. But when that sinister, cruel-lipped elderly man with the strange scar on his temple turns out to have been the wielder of that curiously wrought Eastern knife with which the dead man's throat was cut from ear to ear, our "whodunit" fan sighs happily and snaps off the bedside light. Evil has been smelled out, and the demands of a just world have been satisfied.

Personally, I feel some trepidation in discussing the whys and wherefores of mystery fiction, because, although I have read a fair amount of the best in the field, I am by no means qualified to offer myself as a tried and true fan; most of my reading in that blood-stained category has been done in those infrequent periods when I have been confined to my bed. Of Sherlock Holmes in the days of his prime I make an exception—but then, isn't there Sherlock Holmes,

9

and after him all other detectives; Professor Moriarity, and after him all other diabolic master-minds?

Incidentally, may such an obvious impostor as myself put forth one or two apologetic queries on this sacred ground? I wonder sometimes, for example, why the man from Scotland Yard, or the chief of our homicide bureau at home, must always be presented as having the mental agility of my old friend Zip, whose egg-shaped cranium used to bob above the crowd as it circulated below the platforms of the freaks in the basement of Madison Square Garden. Wouldn't it be possible, just *once*, for the brilliant young attorney, or the debonair young man about town, or the eccentric young Egyptologist, who is always ready at the drop of a hat to forsake his ordinary pursuits and confound those dumb professionals with his cleverness, to be himself the butt of our derision and contempt?

And must the young female who always accompanies the amateur criminologist on his self-appointed rounds be such an adoring nit-wit? Mr. Holmes, it seems to me, whose affairs are not unadorned with personable young women, ordered these matters better, and kept such dear young creatures as he introduced from getting under the feet of the Master.

But no more of these plaintive protests. My correspondent would agree, I think, that besides the triumph of justice and the punishment of the wicked, besides the pleasure of exercising his wits and forgetting his troubles, the mystery reader is held also by the strange fascination which violence in any form has for the human race; the particular appeal which the sadistic and the horrible seem to have for so many people in our time; and the participation in events which lie outside the ordinary round of living. Some or all of these make up, in each reader's case, the appeal of the mystery story.   ←End timing

RECORD HERE THE TIME REQUIRED ON THIS SELECTION: _____ MIN. _____ SEC.

Test Your Comprehension

Which *one* of the following statements most accurately summarizes the *main idea* of the selection you have just finished?

1. Most mystery story readers do not care for adventure books.
2. The appeal of the mystery story lies in the chance it gives a reader to see wickedness punished; to exercise his wits in the solution of a puzzle; to participate vicariously in acts of violence; and to escape from the humdrum patterns of his own living.
3. The popularity of the mystery yarn is due primarily to the opportunity it gives the reader to solve a sort of jig-saw puzzle.

4. Justice always catches up with wrongdoers in mystery and adventure stories.

5. The characters in mystery and detective stories run too much to a pattern.

Key: The answer is given in somewhat cryptic form so that you will not inadvertently discover the correct response before making your own choice. The number of the statement which best summarizes the main idea can be found by subtracting six from seven and adding one.

Compute Your Rate

(Approximate number of words: 850)

TIME	WORDS PER MIN.	TIME	WORDS PER MIN.
1 min.	850	3 min., 45 sec.	227
1 min., 15 sec.	680	4 min.	213
1 min., 30 sec.	567	4 min., 15 sec.	200
1 min., 45 sec.	486	4 min., 30 sec.	189
2 min.	425	4 min., 45 sec.	179
2 min., 15 sec.	378	5 min.	170
2 min., 30 sec.	340	5 min., 15 sec.	162
2 min., 45 sec.	309	5 min., 30 sec.	155
3 min.	283	5 min., 45 sec.	148
3 min., 15 sec.	261	6 min.	142
3 min., 30 sec.	243		

YOUR PRESENT RATE OF READING: _____W.P.M.

Record Your Statistics

We now have a base figure by which to gauge your improvement as you gradually build up your speed, selection by selection and chapter by chapter. Record this figure on the chart on page 392; on the graph below the chart plot your first statistic by marking a heavy dot in the appropriate place on the line labeled *Selection 1.*

As you glance at page 392, you will notice that it contains room for information on selections 1–6 only; when filled in, this first chart and graph will be a quick pictorial representation of your progress during the preliminary period of training—a period in which you will be doing a good deal of new learning; wrestling with, and attempting to use, a variety of new and perhaps unfamiliar techniques; making a start at breaking down comfortable,

11

old, less efficient habits, and replacing them with new and much more efficient ones.

At this point you are probably curious as to how your present rate measures up to the average. The average untrained reader, the typical student beginning his work at any of the adult or college reading clinics spread through the country, invariably covers material pitched on the level of Mr. Adams' article at a rate of 200–250 w.p.m.—he would need anywhere from $3\frac{1}{4}$ to $4\frac{1}{4}$ minutes to read this selection with what he considers adequate comprehension. On the other hand, if our theoretical reader is somewhat above average, if he has learned to perform at, or close to, college level, he would go considerably faster, in the neighborhood of 325–350 w.p.m., so that he would have finished in about $2\frac{1}{2}$ minutes. (Both rates, of course, merely indicate what a certain type of reader *does*, not by any means what he is *capable of doing*.)

Your rate may be, probably is, somewhere between average and college speed. Or it may possibly be slower, even very much slower, than average; or, on the contrary, a good distance beyond college level. Actually, while such comparisons are interesting, they are of no great moment. You read as you read—good, bad, or indifferent, your present rate is roughly whatever this test has indicated. What will be far more interesting, and of far greater significance, as we go on, is how much your rate increases over that of your initial performance—for the extent of the increase will indicate how successfully you are capitalizing on your latent capacities. The comparisons that will interest us most, bear in mind, are those between your later and your earlier performances, between how you function at any given time and how you functioned days or weeks or months previously.

PROOF THAT YOU CAN READ FASTER

I have indicated that *the average untrained person reads much more slowly than he is actually capable of reading.*

Term after term, during the years that I supervised the courses at the Adult Reading Laboratory of City College, I would demonstrate the truth of this statement to my students.

12

Let me ask you to imagine yourself taking part in a typical first meeting of one of these courses. So that you can get the full flavor of what invariably occurred, I shall use the present tense in explaining the procedure we followed and in describing the general reactions of the students.

We start by testing the class on material of about the same length and level of difficulty as the J. Donald Adams article on which you timed yourself in the previous section.

"Read this selection," I say, "exactly as you always read. Pretend you are at home in your favorite easy chair. Just read."

And I time the performance with a stop watch, noting the passage of every fifteen seconds on the blackboard.

The great bulk of the class reads at approximately 200–250 words per minute—the average speed of the untrained adult, *but also the normal reading rate of eighth-grade elementary school pupils.* This result may sound shocking, but the fact is that most adults considerably cut down their reading—especially their reading of books—after leaving school, and for that reason among others their speed drops back from the high school and college level of 295–350 words per minute to elementary-school speed.

The rate of only a few students falls considerably above or below the average. Three or four read at college level (325–350 w.p.m.) or better; one or two, abnormally slow, bumble along at 125–175 words per minute, the same rate at which children of ten or eleven go through the class readers of the fourth and fifth grades.

These adults have come to my class because they are troubled and unhappy about their reading. Slow reading, they realize, is awkward, unsatisfying reading. They see their friends cover the same ground in half the time and with more enjoyment and better retention; and they hope that after a few months of training they can at least make a start at catching up with these speedier readers.

After my students have examined their first statistics and are properly chagrined to learn that they are reading no faster than children in the middle and upper grades of elementary school, they invariably ask the obvious question: "Can we increase our speed by the end of the course?"

"You can do better than that," I answer. "You can increase your speed tonight—before you leave this classroom."

I then pass out to them a second selection of about the same length and difficulty as the first one on which they have been tested.

"Now," I say, "understand this about yourselves. The probability is very great that you are reading slowly partly because you have developed lazy habits. You are unwilling to jog your minds. You find that you can *comfortably* react to the message of print at a certain speed—a comparatively low speed, as you've discovered tonight. You have got into the habit of sauntering leisurely along a mental countryside when you should push along briskly and with a purpose—the purpose of finding the *meat* of an author's ideas in the quickest possible time. You occasionally stop and admire the intellectual scenery, you sometimes retrace your steps to make sure you've seen *everything* instead of pushing ahead with the exclusive desire of getting an over-all view. The result? You read at elementary school speed.

"I am going to let you prove to yourselves that you can do better —much better.

"When the signal is given, jump right into this new selection, follow the main thread of the ideas, keep going at a consciously fast pace. Feel that you're going *fast*, but not so fast, of course, that comprehension is lost. You may miss the full flavor or meaning of certain words, or of occasional sentences. No matter. Keep right on pushing. Try it as an experiment and see what happens. Remember—the idea is to get the main thought of the selection quickly."

I then give the signal and they start to read. If you could watch these people now, you would see an actual *physical* change in them. They are visibly alert—they have mobilized themselves for reading—and it is apparent that they are now concentrating far better than at their first attempt, when they were reading normally, overrelaxed. Now they are working at reading. You can see that they are immersed—totally immersed—in the material; there is an air of concentration about them that was conspicuously absent a few minutes before. As you will shortly discover for yourself when you train to speed up your own reading, it is impossible *not* to have sharper concentration when you consciously read for faster understanding of main ideas, when you purposefully sweep through material looking for the essential points of an author's thinking.

14

After the second test is over, we again gather statistics. When I say to you that my students are astonished, I am making an understatement. Some of them find their new results almost unbelievable.

Those students who read the first selection at 200–250 words per minute get through the second piece in the neighborhood of 300 words per minute—an immediate improvement of 20–50 per cent. The few faster readers also show marked improvement; to use the words of one of these students some years back, it is as if "we had suddenly dropped our shackles." These 325–350-w.p.m. readers discover that they are able, if they really try, to attain a rate of close to 450 w.p.m., a good, efficient, cruising speed. And the one or two very slow readers have also caught fire—they have stopped reading *words* and have begun to look for *ideas*, and the change is clearly reflected in their increased rate.

My students are now convinced that they have the *ability* to perform faster. All they need to do from that point on is practice reading in such a way that the *ability to perform* becomes *habitual performance*.

You, too, have the ability to read much faster if you fall (as you probably do) in the vast average group of 200–250-word-per-minute readers or in the smaller, more select, group of 325–350-word-per-minute readers.

The next few pages will convince you.

Directly below you will find another article by J. Donald Adams, a piece similar in style, difficulty, and length to the one on which you have determined your present reading speed.

While the *material* will be similar, your *attitude* must be very different as you read. Aim to understand the ideas more quickly by mobilizing yourself for quick reading. Get the thoughts *fast*, do not get bogged down in details; just follow the main thread. If occasionally a word eludes you, or a thought is somewhat fuzzy, keep plowing right through nonetheless. Read under slight speed pressure and with a purpose—the purpose of getting the main thought quickly. Get in, get the thought, and get out. Do not read words; rather, absorb *thoughts, ideas*. Move along rapidly, but of course do not lose comprehension, for your primary purpose in all reading is understanding, not speed. But you will be attempting to

15

discover whether you cannot, eventually, be a much faster reader than you are today. Again, time yourself in minutes and seconds.

A Test of Your Potential Reading Speed

Read the following selection through rapidly, aiming at a quick understanding of the central theme.

Selection 2

SPEAKING OF BOOKS
by J. Donald Adams

Start timing→ Much water has gone under the bridge since sedate listings were the norm of publishers' advertising. We have to look sharp these days to make sure whether it is a brassiere or a book we are being urged to buy. I, for one, grow quite bewildered whenever I turn an eye—or is it an ear?—to the hucksters' crying of their literary wares, and I often wonder whether I've wandered into the wrong department. Here is a copy-writer who signals for my attention by asking: "Do you get up in the morning almost as tired as you were the night before? Do you often have to drag yourself through your day's work?" Just as my eye is prepared to find the name of a new patent medicine, it falls somewhere on the word "book," and I discover that I am being invited to buy a volume on how to relax.

Or, finding myself confronted by a line of large and bold-faced type reading "What a woman!" and under it a half-page picture of an equally bold-faced damsel, I am about to look for the name of the theatre where this new super-colossal drama is to open when I discover that this lady is expected to take her place as "one of the unforgettable women of fiction."

Such experiences have become so frequent as to be no longer novel, but the other day I saw an ad which made me realize that we are indeed on or over the threshold of momentous change. On the cover of Publishers' Weekly was a picture of a highly photogenic young woman, and under it the words, "Her novel is the book the entire trade has been waiting for." Nothing strange or new about that; her picture had appeared there before when "Forever Amber" was about to be published. My realization that I was standing on my head came when I turned the page.

From *The New York Times* Book Review. Reprinted with permission of the author.

16

There, on the double-spread advertising Miss Kathleen Winsor's new novel, the picture was repeated in smaller size, and under it were these significant words: "The recurrent theme of all our advertising will be this striking new photograph of the author." It was that word "theme" that shook me to my gizzard. The recurrent theme of all advertising would not be what Miss Winsor's novel was about, or even merely that this was the new work by the author of "Forever Amber." It would be simply the pleasing contours of Miss Winsor's physiognomy.

Surely the handwriting on the wall is plain. The sober prophets who have been proclaiming that we were about to enter a new literary era were speaking more truly than they knew—but for very different reasons than those which they had offered. Here was in the making the literary revolution to end all literary revolutions. The whole basis of literary appreciation for the reader, all the sage advice that has been spoken or written about literary apprenticeship— these are being swept relentlessly into the discard. Henceforth the bedeviled publisher need ask but one question of the aspiring author: "How well do you photograph?"— provided, of course, that there is any visible reason for asking the question at all.

This impending upheaval must necessarily deal a deathblow to the schools of creative writing which have been springing up all over the country. It should bring comfort and reassurance to those sour-visaged and sour-minded pessimists who protest from time to time, "But you can't teach anybody to write." And while the schools will go under, their loss should be the beauty parlors' gain.

There are, it seems to me, quite unexplored avenues along which this new development may take us. If you insist on being logical about the significance of this revolution in book advertising, you must take the position, I suppose, that the use of the author's picture as a recurrent theme is merely a means of halting the wayward reader and causing him to read the accompanying text. Well, then, isn't there more than one way of skinning this particular cat? What's wrong with a publisher discovering an author with a face that would stop a clock, and using that as a recurrent theme? After all, pretty faces are a dime a dozen these days, and they have been displayed to the point of surfeit both on the screen and in the ads. Why not strike a fresh and startling note?

Rightly or wrongly, the craving for novelty is generally held to be one of the touchstones for the understanding of American character. I am willing to wager a complete set of the Elsie Dinsmore books against a single copy of "Star Money" to prove that a face which is the ultimate in ugliness, if used as a recurrent theme, will halt more readers in their tracks than will the repetition of fare, however

17

pleasant, for which our appetite has become a little jaded. Whether that suggestion is adopted or not, it should be apparent to the least concerned reader that a new day is at hand, and that what it will bring us no man knows.   ←End timing

RECORD HERE THE TIME REQUIRED ON THIS SELECTION: _____ MIN. _____ SEC.

Test Your Comprehension

Check the main idea:

1. An ugly face would attract more attention to an ad than a beautiful one.
2. Book publishers are experimenting with new and startling developments in advertising—and Mr. Adams isn't very enthusiastic about them.
3. An author's picture is more important than the title of his or her book.
4. If an author does not photograph well, his or her book will not be successful.

Key: Subtract four from six to determine the number of the correct answer.

Compute Your Rate

(*Approximate number of words: 945*)

TIME	W.P.M.	TIME	W.P.M.
1 min., 30 sec.	628	3 min.	314
1 min., 45 sec.	528	3 min., 30 sec.	264
2 min.	471	4 min.	237
2 min., 30 sec.	376	4 min., 30 sec.	210

YOUR POTENTIAL READING RATE: _____W.P.M.
(*Record this statistic on the chart and graph on page 392.*)
GAIN OVER SELECTION 1 (*page 11*): _____W.P.M.

You have probably proved to yourself, as a result of these tests, that you can read faster—at least 20 to 50 per cent faster.

But, you may be thinking, "It was far from comfortable, and I was not quite as sure of my comprehension as I usually am."

You're right, completely—on both counts. An average, slow reader cannot become a rapid, efficient reader overnight—even

18

though a start in the right direction can be made within five minutes, as you have already discovered for yourself. Your training and practice, from this point on, will aim to make a much faster rate just as comfortable as a slow rate, will aim to make your comprehension far more assured, far more efficient than it is today.

SIX RULES FOR FASTER COMPREHENSION

One of the important goals of your training is to transform your *potential* speed into a normal, comfortable, habitual speed.

To achieve this goal, you will, throughout this book, be constantly and repeatedly asked, encouraged, urged, and expected to follow —you will be prodded, cajoled, and at times even shamed into following—these important rules for improving your reading:

1. *Read more.*

You will have to read much, much more than you are now in the habit of reading. If you're a slow reader, you very likely do little more than go through the daily papers and a few light magazines. You read whenever you happen to have a few spare minutes, you read merely to pass time. Or perhaps you hardly ever read at all unless you absolutely have to.

From now on, *you must make time for reading.* My students always allocated, during their training, at least three evenings every week, and at least two full, continuous hours during those evenings, to the reading of books. Speed can be developed into a permanent habit only if you do what naturally fast and skillful readers have always done, from childhood on: read a lot. That means at least a full book every week; that means several evenings of concentrated reading every week. Unless you develop the habit of reading for two hours or more at a stretch, several stretches every week, do not expect ever to become an efficient or a rapid reader. (But as reading becomes gradually more rewarding and more meaningful and less like a chore, this requirement will turn out to be a lot easier and considerably less taxing than it may sound to you at this moment.)

2. *Learn to read for main ideas.*

Stop wasting time and effort on details. When you read an article, push through efficiently for a quick recognition of the main idea

19

that the details support and illustrate; be more interested in the writer's basic thinking than in his minor points.

When you read a volume of nonfiction, be intent on getting the theme, the broad ideas, the framework on which the author has built his book. Don't let an occasionally perplexing paragraph, page, or chapter slow you up. Keep speeding through. As the complete picture is filled in by rapid over-all reading, the few puzzling details will either turn out to have been inconsequential or will be cleared up as you move along.

When you read a short story or novel, follow the thread of the plot, consciously look for and find the "conflict," skim whenever you feel impelled to—don't meander in poky fashion from word to word and sentence to sentence.

3. *Challenge your comprehension.*

Fast readers are good readers. They're fast because they have learned to understand print quickly, and they understand quickly because they give themselves constant practice in understanding. To this end, they read challenging material; and you must do the same. Does a novel sound deep; does a book of nonfiction seem difficult; does an article in a magazine look as if it will require more thinking than you feel prepared to do? Then that's the type of reading that will give you the most valuable training. You will never become a better reader by limiting yourself to easy reading—you cannot grow intellectually by pampering yourself. Ask yourself: Do I know more about myself and the rest of the world, as a result of my reading, than I did five years ago? If your honest answer is no, then you'd better get started, today, on a more challenging type of reading than you've been accustomed to.

4. *Budget your time.*

Say to yourself: I have this book and I want to finish it by tomorrow night. And then get into it. If you know that you must finish half the book tonight and the other half by tomorrow, you'll speed up, because you'll have to. You'll develop tricks of getting ahead, of skimming parts that are less essential, of looking for main ideas, of reading at your top potential rate. The good reader always has a feeling of going fast, but he's never uncomfortable, for he has developed fast habits. Indeed, after a while, an adult who trains himself to read rapidly will find his original slow pace uncomfortable.

Or say to yourself: I am going to finish this magazine, complete, getting what I want out of it, in two hours. And, such is the adaptability of the human mind under pressure, you *will* finish it in two hours. It is amazing what people can do if they really try. Why not put yourself to the test?

While you are training with this book, give yourself a time limit on whatever you read—and live up to that time limit. In this way you will mobilize yourself for reading as an intellectual pursuit, and only in this way will you train yourself to understand at your highest potential rate.

5. *Pace yourself.*

When you start a new book, read for quick understanding for fifteen minutes. Count the number of pages you've finished in that time, multiply by four, and you have your potential speed for that book in pages per hour. (Of course, some books are slower reading than others—it takes more time to cover fifty pages in a Kinsey report than in *Forever Amber*, though they deal with somewhat the same subject. The more solidly packed the ideas are on a page, the more time it will take to cover that page. But throughout a given book, all the material will likely be on the same level.) Keep to the rate you've set for yourself in pages per hour.

By this means, you will learn to devise personal tricks that will speed you up and that will, at the same time, sharpen your comprehension skill. But you must practice every day, or nearly every day, if you wish to make high speed comfortable and automatic, if you wish to become efficient in quicker understanding.

6. *Develop habits of immediate concentration.*

Nothing makes concentration so easy, so immediate, as the technique of sweeping through material purposefully looking for main ideas and broad concepts.

Every person of normal intelligence can concentrate when he reads, but slow readers put themselves at a disadvantage. If, through laziness, you read at a slower rate than the rate at which you are able to comprehend, there is great temptation for your mind to wander. The brightest child in a class is not always the best student. If the work is too easy for him, he becomes bored and stops paying attention. This is a perfect analogy to explain why a slow reader picks up a book or magazine, goes through a few pages, and, finding his attention wandering, puts it down and turns to something else. By reading always at your top comprehension speed, you constantly challenge your understanding, you stimulate your mind, you get involved in the author's thoughts without half trying. And, as an added dividend, you soon find that the increased concentration you get from speedy reading sharpens your understanding and enjoyment, for every distracting thought is pushed out of your mind.

But reading *about* the principles of efficient and rapid reading is not going to make you a faster or better reader. Only putting those principles *into practice*, over a period of time, can do that for you. How long will it take? That depends on what sort of person you are and how assiduously you apply yourself. Under prime conditions, habits of speed and aggressive comprehension can become automatic after a few months of daily, or almost daily, practice. This is not theory—students in adult and college reading clinics prove it a fact term after term.

And when, as a result of your training, you find yourself not only doing much more reading than ever before, but also getting much more out of your reading, you will agree that it was time and effort well spent.

The important thing is that you now know, from actual self-testing, that you have the ability to read faster than you generally do. The training that lies ahead will show you how to capitalize on this ability, will help you make habitual and comfortable the rapid rate, and the quick and self-assured grasp of main ideas, that characterize the efficient reader. Exercise by exercise, drill by drill, selection after selection, you will learn to eliminate the faulty habits and inefficient techniques that interfere with total concentration, that slow up your comprehension, that keep your rate of reading down to a much lower level than you are potentially capable of achieving.

CHAPTER 2

HOW TO READ FOR MAIN IDEAS *

Preview

You have discovered that you are capable of reading faster if you make a real effort and if you concentrate on looking for main ideas. Now your training moves into high gear, and in this chapter you will learn:

• The conspicuous differences between the performance of the rapid, efficient reader and that of the slow, inefficient reader.
• How to push through a selection briskly, pursuing the gist of an author's communication.
• How to distinguish subordinate details from main ideas.
• How to sense the structure of a piece of writing.
• How well you remember what you read.

In *Chapter 2* you practice intensively on four selections, trying to apply aggressive techniques that will speed up your comprehension.

---

* Throughout the book, the terms *main idea, central theme, central thought, main point,* etc. will be used interchangeably and with identical meaning.

HOW EFFICIENT IS YOUR READING?

The distinction between an efficient and an inefficient reader is so definite and clear-cut that we can graphically chart the differences in two contrasting columns. Think of your own reading habits and techniques as you examine the following chart. In which column do you most frequently see yourself mirrored? Take a pencil and check off your characteristics as you meet them.

THE INEFFICIENT READER	THE EFFICIENT READER
Reads slowly, generally 250 words a minute or less. *Check here if you think this applies to you.* ☑	Has a cruising rate of at least 400 to 500 words a minute. *Check here if you think this applies to you.* ☐
Reads all material, of whatever type or difficulty, at an unvarying rate. ☑	Varies his rate according to the type of material—goes faster on easier material, on narrative stretches, on paragraphs of supporting details, etc. Suits his speed to what he wants to get out of material. ☐
Reads word by word or, in extreme cases, syllable by syllable. ☑	Reads for ideas, is rarely conscious of individual words. Skims or skips unimportant words, paragraphs, sections, or even whole chapters. ☐
Makes many "regressions"—that is, *rereads* syllables, words, or phrases to assure himself that he has seen and understood them correctly. ☑	Has few, if any, regressions—his perception is accurate, fast, dependable, and so nearly unconscious that he can concentrate on meaning rather than on separate words. ☐

24

THE INEFFICIENT READER	THE EFFICIENT READER
Moves his eyes eight to a dozen times or more to cover the average line of print. ☑	Covers the average line of print in three to five eye movements. ☐
May "vocalize," i.e., sound words out with his lips, tongue, or vocal cords, thus keeping his speed down to his rate of oral reading and seriously interfering with smooth comprehension; or he may be excessively dependent on "inner speech," i.e., on hearing the sounds of the words he is reading. ☑	Reads silently in the literal sense of the word—his lips, tongue, and vocal cords are motionless, and he is far more aware of meaning than of sound. ☐
Often gets bogged down in details and subordinate elements at the sacrifice of a clear awareness of salient concepts and important overall ideas. ☐	Pushes briskly through details to grasp main ideas. Is more interested in the basic thinking that shapes an author's writing than in minor points or background information. ☐
Reads passively, sentence after sentence, without any understanding of either the material as a whole or of the relationship of the parts. ☑	Reads with aggressive comprehension, thinking along with the author, interpreting the purpose and function of the broad sections of material, and searching always for the final and total meaning of any piece of writing. ☐
Concentrates imperfectly. Because he is not deeply and actively involved in what he is reading, he is easily distracted by irrelevant thoughts, by external noises, or by the happenings around him. As a result, his retention and recall are poor. ☑	Concentrates immediately and perfectly—becomes so involved with the ideas on a page that he temporarily loses contact with the outside world. Has, in consequence, excellent retention and recall. ☐
Fatigues easily, because reading is —for him—a slow, unrewarding, even a tedious, process. Spends only as much time with books as is absolutely necessary. ☐	Reads for hours at a time without becoming tired. Can—and usually does—complete an entire novel or magazine in a single sitting. ☐

What has brought the inefficient reader to his sorry state? How account for the effortless skill of the efficient reader? Part (but only part) of the answer to these questions can be given in the phrase "perception speed." The inefficient reader has built up and thoroughly refined a set of incorrect eye habits, and by continuous repetition has developed these habits to such a point that they act as an impediment to smooth and rapid reading.

But perception is, keep in mind, only part of the answer.

An equally important part of the answer can be given in the phrase "intellectual habits."

The inefficient reader is often *overconscientious,* to use the term in a special sense. He methodically reads every word in a selection, giving equal weight and time to *all* words, to every single word, no matter how relatively unimportant, instead of using words as a means of grasping the author's ideas.

The inefficient reader doesn't quite trust the adequacy of his comprehension. He reads meticulously, digesting and redigesting every sentence, every paragraph. Paradoxically enough, not only his speed suffers as a result of such extreme care, but his comprehension also, for he gets so involved in details and relatively unimportant minor points that he often misses the main theme of the writing. He is an excellent example of the man who can't see the forest because of the thickness of the trees. If he is reading a book, he may struggle mightily to master every page, down to the last comma and semicolon, and may nevertheless fail to understand the over-all ideas and implications of the chapter. In short, the inefficient reader strives too hard to be perfect in his grasp of every word, every phrase, every detail, instead of pushing through swiftly to follow the basic concepts.

Therefore, he often regresses. Having no confidence in his comprehension, he goes back to check on figures, minor points, statistics, bits of description whose only purpose is to lend atmosphere—and the regressions cut his train of thought, make him overconscious of words, ruin his concentration, break the smoothness of his absorption of ideas, and, of course, wreck his speed. He has never trained himself to plow straight ahead as fast as his understanding makes potentially possible. He has simply never learned to develop the habit of moving along rapidly.

In addition, there are certain other factors.

26

The efficient reader has so large a vocabulary that the words he meets are quick conveyors of thought. The vocabulary of the inefficient reader, on the other hand, is so limited that many of the words he encounters represent a mystery to be puzzled out before ideas can be fully grasped and appreciated.

The efficient reader has already read so much that he can constantly compare and contrast his present reading with his previous literary experiences; he has a background on which to build. The inefficient reader too often has to approach every little bit of reading as a new and unrelated experience.

The efficient reader has developed a strong intellectual curiosity; and all the reading he does helps in some measure to satisfy that curiosity. The inefficient reader's intellectual curiosity has gradually grown weaker because reading has never been a sufficiently comfortable or rapid process to make the satisfaction of his curiosity worth the effort.

If you suspect that you are not normally as efficient, as rapid, or as responsive a reader as you would like to be, let me tell you this—without qualification. The good habits needed for fast and skillful reading can be developed in a comparatively short time. You can train the speed and accuracy of your visual perception; you can learn to attack material with the kind of aggressiveness that will sharpen your concentration and increase your rate of comprehension; you can learn to eliminate regressions, to by-pass your vocal apparatus, to decrease your dependency on inner speech, and to avoid poky attention to minor details—you can, with the proper practice and guidance, learn to plow ahead, speedily absorbing the main ideas, getting the over-all picture. You can start building your vocabulary and stimulating your intellectual curiosity. *And as a result, you will, in all likelihood, make tremendous gains in speed.* Not the kind of forced gain you discovered from your work in the previous chapter, but a permanent, comfortable, habitual gain that will come from radically improved habits and techniques of reading.

You can do all this if you actively *will* it instead of merely *wishing* for it. What is the difference between *willing* and *wishing* in learning? As Dr. James L. Mursell, Professor of Education at Teachers College, Columbia University, explains it in *Streamline Your Mind* (J. B. Lippincott Co.):

The *wish* to learn is diffuse and general. The *will* to learn is concentrated and specific. The wish to learn means that we repeat a thing again and again hoping for something to happen. The will to learn means that we dig down and analyze, that we try to find out exactly what is wrong and exactly how to put it right. Let us take an analogy. A man may have a wish for better physical health and strength. His wish for health becomes a will to health only when he finds out what he must do to become more healthy, and then does it. So the will to learn means an intelligent and persistent search for the conditions of improvement and an intelligent and persistent concentration upon them.

Canny words, those, and important words—words that should condition your entire attitude toward increasing your reading efficiency. And every page in this book aims to help you "dig down and analyze"; aims to help you "find out exactly what is wrong and exactly how to put it right"; aims to show you how you can succeed in your "intelligent and persistent search for the conditions of improvement" of which Dr. Mursell speaks.

MAIN IDEAS AND SUBORDINATE DETAILS

But enough of theory—let's get down to work.

I offer you now four practice selections, and I ask you to read each one a little faster than is completely comfortable. Read with one dominating purpose—to find the main idea and to find it quickly. Push through briskly in a single-minded pursuit of the *gist* of the author's communication—do not waste time on individual words, on details, or on other subordinate elements.

This is a big order, and you may or may not be immediately successful, but a conscious and sincere attempt to move along at a rapid clip, concentrating on main ideas, is more important at this point than success or failure.

As in the two selections of chapter 1, keep a strict time check on your performance. I suggest the following procedure as a means of insuring accuracy:

1. First read the title, author, and source note of each selection (these are not included in the word-count).

2. Then note the time in writing (in the margin of the page, if

28

you like) *to the next minute coming.* If it is, for example, almost 8:43, but not quite, write 8:43 in the margin.

3. Wait until the second-hand of your watch shows *five seconds* before 8:43. (You may have to adjust the hands so that the second hand reaches zero at approximately the same moment that the minute hand reaches a full number.)

4. When the second hand shows that it is five seconds short of 8:43, start reading at the first arrow.

5. Lose all consciousness of your watch, concentrating only on the reading and on a speedy grasp of main ideas.

6. When you come to the terminating arrow, note the new time, subtract, and record, in the blank provided for that purpose, the number of minutes and seconds that your reading required. (The five seconds are allowed for transfer from watch to page and back again.)

7. Take the comprehension test.

8. Then determine your rate from the table that follows the test, and record this statistic on the chart and graph on page 392.

Next study carefully the discussion of each selection, and compare your reactions and comprehension with those that a trained and skillful reader would have. You will thus discover where your technique was good and where it was faulty; selection by selection, you will learn what errors you make, why you make them, and how to avoid making them in the future; you will "find out exactly what is wrong and exactly how to put it right." In this way you will effect gradual changes in your comprehension patterns, and in your method of attack on reading material; and you will pave the way for the acquisition of habits that make fast, efficient, and accurate reading comfortable and assured.

Ready for your first try? Remember the instructions: *read at a consciously accelerated rate, intent on extracting the essence of the piece quickly and with no lost motion.*

Selection 3

CAN THE H-BOMB DESTROY THE EARTH?
by Waldemar Kaempffert

Start timing→ The Atomic Energy Commission has announced that Soviet scientists have detonated a hydrogen bomb with results as frightening as those of last year's test at Eniwetok. When an atomic bomb of either the old A type or the most recent H type explodes, the upward rush of air, visible as the now familiar mushroom-shaped cloud, carries with it an enormous amount of dust which is radioactive. By exploding their H bomb high in the air the Russians left most of the dust on the ground where it belongs

2. It may be that the Soviet procedure will be adopted when next we touch off an atomic bomb. If so, some of the danger from fall-out that geneticists fear will be reduced but not entirely removed. But what of the possibility that bigger explosions of hydrogen bombs may set off a thermonuclear reaction on land or in the ocean and so destroy the earth? The physicists have pooh-poohed the possibility time and time again but without giving reasons. Now comes Prof. M. H. L. A. Pryce of the University of Bristol with an article in the British scientific magazine Discovery in which he explains why the earth is quite safe.

3. The alarmist who has received most attention of late is Sir Robert Robertson, president of the British Association for the Advancement of Science. At the meeting held recently by the association at Bristol, England, he asked: "Do we really know enough about nuclear explosions to be sure that there is no loophole?" He suggested that security regulations forbid physicists from talking openly about the possibility of blowing up the earth.

4. Professor Pryce retorts that secrecy has nothing to do with the case presented. The argument of many who think as Sir Robert does is based on the fact that it is the transmutation of hydrogen into helium that makes the sun and the stars shine. This being so, why should not the same transmutation on earth cause similar results? The answer is that it takes millions of years to fuse hydrogen into helium in the sun by a roundabout process, whereas fusion in a hydrogen bomb occurs in a minute fraction of a second.

5. The explosive materials are carefully selected, and the design of the bomb bears no resemblance to that of a star. Of the materials selected tritium occurs only in traces on the earth. As for deuterium there are

Reprinted by permission from *The New York Times*. Mr. Kaempffert, until his death early in 1957, was science editor of the *Times*.

only a few spoonfuls in a small lake or pond. Both tritium and deuterium must be made at great expense in enormous plants.

6. There is plenty of hydrogen in the ocean but the conditions are not right for the maintenance of temperatures of millions of degrees and pressures of millions of pounds to the square inch. Without the temperatures and the pressures no self-sustaining thermonuclear reaction is possible. ←**End timing**

RECORD HERE THE TIME REQUIRED ON THIS SELECTION: _____ MIN.
_____ SEC.

Test Your Comprehension

Which *one* of the following statements most accurately summarizes the *main idea* of the selection you have just finished? Check your choice without referring to the text.

1. Russian scientists have learned more about hydrogen bombs than have scientists in this country or in England.

2. There is quite a controversy going on in the press as to whether or not the hydrogen bomb can destroy the earth.

3. Conditions do not exist on land or in water to make a self-sustaining thermonuclear reaction possible—hence the earth cannot be destroyed by the hydrogen bomb.

4. By exploding the H-bomb high in the air, some of the danger from fall-out will be reduced, but not completely eliminated.

5. The H-bomb cannot destroy the earth because all its effects are eventually neutralized.

Compute Your Rate

(*Approximate number of words: 485*)

TIME	W.P.M.	TIME	W.P.M.
50 sec.	579	2 min.	243
1 min.	485	2 min., 10 sec.	222
1 min., 10 sec.	414	2 min., 15 sec.	216
1 min., 20 sec.	363	2 min., 30 sec.	194
1 min., 30 sec.	322	2 min., 45 sec.	176
1 min., 40 sec.	291	3 min.	161
1 min., 45 sec.	276	3 min., 15 sec.	148
1 min., 50 sec.	264	3 min., 30 sec.	138

YOUR RATE ON SELECTION 3: _____ W.P.M.
(*Record this statistic on the chart and graph on page 392.*)
GAIN OVER SELECTION 1 (*page 11*): _____ W.P.M.

31

Discussion of the Selection

The selection you have just read is full of words—almost 500 of them. It is full of phrases, sentences, and paragraphs, full of thoughts and ideas. But what are the key words, what are the important paragraphs, what is the central theme around which the article is built, and how do you find it—and, especially, how do you recognize it when you do find it?

One of the basic techniques that your training will aim to develop in you is that of distinguishing, quickly and successfully, between the central theme of a selection and the material that introduces, develops, clarifies, explains, illustrates, or supports that theme. Mr. Kaempffert speaks of many things in his piece—of hydrogen bombs and atom bombs; of mushroom-shaped clouds, radioactivity, fall-out danger, and thermonuclear reactions; of science professors and their disputes; of tritium and deuterium and the temperatures and pressures of the ocean. (Indeed, if a reader hasn't learned to exercise some discrimination in his assimilation of ideas—and every person has to, if material is to be at all intelligible to him—then this jumble of subjects almost reminds one of Lewis Carroll's classical "of cabbages—and kings—/ And why the sea is boiling hot—/ And whether pigs have wings.")

These, and more, are the things Mr. Kaempffert is speaking of, but what is he really saying? How does he combine and sort out and present this apparent jumble so that it has a single meaning, an over-all effect, a central theme? How does he organize it to drive home a final point?

Let's look at the piece together.

The first paragraph is clearly introductory. The author starts with a recent and newsworthy announcement about the Russians and develops that for some dozen or more lines, leading into paragraph 2, in which he first touches on the genetic danger that fall-out presents. He has used about 100 words, or over a fifth of his total material, to catch the reader's attention and lead into his main idea, which he now presents as a question in these words from the second paragraph: *"But what of the possibility that bigger explosions of hydrogen bombs may set off a thermonuclear reaction on land or in the ocean and so destroy the earth?"*

To the efficient reader, this sentence stands out from the bed of

32

surrounding words as if it were printed in black type (or, to use the printer's term, "boldface")—he immediately recognizes its importance because (1) it repeats, more elaborately, the question in the title, and (2) it starts off with *"But what of the possibility that . . . ,"* often a comprehension clue that a main point is on the way.

An author usually raises a question as a springboard toward an answer—and Mr. Kaempffert devotes all the rest of his article, right down to the end, to developing and explaining his answer. Through the middle of paragraph 4 he fills in the background of the answer; and from there through the last two paragraphs he explains that *the earth will not be destroyed by the hydrogen bomb because conditions do not exist on land or in water to make a self-sustaining thermonuclear reaction possible*—this is the main idea of the whole selection, the gist of what the author is saying.

Correct choice on the comprehension test is statement 3.

I want to state again, even at the risk of being tediously repetitious, that your dominating aim in reading these selections is to *cut rapidly through the words, sentences, and details to find and follow the author's main idea.*

This is not as hard as it may at first sound—it is not a bit hard if you will make an honest attempt to alter some of the comfortable and probably inefficient reading patterns you have grown too used to, that you have become too fond of, that it may be unpleasant, even painful, to give up.

Perhaps you have got into the habit of sauntering leisurely, too leisurely, when it's just as easy to run. Perhaps you get bogged down in details instead of concentrating purposefully on finding and understanding the main idea. Perhaps you think that every word has to be chewed and digested before you can go on to the next one, that every sentence has to be mulled over, that every thought has to be studied before you can really understand it; believe me, this is not so. All the words, all the sentences, all the thoughts in any selection add up to a final point, a final effect, a dominant and central idea. *Get into the next selection, get that central idea, and get out.* If you have any success in putting these instructions into practice, both your over-all understanding and your increase in rate will surprise you.

Selection 4

A STUTTERER WRITES TO A FORMER TEACHER
by Irving S. Shaw

Start timing→ Remember me? I came into your classroom more timid than the rest. My first thoughts were: When would I be called upon to recite? How would you react to my hesitance in speech? Would my classmates ridicule me? I hoped you could help me.

2. As the long days passed without my being called on, my anxiety intensified. My back ached, because I was constantly sittting on the edge of my chair.

3. At last you asked me a simple question. Do you remember how I blushed, how everybody in class turned to gaze?

4. The silence of the room, the impatient look on your face, and the stares of my classmates brought on the worst blockage I had ever experienced. My facial contortion brought an uproarious laugh from the class and a puzzled look to your face.

5. Do you remember what you did then? You reprimanded the class and moved me to a side seat—to be forgotten for the rest of the year.

6. You did not know that my stuttering was not caused by a physical defect, but by a personality impediment. You did not understand my problem, and your reaction only aggravated my condition.

7. Because of your attitude of taking my stuttering as a serious and troublesome problem, I became more selfconscious. Had you taken a lighter attitude, encouraged me to speak, and accepted me as one of the class, you would have helped instead of hurt me.

8. I was never encouraged to enter social activities. How I craved for companionship; how I needed self-expression! Except for my stuttering I was like any other pupil, but you made me feel different.

9. How frequently I wanted to speak to you informally, as the others did. Did you perhaps feel that I didn't care to chat? How wrong you were! The teacher who accepts the stutterer and who understands his make-up, can make it easier for him to develop a proper attitude about his problem.

10. I never stuttered when I sang, so singing gave me an opportunity to feel on equal terms with others. Yet even when you discovered I had a good voice, you did not choose me to sing a song in the class

Reprinted by permission from the *National Education Journal*. Mr. Shaw has taught high school classes in Mayer, Arizona, and Owyhee, Nevada.

play. If only you had capitalized on my simple musical talent!

11. Do you remember one particular instance when I requested a pass? I threw in a block, a spasm, which bewildered you as usual. You looked away, believing I would find it easier to speak. This only made things worse, for I felt that you were not paying attention or that you couldn't "take" the speech block. For days after this experience I was depressed, my speech difficulty worse than ever.

12. By the way, is Mrs. Ray still around? I wish she had been my teacher throughout the years. Her way of asking questions was so unusual that even I was able to speak up. She frequently asked for volunteers, and never cared if anyone answered without recognition. By not having to be the center of attraction, and by not thinking of speech, I frequently answered with no regard to my impediment.

13. Talking to Mrs. Ray after class was easy, too. When I did have a block, she just said, "Slow, easy." The fact that she didn't turn away and the realization that she understood gave me a great deal of encouragement.

14. If only you had sensed, as Mrs. Ray did, that the aim in guiding the personality development of the stutterer should be the same as the aim for any other child: to help him acquire a feeling of personal security so that he can face the future with confidence.

15. When I got to high school, my stuttering grew worse than ever, and I became more withdrawn.

The confidence given me by Mrs. Ray could not withstand the treatment I received from others who had no understanding of my problem.

16. Then another teacher came into my life who was interested in me and helped me. He advised me to improve myself by seeking outlets through school activities.

17. After one or two trial efforts at other things, I took up handball. A few pointers from the coach, and in no time at all I was on the team.

18. At last I had something other than myself to think about. I was accepted as one of the group, and my speech was of little concern. I let the ball do all of the talking, and how it did roar! Did you read that I won the city high school championship for two successive years?

19. That teacher's kindly interest changed my life. No longer did I eat alone in the school lunchroom. People gradually became my friends, and I used to tell them that my speech impediment was because of tight shoes. I found that joking about the defect made it less important.

20. My confidence increased, anxiety lessened, and slowly but surely better speech resulted.

21. I hesitate to think what might have happened if I had not encountered *some* teachers who understood my problem and were able to help me!   ←End timing

RECORD HERE THE TIME REQUIRED
ON THIS SELECTION: ___3___ MIN.
          _____ SEC.

35

Test Your Comprehension

Which *one* of the following statements most accurately summarizes the *main idea* of the selection you have just finished? Check your choice without referring to the text.

1. A stutterer needs and craves acceptance—only from this will he gain the feeling of confidence and personal security that will help him improve his speech.
2. Since stuttering is caused by feelings of inadequacy and inferiority, teachers should treat victims of this affliction in an especially considerate manner, constantly pointing out to them the areas in which they excel and the things they can do better than others.
3. Stuttering results from a personality impediment, not from a speech defect.
4. Singing is the best cure for stutterers.
5. Children and teachers can be cruel to someone who is different.

Compute Your Rate

(Approximate number of words: 840)

TIME	W.P.M.	TIME	W.P.M.
1 min.	840	2 min., 45 sec.	304
1 min., 15 sec.	672	3 min.	280
1 min., 30 sec.	558	3 min., 30 sec.	240
1 min., 45 sec.	480	4 min.	209
2 min.	420	4 min., 30 sec.	186
2 min., 15 sec.	362	5 min.	168
2 min., 30 sec.	334	6 min.	140

YOUR RATE ON SELECTION 4: _280_ w.p.m.
(Record this statistic on the chart and graph on page 392.)
GAIN OVER SELECTION 1 *(page 11)*: ___ w.p.m.

Discussion of the Selection

Here, as you no doubt realized while you were reading, is a piece in which a mass of details and narrative incidents is presented in combination with interpretation—and it is the interpretation, of course, which gradually builds up into a strong and inescapable central theme.

The first bit of interpretation occurs in the last sentence of

36

paragraph 7 (*"Had you taken a lighter attitude . . ."*) and the key phrase in this sentence is *"accepted me as one of the class. . . ."* The author has used over 25 per cent of his material to prepare you for his main idea, *that a stutterer craves and needs acceptance* —and then continues with an even larger block of material, right through paragraph 13, elaborating on and pounding home this same central point. In paragraph 14, the writer restates the theme (*". . . that the aim in guiding the personality development of the stutterer should be the same* [i.e., acceptance] *as the aim for any other child . . ."*); and then, in another key sentence of the piece, he broadens his theme to include the idea that *acceptance* results in *"a feeling of personal security. . . ."*

Paragraphs 15 through 17 add more details to support the theme, with paragraph 20 (*"My confidence increased . . . and better speech resulted"*) restating, in different words, the idea of *personal security.*

Correct choice on the comprehension test is statement 1.

No one, of course, goes through this conscious and elaborate type of analysis as he reads. But accurate comprehension of the final meaning of any piece of writing is based on a recognition, perhaps largely subverbal, of how the author has organized his material, how he has knit together the various strands of his fabric, how he combines the parts to produce a total effect. And the efficient reader, intent on extracting the essence of a page as quickly as possible, has always some feeling, whether or not he verbalizes it, of how the broad sections of material are related and of how the important concepts are supported, explained, clarified, or illustrated by subordinate details.

My purpose in asking you to go back over each selection as you study the analysis is to sharpen your sense of the structure of material, to develop your skill in differentiating subordinate elements from main ideas. The more practiced you become in recognizing how details are used to introduce, bolster, pound home, clarify, or illustrate main ideas, the more rapidly and successfully will you be able to pull these ideas out of your reading, and the clearer will be your grasp of the final meaning of what an author is saying to you.

So let us continue this valuable practice on the next selection. Push through the details rapidly, keep on the alert for the main idea, and come out of your reading with an awareness of what *all the words add up to.*

Selection 5

ATOM BOMBS AND X-RAYS

Start timing→ Argument goes on at great length in scientific circles over the effects of U. S. atomic bomb tests on the present population and future generations. Scientists who like to air their views publicly can usually make page one of the big city newspapers or get their pictures in weekly news magazines by viewing with alarm the horrors that may be visited on civilians in super-bomb warfare. Apparently the general public is not greatly impressed by these warnings, for officials complain loudly that civilian defense organizations have not been able to secure support or muster any great following.

2. Of much more practical concern to the average citizen are the by-products of the current H-bomb discussions, which have brought to light the fact that certain peace-time medical practices need to be looked at with a critical eye to determine whether medical X-rays are being applied too freely and, in some cases, too carelessly. Chest X-rays are recommended on a yearly basis in many localities. X-rays are used after accidents and injuries to find broken bones, and they are much used also in diagnosing troubles of the digestive tract. In addition, X-rays are applied in various medical treatments. Dentists often take X-ray negatives for locating cavities in teeth. There is a widely-used fluoroscope device that employs X-rays to determine the fit of shoes, particularly in children.

3. Statistics on radiologists who work with radioactive substances indicate that 8 to 10 times more radiologists die of leukemia (cancer of the blood) than do those who work in other fields. Studies of 10,000 youngsters indicated that radiologists' children suffered more from heart, blood, and eye defects than those in the relatively unexposed group. One outstanding scientist takes the position that the genetic hazards (the effect on future generations) of the actual bomb tests are probably not as great as the genetic dangers of incautiously administered X-rays. It is his view that X-rays, particularly in the abdominal region, will have an adverse effect on the reproductive organs. Furthermore, he points

An editorial from the September 1955 issue of *Consumers' Research Bulletin*. Reprinted with permission.

out, the more radiation a person is exposed to, the more risk there is of occurrence of mutations with adverse effect on health and vigor of future offspring.

4. Knowledge in this field is quite inadequate at the present time and the subject deserves greater attention from medical foundations that spend great sums every year to discover the causes of various human ailments. It is the view of one eminent scientist that genetic damage from medical uses of X-rays could be avoided if proper precautions were taken in their application.

5. Instead of forecasting what will be the probable effect of H-bombs in time of war, it would seem much more practical to take a careful look at current recommendations in the public health field in the use of ionizing radiations. Just how much of a cumulative dose does the person get who customarily has an annual chest X-ray, plus an annual or semiannual dental X-ray, and perhaps other X-ray treatments during a year, and what is a safe tolerance in a given case? This question requires considerably more intensive, unspectacular, expensive, and tedious research, but many would consider it to be of far more practical importance to the population of the United States than the speculative viewings with alarm of the suppositional dangers that would be incurred by the population in this and other countries in the event of an A-bomb or H-bomb attack.   ←End timing

RECORD HERE THE TIME REQUIRED ON THIS SELECTION: _____ MIN. _____ SEC.

Test Your Comprehension

Which *one* of the following statements most accurately summarizes the *main idea* of the selection you have just finished? Check your choice without referring to the text.

1. The public is not sufficiently alarmed over the possible horrors they will suffer from atomic radiation or superbomb warfare.

2. Perhaps we had better give some thought to the current, immediate, and continuing danger of the too free and careless use of medical X rays.

3. People who work with radioactive substances suffer from an abnormal incidence of leukemia, and their children suffer from more bodily defects than do the children of the general population.

4. The genetic dangers from X rays are greater than those from atom-bomb tests.

5. The use of X rays and other radioactive substances must be cut

down drastically, or even stopped entirely, if we are to preserve our health.

Compute Your Rate
(Approximate number of words: 580)

TIME	W.P.M.	TIME	W.P.M.
1 min.	580	2 min.	290
1 min., 10 sec.	498	2 min., 10 sec.	270
1 min., 20 sec.	438	2 min., 15 sec.	260
1 min., 30 sec.	388	2 min., 30 sec.	232
1 min., 40 sec.	348	2 min., 45 sec.	212
1 min., 50 sec.	318	3 min.	194

YOUR RATE ON SELECTION 5: ___348___ W.P.M.
(Record this statistic on the chart and graph on page 392.)
GAIN OVER SELECTION 1 *(page 11)*: ___300___ W.P.M.

Discussion of the Selection

What, in five paragraphs and almost 600 words, was the editorial writer attempting to convey to the reader? What was his essence, his gist, his central thought? Let us look back at the piece and examine its structure.

Paragraph 1 is obviously *introduction*, a means of catching the reader's interest by starting with a problem very much in the day's news—the effects of atomic bomb tests. The trained reader quickly recognizes this as introductory material and moves through it at a rapid pace.

Paragraph 2 starts with a comprehension clue—*"of much more practical concern"*—that alerts the reader to look for a main idea, which he discovers toward the end of the sentence—*"determine whether medical X-rays are being applied too freely . . . too carelessly."*

The reader now expects supporting details for this statement, and these he finds in abundance in the rest of paragraph 2 and throughout paragraph 3.

Paragraph 4 reiterates, with further explanation, the main idea first presented in the second paragraph—*"the subject deserves greater attention. . . ."*

And the last paragraph pounds the thought home—*"requires in-*

tensive . . . research"—with still more details and justification, finally ending with a restatement of the introduction.

What do we have here, then? We have a springboard, *the effects of atom bomb tests,* from which the author jumps into his central theme, that *perhaps we had better give some practical thought to the current and immediate and continuing danger of medical X rays and radiation;* this theme is supported, explained, and repeated with a wealth of specific details, all of them valuable, all interesting, all intended to contribute to the persuasiveness of the central point, but subordinate details nonetheless. And finally we have a concluding sentence that returns to the thought of the introduction, and that ties the piece up neatly into a nice, symmetrical package.

Correct choice on the comprehension test is statement 2.

The skillful reader sees the statements, restatements, and elaborations of the main idea stand out conspicuously, as if in full relief, from the much larger background of narrative details. He sweeps rapidly through these details, consciously searching out the central theme, and realizes, all through the piece, that *here, here, here,* and *here* is where the author is stating or restating a main point— everything else, though valuable, interesting, and effective, is nevertheless detail and therefore subordinate; it contributes to, prepares the way for, or supports the central theme, but the central theme itself is what the efficient reader concentrates on.

If you yourself followed some such pattern of reading in selection 5, then you are beginning to apply efficient techniques, and your rate of reading probably reflected this efficiency. If not, do not be discouraged. There are still chapters and chapters of learning and practice ahead of you.

The next selection, which is considerably longer than those on which you have heretofore practiced, has a broad structure of clearly discernible parts. It is a slightly technical but extremely interesting article, with a well-defined main idea. There is a wealth of details which might seduce an unsophisticated reader into a slow and careful reading quite unwarranted by the broad theme on which the author builds her piece. So push through rapidly looking for this theme—*do not waste time or effort over the somewhat technical details.*

41

JOHNNY, A REJECTED CHILD
by Bertha Padouk

Start timing→ This is the story of Johnny, who is ten years of age and is now in the fifth grade. In September 1951 he was referred to the school nurse because of poor bladder control. He would constantly wet and soil his trousers. He was shy and withdrawn. He was shunned by other children because of his bad odor. He was unresponsive in class and he would never smile.

2. When the school nurse visited Johnny's house, she discovered a "shack without a bathroom." A barber chair served as the living room furniture. Johnny's father, who is highly emotional, is a strict disciplinarian. Johnny is afraid of his father, who feels that his boy is never serious about anything.

3. In addition to Johnny, there are two other children—an older son in the service and a daughter now in the first term of high school. Both parents work.

4. Shortly after the nurse's visit the school guidance counselor interviewed Johnny's father, who refused to get any help from any guidance source—either the Bureau of Child Guidance or some other agency.

5. The school psychologist gave Johnny a Stanford Binet L Test in October 1951. This revealed that the youngster had an I.Q. of 116, had a higher potential for learning than was indicated in his functioning, and had a definite reading disability because of an emotional block. Use of primer materials in reading on a remedial instructional basis was recommended. These were put into effect by his classroom teacher. Only a slight improvement was noted by June 1952.

6. In September of the same year Johnny was assigned to an Opportunity Class (small register) with a most sympathetic teacher. Two months later he became a member of the Reading Club (a remedial reading class was granted to the school at this time).

7. On November 17, 1952, the results of two reading tests (Project Oral Reading and Project Silent Reading) revealed:

Johnny's Reading Age	7.6
" Reading Grade	2.6
" Retardation	3.4

Reprinted by permission from *Understanding the Child*. Mrs. Padouk is a remedial reading teacher in Public School 154, Flushing, New York.

Confusions and Substitutions

their brother for—they brought

wild	"	wide
bed	"	band
fry	"	fire
ounce	"	inch
Rover	"	river etc.

Phonetic Attack on New Words

Johnny could not blend, sound out or figure out by phonetic or contextual clues.

Omissions

He left out several words at a time—as "it began, I know, like ours." These omissions happened most frequently at the beginning and in the middle of a sentence.

Comprehension

When he was asked what he had read, the answer was, "I don't know."

Voice

Monotonous — vocalized — did not stop at a period.

Picture Clues

He did not notice them.

Reading Habits

He pointed during oral reading and vocalized during silent reading. 8. Johnny, who was afraid to express himself, and who handled his conflicts by withdrawal and depressive reactions, had to be reintroduced to reading in a relaxed atmosphere that would promote interest, self-respect, understanding, and achievement. 9. At the beginning of each lesson in the Reading Club ten minutes were given to oral language. The group, consisting of six children, would rhyme funny words, discuss ways of helping other children, tell about experiences over the weekend, and engage in oral picture reading. Statements made by the children were written on experiential charts with the name of the individual child who contributed to the story. At this point Johnny began to show a marked interest. It was necessary to ask Johnny several questions before one sentence could be formed:

Teacher—"What did you do on Sunday?"

Johnny—"I went fishing."

Teacher—"With whom did you go?"

Johnny—"With my father."

Teacher—"What did you catch?"

Johnny—"Carp."

Teacher—"What's that?"

Johnny—"A brown fish."

Teacher—"Are they good to eat?"

Johnny—"Yes."

Teacher—"Johnny, please put all this information in a story so that I can print it on this chart. The other children will then be able to enjoy this wonderful story of yours."

Johnny—"I went fishing with my father on Sunday. We caught six carp. They are a brown fish and are good to eat."

10. Thus, by direct questioning, Johnny became interested in expressing himself and in reading his answers. Furthermore, his status among the other children in the Reading Club improved considerably. A feeling of self-respect and achievement gradually became his. 11. One of the activities in the Reading Club is finger painting,

which is correlated with poetry, music enjoyment, and expressional and creative writing. On one occasion rain poems were read to the group. The children were encouraged to express their reactions to these poems. Johnny contributed to "rain sounds." After a stimulating discussion in which each member of the Reading Club participated, finger painting was introduced. Johnny had never finger-painted before. He started to talk to the boy next to him:

Johnny—"I have never finger-painted."

Richard—"Neither have I."

Paul—"In finger painting you do not use a brush."

Matty—"I think finger painting must be messy."

Paul—"Let's find out."

12. At last Johnny had found some interest—some activity in common with other boys. This was the beginning of his becoming friendly with others.

13. During this period of adjustment for Johnny, who was beginning to enjoy reading and related activities (finger painting, expressional writing in the form of individual and group dictation to the teacher, picture reading, working with Dixie mesh, group discussion, clay work, etc.), the guidance counselor constantly kept the father informed of his boy's progress in school. A very strong plea was made that the rigid discipline at home should be relaxed. The father finally decided to cooperate with the request. He began to notice the changes in his son. Within a short time the odor emanating from Johnny's clothing ceased.

14. Within a period of seven months Johnny, from a reading grade of 2.5, made a year and a half progress in reading with a score of 4.1 in May 1953.

15. On November 19, 1953—Johnny was given a silent and an oral reading test. He made these scores.

Gray Oral—5.9
Stanford Achievement Test D—4.3

16. It is expected that Johnny will do even better in the near future.

17. On Johnny's birthday, the Remedial Reading Teacher phoned Johnny's father. She told the father what fine progress the boy was making in reading and that Johnny was a bright boy. Over the phone she heard the father say to his son: "My boy, that's wonderful. I am very proud of you."

18. Then he asked his son to play a clarinet solo to celebrate the event. This proved to be a turning point in Johnny's social and intellectual development.

19. Utilizing to good advantage the services of the school nurse, the psychologist, the guidance counselor, and the classroom teacher, the remedial reading teacher was able to add her services to stem a severe case of enuresis (a manifestation of Johnny's anxiety over his paternal relationship). The reading club room established an atmosphere of learning conducive to academic achievement and social recognition.

44

20. Thanks to coordinated efforts on the part of the school personnel, a problem which originated in the home is being currently solved. From rejection to acceptance by father and classmates epitomized the story of Johnny. ←**End timing**

RECORD HERE THE TIME REQUIRED ON THIS SELECTION: _2_ MIN. _56_ SEC.

Test Your Comprehension

Which *one* of the following statements most accurately summarizes the *main idea* of the selection you have just finished? Check your choice without referring to the text.

1. Ten-year-old Johnny was a rejected, disturbed, unhappy child who needed psychiatric help.
2. Johnny's difficulties stemmed from a poor home environment and an over-disciplinary and unco-operative father.
3. Johnny had better than average intelligence—his learning difficulties and reading disabilities resulted from an emotional block.
4. When parents make mistakes, it is necessary for the school to interfere.
5. Johnny's reading and other problems were solved because active steps were taken to change rejection to acceptance, both at home and in school.

Compute Your Rate

(*Approximate number of words: 1200*)

TIME	W.P.M.	TIME	W.P.M.
2 min.	600	3 min., 30 sec.	342
2 min., 15 sec.	532	3 min., 45 sec.	320
2 min., 30 sec.	480	4 min.	300
2 min., 45 sec.	436	4 min., 15 sec.	282
3 min.	400	4 min., 30 sec.	266
3 min., 15 sec.	368	5 min.	240

YOUR RATE ON SELECTION 6: _338_ W.P.M.
(*Record this statistic on the chart and graph on page 392.*)
GAIN OVER SELECTION 1 (*page 11*): _283_ W.P.M.

Discussion of the Selection

I am now going to ask you to take a more active part in analyzing the structure of material. Referring to the numbered paragraphs in Mrs. Padouk's article, answer the following questions:

1. Paragraphs 1 through 4 constitute the first major part of this piece. What is the purpose, very briefly, of this section? _how_ _his problem was found out_ _and what was cause_

2. Paragraphs 5, 6, and 7 make up a second section—what is the author doing here? _showing he is alright_ _child and should be doing_ _better_

3. Paragraphs 8 through 13 form the third section—what is this about? _his lessons_

4. What is the author presenting in the next section, paragraphs 14 through 18? _his achievement_

5. Finally, in the last two paragraphs, 19 and 20, what is the author doing? _his growth back to_ _normal_

The article we are working on is full of the kind of statistics and specialized explanations that might well slow down the rate of the untrained reader—minutes can be wasted, and concentration interfered with, by an attempt to wrestle with the technical terminology often found in this type of writing.

The skillful reader, on the other hand, would recognize almost from the first few sentences that he is dealing with a *problem-solution* piece—and he would be interested at once in discovering quickly what the problem is and how it was solved. To this end, he would avoid getting enmeshed in statistics, he would skim through the conversation and narrative details, extracting only the flavor, and since he knows from the start what he is looking for (the solution to Johnny's difficulties), he would whiz through the piece at high speed. (*Skilled reading always involves suiting your pace to the type of material and to what you are trying to get out of it.*)

This article has a simple, clear-cut structure that contributes strongly to rapid comprehension. In paragraphs 1 through 4, the problem is described and the background filled in (answer to ques-

46

tion 1); in paragraphs 5 through 7, the author is tabulating the statistics on Johnny's reading performance and elaborating on his reading disabilities—she is still discussing the problem (answer to question 2); in paragraphs 8 through 13 she describes the therapy used with Johnny (answer to question 3), and if you were at all alert to structure as you read you realized that at this point the central theme of the article was beginning. In paragraphs 14 through 18, the results of the therapy are presented (answer to question 4), and the important point you should have come away with is that these results were good.

And then, in the last two paragraphs, 19 and 20, the author sums up what has been accomplished with Johnny, and by what means (answer to question 5). In the very final paragraph the total meaning of all the facts and details of the piece is explicitly stated. Correct choice on the comprehension test, therefore, is statement 5.

Reflect, for a moment, on what this type of training aims to help you accomplish. You are learning, by actual practice, to look at material not as a conglomeration of words or phrases or sentences, not as a parade of unrelated facts or details or ideas—but rather as an integrated whole with a dominant and over-all meaning. You are learning to move along more rapidly, to push through the details and extract a final meaning, to sense the broad structure of an author's thinking—in short, you are learning to read aggressively, not just take in words.

This ends one phase of your training, and with the next chapter a new phase will begin. And so we are ready, now, to examine the statistics you have been keeping and to see whether we can spot a trend.

Suppose you copy down, from the chart on page 392, your rates on selections 1, 3, 4, 5, and 6.

SELECTION 1 (MYSTERY STORIES): _____W.P.M.
SELECTION 3 (H-BOMB): _____W.P.M.
SELECTION 4 (STUTTERER): _____W.P.M.
SELECTION 5 (X RAYS): _____W.P.M.
SELECTION 6 (JOHNNY): _____W.P.M.

Examine this chart. Your rates may show great variation from selection to selection. If so, this is a good sign—you are suiting your speed to the changes in complexity and style of the material.

Do your rates on the last four selections show a definite gain over your initial rate? This is an even better sign.

Your rates may possibly be fairly constant, after a significant jump over your performance on the first selection. If this is so, there is cause for rejoicing. You have demonstrated your capacity for accelerating your normal and habitual speed of comprehension —you have climbed to a higher plateau where you may remain for a while as you integrate the new techniques you are learning.

Let us do a little arithmetic. Add up your statistics on selections 3 through 6, and divide by 4 to find an average rate during the first phase of your training. How much higher is it than your rate on selection 1? And what is the percentage of increase? To find this last figure, divide the average gain by your initial rate, and carry the answer to two decimal places. For example, if your starting rate was 213 w.p.m., and your average rate on selections 3 through 6 was 295 w.p.m., you subtract 213 from 295, and then divide this answer, 82, by 213, giving you approximately .38, or 38 per cent. Record these statistics below and also in the appropriate spaces on page 392.

Average Gain in Rate: ———————w.p.m.
Percentage Gain in Rate: ———————

A TEST OF YOUR RETENTION AND RECALL

And now let us try an interesting experiment. One of the significant dividends that training promises is an increase in *retention and recall*—and learning to seek out main ideas is one of the chief means of earning such a dividend. Without further reference to the selections you read earlier, how successfully can you recall the gist of each one?

Retention Test

Write out, *very briefly*, the gist of each of the following articles.

1. "Can the H-Bomb Destroy the Earth?" *No because the makeup of the air earth and water would not change in a very long time*

48

2. "A Stutterer Writes to a Former Teacher" _A Stutterer_
blame his teacher for his trouble
and says other teacher helped him
3. "Atom Bombs and X-Rays" _It say that present_
day use of X-Ray might be more
dangerous than future atom bombs
4. "Johnny, a Rejected Child" _is about a boy who_
was depressed and needed a
little attention

Key:

1. Conditions do not exist for a sustained thermonuclear reaction
—the earth is safe. 2. A stutterer needs acceptance and attitudes
that increase his security if he is to speak better. 3. Medical use of
X rays may be dangerous—the question should be investigated
further. 4. Johnny's reading and personality problems were solved
by changing rejection to acceptance.

(Your own language is of course different from that suggested
above—but does it boil down to pretty much the same general
ideas?)

CHAPTER 3

HOW TO TRAIN YOUR PERCEPTION

Preview

In the first two sessions of your training you made an attempt, during your reading, to avoid poky and time-consuming attention to minor details—you tried to sweep briskly through material, speedily following main ideas, sensing the broad structure of the author's thinking, and getting an accurate, over-all, understanding of the *gist* of each selection.

Now we concentrate for a period on a different area of training. In this chapter you will learn:

• How to do productive exercises in the rapid and accurate perception of numbers, words, and phrases.

• How to make greater use of your "peripheral" vision.

• How to increase your "span of recognition."

• How to reduce your "fixation-time."

• How perception training can markedly accelerate your general reading rate.

> *Chapter 3* shows you how to interpret *more* of what you see—and in *less* time.

50

READING AS A VISUAL PROCESS

In one sense, as you may know, we do not read with our eyes at all, but with our minds. The eyes are only a vehicle of transmission —they flash the visual impulses that the brain interprets and the mind reacts to. Such interpretation and reaction may be instantaneous or halting, accurate or erroneous, easy or full of effort, depending not on the sharpness of a reader's vision but on the clearness and richness of his understanding, and on the reflexive perception habits under which he operates.

The eyes are the camera of the mind. Like a camera, they do no more than snap the photograph. From that point on, the brain does all the work—it develops the negative, prints the picture, and stores away the result.

Like a camera, the eyes must focus on the subject before a photograph can be taken. They may focus and refocus three to a dozen times on a single line of print, up to a hundred times or more on an average page, in order to continue feeding successive images to the brain for interpretation.

Sit in front of a reader and peer up into his eyes as they move across a page of print. It is a fascinating process to watch, especially if you have never observed it before. You will see his eyes focus at a point somewhere near the beginning of a line and remain there for a very brief period of time, generally a fraction of a second. It is during this momentary pause that he is reading—depending on his skill, his eyes are photographing a phrase unit, a couple of words, a single word, or maybe only a portion of a word. Then his eyes jerk sharply to the right, focus for a second time, snap a second photograph, and jerk again to the right. These alternating jerks and pauses go on until the end of the line is reached, at which point

51

his eyes sweep back to the left, focus on the following line, and the movement-pause, movement-pause process starts all over again, continuing line by line, paragraph by paragraph, page by page.

Go on watching for a while. Soon you will be able to count the number of pauses made on each line. If the reader you are observing is fairly skillful you may see only three to five pauses. If he is awkward and inexperienced you may be able to count ten to a dozen or more, and on many lines, if not on practically every line, you may see his eyes suddenly reverse and jerk to the left. He is making regressions—he is going back to check on the camera; the picture that his mind developed failed to make sense, or in some way his comprehension momentarily broke down.

Does all this seem vastly complicated? It is, of course. Nevertheless, these constantly alternating movements and pauses are completely reflexive and pretty nearly unconscious, controlled automatically by the ability and speed of the mind in absorbing and integrating what the eyes see. They are as reflexive and automatic as the movements in eating, an activity in which, particularly when one is hungry, there is ordinarily little or no conscious control over, or even awareness of, the separate motions of opening and closing the mouth, raising and dropping the lower jaw, grinding the teeth, or swallowing. In a sense, such motions are directed and controlled by the stomach, which dictates the amount of food it wishes to receive and the rate at which it can comfortably receive it. So also in reading—the mind dictates the portion of print it wishes to interpret at one time, and the rate at which the eyes should continue feeding it these portions.

Reading, then, is accomplished by a continuous alternation of ocular pauses and movements—or what we call "fixations" and "interfixation movements."

"Fixation" is the technical term for the fractional second in which the eyes focus on a portion of a line of print. During a fixation the external movement of the eyes stops, an image is transmitted to the brain, and words are read. Then the eyes move slightly to the right, a new point of fixation is made, and another image is flashed to the brain.

In order to keep reading, the eyes must move; but *while reading*, the eyes are externally motionless. During the movement between

52

two fixations ("interfixation movements"), there is a marked reduction in visual sharpness—vision is clear only when the eyes are stationary, or "*fixated.*" However, owing to the persistence of an "afterimage" in the brain, there is no *sensation* of loss of sight, no sensation even of a blur, as the eyes focus and refocus, moving from one fixation point to the next.

What is "afterimage"? Try staring at an object for thirty seconds, then quickly close your eyes. You can still see the object, can't you, for just the briefest fraction of a second? Or stare at this object again, very rapidly shutting and opening your eyes a half dozen times. Doesn't it seem as if your sight is continuous? It isn't, of course—the optical illusion results from the slight persistence of the afterimage. It is this afterimage during the interfixations that produces an illusion of smooth and continuous vision as you read, even though there are alternating periods of sight and partial blindness. In truth, it is not the vision, but rather the flow of visual impulses to the brain, that is smooth and continuous, for the mind, under conditions of normal comprehension, is fusing the impulses it receives into a steady stream of meaning.

Let us examine the process more closely. A reader is confronted with a page of print. He starts to read the first line:

The eye moves across a printed line and you read. The eye

To begin reading, his eyes fixate at a point somewhere at the beginning of the line and remain there, if he is the average reader, for about one fourth to one half a second. If we attempted to diagram the action, it would look something like this:

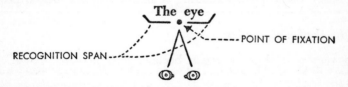

Having photographed the first two words (*"the eye"*) by fixating between them, his eyes then travel to the right and make a second point of fixation, then a third, a fourth, and so on until the end of the line is reached. Then they make a return sweep to the following line and start fixating all over again. For example:

The eye moves across a printed line and you read. The eye
is a very special sense organ because it is a direct extension of
the brain. Consequently reading is almost a direct mental process.

This pattern shows the unconscious eye movements of a reader of average efficiency: a type line about four inches long (the size used in this book) is read in six or seven fixations. A skilled reader might cover such a line in three or four fixations—an extremely inefficient reader, on the other hand, would require nine to twelve fixations, or even more.

Now, oddly enough, the process of making fixations and of moving the eyes is so rapid, or reflexive, so unconscious that you might read eight hours a day and never realize what your eyes are doing. And this is exactly as it should be. *Your are not supposed to feel your eyes fixating and moving. The more aware you are of these movements, the less skillfully you are reading.* Nevertheless, the movements go on—for without them, no reading could be done.

Let us now contrast the reading patterns of the efficient and the inefficient reader.

The efficient reader:

The eye moves across a printed line and you read. The eye
is a very special sense organ because it is a direct extension of
the brain. Consequently reading is almost a direct mental process.

The inefficient reader:

is a very special sense organ because it is a direct extension of
the brain. Consequently reading is almost a direct mental process.

By being able to cover a book-length line of type at an average of three to four fixations to a line, with three to four medium-sized words to each eye span, the efficient reader not only saves time; he also works less hard and has fewer periods of nonreading. The

54

skillful reader does not take any longer to absorb three or four words than the inefficient reader needs for a single word. The former's fixations are certainly no longer in duration than the latter's, and generally are much shorter.

The inefficient reader whose patterns are illustrated above is the word-by-word reader. The reason his eye spans take in only a single word at a time is no fault of his vision: word-by-word reading is simply a habit he has perfected through constant practice. As a result, the meaning of the page comes to him choppily, and thinking is made difficult, for normal thought does not occur by words, but by phrases and pictures. A picture is much more quickly drawn in the mind by several combined words than by individual ones.

(The pattern we have just been studying does not by any means represent the worst possible reader. Many poor readers have such short eye spans that they cannot even take in a whole word at one fixation. Such undisciplined readers may even go so far as to attack a line of type syllable by syllable, or even letter by letter.)

You now understand the broad outlines of reading as a visual process, you now have an idea of how the eyes function in feeding images to the brain for translation into meaning. *What has all this to do with your own training to speed up comprehension?* The answer will be found in the following excerpt from *The Air University Reading Improvement Program:*

NATURE OF READING *

The eye moves across a printed line and you read. The eye is a very special sense organ because it is a direct extension of the brain. Consequently reading is almost a direct mental process. The eye, however, does not read while it moves. Decades ago physiologists learned that the eye sees only when it stops.

Reading, therefore, consists of a series of fixations which the eye makes while viewing a printed line. During these fixation pauses, the material viewed is translated into meanings by the brain. A good reader will make three to four fixations for an ordinary line of print; the poor reader eight to twelve or more. Ability to cover a wider span, to view a large field, is directly related to reading ability. The span is also related to speed of reading, since the eye travels about

* From *The Air University Reading Improvement Program*, The Air University, Maxwell Air Force Base, Montgomery, Alabama, June 1948. Reprinted with permission.

6 per cent of the time between fixations and spends about 94 per cent of the time on the fixation pauses.

The good reader is also able to spend a shorter time on each fixation. He will stop only about a fifth of a second on each fixation; the poor reader will take twice as long.

Finally, the good reader makes fewer regressions per line or, in other words, his eye travels back over material less frequently. As a result, the rapid reader is able to read continuously and thus follow the meaning of the writer more easily.

To improve reading ability, it is necessary to have training to develop these characteristics: (1) a wide recognition span, (2) few fixation pauses per line, (3) short fixation pauses, and (4) few regressions.

AN EXPERIMENT IN FIXATIONS

Now, for just a few minutes, let us attempt to make the interdependence and interaction of your own eyes and mind a bit more conscious, so that you will thoroughly understand the basis and the reason for the training that will be offered to you in later sections of this chapter. I ask you to experiment personally with a single line of print in order to realize what is actually happening as you read.

This is the line of print on which you will work:

Our eyes move across the page in jerks and pauses as we read.

1. *First, focus at the beginning of the line as you normally would in starting to read.*

What did you see? Perhaps two words—*our eyes*. You made your initial fixation by focusing your eyes at a point approximately in the middle of the space occupied by the two words, and in a fraction of a second you read the print on both sides of that point. This was accomplished, you realize, not by sweeping from the O in *Our* through to the s in *eyes*, but by taking a single, instantaneous picture of the entire space.

2. *Now start the line again. Make your initial fixation as you did before, then move your eyes to make a second fixation.*

What did you see this time? Perhaps two more words—*move across*. After interpreting the first photograph snapped by your eyes, your mind called for more material, and your eyes automatically responded by feeding a second image to your brain.

3. *Take your pen or pencil, and go back once again to the line of print. This time read it through completely by making conscious and deliberate fixation after fixation until you have finished the last word. Mark off each of your recognition spans with a slanting line as you move from the beginning to the end of the line.*
Did it work out somewhat as follows?

Our eyes/move across/the page/in jerks/and pauses/as we/read.

If so, you made seven fixations to the line—or perhaps you did better, or perhaps not as well. No matter. We are more interested in what you eventually *can* do, after perception training, than in what you *have done* at this point. So let us approach the culmination of our experiment by taking step 4.

4. *The line has been broken up below into longer portions. Attempt to read each portion in one fixation by consciously focusing your eyes above the black dot in the center of the phrase.*

Our eyes move
•

across the page
•

in jerks and pauses
•

as we read.
•

What did you discover? By consciously fixating at the black dot, were you able to read the entire phrase without moving your eyes? Probably so. Or were the outer edges of each phrase less clear than the center word or words? Or was it perhaps impossible to see anything but a few letters to the left and right of the fixation point? (Your answer will depend not on the efficiency of your eyes but on the mental habits you have built up through years of reading.)

No matter how successful or unsuccessful you may have been in interpreting the complete phrases above in single fixations, you can now understand the final goal of your perception training: the building up of such strong and deep-seated habits that you will automatically and reflexively read with wide recognition spans, and your fixations will be made, without conscious control on your part, in *phrase units*, rather than in *one- or two-word units*.

5. Now read the entire bold-face line on page 56 one final time. Read it rapidly and without any thought or awareness of fixations or of eye movements.

I have asked you to take this last step in order to close the experiment by disabusing you of the notion that you can learn to read more rapidly by consciously controlling your fixations. It is perfectly possible to read with such self-directed fixations—but at the end of half a page fatigue will set in, comprehension will suffer drastically, and reading will degenerate into a mechanical chore. Your fixations are automatically controlled by your comprehension, and the only kind of training that will work is the steady practice of habits that will condition your mind (1) to accept more material from your eyes at each fixation and (2) to react more speedily to this material as it is fed in.

A NOTE ON FIXATION TIME

An extremely poor reader may linger on an individual word for as long as a full second—he may fixate on the longer words syllable by syllable before he is able to interpret the total picture. *And each of his fixations may take twice as long as a skilled reader requires for interpreting a complete phrase.*

I want to give you an opportunity to identify momentarily with an extremely poor reader—I want you to experience personally a small degree of the laborious, the almost agonizing, effort involved when you have to extract meaning through exceedingly slow and awkward fixations and narrow recognition spans. *Without reversing the book, read the next two paragraphs, which, as you will notice, are printed upside down.*

culty and slow rate. (Left to right printing is merely a tradition— tion you are accustomed to, but this is not the reason for your diffi- You are now fixating from right to left, rather than in the direc-

58

with a little experience one can read just as competently from right to left, as in Hebrew, or straight down, as in Chinese; or even, if material were so printed, straight up from the bottom of a page, or left-to-right and then right-to-left on alternating lines. Indeed, some of these odd systems have much to recommend them as time-savers.)

You are having trouble, and probably also experiencing some discomfort, in extracting meaning from these paragraphs solely because the shapes and configurations of the words are so peculiar and unfamiliar to you that only a very short recognition span combined with a long fixation time permits your mind to interpret with any accuracy what your eyes are photographing.

The poor reader's fixation times may be comparatively long for another reason. In order to comprehend, he must move his tongue or lips or vocal cords, or even whisper audibly, for he has learned to understand meaning only by recognizing the shape or feel or sound of words. His speed, as a result, is limited to not much more than the rate at which he can read aloud. And this is far slower, of course, than the rate at which he could interpret meaning by completely by-passing the vocal apparatus—far slower and far, far less efficient.

You are not, of course, a pathologically slow and awkward reader. You do not have to puzzle out most words, your fixations probably last no more than two fifths of a second, and your recognition span covers generally at least two words, sometimes more. You doubtless never whisper or move your lips or tongue when you read, and, if your rate is now over 250 w.p.m., you do not rely on your vocal cords to assist you in interpreting meaning.

But possibly you are a little overdependent on *thinking* the words as you read them, a little too conscious of *hearing* them in your mind's ear. (Such "inner hearing" or "inner speech" goes on to a certain extent in all readers, but with less and less consciousness of the individual words or phrases as speed increases and concentration deepens.) Possibly, also, there are some slight vestiges of vocalization still accompanying your reading performance—so slight that you are rarely if ever aware of them, but nevertheless serving to keep your fixations significantly longer, and your recognition spans significantly narrower, than necessary.

59

If these possibilities exist, as they do in most untrained readers, then the perception exercises that follow in the next sections will help you break a pattern of interpreting visual impulses less rapidly and less efficiently than you are capable of doing.

We proceed, now, to the first step in perception training by aiming for an increase in accuracy—and for this purpose, we shall start with *numbers*. (*Number drills*, and then *word drills*, will prepare you for *phrase drills*. The final goal of perception training is reflexive and instantaneous interpretation of complete phrases in single, quick fixations.)

TRAINING IN DIGIT PERCEPTION

Practicing on the rapid perception of numbers trains your mind to interpret accurately and instantaneously the *total* photograph snapped by your eyes. Since the element of familiarity on which you naturally rely in the rapid reading of words is essentially lacking in digit combinations—rows of random numbers, unlike words and phrases, are practically, if not completely, meaningless—you will be learning, during this practice, to interpret *all*, rather than some or most, of what you see.

The type of exercises on which you will shortly start working is usually called "tachistoscopic (ta-kiss-ta-SKOP-ik) training," after the device known as a "tachistoscope" (ta-KISS-ta-skope), which flashes digits, words, and phrases on a screen at exposures varying from one full second down to as low as $\frac{1}{100}$ of a second.

An improved form of the tachistoscope, manufactured by the Keystone View Co., of Meadville, Pennsylvania, consists of a lantern and a Flashmeter.* The lantern provides enough light to project the material on the screen, and the Flashmeter, working on a spring principle, limits the exposure to the fraction of a second determined by the operator. The Keystone tachistoscope is used throughout the country in elementary and high schools, and in the reading clinics of colleges and universities, to provide the kind of training in quick perception that is so valuable in increasing rate of reading. In a supplement to the *Keystone Tachistoscope Manual*, William B. Greet and John H. Eargle of the Keystone

* This is the registered trade name of the Keystone View Co.

60

School and Guidance Center, San Antonio, Texas, explain the principle behind such training as follows:

> Since we use but a fraction of our capacities, according to research psychologists, and since approximately 80 per cent of our knowledge comes to us through our eyes, increasing usable vision and broadening spans of perception and recognition . . . [has as its purpose to] increase speed, comprehension, accuracy, and self-confidence in reading. . . .
>
> By gradually increasing the speed of the flash and the amount of material to be perceived, unnecessary eye movements are eliminated and the spans of perception and recognition broadened. This technique drives vision impulses to lower reflex levels, where, as learning proceeds, the interval necessary between reception and interpretation is reduced.

A similar explanation is offered by *The Air University Reading Improvement Program,* from which the following excerpts are quoted with permission:

> The use of the tachistoscope in rapid recognition was developed by Dr. Samuel Renshaw at The Ohio State University. When the armed services realized the need for speed-up training in aircraft recognition, Army and Navy pilots used the tachistoscope with outstandingly successful results. Dr. Renshaw is one of our most prominent leaders in experimentation with visual problems and has tested the tachistoscope widely for reading benefits. . . .
>
> The tachistoscope helps the reader approach his limit of precision of vision and peripheral span. The untrained eye has a limited field of vision but with training on quick recognition this field of functional recognition expands.
>
> The tachistoscope has other values. It provides training in several visual processes simultaneously. Not only does it increase the eye span, it also decreases the length of eye fixation. The shutter of the Flashmeter can be controlled so that an interval as short as $\frac{1}{100}$ of a second can be obtained. For purposes of training in the Reading Laboratory $\frac{1}{100}$ second gives enough speed to provide practice in quickening the eye fixation, since the shortest recorded fixation during reading is several times as long as $\frac{1}{100}$ second.
>
> Another value of the tachistoscope is that it forces the reader to grasp material as a form-field, seen as a whole. With such a quick flash he cannot vocalize or get side-tracked on elements of the visual pattern; he must take it in at once or it is gone as soon as the after-image fades. . . .

61

Progress on the tachistoscopic training occurs in three stages: (1) ability to see part of the digit sequence, usually the first part; (2) ability to see the form of the sequence, getting all digits but with reversals in order; and (3) ability to see the content of the sequence, getting all digits and getting them in the right order.

The digit exercises that appear below and at numerous points throughout the remaining chapters of the book are an adaptation of the Keystone slides, which I have made for self-training. Be careful to observe the following instructions carefully whenever you work with these exercises.

Instructions for Training in Digit Perception

1. Place the Flashmeter card (which you will find between the pages of the book) in such a way that the digit window is just above the first number and the digit arrow squarely meets the arrow on the page.

13856   ←_____

2. Pull down the card just far enough to expose the number, *and immediately push the card back* so that the number is again hidden.

3. During the time the number is exposed, glance at it quickly. *Do not say the number to yourself.*

4. As soon as the number is concealed, attempt to reproduce it, *in writing,* in the blank to its right.

5. Then pull the card down a second time and check your answer.

6. Now repeat the process by exposing the next number. To do this pull the card down one line, exposing the number for a fraction of a second, and quickly cover it with an upward movement. Expose the numbers in the left-hand column before doing those in the middle and right-hand columns.

7. Allow only enough time to make one fixation at each exposure. There is no need to rush the movement of the card, but you must expose and conceal quickly enough to permit only one fixation. As you become skillful, you will expose for less and less time, always considerably under a second.

8. There is a broad black arrow pointing to the center of the digit window, and this point will be approximately in the middle of the space occupied by the digits. Fixate at that point, and you will

be able to see a certain distance on each side. (This is called peripheral vision.)

9. As you get into the longer numbers, you will at first be able to reproduce only a certain portion of the digits. Don't let this phenomenon disturb you; accept it as a challenge and expect eventually, with further practice, to perceive a greater and greater proportion, until you will see the complete number in one fixation. That is the pattern of progress. Starting on five-digit numbers, you may at first see only the three central digits, or perhaps the first or the last three digits; with more practice, you'll perceive four, and finally all five digits.

10. You may also note the phenomenon known as "reversal." When you flash, for example, 63218, you may see all five digits but reproduce them as 62381—reversing the order of some of them. This, too, is a natural step in progress, an indication that you're approaching, but have not yet achieved, perfect accuracy. With further practice, reversals will gradually be eliminated.

11. Bear in mind that you are training to respond instantaneously to a *visual* stimulus. Therefore do not, under any circumstances, *say* the numbers you see—and, if possible, do not even think them. Rely, as much as you can, on the visual image you get, plus the afterimage. (The eye transmits the image to the brain, instantaneously, and for the merest fraction of a second that image will continue after the number has been hidden. It is this afterimage that will help you to reproduce the number in writing.) Predominantly visual response, once made habitual, will be of incalculable benefit in eliminating vocalization and lip movements, and in learning to absorb ideas at a rapid rate.

Such are the eleven steps to follow in every digit exercise. Remember that you expose the number for only a fraction of a second, that you do not attempt to vocalize what you have seen, that you reproduce it as accurately as you are able, and that you check your response after each exposure. Practice on the following six numbers before you start exercise 1, so that you are sure your technique is correct.

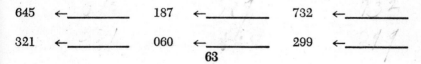

645 ←_____   187 ←_____   732 ←_____

321 ←_____   060 ←_____   299 ←_____

Perception Exercise 1

Using the Flashmeter card, expose each number for a fraction of a second, getting a *visual* impression. Do not say the digits to yourself. Reproduce the number in the blank to the right and then check your result. Mark each error so that you can tally your score at the end of the exercise.

625 ←_____		948 ←_____		802 ←_____	
847 ←_____		029 ←_____		802 ←_____	
948 ←_____		190 ←_____		902 ←_____	
872 ←_____		938 ←_____		602 ←_____	
951 ←_____		739 ←_____		784 ←_____	
092 ←_____		283 ←_____		393 ←_____	
851 ←_____		502 ←_____		593 ←_____	
982 ←_____		914 ←_____		511 ←_____	
939 ←_____		802 ←_____		151 ←_____	
985 ←_____		502 ←_____		477 ←_____	
839 ←_____		803 ←_____		586 ←_____	
041 ←_____		840 ←_____		392 ←_____	
982 ←_____		192 ←_____		864 ←_____	
041 ←_____		845 ←_____		211 ←_____	
092 ←_____		902 ←_____		189 ←_____	
804 ←_____		100 ←_____		468 ←_____	
827 ←_____		010 ←_____			

NUMBER CORRECT OUT OF 50: _____

ONE KEY TO RAPID READING

Actual reading, you recall, is done during the fractional seconds in which the eyes fixate. The efficient reader reacts to a number of words at a single fixation: his unit of comprehension is a complete phrase, a thought sequence. The inefficient reader responds to single words, one at a time; or, if his reading is very poor, parts of words, individual syllables.

Thus, to cover a line of print such as is used in this book, a highly skilled reader might make three or four fixations. After coming to rest at the first point on a new line, his eyes need move only twice or three times more before he is ready to make a return sweep to the beginning of the next line. After that first fixation, then, there are at most two or three moments of nonfocusing, only two or three fractional seconds in which his eyes are not reading. The unskilled reader, on the other hand, may have to move his eyes eight or nine or more times before he has read the whole line: there is a correspondingly greater number of moments of nonreading. This extra time allotted by the poor reader to nonreading accounts in part for his slowness.

But only in part.

Suppose there are two boxes in front of you, both nailed to the top of a table. Box A contains a thousand marbles. Box B is empty. It is your job to transfer the marbles from one box to the other. How would you do it?

You could, if you liked, pick up the marbles one by one, dropping each into the second box before you picked up another from the first one. That would take a long time. The muscles in your arm and hand would become tired long before you finished. You would be doing your task in as inefficient a way as possible.

Or you could pick up the marbles two at a time. That would

double your speed. But to do the job as quickly and as efficiently as possible, you would grab up handful after handful. The more you grabbed each time, the sooner you'd be through, and the less you would be likely to tire.

This analogy is admirably applicable to reading. If your eyes photograph only one or two words at a time, the process must perforce be a slow and painful one. However, if your eyes grab up "handfuls" of words, you can read like the wind. *The more words you absorb in a single fixation, the faster you read.* That is the second part of the reason that increased efficiency in perception can so radically speed up your reading.

There is a third, and very significant, factor.

Reading is not actually done with the eyes, as I have pointed out; reading is a mental activity. It is done with the mind—the eyes acting as sensory extensions of the brain, as a transmitting belt carrying images of words to the brain. (A blind person, as you know, can read, even though he has lost, or has never had, the use of his eyes. He can train his *fingers* to substitute for eyes, his fingers can become the sensory extensions of his brain.)

If your eyes feed your mind one word at a time, you grasp the thought of a printed page choppily, disconnectedly; for thought normally comes in phrases, not in single words. There is practically no meaning at all in the single word *one*. There is very little thought in the single word *bright*. The word *morning*, although it has a fuller significance by itself than either *one* or *bright*, contains a good deal less meaning than the complete phrase, *one bright morning*.

The word-by-word reader forces his mind to slow up because his eyes are continually feeding it words that are devoid, or nearly devoid, of meaning. His mind receives the impulse *one*—and must wait patiently for the second impulse, *bright*—and must wait still again for the third impulse, *morning*—before it has something definite to work on.

The eyes of the efficient reader feed his mind, in a *single* impulse, a complete thought, *one bright morning*. No dead spots. No waiting. No interruption to the process of thinking. And no waste of time—for the idea, *one bright morning*, can be photographed by the eyes and registered in the mind *more quickly as a single unit* than can the three separate words, one after the other, that make up that thought.

In reading, the whole is more significant than the sum of its parts.
The "whole" is a phrase, a thought; the parts are individual words
which, by themselves, one by one, are often useless for comprehension.

The third factor, then, is that the reader who takes in *more* words
in a single fixation understands more quickly; and, since the final
purpose of reading is to understand, the more nearly instantaneously the thought of a printed line is grasped, and the more
smoothly the eyes and mind co-operate, the more rapid and efficient the entire process becomes.

One key to rapid reading is the perception and interpretation of
large numbers of words at each fixation.

Merely knowing this fact is not enough.

Expert as you may become at understanding the principles of
rapid, efficient reading, you cannot become a fast reader until you
are able, as a result of constant, hard practice, to apply these principles as a matter of automatic habit. You can say to yourself, "I am
now going to use wide fixations; I am going to perceive quickly and
accurately; and thus I am going to read faster," but you will have
as little success as the person who has memorized the principles of
expert swimming and then jumps into the water for a half-mile
race. If he has never been in the water before, he will likely thrash
around awkwardly and perhaps eventually drown, for his knowledge of the rules *intellectually* would not, by itself, make his body
respond *physically*.

The person who intends to become an expert swimmer must
practice one skill after another until the correct bodily movements
become habitual and automatic; he must build up such an excellent
set of co-ordinating reflexive habits that his body does the proper
things without any conscious direction from his mind. In first learning how to swim, he must go through each part of the act consciously. Then, by practice, by more and more and more practice,
by constantly and patiently refining his good habits and by ruth-
lessly weeding out his bad ones, he trains his body to function by
itself.

Becoming a fast reader requires the same continuous, intelligent practice, the same single-minded diligence that are essential
to the conquest of any high-order skill; it requires the building
up and refinement of good habits to the point where instantaneous

perception and wide fixations; lack of vocalization, regressions, and lip movements; and rapid mental reaction to the *ideas* on the printed page become so nearly automatic that the mind can be left entirely free to concentrate on what an author is saying.

MACULAR AND PERIPHERAL IMAGE

In adult reading courses, and in the reading clinics of American colleges and universities, students are taught, through tachistoscopic training, to perceive and interpret more words in a single fixation and to reduce to a minimum the time spent on making that fixation. They are trained to make greater use of their peripheral vision, and thereby to increase the width of their interpretable eye spans while reading.

You can find out quickly what peripheral vision is by holding your forefinger up in front of your eyes at a comfortable distance— say ten to twelve inches.

When you do that, and stare at your finger, what do you see?

Your finger, of course. You see your finger clearly and sharply because your eyes are focusing on it. This image comes to you through the macula of the retina of your eyes, that portion of the optical equipment which sees objects in the direct line of vision. We might call your finger, in this instance, your macular image.

But do you see only your finger? Look again, and you will notice, though not so clearly, many things on all sides of your finger. Don't shift your gaze, keep focused directly on your finger, and yet you can see, though perhaps vaguely, many objects above and below the macular image and to the right or left of it, possibly for quite a distance in all directions.

Everything you see in addition to your finger is being photographed by your peripheral vision; or we may say that the less distinct images you receive on all sides of your finger are the peripheral images.

Perception training, both on digits and on words or phrases, is intended to help you react more accurately to the peripheral images you receive while reading.

Perception training is purely psychological—it has no effect whatever on the organic structure or on the efficiency of your eyes, but rather sharpens and accelerates your mental interpretations of the ocular images that are sent to your brain during each fixation. Sloppy, slow, or awkward seeing, in reading as in anything else, is the result of poor development of *mental images* and not necessarily a sign of poor vision. By means of perception exercises on digits, words, and phrases you are attempting to teach your mind to interpret as quickly and completely as possible the image transmitted to it by an ocular fixation.*

Take, for example, a number of seven digits: 8321689.

Before training, you fixate on this number and interpret only the macular image of—216—; the interpretation of the peripheral image is lost. As your training begins to produce results, you learn to react mentally to more and more of the peripheral image, until finally you can interpret accurately all seven digits in a single quick fixation: three of them (2, 1, 6) perhaps as a macular image, the other four—two on each side of the central digits—as a peripheral image.

A similar phenomenon occurs in phrases. Macular vision transmits the center of the phrase as a stimulus to the brain, and peripheral vision transmits those parts which are to the left and right of the center. A phrase such as *in the reading clinics* can be grasped as an entity if the reader has trained his peripheral vision, but actually there are two kinds of image, macular and peripheral, as follows:

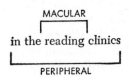

It thus stands to reason that the sharper and more efficient your interpretation of peripheral vision becomes, the wider your usable eye spans will be, and the more material you will be able to interpret at each fixation.

The Flashmeter (or tachistoscope), as you know, exposes a word

* Needless to say, I am taking for granted that your eyes are capable of good vision at reading distance or have been corrected through glasses or other means. If you feel that your vision is faulty, I strongly recommend a thorough checkup by a competent oculist or optometrist before you proceed with your training.

or phrase for an amazingly minute space of time, down to as little as one one-hundredth of a second. In that merest fraction of a moment the student must perceive and interpret as many words as the merciless operator of the machine wishes to present to him. And since the machine is adjustable both as to the number of words to be exposed and the length of time of their exposure, the reader can slowly and methodically be trained to increase the length of his recognition span while he decreases the time of his fixation.

Let me describe the use of the Flashmeter with a typical class during the years I supervised the Adult Reading Laboratory at City College.

The students sit in front of a large white motion picture screen, their eyes focused on a particular point on the screen. The operator touches the Flashmeter control, and a word flashes on the screen— flashes on and then flashes off again so quickly that you can scarcely believe it has been there at all. The word has been exposed for the merest fraction of a second. Yet it is time enough, for these students through practice have learned the art of instantaneous recognition.

Each student writes the word on a sheet of paper in front of him, and then looks back at the screen for the next word. The process is repeated several times, and then the operator adjusts the Flashmeter so that an entire phrase, instead of an individual word, will now be projected on the screen. Since no increase of exposure time is made, the student is unable to use more than a single fixation, even if he is tempted to do so. Unless the phrase is absorbed in one quick glance, no comprehension will result.

And the effect? Most of the class within a few weeks has become adept at reading complete phrases in single instantaneous fixations.

It is true that these students have worked methodically through-out these weeks. Without exception they have devoted numerous practice periods at home to working on mimeographed sheets of digits, words, and phrases—sheets containing the same material you will find in the succeeding pages of this book. Their excellence is produced not by the magic of the machine but by the constant practice they have engaged in both at home and in class—practice you will have to engage in also if you wish to achieve similar results.

TRAINING IN FASTER WORD PERCEPTION

In the section on digit perception I have already described how to practice for best results. The methods here are essentially the same, but I wish to repeat them, briefly, so that you will be sure to do the right thing.

The Flashmeter card, which you have been using for training in digit perception, contains wider windows for word and phrase perception, and will simulate for you all the conditions of reading with an actual Flashmeter. This is how to use it: Place the card over the first word in exercise 2 so that the arrow of the "word window" aligns with the arrow on the page. When you are ready to start your practicing, pull the card down just enough to expose the first word in the window.

As fast as you can move your muscles, push the card up again so that the word is once more concealed. Thus you will be acting as a human Flashmeter, with the page of the book taking the part of the motion picture screen. Now, in that slight fraction of a second in which the word is exposed, it is up to you to interpret it *accurately*—and this will be no mean task, for each word will be somewhat similar, but not exactly identical, to one or more words that precede and/or follow it. If you have a little trouble at first, *do not slacken your speed of exposure and concealment;* the idea is not to decrease the speed of your arm movement until it coincides with the speed of your perception, but, on the contrary, to accelerate your speed of perception so that it will equal the swiftness of your arm. Your job, in other words, is to prove the falsity of the old adage that the hand is quicker than the eye.

Perception Exercise 2

Use the Flashmeter card according to previous directions, with the "word window" at the top, aligning the arrow at the right edge of the card with the arrow on the page. As soon as a word has been exposed and immediately concealed, attempt to reproduce it, in writing, in the blank to its right. Then pull the card down again and check on your accuracy. Mark each error so that you can tally your score at the end of the exercise.

71

fits	← _____	slough	← _____
fists	← _____	slit	← _____
fights	← _____	slink	← _____
flights	← _____	slosh	← _____
flits	← _____	sash	← _____
slats	← _____	slips	← _____
slash	← _____	slaps	← _____
slams	← _____	slakes	← _____
slants	← _____	bright	← _____
slow	← _____	bricks	← _____
first	← _____	breaks	← _____
frost	← _____	brink	← _____
front	← _____	pain	← _____
flint	← _____	pane	← _____
fought	← _____	pram	← _____
flirt	← _____	prom	← _____
frets	← _____	prime	← _____
fasts	← _____	prong	← _____
fluster	← _____	plant	← _____
flutter	← _____	plank	← _____
flitter	← _____	brittle	← _____
fritter	← _____	bottle	← _____

battle	←_____	blocks	←_____
bitter	←_____	blinks	←_____
black	←_____	bleats	←_____

NUMBER CORRECT OUT OF 50: _____

TRAINING IN PHRASE PERCEPTION

Perception Exercise 3

Focus your eyes just above the broad arrow pointing to the "phrase window" on the Flashmeter card. This arrow indicates the approximate center of each phrase, and through a combination of macular and peripheral images you will eventually, after some periods of training, be able to interpret the entire phrase. Rely on your vision, not your speech, in doing this exercise; *refrain, if possible, from repeating the phrase in your mind after you have seen it.* If necessary, allow yourself two or more exposures on a phrase if the first exposure is not successful. However, at each successive exposure, attempt to see the entire phrase, not just that portion you may have missed in the first exposure. Remember to keep the time of exposure so small that you will be able to make only *one* fixation on each phrase.

→	a basic need	→	a single woman
→	a basic idea	→	a single cup
→	a third meaning	→	a lonely woman
→	a fourth meaning	→	a lonely man
→	type of learning	→	an only son
→	need of warming	→	gave her life
→	my real purpose	→	took his wife
→	his first purpose	→	with a knife

73

→	unnecessary strife	→	a sure cure
→	not too unusual	→	a strange cure
→	hardly unusual	→	telephone connection
→	most unusual	→	hold the line
→	they tell me	→	hold it tight
→	he tells me	→	hold it taut
→	I tell them	→	come to naught
→	don't tell me	→	came at night
→	I may never	→	do it right
→	I rarely do	→	right this way
→	I surely do	→	can you wait
→	I certainly don't	→	read the book
→	a great idea	→	fire the cook
→	a foolish idea	→	cook for two
→	two good ideas	→	find the book
→	some strange ideas	→	book the band
→	no good idea	→	beat the band
→	no possible idea	→	boot the cook
→	a cute idea	→	bake the cake
→	a cure for all	→	take the cake
→	a city of stone	→	took the cake
→	a cure-all	→	hold a wake

Perception Exercise 4

Now that you have warmed up with the phrases in exercise 3, you are ready to be a little more demanding of your powers. You allowed yourself to make more than one exposure, if you found such multiple exposure necessary. From now on, consider your training successful only if you see the complete phrase *the first time;* if you do not, go directly to the next phrase and continue working, phrase by phrase, exercise by exercise, until success is achieved.

→	he won't marry	→	one cup only
→	we won't tarry	→	one enchanted evening
→	can you carry	→	one strange evening
→	you can carry	→	this rare evening
→	with whom I share	→	a spare evening
→	he'll get along	→	spare an evening
→	good to know	→	spare a day
→	good to see	→	spare some time
→	food for thought	→	take some time
→	he had thought	→	an inconvenient time
→	because of him	→	too much time
→	with all the contacts	→	full of lime
→	with many contacts	→	the salty brine
→	with few contacts	→	rare old wine
→	try to relax	→	sparkling wine
→	much more lonely	→	very strong wine
→	much less lonely	→	this strong wine

→	a time of stress	→	Ford has everything
→	a time to play	→	a fine car
→	the time to go	→	a complete lemon
→	continue the work	→	broken-down hack
→	hard work to do	→	money can't buy
→	well-paid work	→	love and kisses
→	old work-horse	→	down the street
→	kind of work	→	fine and dandy
→	rare old jerk	→	not a treatment
→	good old jerk	→	not a reaction
→	jerked his finger	→	a bad cold
→	made a ringer	→	good as gold
→	took the ring	→	gold and silver
→	joined the army	→	copper and bronze
→	old army game	→	wire and spit
→	an exciting game	→	a new ingredient
→	big game hunter	→	smoother performance
→	hunted big game	→	it really is
→	smelled a rat	→	like a bank
→	on a bat	→	like a baby
→	weird old house	→	like a baby's bank
→	two-story house	→	like a piggy bank

76

→	like a stuffed owl	→	thin as a bug
→	like a stuffed pig	→	snug as a bug
→	like a stuffy pig	→	thin as a rail
→	like a wise owl	→	built like a house
→	a wise old owl	→	gone and forgotten
→	a prize owl	→	permanently ruined
→	air conditioning	→	completely bereft
→	Elgin watch	→	no single stone
→	the night watch	→	had actually seen
→	the new watch	→	blinked his eyes
→	a few watches	→	you rich folks
→	truly yours	→	we poor people
→	yours truly	→	we the people
→	a crowded car	→	in order to get
→	the back seat	→	twice a week
→	the window seat	→	on first seeing
→	filled with love	→	without real fun
→	fat as a rail	→	What's wrong?

You have made a start, now, at training your perception—at learning to interpret quickly and accurately what your eyes see, and at permitting your eyes to feed your mind a wider portion of print, during each fixation, for such interpretation.

This is, of course, only the beginning of such learning and training—to develop any degree of skill and accuracy in rapid percep-

77

tion, you must devote a great deal of practice to the scores of perception drills that you will find spread throughout the book.

Intensive and continuous practice on these drills will reduce, perhaps almost to the vanishing point, any *time lag* between your reception of, and your mental response to, the visual images offered by a line of print—will make your interpretation of the meaning of such images as immediate, indeed as nearly instantaneous, as possible.

So do all perception exercises religiously, unfailingly, whenever you come upon them. I cannot overemphasize their importance, I cannot overrate their value in your total training program; as you gradually build your skill you yourself will realize from personal experience how effectively instantaneous responses, fewer fixations, and wider recognition spans can increase your reading speed.

Certain factors in the reading process may, singly or in various combinations, drastically interfere with the nearly instantaneous reaction to meaning that perception training aims at—may act as circuit breakers, so to speak, of the electrical impulses that the eyes flash to the brain. The most serious of such factors are (1) lip movements, (2) vocalization, (3) excessive reliance on inner speech, and (4) addiction to unnecessary regressions. How these factors operate to retard interpretation and thus slow up the rate of comprehension will be the subject of the next chapter.

INNER SPEECH, LIP MOVE-
MENTS, VOCALIZATION,
AND REGRESSIONS

Preview

Training to become a rapid reader involves not only the constant practice of *efficient* techniques, but also the ruthless elimination of any *inefficient* habits that hold your comprehension down to a rate far lower than you are actually capable of.

And so, in this chapter, you will learn:

- How to reduce your dependency on inner speech.
- How to read without lip movements or other forms of vocalization.
- How to stop making frequent and unnecessary regressions.

> *Chapter 4* explains in detail how to give up three bad habits that drastically reduce speed of comprehension.

INNER SPEECH

According to J. A. O'Brien, an expert in the field of improved reading habits, there are essentially three kinds of readers: *motor* readers, *auditory* readers, and *visual* readers.

The *motor* reader is the lip mover, the vocalizer. He accompanies his reading with various (and quite unnecessary) movements of the muscles of articulation. "In other words," as O'Brien explains it, "reading is not confined to the visualization of the printed symbols. Concomitant with this visualization there occur movements, more or less incipient in character, of the tongue, lips, vocal cords, larynx, inner palate, throat, and the general physiological mechanism that functions in oral speech. The reader goes through the form of saying the words to himself." *

The *auditory* reader relies on *hearing* a page of print—he is aware of pronouncing words in his mind, although his speech organs are completely at rest.

The *visual* reader, in contrast, not only completely by-passes the vocal apparatus in his response to meaning—he is also, for the most part, largely unaware of the individual words that combine to make up such meaning. He can, in short, understand words and phrases without first stopping either to say them or to listen to their sound; he reads with his eyes and mind, not with his mouth or ears.

These three types of readers—motor, auditory, and visual—are, as you can guess, listed in ascending order of skill. The *lip mover* or *vocalizer* is an extremely slow reader, for he is artificially keeping his speed down to the rate at which he can pronounce words— and this is about one fourth as fast as he could read them silently.

* J. A. O'Brien, *Silent Reading*, The Macmillan Company, New York. Reprinted with permission.

He tires quickly because there is so much muscular activity. He makes frequent regressions, for the eyes tend to rush ahead and the voice stays behind. Often he uses his finger to point, so that he can keep his eyes back where his voice is. He tends to be a word-by-word reader, for the unit of pronunciation is a word, or even a syllable, although the unit of meaning is usually a phrase and sometimes a whole sentence. He makes numerous fixations on a line, since his eyes must focus on every syllable or word which his lips pronounce. And, finally, his comprehension is poor, for his mind is as much involved with the mechanics of reading as it is with the ideas—if not more so. In fine, the whole reading process is a chore, and the less he reads the happier he is.

The *auditory* reader is much more skillful, much more rapid. His speed need not be unduly hampered, for he is not actually pronouncing the words he "hears," but only imagining their pronunciation. If his awareness of, and reliance on, the *sounds* of words is not very great, his rate of comprehension does not suffer to any alarming extent; however, if he cannot easily increase his speed to over 400 words per minute he is undoubtedly much more dependent on inner speech than he should be.

Inner speech probably occurs to some extent in all readers, even the fastest and most skillful—but the visual reader does not have to *lean* on it before he can respond to meaning. The auditory reader does—that is the significant difference between them.

Strong dependence on inner speech is not necessary for understanding. When you listen with keen interest to someone who is talking, when you become really involved in what he is saying, you are, as you know, almost totally unaware of the individual *words* he is using—for you are concentrating on the *ideas* that his words add up to. You respond to his words not as *words,* but as conveyors of *meaning.* You think along with him, you react intellectually and emotionally to the thoughts he expresses, you agree or disagree, you may even interrupt at times to express the thoughts and reactions that he stimulates in you. *But one thing you do not do is consciously repeat the speaker's words in your mind before you understand what they mean.* You don't do this because you obviously don't have to—in reading, *conscious* mental repetition of the words on a page is equally unnecessary.

Have you ever watched an expert stenographer taking rapid

dictation? Her pencil whizzes across her shorthand notebook at a rate that clearly rules out any possibility that she is repeating what she hears before writing it down. The dictator's words stimulate impulses in the stenographer's brain that are immediately transmitted to her flying fingers—there is no time for conscious repetition.

The interested listener and the expert stenographer respond to the meaning of *auditory* stimuli without conscious reliance on inner speech—is it possible to react similarly to the meaning of purely *visual* stimuli?

Let us consider this question at some length.

Suppose that an experiment is set up in which you are asked to press one lever when a *red* light flashes, a different lever when a *green* light flashes. Imagine yourself sitting at a table with your right hand resting on the lever for red, your left hand on the one for green.

The light flashes. What do you do?

First, of course, you interpret the color. Is it red, or is it green? (If you are color-blind, this experiment is not for you.) Having made your decision, you next recall which hand is for which color. Then, finally, you press the correct lever.

How long a time interval elapses between the flashing of the light and your manual response? I think you know the answer. After a few warm-up tries (and the requirements of the experiment are so simple that these may not be necessary), you respond almost instantaneously—you are able to press the proper lever each time in no more than one tenth of a second. (I have tried this experiment over and over with my students, and that's the longest it ever takes.)

Now we may ask, how can you react so quickly if you first have to make all these conscious and verbalized decisions? (Just saying to yourself *Is it red or green?* takes almost a second.)

And again you know the answer. *You do not consciously verbalize your decisions.* Instantaneously after the flash, your brain interprets the color of the light, remembers that *red* is *right, green* is *left,* and transmits a pressure impulse to the proper hand—all this wordlessly and in one tenth of a second or less!

Suppose, however, that you were in the habit of consciously verbalizing all your bodily responses to visual stimuli, something clearly improbable and abnormal. When the light flashed you might say to yourself, *"red—right"* or *"green—left,"* and then press. Would you still be able to react as quickly? Obviously not—you would take at least twice as long.

Most bodily responses to visual images occur, as you know, without consciously *verbalized* recognition or direction. When you raise your arm to ward off a blow, jump out of the path of an oncoming car, or stamp on the brake or twist the steering wheel of an automobile to avoid a sudden obstacle, your brain, reacting to the visual danger signals, instantaneously shoots impulses through the proper nerve pathways—and this, too, happens apparently wordlessly and in the merest fraction of a second. Indeed it is only if the perception of peril causes momentary muscular paralysis that inner speech may take the place of action. You see the danger, but for some reason you are frozen into petrified immobility; and yet you may be conscious, during such an awful moment, of thinking wildly to yourself, in actual words, *He's going to hit me!* or *I'm going to hit it!* And sure enough he does, or you do.

Let us get away, now, from physical responses and consider a form of thinking that more closely approximates the mental activity involved in silent reading.

Here, as an instance, is a simple example in addition for you to work out. As you figure the sum, pay close attention to the amount of conscious inner speech you use.

$$5 + 6 + 3 + 8 + 4 + 2 = ?$$

What did you say to yourself in order to get the correct answer? Did you say, *five and six are eleven, eleven and three are fourteen, fourteen and eight are twenty-two, twenty-two and four are twenty-six, twenty-six and two are twenty-eight?* If you did, you have never learned the quick and efficient way to do your sums.

Or did you, perhaps, cut down your inner speech to the following: *eleven, fourteen, twenty-two, twenty-six, twenty-eight?* If you did (and anyone can work this way with a little practice) you were responding to the visual impulses set up by the numbers 5, 6, 3, 8, 4, and 2 without once verbalizing what you saw.

As it happens, there is an even more rapid and more efficient way to add these six numbers, namely, *eleven, twenty-two, twenty-eight.* What have we done this time? To the sum of the first two numbers,

83

eleven, we've added the sum of the next two to get *twenty-two,* then added the sum of the last two to get *twenty-eight*—even less conscious inner speech than before. (This method, too, can be made habitual with a little practice.)

Try a few addition problems on your own now, using either of the two efficient methods described above, so that you will clearly understand how *reduced reliance on inner speech and verbalization can speed up your responses to visual images.*

$$2 + 9 + 1 + 7 + 3 + 6 = ?$$

$$5 + 5 + 3 + 7 + 2 + 8 = ?$$

$$9 + 1 + 4 + 6 + 7 + 3 = ?$$

$$4 + 5 + 1 + 8 + 9 + 9 = ?$$

$$5 + 3 + 2 + 6 + 1 + 7 = ?$$

Reading a page of print is, admittedly, not exactly the same as pressing a lever when you see a light flash, moving your body to ward off perceived danger, or computing sums in arithmetic. But there are two important areas of similarity, namely: (1) reading, like these other activities, consists of responding to the *meaning* of visual images; and (2) the less inner speech or conscious verbalization, the quicker the response.

A certain amount of inner speech, as I have said, probably accompanies all silent reading. This may be so partly because, as children, we understood words as meaningful *sounds* long before we were able to read them as written or printed symbols. A child learns to read by connecting the picture of a word with some sound that he is familiar with—and all reading is dependent, in the earliest stages of learning, on sounds and on oral activity. When a child becomes more experienced with words as visual symbols, he finds that he can gain meaning without making any very audible sounds, although for a short time, as a kind of transitional stage, he will either whisper faintly or move his tongue and lips silently. (And this is a stage that some poor readers never manage to progress beyond.) As his skill and experience increase, he gives up his dependence on the vocal mechanism and relies solely on inner speech. Eventually, if he matures into an efficient and rapid reader, he gradually loses a good deal of his awareness even of inner speech.

He can now respond to the meaning of words without consciously depending on their remembered sound—indeed, as I have pointed out, he is largely unaware of the presence of the individual words that make up the meaning of a page of print. The occurrence of at least some degree of inner speech in all silent reading may be partly due, also, to the fact that in most languages the written or printed symbols represent the actual spoken sounds of words—hence it may be impossible for anyone to eliminate completely in his mind the connection between sound and meaning.

Obviously, then, you cannot totally eradicate the auditory reactions that may attend your own reading. However, you can considerably reduce your reliance on them, you can cut them down to a point where they no longer retard, even to the slightest amount, your immediate response to meaning.

How can you do this? Largely by intensive and frequent practice on instantaneous perception; and by consciously attempting, during your work on digit, word, and phrase drills, to verbalize less and less the visual image that you expose for a fraction of a second in the window of the Flashmeter card.

If you are *excessively* dependent on inner speech as you read (and a rate of under 400 w.p.m. would indicate that this may be so), increasing the speed of your mental responses to visual images by means of perception exercises will be of tremendous benefit to you.

However, let me issue a note of warning at this point: the conscious inhibition of auditory reactions, immensely valuable and profitable during perception practice, *is pointless and may even be dangerous when applied to actual reading.*

For when you read for meaning your mind should be entirely occupied with the pursuit of ideas. If part of your mind is concerned with suppressing inner speech, comprehension will suffer and the comfort and enjoyment so vital to skillful reading will be lost. On the other hand, if you constantly read as fast as your comprehension permits, the perception training you are getting will be transferred, without conscious effort on your part, over into your general reading. The more involved you become in the *ideas* on a page, the less will you be aware of the individual *words* in which these ideas are expressed. As you increase your ability to grasp ideas quickly and to respond to them actively, you will gradually decrease your dependence on "hearing" the words and sounds that make up ideas.

LIP MOVEMENTS AND VOCALIZATION

If you are a motor reader, you have to attack your problem in a different way. *You must consciously inhibit every last vestige of movement in the vocal mechanism not only during perception practice but in all your reading.*

How can you tell whether a page of print elicits any degree of motor responses in you? To begin with, if your rate is 250 w.p.m. or better, you may rest assured that you have given up the childhood crutch of saying or whispering words, or of forming them with your lips and tongue, in order to understand them. (And if this is so, the rest of this section will be of only academic interest to you.)

If, however, your rate is considerably below 250 w.p.m. on material well within your comprehension, the chances are good that vocal movements of some sort are interfering with normal speed.

Pay close attention to your lips and tongue as you read the following italicized words: *Tick, tack, toe; drip, drop, drape; sit, sat, set; limp, lump, lamp; pit, pat, pet; bass, base, bus; past, pressed, post; must, massed, mussed; fist, fast, fussed.* Did you feel any motion at all in the vocal mechanism? Did your tongue move, even the least bit, to sound out the consonants *t* and *d*? Did your lips move, even ever so slightly, on the consonants *p, b, m,* and *f*? Did you make any sounds, however barely audible, or detect even the hint of whispering?

If the answer is *yes* to any of these questions, you are a lip mover or a vocalizer or both; and you will never be able to grasp the meaning of a page with even average speed until you completely eliminate every slight remnant and trace of vocal movement and sound from your silent reading.

This is not hard to do if you are willing to undergo a short period of discomfort. Louella Cole, in her book *Improvement of Reading,** makes two suggestions for teaching a child to read without vocalization. They are suggestions which are also adaptable to the adult. Here they are, in her own words:

* Rinehart & Company, Inc., New York. Reprinted with permission.

The simplest method is to render the speech mechanism incapable of pronouncing words, even partially. A simple and effective means of bringing about this result is to have the child put two fingers into his mouth, using them to separate his upper and lower teeth and to hold down his tongue. Nobody can articulate words with his mouth hanging open. If the child, through force of habit, moves his jaws to articulate, he bites his fingers. With the tongue and the jaws both out of commission, there will be no pronunciation. Instead of his fingers a child may may use his ruler or a large-sized eraser. The fingers are better than either wood or rubber, however, partly because the pupil is unwilling to bite them and partly because he always has them with him!

Another, if even less elegant, procedure is to let the child chew gum while he is reading. His speech mechanism is out of commission, not because it is at rest but because it is doing something else. No one can pronounce words and chew gum simultaneously. Naturally, a pupil should not persist in these techniques until they become habits. They should be used only until the tendency to pronounce words has been broken.

Dr. Cole cites this interesting case:

John was a loud vocalizer. Whatever else might be wrong with him, it was evident at once to the teacher of the remedial class that something must be done to stop the noise John made, if the other children were to get their work done. Without waiting to make any analysis, Miss A. promptly recommended the finger-in-the-mouth technique. There ensued a silence—but almost no comprehension of the reading matter. John seemed unable to recognize even the simplest words unless he could pronounce them. In order to find something that John could read without vocalizing, it was necessary to use a second-grade book. During the first week John had his doubts about the value of this method but agreed to give it a fair trial. Before the end of the second week he had begun to feel that his reading was much less labored than ever before. Instead of being work, the simple book he was using became play. At about this time the boy appeared one morning with a neatly whittled and sandpapered piece of wood, all wrapped up in a clean handkerchief. During the following six weeks John kept the piece of wood between his teeth whenever he was reading. No other treatment was used for this boy. Yet in two months' time he improved nearly three years in speed and over a year in comprehension. Moreover, he reported a great increase in the ease with which he read. After leaving the class, John continued to carry the wood around with him, but he used it less and less. At the end of the year he was reading without any artificial aid to keep him from vocalizing.

I have found, from my own experience with adult students who were motor readers, that maintaining a rigidity in the vocal apparatus while reading will eliminate lip movements and vocalization within two weeks. During *every bit* of reading in this two-week period, the jaws must be clamped shut, the tongue held rigid against the roof of the mouth, and the lips maintained absolutely motionless, even if, in difficult cases, the student must use the thumb and forefinger to hold his lips in a viselike grip.

This is the one bad habit of reading that is the quickest to disappear when an inhibiting set of conditions is put into effect. At first the student is comically uncomfortable. His eyes pop, he is the very picture of misery. His whole being cries out to be allowed to relapse into the comfortable habit of accompanying his reading with muscular activity. But if his spirit is stronger than his flesh, he very shortly finds nonvocalized reading decreasing in discomfort. Soon he needs to exert less force to keep his vocal apparatus still, and he then discovers what every good reader has long since learned and forgotten—that words can be understood without sounding them out, without whispering them, without even forming them silently with the lips and tongue. At this point comprehension becomes so much more efficient, so much faster, and so much easier, that he is ready to relinquish permanently an infantile pattern that has unnecessarily persisted into adulthood, a pattern that *compels* an extremely slow rate of reading, that, indeed, makes reading an awkward and unpleasant experience. He has, maturely, been willing to suffer some pain in the expectation of future rewards—and he is not disappointed.

If you are a lip-mover or vocalizer, you too must be prepared to undergo a short period of discomfort. Possibly, in the beginning, you will get little or no meaning from a page if you totally suppress your motor reactions. But persevere. If necessary, practice on the simplest kind of material you can find—even a child's second or third grade reader, or juvenile books written for seven- or eight-year-olds, or picture books with only the most elementary kind of text. *But read with your eyes only, not with any part of your mouth.* And eventually full comprehension will return. When it does, and

88

with it far greater speed and ease, the rewards will more than compensate for the pain.

REGRESSIONS

The habitually or compulsively regressive reader does not fully trust his comprehension—perhaps he does not quite trust his ability in any area in which he functions.

Let us look at an extreme case: Miss X, a spinster of thirty-eight, did well in many aspects of training at the Adult Reading Laboratory, but always her progress was impeded by a compulsive need to regress. If a selection contained figures or statistics, she would have an incomplete feeling unless she went back, time and time again, and reread them, often breaking the trend of her comprehension in order to reassure herself that she had seen them correctly the first time. On any one line of print she would return several times to the first few words before she reached the last one. In the normal person, regressions are caused mainly by faulty comprehension or by an unfamiliarity with vocabulary, but with Miss X they appeared to be an almost neurotic pattern.

Further discussions with her turned up the fascinating fact that she was a habitual "regressor" (if we may extend the term to non-reading acts) in everything she did. After she stepped out of her apartment, and locked the door behind her, she would open it again, and walk back into her rooms to make sure the lights were turned out, her last cigarette extinguished, the radio shut off, and the windows closed. If she went to the ladies' room in a public place, she would no sooner pass the threshold than she would have to rush out in a panic to make sure that the door had, indeed, been marked "Ladies" and not "Men." After making a business phone call (she was the secretary to the vice-president of a small bank), she would often put a call through a second time to the same person to ask him if she had remembered to tell him so-and-so (of course, she always had). She was a neat, methodical worker, but lost an immense amount of time, energy, and efficiency by constantly checking up on herself.

And this pattern carried over, naturally, into her reading. Though her intelligence was considerably above average and her comprehension good, she never trusted either—so she was a slow reader, with poor concentration and four to six regressions on every line of print.

If you yourself are conscious of making only occasional regressions, pay no further attention to this aspect of the reading act. But if you feel that usually you cannot understand a page of print to your full satisfaction without frequently going back to verify your first impressions, then take warning. You may be regressing *because of habit and anxiety,* not because your comprehension was inadequate.

The most effective means of breaking a habit is to set up conditions that will encourage the contrary and opposing habit.

Thus, when we wish to teach a child not to misspell a word, the most effective method is to have him practice on the correct spelling until the incorrect one fades from his memory. (What is habit but reflexive and automatic memory of previous acts?)

To teach an aviator *not* to pull back the stick and attempt to climb when he feels his plane going into a stall or a spin (for such an action, logical as it may seem, makes him lose control over his plane and in many cases results in a fatal crack-up), we must enable him to gain such complete mastery over the reverse habit—that is, pushing the stick forward and forcing the plane into a more rapid descent—that his muscles will react instantaneously, and the former habit will fade from his memory because a new habit is taking its place.

So with *regressions.* To inhibit and finally destroy the habit of reading backward—that is, letting the eyes return to words or phrases previously read in a line of print—you must set up the contrary and opposing habit of *constantly reading forward.*

Reading, like most other skills, is a whole complex of automatic habits. When the habits are good, reading is efficient and rapid; when the habits are bad, reading is slow, awkward, unsatisfying. The habit of frequent and unnecessary regressions not only reduces the speed of reading (obviously); but by disrupting the smooth and continuous flow of meaning it also interferes with comprehension—which is ironic, for the severely regressive reader, by unceasingly checking up on his understanding, succeeds only in ruining it.

90

The skillful reader may make occasional and *voluntary* regressions, but solely out of actual and realistic need, never from habit or compulsion or because he doesn't entirely trust his ability to comprehend. He goes back to reread a word or phrase only if he is certain that it is utterly useless to go on without doing so; otherwise he keeps pushing rapidly ahead, for he is far more interested in total meaning and in ideas than he is in individual words or phrases or details.

Of course, if ideas are expressed ambiguously or confusingly, or in extremely complicated or involved language, meaning will be elusive, and rereading and still further rereading may be necessary —but then the fault lies with the writer, not with the reader. S. N. Behrman, in a short story that appeared in a recent issue of the *New Yorker*, touchingly describes the reaction of one of his characters to such elusive writing:

> Reflecting on these miseries, yet struggling also to keep his mind on the words he was reading, Mr. Weintraub took off his glasses and polished them again. Because his formal education had been sketchy, he did not know that he had a right to demand clarity and simplicity from an author, or that the relationship between writer and reader was a reciprocal one and the responsibility for understanding divided equally between them. He cursed himself for being stupid, and he felt a certain pride that for [his son] Willard, presumably, these massive and coagulated paragraphs were hammock reading.

Regressions, then, are by no means forbidden—*if they are absolutely necessary.* When you have an impulse to regress, test your needs against reality. Ask yourself, *have you really not understood what you have just read, or are you merely indulging a bad habit? Is it positively essential to check up on that word, or phrase, or detail you don't feel too sure of, or can you go on notwithstanding, and with no great loss?* Try this a few times and you may be surprised to discover that regressions are seldom as vital as they may at first seem. Try building up the habit of *constantly reading forward* so long as comprehension is not totally impossible—again you may be surprised to discover, if you have the courage to take the gamble, that your understanding is better than you give it credit for and does not need frequent checking up on!

PERCEPTION TRAINING II

In chapter 3 you began your perception training on numbers of three digits, and possibly you had little difficulty making a high score. True learning, however, occurs only when a problem is just a little beyond a student's ability. To solve such a problem, he must draw on his innate *capacities* so that he can increase his present *ability* just a bit. (As you know, I make a clear distinction between *ability* and *capacity*, especially in reading—*ability* reflects the level of your actual performance, as of this moment; *capacity* refers to what you can do eventually, if you keep on trying.) And so, if reacting accurately to three-digit numbers in split-second fixations was easy for you, if it involved no particular effort, then very little real learning occurred. (You were, however, being prepared for the more difficult digit drills that will occur in this and in later chapters.)

Four-digit numbers, on the other hand, are a horse, to coin a phrase, of an entirely different hue. The average untrained reader has to mature a little in his perception-interpretation abilities before he can invariably react accurately to four-digit combinations in single, quick fixations—he has to draw on his *capacity*, and keep practicing, before success is achieved. (With enough practice and with intelligent effort, the recognition span can easily be pushed as high as six to nine digits.)

The problem ahead of you, now, is probably just slightly beyond your present ability. Let us see how long it will take you to increase that ability.

Perception Exercise 5

Use the Flashmeter card according to the instructions on page 62. (I suggest that you reread these instructions before you start to work so that you will be sure to practice correctly.)

Keep a record of your errors in order to be able to tally your score at the end of the exercise. And remember in this, as in all other perception drills, to try to keep your reactions as exclusively *visual* as you possibly can.

6234 ←_____	1930 ←_____	9411 ←_____
1876 ←_____	9872 ←_____	9432 ←_____
9845 ←_____	9031 ←_____	9440 ←_____
3472 ←_____	9032 ←_____	9288 ←_____
7850 ←_____	0921 ←_____	3820 ←_____
9075 ←_____	9832 ←_____	6782 ←_____
8793 ←_____	9032 ←_____	9280 ←_____
8675 ←_____	8940 ←_____	9380 ←_____
6432 ←_____	7802 ←_____	7277 ←_____
0946 ←_____	3012 ←_____	9288 ←_____
6472 ←_____	9402 ←_____	0311 ←_____
5321 ←_____	5793 ←_____	9320 ←_____
1560 ←_____	8502 ←_____	9387 ←_____
9081 ←_____	1592 ←_____	7356 ←_____
4560 ←_____	0499 ←_____	9278 ←_____
6728 ←_____	8492 ←_____	0596 ←_____
0982 ←_____	0293 ←_____	

NUMBER CORRECT OUT OF 50: _____

Perception Exercise 6

Hold the Flashmeter card with the "word window" at the top, aligning the arrow at the right edge of the card with the arrow on the page. Allow yourself only one split-second exposure of each line, strongly relying on your visual impression. As soon as a word has been exposed and immediately concealed, attempt to reproduce it, in writing, in the blank to its right. Then pull the card down again and check on your accuracy. Mark each error so that you can tally your score at the end of the exercise.

ankle	←_____	archness	←_____
uncle	←_____	black	←_____
ankles	←_____	block	←_____
anger	←_____	blackhead	←_____
answer	←_____	blockhead	←_____
answered	←_____	blackguard	←_____
ants	←_____	blackguardly	←_____
antrum	←_____	blackhearted	←_____
arty	←_____	blackish	←_____
artist	←_____	blackly	←_____
architect	←_____	blackness	←_____
archer	←_____	blocker	←_____
archaic	←_____	bladder	←_____
architecture	←_____	bleeder	←_____
arches	←_____	bleeding	←_____
arching	←_____	blink	←_____
architectural	←_____	blank	←_____
archives	←_____	blasted	←_____

bleaker	←_____	bland	←_____
bleacher	←_____	blond	←_____
bleeder	←_____	blonde	←_____
bloody	←_____	blindness	←_____
blooded	←_____	blindly	←_____
blend	←_____	blob	←_____
blender	←_____	bloodily	←_____

NUMBER CORRECT OUT OF 50: _____

Perception Exercise 7

Proceed according to instructions on page 75.

→	what's so new	→	my wife and child
→	that's too good	→	my child and wife
→	can also provide	→	my new husband
→	beyond the walls	→	her new couch
→	beyond the horizon	→	her new husband
→	the French have	→	his new mate
→	the British have	→	to produce rice
→	the English know	→	to produce results
→	the Germans say	→	known for value
→	the French believe	→	tears and sweat
→	we are sure	→	lost and found
→	we aren't sure	→	pulled his leg
→	we weren't sure	→	caught his man

95

→ loved not wisely	→ lost his dog
→ dug the grave	→ will lose his cash
→ the man cried	→ a gallant gesture
→ the little dog	→ Sinclair Lewis
→ an awful dope	→ new Chevrolet
→ no sooner than	→ old Buick
→ much less pain	→ beautiful blonde
→ much less gain	→ glamorous blonde
→ far less strain	→ skinny blonde
→ no less rain	→ dirty brunette
→ clean and neat	→ famous in radio
→ neat and clean	→ words of love
→ far and wide	→ toil and trouble
→ far and near	→ taken for a ride
→ near and far	→ opened his purse
→ rich or poor	→ found the answer
→ poor and rich	→ loved not well
→ man or boy	→ fought the war
→ girl or boy	→ the man laughed
→ girls and boys	→ the big ape
→ Sam and Tom	→ a big dose
→ lost his nerve	→ in the dark

→ better and faster

→ a better time

→ playing safe

→ when germs hit

→ exciting story

→ I was there

→ were you there?

→ natural result

→ important difference

→ the long cigarette

→ smart window dressing

→ you can't miss

→ what's new?

→ key to power

→ if you ever stood

→ the teacher said

→ as you move

→ how are you?

→ in this field

→ he can figure

→ richest of all

→ try to visualize

→ you have claimed

→ no longer alive

→ now quite dead

→ during the winter

→ during the summer

→ during the fall

→ through the spring

→ back at home

→ back in town

→ lost for years

→ when I finish

→ then I began

→ then he started

→ then we began

→ then she stopped

→ no greater sacrifice

→ happen to you

→ can happen to you

→ could happen to you

→ that violet hue

→ that violin tone

→ that violent man

97

CHAPTER 5

HOW TO GET THE GIST
QUICKLY

Preview

Now you resume your training in attacking material more aggressively. Your practice in this chapter will help you:
- Whip through material looking for total meaning.
- Eliminate from your reading habits any excessive regard for minor details.
- React quickly and accurately to the *gist* of a piece of writing.

> *Chapter 5* offers you practice in responding rapidly to the main ideas of 12 short selections.

★ SESSION 7

THE DETAILS WILL TAKE CARE OF THEMSELVES

Let us pause, now, for a partial review.

The average untrained adult, we have decided, reads at a speed much lower than his innate ability to understand should make possible.

His slowness may be caused, in part, by unnecessarily short recognition spans, so that he habitually interprets print almost word by word rather than by phrases or by thought-units of several words. Not only is his speed thus curtailed—it obviously takes more time to read three or four words in separate fixations than to read them all in one fixation—but his comprehension is also likely to suffer, for his attention is focused on individual words instead of on ideas and total meaning.

His speed may also be held back—even drastically reduced—by certain other bad habits and inefficient techniques. He may move his lips, or tongue, or vocal cords in order to react to meaning. Or he may rely excessively on auditory responses, so that he does not react as instantaneously as he should to the visual images that his eyes flash to his brain. Or he may have a psychological compulsion to *study* every word, to read and reread and then re-reread words and phrases and lines before he is convinced that he has properly understood them. Or he may dwell unnecessarily long on minor details, get lost in a patch of daydreaming stimulated by a chance idea that occurs in a paragraph, or become so easily distracted by his external environment or his internal ruminations that he continues reading without absorbing meaning, and finally has to go back to pick up the thread that his mind in effect dropped paragraphs or pages back. Any one of these characteristics can serve as a massive obstacle to efficient, aggressive, and rapid comprehension.

Or the obstacles may be of a more subtle variety.

Perhaps he has simply become accustomed to reacting comfortably or lazily to the message of print at a uniformly slow and meandering rate—a rate not only slower than he needs for excellent and accurate comprehension, but slower even than most types of material demand. (The rate of the trained reader, you will recall, is highly flexible, changing as the material changes.)

Or perhaps he lacks experience in differentiating between details and main ideas, and has never learned to push rapidly through the subsidiary embellishments and decorations of an author's writing and get down efficiently to the important points.

Or perhaps he does not read *widely* enough, maintaining little, if any, contact with the type of magazine that stimulates thinking and jogs the intellect; only infrequently, if at all, willing to accept the challenge of a good book of nonfiction or of a deep and thoughtful novel. Or he may not read *continuously* enough, often letting weeks or months slip by without doing anything more than superficially perusing the daily and Sunday papers. (Stop and think for a moment—how many complete books have *you* read in the last few months? And how many of these were general books, rather than novels? And if you add them up, how many hours would you say you devote on the average to leisure reading, other than newspapers, every week?) When reading is so occasional, or so restricted in scope, a high order of skill can never be developed, or even maintained. How long does a professional typist remain skillful and speedy after she leaves her job to become a housewife or mother, if for years her only contact with her machine is to tap out an occasional letter or shopping list? How skillful can a surgeon be if he does only an occasional operation, or if he restricts himself to the simplest and least demanding type of work? Or, finally, not to belabor the matter, how skillfully will a pianist play who only occasionally sits down at the keyboard? (The following statement, variously attributed to Paderewski, Josef Hofmann, Mendelssohn, and any number of other musicians, is very much to the point: "If I skip one day's practice, only I know it; if I skip two days, my teacher knows it; and if I skip three days, everyone in the audience knows it.")

What it all boils down to, of course, is that the slow reader rarely sets up for himself those conditions that will require him to operate at the peak of his efficiency, that will force him to make maximum use of his intelligence, talents, and capacities. The kind of training you are now receiving sets up such conditions for you, shows you how to operate under them, and demands that you make every effort to draw on your latent capacities and thus increase your actual operating ability.

The basic training in this chapter, for example, will set up conditions under which you will be required to understand material at a rate substantially faster than you were accustomed to when you started this book—substantially faster than the normal, comfortable, perhaps lazy rate at which you read the first J. Donald Adams selection in Chapter 1.

The exercises you will shortly work on will continue to chip away at any tendency you may have to read more slowly than you are able to comprehend. With the perception exercises on which you practiced in previous chapters (and which will occur profusely also in this and later chapters), you made a start at removing certain *visual* obstacles to quick comprehension; now you will begin to remove certain *psychological* obstacles.

The purpose of these new exercises is to train you to get into a selection without delay, get the gist of it quickly and correctly, and then get out without waste of time or effort, and with full assurance that you understood exactly what the author was saying to you.

In order to accomplish this, you must submit, emotionally as well as intellectually, to this principle: *If you read for main ideas, the details will take care of themselves.*

You may be reluctant to accept this principle. You may be conditioned, because of previous habits and experience, or because of the type of professional reading you now do (proofreading, editing, reading of technical material such as contracts, legal briefs, estimates, specifications, medical or dental literature, etc.) to consider all details of supreme importance—and you may be emotionally opposed (whether consciously or unconsciously is of no importance) to reading for main ideas.

Or you may be a perfectionist in your daily life, a stickler for details, a person who prefers to be slow but sure.

In short, it may be a psychological wrench, because it runs so counter to your ingrained patterns and attitudes, to adjust to reading rapidly, to cruising along at a good clip with speedy comprehension of the main ideas.

I wish only to point out that you can't have your cake and eat it too.

If you wish to be a rapid, efficient reader, you must give up your excessive attention to details, your superfluous regard for minor points, and be willing to develop a mind-set that concentrates on central themes.

In your professional capacity you may read with the proper slowness and meticulousness that your job requires. But the efficient reader has a variety of speeds, a diversity of approaches to material, depending on the purpose for which he reads and on the type of material he is reading.

In work that requires infinite, close scrutiny, that is what he gives it.

In reading for information, relaxation, or entertainment, he reads swiftly for main ideas, knowing that the details will take care of themselves.

As an efficient reader, he chooses the tool best suited to the reading task. It would be a poor carpenter, for example, who relied on a surgical scalpel to do all the cutting of lumber which his job requires. (Indeed, it would be a poor surgeon who used only one scalpel no matter what type of tissue he was cutting.) And so it is a poor reader who reads everything the same way, with the same careful attention to details. The good reader has a large supply of different tools and uses that one which will best do the job. He can read slowly when the job requires it; that is, when the details are of special importance or when he wants to savor the emotional impact of every word. But he can read like the wind when he wants the ideas of a selection, and wants them quickly.

Sometimes, also (and this may at first sound paradoxical), the reader who pays excessive attention to details loses a lot of the impact of the main theme of a piece—so that slow, finicky reading may actually not result in as good comprehension as one would logically suppose.

So you must be willing, if the practice in this chapter is to be of maximum effectiveness, to accept the validity of the principle that if you read for main ideas the details will take care of themselves.

GETTING THE AUTHOR'S POINT

You will begin your practice very shortly—but, as in previous exercises, it is important that you thoroughly understand the technique under which you are to operate, and that you follow that technique exactly as directed.

I shall set down the rules clearly. Make sure you understand them, and then make sure that you apply them when you start working.

Rule 1. Do not aim to go as fast as is humanly possible—such an impatient rush to achieve in a few minutes a goal that normally requires many weeks or months will only cause fatigue and result in very great, or even total, comprehension loss.

Rule 2. Pay no attention to fixations or eye movements as you read—comprehension and concentration are interfered with if part of your mind is concerned with what your eyes are doing. Aim only at understanding the author's main idea in a satisfyingly rapid manner.

Rule 3. Feel that you are going a little faster than you usually do. Jump into a piece, look for and follow the author's main idea (do not worry about the minor points), and finish without wasting time.

Rule 4. If you happen to lose a word, a phrase, or a minor point here or there, do not regress—keep reading for the main idea.

Rule 5. Get the thoughts quickly, but don't rush. Rushing produces tension, and tension inhibits, rather than aids, quick comprehension.

Rule 6. In a sense, you can "read" as quickly as you're able to turn pages—but you're not really reading unless you follow, with understanding, the gist of what an author is saying. So read quickly enough to realize you're getting the author's thoughts rapidly, but not so quickly that you feel panic, become confused, or lose all comprehension.

Rule 7. Do not worry about auditory responses; the more conscious you are of inner speech, the more inner speech you'll have. Think only of the main ideas—the more involved you become in main ideas, and the less you concentrate on minor points, the better the chances are that inner speech will be reduced.

These are the seven general principles for you to follow in your training. Specific rules applying directly to the material that will be presented will be offered at the proper place.

Rapid Comprehension Exercise 1

Let us start with a selection written back in 1949 by Sylvia F. Porter, financial columnist on the *New York Post*. The style is simple and clear and the piece can be read rapidly if you look for the main thought and do not get bogged down in the various statistics that Miss Porter will offer.

The selection will explain why, as of 1949, more people do not invest their surplus capital in stocks. Read with a mind-set to discover, quickly and without wasting time on details, what that reason is. Remember, no panicky rushing, no zooming through the print at such a breakneck speed that you won't understand what the author is trying to communicate to you. On the other hand, try to understand the point of the piece quickly, with no lost time or motion.

(In this set of exercises, we will dispense with time-charts—for the moment we are less interested in your actual word-per-minute rate than in two other factors: (1) Can you read with the dominant aim of seeking the main thought? (2) Can you do this rapidly and efficiently, that is, with a feeling of increased speed and good over-all comprehension?)

OWNING STOCKS
by Sylvia F. Porter

If your income is more than $3,000 a year and you have some money left over for savings, why aren't you putting part of this hard-earned, extra cash into stocks? I'll tell you two main reasons why:

You don't know much about "Wall Street," you may not even be quite sure what a stock is, and so you're not fiddling around.

Or you think stocks aren't safe and you're against taking any unnecessary risks with these precious dollars of yours.

If your income is more than $5,000 a year and you have some of your accumulated cash in Government savings bonds, some in insurance and some in the bank, why aren't you diversifying your assets a bit more and holding a few stocks too? I'll tell you again two main reasons why:

You're convinced you could be successful in the stock market only if you had an intimate knowledge of financial problems or if you had friends among the financial experts. You have neither.

Or you're old enough to recall the 1929 stock crash and to have developed a strong antagonism toward "Wall Street" which neither the stock brokers nor businessmen have tried or been able to overcome.

This isn't I pontificating on your assets and attitudes. What I have summarized here are the results of a survey just released by the Federal Reserve Board on how families with incomes of $3,000-and-up invest their extra cash and why.

It makes me wince—the disclosures and implications here. For how

From the *New York Post*. Reprinted with permission of the author. Miss Porter is Financial Editor of the *Post* and the author, with J. K. Lasser, of *How to Live Within Your Income*.

many times have I heard bankers, businessmen, brokers denounce the policies of the Roosevelt and Truman Administrations as responsible for the relative unpopularity of Wall Street!

Fiddlesticks. What this survey shows is that Wall Street is still unpopular among the great majority because Wall Street itself has done a fantastically bad job of explaining itself, its operations, and its purposes to that vast majority.

How often have I heard supposedly informed industrialists condemn our tax laws or Government regulations as responsible for the fact they can't issue new stocks as easily as they once could and thus can't raise new money through the stock market?

Poppycock. What this study reveals is that overwhelming numbers of Americans are simply afraid to put their savings in stocks. They're talking "safety."

And how many times have I read speeches by leading businessmen and financiers appealing to stockholders to vote against Administration policies, rise up against the welfare state philosophy?

Futility as of now. For what these findings emphasize is that the appeal is touching only a tiny fraction of our voting population. Stock ownership as a percentage of our total population is now at the lowest level in over a quarter-century.

Here are some of the startling facts uncovered for the Reserve Board by the University of Michigan Survey Research Center:

Only 4,000,000 families—8 per cent of the total—hold stocks of American corporations today.

Of this 8 per cent, half figure the value of their stocks at less than $1,000. Only 2 per cent estimate their holding as worth more than $5,000. (That 2 per cent, of course, is in the highest income bracket.)

There is money around, plenty of it, but it's going into other things—savings bonds, insurance, bank accounts, real estate.

In the measured words of the Reserve: "Early in 1949 there was no lack of funds potentially available for consumer investment in corporate equities either among individuals who owned no corporate stock at that time or among those who were already participating directly. . . ."

Why, then, was this money not going into stocks? Because 28 per cent felt that this market was "not safe" and another 34 per cent answered, they were "not familiar with" this market. Only 8 per cent gave any positive reason for stock ownership. The remaining, overwhelming 92 per cent either were openly against or were indifferent.

If Wall Street wants to bring us into the stock market, let its representatives stop grumbling about taxes and rules and the like—and get out and explain stocks to that 34 per cent who are "not familiar with" securities. If industry wants a revived market so it can sell more new issues, let its representatives give an acceptable answer to that 28 per cent who think stocks are "not safe."

But I'll make a bet. I'll wager only a handful among businessmen and financiers will even bother about this vital message to them—unless or until they read this.

Test Your Comprehension

Which of the following statements, in your opinion, most closely approximates the main idea of the selection?

a. If you make more than $3,000 a year, you ought to buy some stocks.

b. The stock market is safer than it used to be.

c. Wall Street is unpopular because of administration policies of the Roosevelt and Truman administrations.

d. Only 8 per cent of American families own stocks.

e. Less money is being invested in stocks than is available for such purposes because Wall Street has done a bad job of explaining its operations and purposes to the majority of Americans.

f. We must do something about making stocks safer if we wish to attract the average person into the market.

Note carefully these possibilities:

1. If you had a feeling that you were going along at a good clip, understanding the point Miss Porter was making; and if you readily checked answer *e* in the choices above, then the conditions are excellent, as of now, that training of the sort offered in this chapter can produce good results for you, both as to speed and comprehension.

2. If you went as slowly as usual (I'll rely on your subjective reactions at this point), but still saw the main point of Miss Porter's argument, then you will have to adjust more successfully to faster comprehension before this training can show results.

3. If you read rapidly, but missed the point, reread the selection, now that you know the central thought, and try to understand how everything in the piece is intended to get that thought across to you.

In all likelihood, possibility 1 or 2 applies to your reading; but if possibility 3 is true, then the training in this chapter, like the preliminary training in Chapter 1, is of the utmost importance to you, for you must learn to push aside the details and get to the meat of an author's ideas. The ability to do this is, as you know, a prime requisite for efficient reading, and, once achieved, it is an ability that can have a radical effect on your speed.

Rapid Comprehension Exercise 2

A clear central theme, surrounded by explanatory details, runs through the next selection. Read the piece rapidly, aiming for an accurate understanding of the author's final meaning.

FRIED FOODS
by Irving S. Cutter, M.D.

Fried foods have long been frowned upon. Nevertheless the skillet is about our handiest and most useful piece of kitchen equipment. Stalwart lumberjacks and others engaged in active labor requiring 4,000 calories per day or more will take approximately one-third of their rations prepared in this fashion. Meats, eggs, and French toast cooked in this way are served in millions of homes daily. Apparently the consumers are not beset with more signs of indigestion than afflict those who insist upon broiling, roasting, or boiling. Some years ago one of our most eminent physiologists investigated the digestibility of fried potatoes. He found that the pan variety was more easily broken down for assimilation than when deep fat was employed. The latter, however, dissolved within the alimentary tract more readily than the boiled type. Furthermore, he learned, by watching the progress of the contents of the stomach by means of the fluoroscope, that fat actually accelerated the rate of digestion. Now all this is quite in contrast with "authority." Volumes have been written on nutrition and everywhere the dictum has been accepted—no fried edibles of any sort for children. A few will go so far as to forbid this style of cooking wholly. Now and then an expert will be bold enough to admit that he uses them himself, the absence of discomfort being explained on the ground that he possesses a powerful gastric apparatus. We can of course sizzle perfectly good articles to death so that they will be leathery and tough. But thorough heating, in the presence of shortening, is not the awful crime that it has been labeled. Such dishes stimulate rather than retard contractions of the gall bladder. Thus it is that bile mixes with the nutriment shortly after it leaves the stomach. We don't need to allow our foodstuffs to become oil soaked, but other than that there seems to be no basis for the widely heralded prohibition against this method. But notions become fixed. The first condemnation probably arose because an "oracle" suffered from dyspepsia which he ascribed to some fried item

From *Your Life*. Reprinted with permission.

on the menu. The theory spread. Others agreed with him and after a time the doctrine became incorporated in our textbooks. The belief is now tradition rather than proved fact. It should have been refuted long since as experience has demonstrated its falsity.

Test Your Comprehension

Which of the following statements, in your opinion, most closely approximates the main idea of the selection?

a. More Americans eat fried foods than any other kinds.

b. It is not true that frying foods makes them indigestible.

c. Children should not eat fried foods.

(The key to this and following comprehension tests will be given after exercise 5; wait until you reach that point before checking your answers.)

Rapid Comprehension Exercise 3

YOUR DIARY

Your diary, if you keep the right kind, may be a lifesaver if you turn it over to your doctor when illness strikes. He isn't interested in what Jim said under the moon, but he would like to know details of your past that can give him important information on your health history. This recommendation comes from Dr. H. E. Robertson of the Mayo Foundation. Did you turn yellow after taking that worm medicine a few years ago? There may be a clue to liver injury there. How often have those troublesome stomachaches been occurring—how many days between them? How many colds do you have a year? Were you bedridden for a day or so with a mysterious fever—and, if so, what kind of activities had you been engaging in previously? When was the last time you called a doctor and for what? This unromantic information can be very helpful indeed when you need a doctor's services.

From *Your Life.* Reprinted with permission.

Test Your Comprehension

Which of the following statements, in your opinion, most closely approximates the main idea of the selection?

a. People should keep diaries if they wish to stay healthy.

b. Your diary will save your doctor time when he treats you.

c. An account of previous illnesses and physical reactions will help the doctor to diagnose and treat your ailments more efficiently.

Rapid Comprehension Exercise 4

THE BEST LEARNING
by Cyril O. Houle

The best learning is that which occurs in adulthood. Our psychologists have demonstrated fairly conclusively that, for most people, the ability to learn is at its peak in the years from eighteen to forty-five. There is evidence to show that, even after forty-five, learning power remains high if it is exercised carefully and systematically. Adults can learn better than children; maturity is not a bar but an incentive to the person who wishes to develop his own potentialities. It is significant to recall, among other things, that virtually all the really great teachers, both religious and secular, have taught adults, not children. Naturally, the elementary school and the high school should do something more than keep children warm and dry. They can do little more, however, than prepare their pupils for the real education which maturity will bring.

From *Classroom Techniques in Improving Reading,* compiled and edited by William S. Gray, University of Chicago Press, Chicago. Reprinted with permission.

Test Your Comprehension

Did you get the point? Check the statement which best summarizes the gist of the paragraph:
a. Adults cannot learn properly unless adequately prepared in childhood.
b. Adults are better learners than children.
c. The most famous teachers have always taught adults.

How are you doing? Do you begin to see how you can gain speed and assurance as you aim to find the gist of a selection with no loss of time, with no dawdling or minute examination of details?

Continue your practice now on the next short selection, reading with a sense of deliberately going fast, and looking for the main point, the gist, the total meaning.

Rapid Comprehension Exercise 5

THOUGHT AND LANGUAGE
by Edward Sapir

Most people, asked if they can think without speech, would probably
answer, "Yes, but it is not easy for me to do so. Still I know it can be done."
. . . No one believes that even the most difficult mathematical proposition is inherently dependent on an arbitrary set of symbols, but it is impossible to suppose that the human mind is capable of arriving at or holding such a proposition without the symbolism. The writer, for one, is
strongly of the opinion that the feeling entertained by so many that they
can think, or even reason, without language is an illusion. The illusion
seems to be due to a number of factors. The simplest of these is the failure
to distinguish between imagery and thought. As a matter of fact, no sooner
do we try to put an image into conscious relation with another than we
find ourselves slipping into a silent flow of words. Thought may be a
natural domain apart from the artificial one of speech, but speech would
seem to be the only road we know that leads to it.

Test Your Comprehension
Did you get the point? Then decide which of the following statements most closely paraphrases the gist of the paragraph.
a. Most people imagine they can think without language.
b. Mathematics is dependent on symbolism, a form of language.
c. It is not true that people can think without language.
d. There is a difference between imagery and thought.

> KEY: Now check your work. The correct
> answers to the comprehension tests on the
> last 4 exercises are as follows: ex. 2-b, ex.
> 3-c, ex. 4-b, ex. 5-c.

Before continuing with this very productive type of comprehension exercise, let us pause for further practice in rapid perception and accurate interpretation of numbers, words, and phrases.

★ SESSION 8

PERCEPTION TRAINING III

Perception Exercise 8

Rapid perception and interpretation of four-digit numbers is not, as I have said, easy. But, as I have also said, true learning takes place only when the problem is just slightly beyond the ability of the student. So let's do battle again with four-digit combinations. By now you are probably quite familiar with the proper technique; if you are not, refresh your memory by referring to page 62.

Keep a record of your errors to see whether you can, at this time, improve on the score you made on the previous four-digit exercise (page 93). And remember that your aim is to keep your reactions as exclusively visual as possible.

2954	←_____	2061	←_____	3186	←_____
9315	←_____	0621	←_____	5672	←_____
4386	←_____	6210	←_____	3175	←_____
5313	←_____	3938	←_____	5817	←_____
2745	←_____	9833	←_____	1857	←_____
8594	←_____	2467	←_____	7185	←_____
1062	←_____	9246	←_____	8751	←_____
2601	←_____	8146	←_____	0158	←_____

6213	←_____	2054	←_____	2226	←_____
1362	←_____	9316	←_____	7850	←_____
3389	←_____	3169	←_____	0857	←_____
8393	←_____	1639	←_____	8570	←_____
8399	←_____	6391	←_____	1987	←_____
9983	←_____	3612	←_____	7891	←_____
4025	←_____	3126	←_____	5386	←_____
0245	←_____	2236	←_____	9176	←_____
5042	←_____	6322	←_____		

NUMBER CORRECT OUT OF 50: _____

IMPROVEMENT OVER PREVIOUS TRY (*Page 93*): _____

Perception Exercise 9

Here again are words somewhat similar to each other, but not exactly alike. Follow the usual procedure with the Flashmeter card; keep your exposures infinitesimally short and your reactions as exclusively visual as possible. Write your response in the blank to the right after concealing each word, and then immediately check on your accuracy. Keep a record of your errors.

bridle	←_____	Brittany	←_____
briery	←_____	broccoli	←_____
bristly	←_____	brochette	←_____
bristled	←_____	brochure	←_____
British	←_____	broken	←_____
Britain	←_____	brogan	←_____
brittle	←_____	brogue	←_____

brokage	←_____	brownette	←_____
brokerage	←_____	Brunhild	←_____
broiler	←_____	brushwood	←_____
broiling	←_____	brushing	←_____
bronze	←_____	blushing	←_____
brook	←_____	blusher	←_____
Brooklyn	←_____	Brussels	←_____
Brookline	←_____	brutal	←_____
brownish	←_____	brittle	←_____
browser	←_____	brutish	←_____
blubbery	←_____	bitterish	←_____
blueberry	←_____	bitterly	←_____
bruiser	←_____	Brutus	←_____
bruised	←_____	budding	←_____
Brownie	←_____	bulbous	←_____
browner	←_____	Buddha	←_____
browned	←_____	buddy	←_____
brunette	←_____	bubble	←_____

NUMBER CORRECT OUT OF 50: _____

Perception Exercise 10

Proceed according to instructions on page 75. It is important at this point to attempt to keep your reactions more visual than auditory, even on phrase perception. This will not be easy—but it is not impossible.

→ Mairzy Doats → Eat and be merry

→ we the people → God save the king

→ for which it stands → The king is dead

→ of the people → Long live the king

→ by the people → lived in a shoe

→ postwar plans → cupboard was bare

→ the Electoral College → Mary had a little lamb

→ professorial dignity → Can spring

→ while the sun shines → be far behind?

→ clutching at straws → It's toasted

→ broke the camel's back → hickory dickory dock

→ Yanks are coming → Ten little Indians

→ old woman who → live and let live

→ To be or not to be → Thomas E. Dewey

→ that is the question → the end of the road

→ the City of New York → half a loaf

→ Emperor Hirohito → In Bed We Cry

→ *The New York Times* → liddle lamzee divy

→ the life of Reilly → Hungary is tense

→ a wonderful time → phones are cut

→ Wish you were here → U.S. protests curb

→ the time of your life → a non-Communist oath

114

→ the criminal code → two college groups

→ Home on the range → vie for state aid

→ read better and faster → major fight brews

→ How to make friends → between public schools

→ and influence people → on missing airliner

→ a stitch in time → debate is bitter

→ a needle in a haystack → within a week

→ Buy more bonds → the principal provision

→ in the nick of time → the Asian resolution

→ a pair of Kilkenny cats → it is what happened

→ poor cock robin → tension gripped the city

→ Watch the Fords go by → most of the city

→ They satisfy → police squad cars

→ crazy as a coot → during the day

→ as happy as a lark → U.N. chief urged

→ a severe cold → go to Moscow

→ such unexpected promises → to bolster reserves

→ an unexpected provision → has already emphasized

→ paralyzes Haiti's capital → other rights granted

→ British in Egypt → begun by Dulles

→ violates the cease-fire → bars tariff rise

→ Egyptian sources predicted → his basic opposition

115

→	rules are drafted	→	drinking law proposed
→	police extend efforts	→	traffic accidents rise

(Some of the above phrases were excerpted from the news columns of the *New York Times*.)

★ SESSION 9

CONTINUED PRACTICE ON SHORT SELECTIONS

You are practicing, in these rapid comprehension exercises, to refine and sharpen an ability you already possess, an ability that every normal person possesses—the ability to understand the *central* meaning of what you read. You have this ability, believe me— if you did not, none of your reading would ever make sense to you. What I am demanding of you, as I present selection after selection, is well within your power; it is only a matter of your using that power more determinedly, more aggressively, more efficiently. And this you will learn to do through practice, through more and more and still more practice, until you have formed the reflexive habit of attacking a piece of writing with the psychological mind-set of discovering, as quickly as you can, the answer to one overriding question, namely: "What, *in total*, is the author trying to say?"

Whip through the following pieces with the conscious aim of grasping *total* meaning, of responding to the *essence* of the author's communication—don't linger on individual words, don't let yourself get sidetracked by details.

Rapid Comprehension Exercise 6

When the individual photographs of a motion-picture film pass before our eyes at the rate of approximately twenty frames per second, we enjoy

Delwyn G. Schubert, director of the Reading Clinic at Los Angeles State College of Applied Arts and Sciences. From the *Clearing House*. Reprinted with permission.

116

a continuous flow of meaning. But if the process slows down so that each photograph remains before us for a second or more, the movie becomes absurd, boring, and almost meaningless.

The word reader perceives isolated word pictures at a slow rate of speed. These impressions fail to blend into a meaningful pattern in exactly the same way as do the individual photographs of a slowed-down movie. The word reader sees the trees, perhaps, but the forest escapes him completely. As the psychologist puts it, "The whole is more than the sum of its parts."

Test Your Comprehension

Which of the following statements best expresses the *total meaning* of this selection?

a. If the individual photographs of a motion picture are presented too slowly, the movie loses meaning.
b. The word-by-word reader does not get a continuous flow of meaning from material.
c. The faster a movie is run, the more sense it makes.
d. The whole is more than the sum of its parts.

Rapid Comprehension Exercise 7

It is nothing new that the world is full of hate, that men destroy one another, and that our civilization has arisen from the ashes of despoiled peoples and decimated natural resources. But to relate this destructiveness, this evidence of a spiritual malignancy within us, to an instinct, and to correlate this instinct with the beneficent and fruitful instinct associated with love, this was one of the later flowers of the genius of Freud. We have come to see that just as the child must learn to love wisely, so he must learn to hate expeditiously, to turn destructive tendencies away from himself toward enemies that actually threaten him rather than toward the friendly and the defenseless, the more usual victims of destructive energy.

Karl Menninger in *Man Against Himself*. Reprinted by permission of the publisher, Harcourt, Brace and Co.

Test Your Comprehension

Which of the following statements best expresses the *total meaning* of this selection?

a. The world is full of hate.
b. Our civilization has arisen from destruction.

c. Destructiveness is an evidence of our spiritual malignancy.

d. The child must learn to turn his destructiveness against actual enemies.

Rapid Comprehension Exercise 8

Psychiatrists have observed that no other inadequacy creates as great a sense of frustration and failure as a reading difficulty. This is partly due to the fact that everyone is expected to be able to read adequately in order to advance in his schooling. Reading is also considered a criterion, in the cultural sense, of an individual's mental ability. If a person is deficient in some academic subject such as arithmetic or geography, he can avoid facing his inadequacy by avoiding those subjects. A reading defect cannot, however, be easily circumvented. His disability is brought to his attention, not only when he attends school, but in almost every other situation. He finds himself culturally in an inferior position because he cannot read books as ably as others, nor in some cases can he even read the newspapers with a semblance of competence. In one sense, therefore, the person with a serious reading defect finds himself in the same cultural position as the illiterate. He is reputationally classified by his fellow-men either as an inferior individual or as a queer person. As he grows older he is less able to rationalize the defect or to avoid the conflict associated with his deficiency and therefore accumulates further and further frustration.

Mandel Sherman, in *Clinical Studies in Reading*, copyright 1949 by the University of Chicago. Reprinted by permission of the University of Chicago Press.

Test Your Comprehension

Which of the following statements best expresses the *total meaning* of this selection?

a. A reading difficulty creates a greater conflict and sense of frustration than any other inadequacy.

b. All people are expected to be able to read competently.

c. The ability to read is a yardstick of a person's mental ability.

d. Anyone who has difficulty in reading is considered either inferior or peculiar.

Rapid Comprehension Exercise 9

The majority of Americans have not read a book in the last year. This is the startling conclusion from a survey by the American Institute of Pub-

From the *Reader's Digest.* Copyright 1956 by the Reader's Digest Association, Inc. Reprinted with permission.

lic Opinion. Six out of ten adults questioned said that the last time they could remember reading a book—other than the Bible—was a year ago or more. Even among college graduates, one out of four had not read a book in the last 12 months.

Fewer books are read in the United States than in any major English-speaking democracy. In England about three times as many people are to be found reading books at any given time as in America. One survey recorded the following percentages of book readers: Great Britain, 55 per cent; Australia, 34 per cent; Canada, 31 percent; United States, 17 per cent.

Test Your Comprehension

Which of the following statements best expresses the *total meaning* of this selection?

a. Many Americans did not read a book in the last twelve months.
b. More people read books in England than in this country.
c. Only college graduates have developed the habit of book-reading.
d. We do not read enough books in this country.

Rapid Comprehension Exercise 10

Seeing is a complex act wherein the optical system of the eye takes light emanating from the object and forms an image on a light-sensitive layer, the retina. This light energy through a photochemical process is transformed into nerve energy and passes through the visual pathways to the brain. In the broadest sense seeing is not complete until what is seen is interpreted by the observer. This interpretation is based on past experience; hence, to a considerable extent seeing is a learned skill.

Fred W. Jobe, in *Clinical Studies in Reading*, copyright 1953, by the University of Chicago. Reprinted with permission.

Test Your Comprehension

Which of the following statements best expresses the *total meaning* of this selection?

a. In seeing, the eye takes light from an object and forms an image on the retina.
b. In seeing, nerve energy is passed through visual pathways to the brain.
c. Seeing is a mental activity.
d. Seeing is, to a large extent, a learned skill.

Rapid Comprehension Exercise 11

An early stage in learning to read is recognizing simple printed words and what they mean. With practice, recognition gradually embraces more complicated words and ideas. Then when some ideas can be understood more easily than others, a further skill is very helpful—matching speed to understanding, so that simple passages take less time to read than difficult ones. However, most people do not acquire this knack of flexibility; they maintain a constant rate regardless of its efficiency. Especially in college, where reading is the chief tool for gathering information, a student stuck in low gear is handicapped. Formulas, poems, short stories, and historical documents may all have to be understood, but understanding need not come at the same rate for all. Efficiency, therefore, implies knowing when to change speeds, and then being able to do so without undue trouble.

Frank Laycock, in the *Journal of Experimental Education.*

Test Your Comprehension

Which of the following statements best expresses the *total meaning* of this selection?

a. Reading efficiency implies knowing how, and being able, to change speed in accordance with changing material.
b. Not everybody understands at the same rate.
c. College students who read slowly are handicapped.
d. To learn to read, one must be able to recognize simple words and understand what they mean.

Rapid Comprehension Exercise 12

One does not have to learn to read. But, one does have to learn to read certain things and in more or less certain ways. The reading process is not initiated by school instruction nor does it emerge as a phenomenon of development after infancy. The reading process is comparable to other fundamental native processes such as respiration and nutrition. The innate reading process has to be developed and implemented just as do the other processes in order to make them effective for the needs of the organism.

Peter L. Spencer, in *The Yearbook of the Claremont College Reading Conference.*

Test Your Comprehension

Which of the following statements best expresses the *total meaning* of this selection?

a. Reading is a natural process.
b. Reading has to be developed and implemented to be of greatest use to the reader.
c. Reading is not started by school instruction.
d. Reading is like respiration or nutrition.

KEY: The correct answers to the comprehension tests on the last seven exercises are as follows: 6-b, 7-d, 8-a, 9-d, 10-d, 11-a, 12-b.

A CHALLENGE TO YOUR READING HABITS

By now, since you are well into your training, there should have occurred at least a slight, and perhaps even a decided, change in your intellectual and psychological attitudes to reading. Let me catalogue, briefly, the factors in this change:

1. A realization that reading is not directly concerned with *words,* or even *phrases,* but only with *ideas.*

2. A realization that main ideas are more important than minor details.

3. A realization that the desire to get the main idea quickly will speed up your rate so appreciably that you can actually *feel* yourself going faster—and with little loss in comfort and very likely a substantial gain in comprehension skill.

4. A realization that you can significantly enlarge your recognition span and interpret more accurately and more rapidly what your eyes feed your mind in each fixation—that you can do this by the simple process of making greater demands on your perception capacities—that, in short, you can actually train and educate your vision.

As your general training continues day by day, page by page, this change in your *attitudes* will finally be translated into a change in your *habits and techniques;* with still further training and with continuous daily practice, efficient habits and aggressive techniques will become reflexive, second nature, almost automatic.

But of course you need not, and should not, rely for your practice

121

exclusively on the material in this book—*nor, during your training, should you restrict your reading to this book.* In all your reading from now on—and the *amount* of reading you do should increase as your skill sharpens and your rate accelerates—it is important that you practice the techniques you have been learning. Read— whether it be a magazine article, a newspaper columnist, or a book of nonfiction—for the main ideas, and read to get those main ideas quickly. And if you're reading a novel, follow the general lines of the plot rapidly, instead of getting bogged down in any of the de- tails. It is true that some novels are of such depth, or stylistically so delightful, that you may wish to read for more than the plot- line, but this is no justification for being poky. The important thing to keep in mind is that your *method* of reading and your *rate* of reading should be suited to the material at hand. A trained reader, you will recall, has a variety of speeds and techniques, and uses whichever is required by the *type* of thing he is reading; but what- ever the type, he pushes along at the maximum speed that the ma- terial and what he wants to get out of it permit. The untrained reader, on the other hand, is likely to use the same technique and the same speed for everything—light or heavy, easy or hard, simple or complex, all reading gets the same treatment.

You are on your way, now, toward becoming a trained reader. And so you are ready, I believe, to meet a challenge that I wish to confront you with.

Sometime today or tomorrow choose a novel of the sort that ap- peals to you. It can be one of the popular reprints that you will find in any stationery or drugstore; or perhaps you've had something lying around the house that you've meant to get to, but somehow never did; or stop at a bookstore to rent or buy one of the current best sellers; or ask the librarian at the local library to make a rec- ommendation. Nothing heavy, no historical novel a thousand pages long; just a short, interesting, fast-paced, readable novel. Next find an evening, preferably within the next day or two, when you will have a few hours at your disposal. Then see if you can meet this challenge: *read the entire novel through in one evening,* rapidly following the general lines of the plot, skimming or skipping where you can, but aiming to get through. You may find that you will get just as strong an emotional satisfaction from such fast cruising as from more leisurely reading, and you will be practicing the kind of rapid reading that you are attempting to master.*

If you can meet this challenge, you will have an experience no reader should miss. You will discover that it is possible to get the gist and the flavor of a novel in a few hours, you will learn that it is far from necessary to indulge in the slow, poky reading that causes the untrained reader to take days or weeks before he turns the last page of a book.

And even if you do not meet the challenge completely, the effort, however short of total success it may fall, will be beneficial to you. Try it—*soon.* You will realize that you do not have to read as slowly as you used to!

A SECOND TEST OF YOUR RETENTION AND RECALL

One of the chief means of increasing your retention and recall, as I pointed out at the end of chapter 2, is training in seeking out and successfully discovering the main idea of a selection.

The reason for this is obvious—one can always remember *meaningful* material with greater ease, efficiency, and clarity than material with little or no meaning. (Psychological experiments show that it takes considerably longer to memorize nonsense syllables, and that the period of retention is considerably shorter, than in the case of related words, or poetry, or running text.)

When you read to find, and follow, the main ideas of material, and when you can sense, during your reading, how the structure of a piece is built around these main ideas, you cannot fail to extract more meaning than when you passively absorb word after word, sentence after sentence.

Determine for yourself if this is not true in respect to your own reading. Below are twelve questions that explore your ability to recall the gist of the short selections that you have read in this chapter. You may again be surprised to discover, as you perhaps were

---

* When you do your reading, keep a record of the amount of actual time spent on the novel, the total number of pages, the approximate number of words in the whole book, and your average rate of reading. Instructions for gathering these statistics will be found on pages 163–164.

when you took your first retention test, that your memory is keener than you realize.

1. Why, as of 1949, was less money being invested in stocks than was available?_____

2. Are fried foods indigestible? □yes □no
3. How can your diary help your doctor?_____

4. Which are better learners, *adults* or *children?*_____
5. Can people think without language? □yes □no
6. What kind of reader does *not* get a continuous flow of meaning from material?_____
7. What instinct does Freud correlate with the instinct of love?____

8. What feeling, according to Mandell Sherman, does a reading difficulty create?_____
9. Do we read enough books in this country? □yes □no
10. Is seeing to a considerable extent a *learned* skill? □yes □no
11. Does reading efficiency imply the ability to change speed in accordance with material? □yes □no
12. Must the reading process be trained in order to become effective for one's needs? □yes □no

Here are the correct answers—your *language* may of course differ in some instances, but the *essence* should be the same. How well did you do?

Key: 1. Wall Street was doing a bad job of explaining its operation and purposes. 2. No. 3. By giving him an account of your previous illnesses and physical reactions so that his diagnosis and treatment will be more efficient. 4. Adults. 5. No. 6. The word-by-word reader. 7. The instinct of hate and destructiveness. 8. A feeling of frustration and failure. 9. No. 10. Yes. 11. Yes. 12. Yes.

NUMBER RIGHT OUT OF 12: _____

PERCEPTION TRAINING IV

Perception Exercise 11

We return now to further practice in rapid perception and accurate interpretation of four-digit numbers. Follow the usual procedure, and keep a record of your errors, if any.

1056	←_____	4962	←_____	9246	←_____
0538	←_____	3508	←_____	6429	←_____
1605	←_____	6227	←_____	2964	←_____
5061	←_____	2276	←_____	5803	←_____
6015	←_____	7622	←_____	8035	←_____
2386	←_____	7309	←_____	0210	←_____
6823	←_____	0937	←_____	2100	←_____
8623	←_____	3790	←_____	2001	←_____
3268	←_____	9037	←_____	1020	←_____
3417	←_____	8251	←_____	2664	←_____
1743	←_____	2518	←_____	6624	←_____
4731	←_____	5812	←_____	4662	←_____
7134	←_____	1852	←_____	9443	←_____

9344 ←_____	3568 ←_____	0469 ←_____
4439 ←_____	5386 ←_____	4690 ←_____
4394 ←_____	6904 ←_____	4096 ←_____
4943 ←_____	9046 ←_____	

NUMBER CORRECT OUT OF 50: _____

Perception Exercise 12

Here are words somewhat similar one to another. Follow the usual procedure, and keep a record of your errors, if any.

cabala ←_____	cadenced ←_____
caballero ←_____	cadger ←_____
cabana ←_____	cadgy ←_____
cabinet ←_____	cagey ←_____
cabaret ←_____	cameo ←_____
cabbage ←_____	cameleer ←_____
garbage ←_____	camellia ←_____
cablegram ←_____	camelopard ←_____
cabriolet ←_____	camels ←_____
cacao ←_____	cameral ←_____
cocoa ←_____	camisole ←_____
cackle ←_____	camomile ←_____
cackler ←_____	camphorate ←_____
cadency ←_____	Canada ←_____
cadenza ←_____	Canadienne ←_____

comedienne	←_____	candlefoot	←_____
Canadian	←_____	candied	←_____
canary	←_____	candled	←_____
cancerous	←_____	canfield	←_____
candescence	←_____	canine	←_____
candidly	←_____	canister	←_____
candidature	←_____	cankerous	←_____
candlenut	←_____	cannery	←_____
candler	←_____	cannonade	←_____
candlestick	←_____	carom	←_____

NUMBER CORRECT OUT OF 50: _____

Perception Exercise 13

The material below is from *Journeys Through Wordland* (copyright, 1942, by Amsco School Publications, Inc., New York; reprinted by special permission), and the phrases will continue in meaningful succession.

Aim, as before, for instantaneous recognition of each line which appears in the card window, and move the card quickly enough so that you will be able to make only one fixation for each exposure. The criterion of your success in this training will be that the selection continues to make sense as the phrases flash through the card window.

Avoid, as much as you can, excessive auditory reactions to the *words* in the selection—try to decrease, as much as possible, your reliance on inner speech as you follow the *ideas* into which the phrases combine.

This may not be easy. If strong auditory reactions are an ingrained part of your comprehension, you will not be happy when you reduce your dependency on them. But persevere. If you are at all successful at this time (and eventually success is quite attain-

127

able) you will be able to shorten significantly the fraction of a second you spend on each fixation—your mind will not have to wait until the words are *heard* before it calls for more material.

→ At Saratoga	→ were not
→ are acres and acres	→ growing properly.
→ of ground where	→ They soon learned
→ the State	→ that the reason
→ of New York	→ for this
→ grows thousands	→ was that
→ of trees	→ fierce little
→ every year.	→ grub worms
→ These trees	→ had been feasting
→ are grown	→ on the tender
→ from little seedlings	→ young plants.
→ which are planted	→ It was not known
→ in the ground	→ where the grubs
→ in early spring.	→ had come from,
→ One year	→ but there they were,
→ the men	→ and no one knew
→ in charge	→ how to get
→ of the trees	→ rid of them.
→ became aware	→ Just then
→ that many seeds	→ a little skunk

→ happened by

→ —just an ordinary

→ everyday little skunk.

→ Now, there's nothing

→ a skunk

→ loves better

→ for his breakfast,

→ lunch, and supper

→ than nice fat

→ juicy grubs.

→ There were millions

→ of grubs,

→ and only

→ one skunk

→ but the skunk

→ had a

→ wonderful appetite;

→ it was not long

→ before the last

→ of the grubs

→ had disappeared

→ and the trees

→ were out

→ of peril.

→ The gardeners

→ at Saratoga

→ named the

→ skunk Eric,

→ built him

→ a warm house

→ for winter,

→ made sure

→ he always had

→ a generous supply

→ of food

→ and, in short,

→ did their best

→ to overcome

→ any desire

→ he might have

→ to go away.

→ Eric stayed—

→ maybe he

→ knew that

129

→ all by himself   → of thousands

→ he could save   → of young trees

→ the lives   → every year.

How was your comprehension under the conditions required?
☐good ☐fair ☐poor

Perception Exercise 14

Now we shall dispense with the Flashmeter card as we practice on another selection from *Journeys Through Wordland.* Simply run your eyes down each column, making one fixation to a line, reducing any excessive dependency on inner speech, and yet adequately following the ideas. You have no doubt noticed that this material is on an unusually easy level of vocabulary and sentence structure (*Journeys Through Wordland* is a vocabulary-builder for the sixth and seventh grades of elementary school). I have purposely chosen such simple material so that nothing will interfere with your efforts to decrease your reliance on auditory reactions. Later exercises of this type will be of a more difficult and adult character.

As in the two previous exercises, the criterion of success is that the selection continues to make sense as your eyes sweep down the columns.

↓	↓	↓
There is a man	is mechanical,	toss its head,
in Seattle, Washington,	but it can do	and stamp
who has made	so many things	its foot.
an ape.	that it is	It can even
"How can anyone	very much like	grasp an accordion
make a real ape!"	a real ape.	in its
you will	It can sit	hairy fingers
promptly exclaim.	in a cage,	and play
Well,	roll its eyes,	a tune.
Bob Seymour's ape	move its ears,	What is

130

↓ ↓ ↓

the explanation
of this wonderful
life-like animal?
It moves
by electricity.
Mr. Seymour,
an expert electrician,
spent four years
and $5,000
on his

mechanical ape.
Its appearance is
so real
and its actions
so ape-like
that if you
saw it
in a zoo
you would
undoubtedly assume

that it
was alive.
Mr. Seymour
has not yet
named his ape.
Can you think
of an
appropriate name
for this
uncommon creature?

How was your comprehension under the conditions required?
☐good ☐fair ☐poor (Check one.)

HOW TO BUILD A BETTER
READING VOCABULARY

Preview

Aggressive comprehension; swift and accurate perception; complete absence of all forms of vocalization; little, if any, dependency on inner speech; infrequent regressions; and general habits of cutting efficiently through the details of material to the hard core of main ideas: these are some of the hallmarks of the skillful reader. Equally characteristic of such a reader is a large and ever-increasing vocabulary. And so, in this chapter, you:

• Discover why a large reading vocabulary is an aid to rapid comprehension.

• Take a five-part test that will indicate whether your vocabulary is as good as it should be.

• Learn how easy it is to bring your vocabulary up to efficient levels.

> *Chapter 6* will explain the techniques to use for adding scores of new words to your reading vocabulary.

HOW GOOD IS YOUR READING VOCABULARY?

To a skillful reader, a page of print contains not words, but rather action, color, movement, scenery, ideas, thoughts, and feelings. Nevertheless the vehicle on which all these things ride *is* words—individual English words or combinations of words.

The more familiar a reader is with the words he is reading, the less conscious he is that he is reading words, and the less he realizes that it is by means of words that he is reacting to the content of a sentence or paragraph or page. So, obviously, one of the factors that contribute to efficient and rapid reading is a large recognition vocabulary; conversely, and equally obviously, one of the factors that may reduce comprehension and slow down the rate of reading, that may even encourage regressions and vocalization, is a weak vocabulary.

How about your own vocabulary? Is it as large as it should be for skillful and effortless reading? Let's find out.

Take This Vocabulary Test

You may make an intelligent guess whenever you feel that you are familiar enough with a word to have an even chance of arriving at the correct answer. *Do not guess wildly.* If you have never in your life seen a particular word, or if you haven't the foggiest notion of its meaning, do not attempt an answer, as baseless guessing will invalidate your score.

PART I

Directions: Next to each of the key words in column *A*, copy the letter of the correct definition to be found in column *B*.

A	B
1. to recline	a. to chew
2. to hazard	b. to be sorry
3. to munch	c. to make fun of
4. to utilize	d. to shift one's course
5. to saturate	e. to take a chance
6. to lament	f. to erase
7. to distort	g. to put out of focus
8. to mock	h. to soak completely
9. to veer	i. to use
10. to eradicate	j. to lie down

PART II

Directions: Write to the left of each number the letter of the meaning which most clearly defines each word.

1. egoism: *a*—self-interest, *b*—knowledge, *c*—optimism
2. concoction: *a*—refusal, *b*—mixture, *c*—prayer
3. pollution: *a*—doing away with, *b*—corruption, *c*—coloring
4. candor: *a*—frankness, *b*—sweetness, *c*—inability
5. arrogance: *a*—refusal, *b*—fear, *c*—pride
6. extricate: *a*—complicate, *b*—release, *c*—imprison
7. agile: *a*—happy, *b*—talkative, *c*—spry
8. coherent: *a*—powerful, *b*—well-connected, *c*—rambling
9. mediocre: *a*—ordinary, *b*—poor, *c*—necessary
10. abstain: *a*—ask, *b*—splotch, *c*—refrain

PART III

Directions: Check the correct answer to each question.

1. Does a *phlegmatic* person become easily excited? YES NO
2. Do excessive eaters lead an *abstemious* life? YES NO
3. Do *complacency* and anxiety usually go together? YES NO
4. Is a *diffident* person self-assertive? YES NO
5. Does *inadvertently* mean the same as purposely? YES NO
6. Is a *voluble* person generally silent? YES NO
7. Is a *panacea* a cure-all? YES NO
8. Is a *consummate* liar a skillful liar? YES NO
9. Does a *martinet* insist on strict obedience and discipline? YES NO
10. Does a *misogynist* enjoy the company of women? YES NO

134

Directions: If word and definition are nearly the same in meaning, check *S;* if they are more nearly opposite in meaning, check *O.*

1. veracious   S—O truthful
2. parsimonious   S—O generous
3. stolid   S—O sluggish
4. contrite   S—O sorry
5. vitriolic   S—O mild
6. pathological   S—O diseased
7. disparage   S—O praise
8. asceticism   S—O self-denial
9. obfuscate   S—O clarify
10. equivocal   S—O clear

Directions: If the statement is generally true, check *T;* if it is generally false, check *F.*

1. Industrial *peonage* is an important aspect of American life.

                                                     T F

2. Medicine has *therapeutic* value.   T F
3. The automobile is an *anachronism* in America.   T F
4. Crooked business houses try to *mulct* the public.   T F
5. *Summary* justice is dealt out to military offenders.   T F
6. A *ukase* is commonly disobeyed.   T F
7. A *plethora* of money forces people to live in poverty. T F
8. A *paean* is a song of lamentation.   T F
9. Delight in *panoply* indicates a love of simple things. T F
10. A *truculent* person is fierce and quarrelsome.   T F

Key:

Part I: 1—*j,* 2—*e,* 3—*a,* 4—*i,* 5—*h,* 6—*b,* 7—*g,* 8—*c,* 9—*d,* 10—*f.*

Part II: 1—*a,* 2—*b,* 3—*b,* 4—*a,* 5—*c,* 6—*b,* 7—*c,* 8—*b,* 9—*a,* 10—*c.*

Part III: 1—6: all NO; 7—9: all YES; 10—NO.

Part IV: 1—S, 2—O, 3—S, 4—S, 5—O, 6—S, 7—O, 8—S, 9—O, 10—O.

Part V: 1—F, 2—T, 3—F, 4—T, 5—T, 6—F, 7—F, 8—F, 9—F, 10—T.

Scoring

Allow two points for each correct answer. Add up the scores you made on the five parts, and consult the chart below for a rough gauge of the present state of your vocabulary.

> 90–100—EXCELLENT (college graduate level)
> 70–88—GOOD (college sophomore level)
> 50–68—FAIR (high school level)
> 30–48—POOR (elementary school level)
> 0–28—VERY POOR

The lower your score on this test the more important it is to start building your vocabulary *immediately*. The exercises in this and later chapters will get you started—do them carefully and conscientiously.

If your score was high (80 to 100 per cent) you will probably be able to breeze through these exercises with great rapidity, for you have a rich background; adding to your vocabulary has never been a chore. But do not, for that reason, ignore any of the word-study material. As anyone with a rich vocabulary will agree, every interesting word that can be added to one's personal treasury is grist to the mill. No matter how large your vocabulary may be, every word you add to it will help, in some small way, to make your reading more efficient and more satisfying.

The success of your learning will constantly be tested, and the more actively you participate in these tests the more surely will the new words become permanent and valuable aids to your reading skill.

A STARTER SET OF WORDS

Back in 1942, when I began to work on the first edition of this book, I realized that it was necessary to prepare a short list of words which are not usually found in the poor vocabulary, but which occur with sufficient frequency in general writing to be of immediate usefulness as aids to reading comprehension.

And so, for a period of about a year, I collected such words from the following sources:

1. The editorial pages, book reviews, and signed columns of three representative New York newspapers: the *Times,* the *Herald Tribune,* and the *Post.*

2. A number of widely read magazines, including *Harper's,* the *Atlantic Monthly, Life, Fortune,* the *Reader's Digest,* the *Saturday Evening Post,* the *New Yorker, Esquire,* and *Coronet.*

3. Eight popular nonfiction books.

4. Five popular novels.

The problem was to discover whether professional writers use any group of uncommon words with enough frequency and regularity to permit the construction of a definite and not too cumbersome list which could most quickly, surely, and successfully aid a serious student in building an effective reading vocabulary.

To solve this problem, I kept an alphabetical list of all the uncommon words I encountered during my investigation of the sources indicated, and each successive time a word appeared in any of my sources, I made a notation next to it so that a total of frequency could later be calculated.

At the end of the investigation I found that there were 1,743 uncommon words which I had encountered five or more times in the various books and periodicals I was using. In order to narrow the list still further, I then rearranged the words in order of their frequency and chose the 500 which had appeared most often. How frequently these top 500 occurred can be judged from the following table:

109 words	35 to 51 times
158 words	25 to 34 times
214 words	20 to 24 times
16 words	15 to 19 times
3 words	14 times

Since these 500 words are the ones which I most frequently encountered over a twelve-month period in a representative cross section of American reading matter, I offer them to you, in alphabetical order, as a useful starter set for vocabulary improvement.

I feel that an adequate understanding of the words on this minimum list is critically important to the reader who wishes to develop his comprehension skill. Without a complete mastery of at least these words, a reader will frequently meet blind spots—that is, words which are keys to the author's thought but which, because of the reader's unfamiliarity with them, convey little or no thought to him.

You might, at this point, skim rapidly through the list to see how many of the words are totally unfamiliar to you. Then, in the next section, I shall choose twenty of the words for discussion and learning, and explain, step by step, how to use a dictionary most effectively in adding these words to your vocabulary. In later chapters we will cover successive groups of ten to thirty words in daily practice sessions, and by the end of the course you will have mastered about a third of the complete list. You will then be asked to continue, by the same technique, mastering the remaining words, and a number of specific vocabulary manuals will be recommended so that you may still further add to your reading vocabulary.

500 Words That Belong in Your Reading Vocabulary

* aberration	amenable	assuage
* abject	amenities	astute
abominable	amorphous	atavistic
abortive	anachronism	atheist
abstemious	analogous	attrition
* abstruse	anathema	augment
* acerbity	animosity	
acme	anodyne	auspicious
acrid		* austere
acrimonious	* anomaly	* autonomous
	* anthropoid	avarice
* acumen	* anthropology	avidity
* adamant	anticlimax	badinage
adroit	antipathy	* baleful
adulation	antithesis	* bathos
* affluence	aphrodisiac	belated
agnostic	aplomb	benediction
alacrity	apocryphal	
alleviate	arbitrary	beneficent
* altruism		benevolent
ambidextrous	archaic	benign
	* argot	* blithe
* ambiguous	ascetic	bovine
* ameliorate	assiduous	* bromide

* Starred words are offered for study in this and later chapters.

138

* bucolic
bumptious
* cacophony
cadaverous

cadence
* cajole
calumny
capricious
* captious
* carnivorous
carte blanche
* castigate
catholic (adj.)
* cavil

celibate
* chauvinism
chicanery
chimera
clairvoyant
clandestine
* claustrophobia
coerce
cogent
* cogitate

commiserate
* complacency
compunction
concomitant
* condone
consummate (adj.)
* contentious
contrite
* convivial
* corpulent

corroborate
cryptic
culinary
culpable
cupidity

cursory
cynosure
dearth
* debauchery
decimate

decorum
* defunct
deleterious
deprecate
depredation
desultory
detract
* dexterity
* diffidence
dilettante

* dipsomaniac
dishabille
disparage
disparity
docile
dogmatic
* dormant
dour
dubious
dulcet

* duplicity
* ebullience
effervescence
* effete
egomaniac
* egregious
emasculate
empirical
* emulate
* encomium

* enervation
enigmatic
ennui
ephemeral

epitome
* equanimity
equivocal
* eschew
* esoteric
esthetic

ethereal
* eugenics
* eulogy
euphemism
* euphony
evanescent
execrable
exigency
exotic
expedite

expiate
* expostulate
* extirpate
extrovert
fatuous
fecund
* fetid
fetish
fiasco
fiat

flagrant
fortuitous
* fracas
* fractious
frugality
* fulminate
functional
furtive
futilitarian
* germane

grandiose
* gregarious
* gullible

* gynecology
* halcyon
* harass
  harbinger
* hauteur
  heterogeneous
* histrionic

  holocaust
  homogeneous
  hyperbole
* hypochondria
* iconoclasm
  idiosyncrasy
  ignominy
  illusory
  imbroglio
* immolate

  imperturbable
  impious
* implacable
  implicit
* impugn
  impunity
  impute
  inadvertent
* inane
  incipient

  inclement
* incompatible
  incongruous
  incorrigible
  incredulous
  indefatigable
  indigent
  indolence
  ineffable
* inexorable

  ingenuous
* iniquity

* innocuous
* insidious
  insipid
* insouciant
  intractable
  intransigent
  intrepid
  introversion

  inundate
* inure
  inviolate
  irascible
  itinerant
* jingoism
* jubilation
* kleptomania
  laconic
  lampoon

  lascivious
  latent
* lechery
  lethargy
  levity
* libidinous
* limbo
  limpid
  lithe
* loquacious

  lugubrious
  Machiavellian
* malaise
* malediction
* malefactor
* malevolent
* malign (vb.)
* malignant
* malinger
  manic

  martinet
  maudlin
  mayhem
  megalomania
  mélange
  mellifluous
* mendacity
  Mephistophelian
* mercurial
* meretricious

  metamorphosis
  metaphorical
  meticulous
* militate
  mirage
* misanthropy
* misogyny
  mitigate
  mollify
* mordant

  moribund
* mulct
  mundane
  myriad
  nadir
* naïve
  nebulous
  nefarious
  nepotism
* nostalgia

  novitiate
* nuance
  nymphomania
* obdurate
  obfuscate
* oblique
  oblivion
* obloquy
* obsequious
* obstetrician

obtuse
* occult
ominous
* omnipotent
* omnipresent
* omniscient
* omnivorous
opinionated
* opulence
orthodox

orient (vb.)
ostracize
paean
palliate
* pallid
palpable
panacea
panegyric
paragon
paranoia

paroxysm
parsimonious
patent (adj.)
pathological
pedantic
* pediatrician
penchant
penurious
peonage
perfidious

perfunctory
peripheral
* persiflage
* perspicacity
* perspicuity
philander
phlegmatic
pique
* placate
* plaintive

platitude
plebeian
plethora
poignant
* polyglot
pompous
portentous
* posthumous
pragmatic
* preclude

predatory
predilection
pre-empt
* presage
presentiment
presumptuous
* prodigal
prodigious
* prolific
prolixity

promiscuity
* propinquity
* propitiate
prosaic
prurience
pseudo
psychotic
puberty
puerile
pugnacious

punctilious
pungent
pusillanimous
* pyromania
* querulous
* quintessence
* quixotic
rampant
rationalize
* raucous

recalcitrant
recondite
recrimination
redolent
redundancy
regimen
regurgitate
relevant
renegade
repudiate

resilient
respite
* retribution
revulsion
* ribald
* risible
* risqué
rotund
rubble
rudimentary

ruminate
rustic
saccharine (adj.)
sacrilegious
* sadism
* sagacity
salient (adj.)
* sanctimonious
sanguinary
* sanguine

sardonic
saturnalia
saturnine
schizophrenia
scourge
sedate
sedulous
senile
sententious
* sepulchral

shambles	* taciturn	* urbane
simulate	tantamount	utilitarian
sloth	* tedium	vacillate
sobriquet		* vacuous
* solicitous		
sonorous	temerity	vagary
sophistry	temporize	vapid
soporific	tenet	vegetate
specious	* tenuous	
sporadic	therapeutic	venomous
	titanic	veracity
	titillation	verbatim
stilted	torpid	* verbose
stoic	toxic	verisimilitude
* stolid	* translucent	* vicarious
stratum		vicissitude
* strident	travesty	* vindictive
stringent	* trenchant	virile
* suave	trepidation	virtuoso
subterfuge	truculent	
subversive	truism	virulent
succinct	turgid	* visceral
	tyro	vitiate
summary (adj.)	* ubiquitous	* vitriolic
* supercilious	* ukase	vituperative
surfeit	* unctuous	volatile
surreptitious		* voluble
sycophant	unrequited	vortex
synthesis	* unwitting	wanton
* tacit	upbraid	zenith

VOCABULARY STUDY I

Let us get down to work by considering twenty words chosen at random from the list.

1. anomaly
2. incompatible
3. encomium
4. panegyric
5. eulogy

6. jubilant
7. sporadic
8. vicarious
9. gregarious
10. egregious

142

11. ukase
12. captious
13. misanthropy
14. philanthropy
15. anthropology

16. anthropoid
17. misogyny
18. gynecology
19. obstetrician
20. pediatrician

John Chamberlain, formerly literary critic of the *New York Times*, called *A Preface to Peace*, by Harold Callender, "an *anomaly* among books of its type in that it seeks to base its hopes for the future on the fair and accurate reporting of present facts." Apparently, out of his wide experience with such books, Mr. Chamberlain finds this one distinctly different, contrary to what might be expected, unusual in that it deviates from the general rule for such books.

An editorial in the *New York Herald Tribune* in February 1944 claimed that the international situation proved that the Falangist State, meaning Spain, was *incompatible* with the United Nations. In other words, the two simply could not get along.

The *Tribune* editorial pointed out, in addition, that Franco of Spain heaped *encomiums* on Hitler when the German armies seemed to be within sight of victory. An *encomium* is a formal, generally public, expression of warm praise; usually the plural form, *encomiums*, is used. Synonyms of this word which are worth knowing are *panegyric* and *eulogy*; these may be used in the singular.

In February 1944 Admiral Fletcher's Task Force bombarded Paramushiru, part of the Japanese homeland. This was no *sporadic* raid, said the *New York Times*, but rather a part of a systematic pattern. It would seem, then, that *sporadic* and *systematic* are contrasted words, for anything *sporadic* occurs only occasionally and in no particular pattern.

People who feel happy over something they have accomplished, who feel triumphant and joyful over the outcome of a struggle, a contest, or a conflict, are *jubilant*—they've got what they wanted and as a result they feel set up, elated.

If you cannot experience certain things in life directly, you will have to be content with experiencing them *vicariously*. One can travel *vicariously*, by reading books about foreign lands. Romantic movies provide a *vicarious* thrill for people whose lives are barren of love and adventure. Any feeling is *vicarious* which springs, not from a direct and personal participation in some act or experience, but from reading or hearing about it, or in some way being an inactive spectator.

Human beings are by nature *gregarious*. They enjoy the company of others, they like to be part of the crowd, and prefer friendship and social intercourse to solitude. The important syllable of this word, *greg*, comes from a Latin root meaning flock of sheep. *Gregarious* people like to flock together, the way sheep do. A con*greg*ation is a group of people who have flocked together to listen to their religious shepherd, or pastor. Anything or anyone taken out of the flock is se*greg*ated. And finally a most useful word: *egregious*. Anything is *egregious* which is so bad that it stands out (*ex*) from the flock (*greg*) of bad things, like an *egregious* error, an *egregious* crime, or an *egregious* insult.

Strikes are not prevented by *ukases*, editorializes the *New York Post*, but by eliminating the causes of labor troubles. A *ukase* is any official decree having the force of law.

The *Saturday Evening Post* opines that conflict is an important element of education, and that those boys and girls who want education badly enough to make great sacrifices to get it will derive the most benefit from it. This point is raised in no *captious* spirit, writes the editor, who had just attended a conference on education and didn't quite like what he heard. A person is *captious* who easily finds fault, especially over trifles.

Hitler was sometimes called a *misanthrope* because his actions often seemed indicative of a deep and unwavering hatred for mankind. *Misanthropy*, a hatred for the human race, is opposed to the more common term, *philanthropy*, a love for, and charitable acts toward, humanity. If you know the root *anthrop*, mankind, you will be able to recognize two other words: *anthropology*, the study of the development of the human race; and *anthropoid*, manlike, as in the phrase, *anthropoid apes*.

Schopenhauer, who called women the "long-haired, short-brained sex," was one of the most famous pessimists and *misogynists* among philosophers. A misanthrope hates all mankind; more discriminating

144

in his aversions, a *misogynist* hates women only. The name for the philosophy is *misogyny*. The root *gyn,* meaning woman, is also found in *gynecology,* the study of women's diseases. A *gynecologist* is a doctor who specializes in the treatment of female disorders, and should not be confused with the *obstetrician,* who delivers babies, nor with the *pediatrician,* the doctor who cares for infants after they are born.

No attempt is being made at this point to delve very deeply into the meanings of the words we are discussing. (That is more properly the province of a dictionary or of a vocabulary-building manual.) However, enough of an indication of the meaning and emotional flavor of the words has been given so that you can understand what an author is trying to say when he uses them. And every time you meet these words, in varying contexts, in your everyday reading, you will become a little more keenly aware of their hidden overtones, of their significant implications, of their subtle emotional shadings.

Right now, our interest is in testing the success of your learning. If these twenty words have made at least a surface impression on your mind, you should be able to mark each of the following statements either *true* or *false*.

Test Your Learning

1. *Anomalies* are, by their very nature, rare.　　　TRUE? FALSE?
2. *Incompatibility* makes for a happy married life.　TRUE? FALSE?
3. Newspapers heap *encomiums* on our military heroes.

　　　　　　　　　　　　　　　　　　　TRUE? FALSE?
4. A *panegyric* is insulting.　　　　　　　TRUE? FALSE?
5. It is customary to *eulogize* the deceased in the funeral oration.

　　　　　　　　　　　　　　　　　　　TRUE? FALSE?
6. News of a victory makes us *jubilant*.　　　TRUE? FALSE?
7. Early in World War II we made *sporadic* air raids on Europe.

　　　　　　　　　　　　　　　　　　　TRUE? FALSE?
8. *Vicarious* pleasure is always keener than direct pleasure.

　　　　　　　　　　　　　　　　　　　TRUE? FALSE?
9. Hermits are *gregarious*.　　　　　　　TRUE? FALSE?
10. Some nations have made *egregious* attacks on an unprepared country.　　　　　　　　　　　　TRUE? FALSE?
11. The Nazis ruled by *ukase*.　　　　　　TRUE? FALSE?

12. *Captiousness* often creates resentment.   TRUE? FALSE?
13. *Misanthropy* is a widely held philosophy.   TRUE? FALSE?
14. Kind people are usually *philanthropic*.   TRUE? FALSE?
15. *Anthropology* is the study of insects.   TRUE? FALSE?
16. Fish are *anthropoid*.   TRUE? FALSE?
17. Casanova was a *misogynist*.   TRUE? FALSE?
18. A *gynecologist* is a woman-hater.   TRUE? FALSE?
19. An *obstretrician* treats young infants.   TRUE? FALSE?
20. A *pediatrician* is a foot doctor.   TRUE? FALSE?

Key: 1—T, 2—F, 3—T, 4—F, 5—T, 6—T, 7—F, 8—F, 9—F, 10—T, 11—T, 12—T, 13—F, 14—T, 15—F, 16—F, 17—F, 18—F, 19—F, 20—F.

We have, as I have indicated, so far only scratched the surface of these 20 valuable words. Now I ask you to dig a little deeper, using a good dictionary as a help.

(If you find your present dictionary inadequate in any way, I suggest any one of these, which are among the best published today:

1. Webster's New World Dictionary, College Edition [World Publishing Co., $6.75 thumb-indexed]

2. American College Dictionary [Random House, $6.75 thumb-indexed]

3. Webster's New Collegiate Dictionary [G. & C. Merriam Co., $6.00 thumb-indexed]

4. Thorndike-Barnhart Comprehensive Desk Dictionary [Doubleday and Co., $3.50 thumb-indexed])

With the dictionary as your guide, you will make a concerted attack on these words. Here are the first ten, in alphabetical arrangement—look each one up, find the information that will help you answer the questions below, and write your answers either in the margin of the page or on a scratch pad, or, if you wish to keep your vocabulary-study in a more permanent form, in a bound notebook.

1. *anomaly*
a. First, read and understand the nontechnical definition. Then, in your own phraseology, write briefly the general meaning of the word.
b. Write two forms of the derived adjective, which you will find either with the word or in preceding entries.

c. Write that form which means the *state of being an anomaly,* which you will find in a preceding entry.

2. *anthropoid*

a. Write briefly, in your own language, the general meaning of the word.

b. What does the Greek root *anthropos* mean?

c. Name an animal that may be called *anthropoid.*

3. *anthropology*

a. Write briefly the general meaning of the word.

b. What is the word for a student or expert in *anthropology?*

c. Write the adjective form of *anthropology.*

4. *captious*

a. Write briefly the general meaning of the word.

b. What part of speech is this word?

c. Write a synonym of the word.

d. Does the word connote a *pleasant* or an *unpleasant* characteristic?

5. *egregious*

a. Write briefly the general meaning of the word.

b. Now make sure you can pronounce it correctly. Say it aloud.

c. What does the Latin root *grex, gregis* mean?

6. *encomium*

a. Write briefly the general meaning of the word.

b. Find, in preceding entries, the following:

    (1) the form denoting a writer or speaker of *encomiums.*

    (2) two adjective forms of *encomium.*

c. Write two synonyms of *encomium.*

7. *eulogy*

a. Write briefly the general meaning of the word.

b. Find, in preceding entries, the following:

    (1) a speaker or writer of *eulogies.*

    (2) the adjective form of *eulogy.*

    (3) the verb form of *eulogy.*

8. *gregarious*

a. Write briefly the general meaning of the word.

b. What does the Latin root *grex, gregis* mean?

c. Is it normal to be *gregarious?*

9. *gynecology*

a. Write briefly the general meaning of the word.

147

b. What does the Greek root *gyne* mean?
c. Find, in preceding entries, the following:
    (1) two adjectival forms.
    (2) the term for the specialist in *gynecology*.
10. *incompatible*
a. Write briefly the general meaning of the word.
b. On which syllable does the accent fall?
c. Write two noun forms.

Key:

1.—b. anomalous, anomalistic; c. anomalism, or, of course, anomalousness.

2.—b. man or mankind; c. ape, chimpanzee, gorilla, orangutan, gibbon, etc.

3.—b. anthropologist; c. anthropologic or anthropological.

4.—b. adjective; c. critical, carping, caviling, etc.; d. unpleasant.

5.—c. herd or flock.

6.—b. (1) encomiast; (2) encomiastic or encomiastical; c. eulogy, panegyric, praise, laudation, commendation, plaudits, etc.

7.—b. (1) eulogist; (2) eulogistic; (3) eulogize.

8.—b. flock or herd; c. yes

9.—b. woman or female; c. (1) gynecologic or gynecological; (2) gynecologist.

10.—b. third; c. incompatibleness or incompatibility.

Test Your Learning

After reading over the notes you made, answer the following questions *yes* or *no*.

1. Does one generally find *anomalism?*_____
2. Are birds *anthropoid?*_____
3. Would an *anthropologist* necessarily know much about primitive cultures?_____
4. Is a *captious* person likely to be popular?_____
5. Is murder an *egregious* crime?_____
6. Does an *encomiast* have a low opinion of his subject?_____
7. Does one generally *eulogize* one's enemies?_____
8. Are sheep *gregarious?*_____ How about wolves?_____ cats?_____ people?_____
9. Does a *gynecologist* have mainly male patients?_____

148

10. Does *incompatibility* between husband and wife often lead to thoughts of divorce?_____

Key: 1—no, 2—no, 3—yes, 4—no, 5—yes, 6—no, 7—no, 8—yes, yes, no, yes, 9—no, 10—yes.

Now that you have a good grip on these ten words, let us follow the same procedure with the next ten. I shall not take space to ask you specific questions because you have already learned, from your previous work with the dictionary, the general routine to follow with these words. In each instance rewrite the meaning in your own language; write the derived forms, if any; note the pronunciation, and say the word aloud; and see whether the word is built upon a Greek or Latin root that would be useful to you in figuring out the meanings of related words. Please be sure to follow these directions exactly, and make your notes *in writing* on your scratch pad or in your notebook. Here are the ten words on which to work.

1. jubilant	6. pediatrician
2. misanthropy	7. philanthropy
3. misogyny	8. sporadic
4. obstetrician	9. ukase
5. panegyric	10. vicarious

Test Your Learning

Reread the notes you have made on these ten words, then answer the following questions *yes* or *no*.
1. Is *jubilation* over failure a normal reaction?_____
2. Does a *misanthrope* love people?_____
3. Does a *misogynous* attitude attract women?_____
4. Are labor pains an *obstetrical* phenomenon?_____
5. Are great men often *panegyrized* by their biographers?_____
6. Does a doctor engaging in *pediatrics* have infants as patients?

_____

7. Is a *philanthropist* interested in the welfare of others?_____
8. Are *sporadic* and *constant* synonymous?_____
9. Is a *ukase* usually obeyed?_____
10. Do parents sometimes enjoy youth *vicariously* through their children?_____

Key: 1—no, 2—no, 3—no, 4—yes, 5—yes, 6—yes, 7—yes, 8—no, 9—yes, 10—yes.

PERCEPTION TRAINING V

Perception Exercise 15

To help you prepare for training in five-digit perception, this exercise in "jumping digits" is presented. The span occupied by the following three- and four-digit numbers is equal to that occupied by five-digit numbers, but one or two digits are omitted in each instance. When you can do this and the following exercise comfortably, you will be prepared for complete five-digit training.

Follow the usual procedure, as explained on page 62, and keep a record of your errors, if any.

7 2 8 ←_____	5 0 9 ←_____	77 2 ←_____
1 9 0 ←_____	32 6 ←_____	3 0 5 ←_____
8 6 4 ←_____	9 1 3 ←_____	329 1 ←_____
32 6 ←_____	32 7 ←_____	7 386 ←_____
98 1 ←_____	4 1 2 ←_____	9 542 ←_____
9 18 ←_____	3 7 1 ←_____	06 65 ←_____
5 76 ←_____	88 0 ←_____	43 45 ←_____
40 7 ←_____	1 56 ←_____	6 553 ←_____
7 2 8 ←_____	7 3 9 ←_____	53 96 ←_____
63 1 ←_____	11 4 ←_____	23 63 ←_____
2 19 ←_____	3 1 2 ←_____	386 1 ←_____

764 0 ←_____ 5 047 ←_____ 3 927 ←_____

534 8 ←_____ 23 69 ←_____ 1 057 ←_____

579 1 ←_____ 02 39 ←_____ 89 97 ←_____

62 31 ←_____ 562 4 ←_____ 1 690 ←_____

7 207 ←_____ 9 153 ←_____ 624 3 ←_____

329 1 ←_____ 21 07 ←_____

NUMBER CORRECT OUT OF 50: _____

Perception Exercise 16

As further preparation for five-digit training, here is an exercise combining four digits with a letter. Follow the same procedure as before.

1M302 ←_____ 52D20 ←_____ 3B307 ←_____

2B605 ←_____ 86G55 ←_____ 4D170 ←_____

9L820 ←_____ 93M92 ←_____ 6F132 ←_____

4C312 ←_____ 68N84 ←_____ 7G196 ←_____

8F102 ←_____ 6P108 ←_____ 42Q42 ←_____

9B607 ←_____ 9Q307 ←_____ 77Z24 ←_____

3X404 ←_____ 8R202 ←_____ 84L46 ←_____

5V902 ←_____ 6P070 ←_____ 93P30 ←_____

1A043 ←_____ 4A103 ←_____ 22Q90 ←_____

9B706 ←_____ 9T307 ←_____ 78J08 ←_____

3C405 ←_____ 8R100 ←_____ 92K04 ←_____

34C10 ←_____ 7Q707 ←_____ 44N62 ←_____

67R77	←_____	2R225	←_____	L5507	←_____
82S55	←_____	61F38	←_____	6P075	←_____
49U93	←_____	93P07	←_____	67Q82	←_____
77A82	←_____	6P108	←_____	527L6	←_____
8H522	←_____	82B04	←_____		

NUMBER CORRECT OUT OF 50: _____

Perception Exercise 17

You are now ready for training in five-digit perception. Proceed as before, remembering to keep your exposures as brief as possible and your responses as exclusively visual as you can.

64582	←_____	62111	←_____	19382	←_____
63218	←_____	66966	←_____	83921	←_____
74521	←_____	83623	←_____	93862	←_____
89361	←_____	98931	←_____	45674	←_____
73652	←_____	75231	←_____	62590	←_____
90013	←_____	63923	←_____	82730	←_____
09091	←_____	84721	←_____	94194	←_____
83670	←_____	14729	←_____	10982	←_____
76283	←_____	84720	←_____	84013	←_____
89321	←_____	84982	←_____	94821	←_____
89209	←_____	87210	←_____	95726	←_____
98721	←_____	09370	←_____	72639	←_____
83200	←_____	83920	←_____	83729	←_____

84730	←_____	94729	←_____	92836	←_____
09412	←_____	84729	←_____	94821	←_____
87291	←_____	64820	←_____	36258	←_____
93821	←_____	84720	←_____		

NUMBER CORRECT OUT OF 50: _____

Perception Exercise 18

Without using the Flashmeter card, run your eyes rapidly down each column, allowing only one fixation in the center of each line, as indicated by the arrow, and with decreased reliance on inner speech. The criterion of success is whether comprehension is clear and continuous. The material in exercises 18 and 19 is again from *Journeys Through Wordland* (copyright 1942 by Amsco School Publications, Inc.; reprinted by permission).

↓ ↓ ↓

In the	reaches it	and 25 pounds
Bronx Zoo,	quite often,	of hay.
New York City,	because he	That's a
lives Jack,	likes to lick	considerable amount
a 21-foot giraffe.	the paint	of food,
You will have	with his	isn't it?
no difficulty	12-inch tongue!)	But if you weighed
recognizing him	Would you like	over 2,000 pounds
—he has such	to know	(as Jack does)
a long neck!	what Jack eats?	you'd doubtless need
You can imagine	Here is	just as much
how little	his daily menu:	food.
he has	1¾ pails	Giraffes belong to
to exert himself	of oats,	a vanishing race,
to reach	12 potatoes,	and can be found
the top	an apple,	in just
of his cage.	3 carrots,	a few places
(And he	half a cabbage,	in Africa.

153

↓ | ↓ | ↓

They are timid, | on the top leaves | that's the way
can run swiftly | of trees. | they acquired
and like | Do you think | their long necks?
to feed | perhaps |

How was your comprehension under the conditions required?
☐good ☐fair ☐poor

Perception Exercise 19

Continue as before.

↓ | ↓ | ↓

Most of us | and selling them | to find out why.
think of sharks | at $210 a ton | He went to
as fearful fish | in the San Francisco | San Francisco
that chew off | market. | and learned
swimmers' legs | Harlan Major, | that the livers
and in other | a New York | of soup-fin sharks
disagreeable ways | fishing authority, | (the kind
make general nuisances | stopped at | around Fort Bragg)
of themselves. | Fort Bragg | had proved to be
But the people | when he made | uncommonly rich
of Fort Bragg, | a fishing tour | in Vitamin A
California, | of the country. | (something that
will tell you | He was amazed | keeps people
with no uncertainty | at the great activity | strong and healthy).
that sharks are | going on there, | Chemical laboratories
their best friends— | for Fort Bragg, | were buying
many a | once a sleepy little | all the soup-fin
local fisherman | fishing village, | shark livers
has become richer | was now experiencing | they could
catching the huge | unusual prosperity. | get hold of
creatures | Mr. Major decided | to make into

↓	↓	↓
little pills for people who wish to avoid illnesses.	And so every day the Fort Bragg fishermen put out to sea to look for	the fearful creatures whose livers are keeping a nation in good health!

How was your comprehension under the conditions required?
□good □fair □poor

★ SESSION 13

HOW TO BUILD YOUR VOCABULARY WHILE READING (VOCABULARY STUDY II)

It is safe to say that, unless you are an exception to the rule, your greatest period of vocabulary growth was during the first twenty years of your life—granting that you are now over twenty.

Why then?

First, because that was the period of your formal schooling. Second, because that was the period in which the world held its greatest and freshest novelty for you—you wanted to learn, because learning is natural to childhood, youth, and adolescence, and words are the symbols of learning, the means by which curiosity is satisfied. Third, because you read more books (again, unless you are an exception to the general rule) in your first twenty years than you will read all the rest of your life unless you consciously plan otherwise.

A large vocabulary results from wide learning and varied reading.

This much is definitely known: for most people vocabulary grows at a phenomenal rate for the first twenty years. After that, by comparison with the former rate of growth, it slows down so radically

155

that for practical purposes one might almost say that it comes to a dead stop.

The reason is this: after twenty, the average person who has finished his formal education grows greatly in experience, but comparatively little in *pure knowledge*.

How, then, can you accelerate your vocabulary growth once you've passed your twentieth birthday?

Partly by means of vocabulary-building manuals, examples of which will be suggested later, or by a direct study of the dictionary. Mostly through doubling, tripling, quadrupling the amount of reading you do; through changing your reading habits to include the better magazines, the more adult newspapers, a greater range of nonfiction books in a wider variety of fields.

And through being on the alert for new words while reading.

Exactly how do you go about it?

The *seemingly* logical method to suggest is that you read with a dictionary at your side.

There are some conscientious individuals who follow this practice —and they doggedly thumb through their dictionaries for any word whose meaning they cannot immediately grasp. This is an excellent idea, admittedly, in so far as vocabulary-building is concerned. However, constant shifting from book or magazine to dictionary not only obviously slows reading to a snail's pace, but, more important, sets up numerous interruptions to complete concentration. In addition, it takes much of the joy out of reading, because the dictionary-thumber is not reading at all, but practically translating a foreign language; and this, if you remember your high-school experiences with your French or German reader, or your copy of Caesar or Cicero, is not the most delightful mental activity one can imagine.

So that throws out the seemingly logical method. And leaves us searching for a method that is more practical.

A completely practical method is this:

1. Let any new word you encounter in your reading register, for a second or so, in your mind.

2. Spend a few more seconds puzzling out its probable meaning from the context in which you find it.

That's all.

Just two steps.

Then go right on with your reading. Until, of course, you come across another new word.

The rest happens without any further effort on your part. Because you spend a few seconds registering a new word in your mind, and puzzling about it, the next time you meet it it will hit you a little more strongly than it did the first time.

And you will meet it again—because you are now conscious of its existence, and are, without realizing it, on the alert for its next appearance.

Each time you meet it in a different context, its meaning will become a little clearer to you. Or, if you misunderstood its meaning the first time, the second appearance will begin to set you straight. And the third and fourth and subsequent appearances will add more and more to its meaning.

Eventually, it will be an old friend.

Then subsequent encounters will not detract from your reading speed, and will add to the completeness of your comprehension.

Remember: until you become alert to new words, your mind will skip over them, will be unaware of their existence, no matter how often you may meet them.

Increasing your vocabulary by this simple process of staying on the alert for new words as you meet them in your reading actually works. Without a conscious mind-set, you might encounter an unfamiliar word—the same word—a dozen times in a month and be completely blind to it. Then something external opens your eyes. Perhaps you hear some friends discussing the meaning, derivation, or spelling of the word. Perhaps you read an explanation of it in some such book as this. One of a number of possible things might happen to wake you up. In any case, a "dead" word suddenly comes "alive" for you; a meaningless combination of syllables becomes pregnantly meaningful.

Then what happens? Everywhere you turn you see the word. Every book, magazine, or newspaper writer seems tenaciously bent on using just that word in a hundred varying contexts.

To explain this phenomenon, let me draw an analogy. You spend $150 for a new overcoat—more, let us say for the sake of argument, than you have ever spent before. Or, if you are a woman, you buy a new and expensive fur coat. Then what happens? Your eyes are opened to coats. Where once before you saw men and women walking down a street, you now see coats, each with a comparatively unimportant man or woman inside it. You notice color, shape, material; you notice which ones are new, and which ones look shabby. In a word, you are, for as long as your own coat retains its novelty, "coat-conscious."

And that's the way it is with a new word. So long as a new word, say *vicarious,* retains its novelty for you, you are "*vicarious*-conscious." Every time you meet it, it gives you a warm thrill of recognition. Its meaning becomes clearer and clearer at each new encounter, its use more and more understandable. *Vicarious* is alive for you.

You have probably observed this phenomenon over and over in your personal experience.

So as you continue your direct study of words, let the new words sink in deeply. Become hyperconscious of the new words you learn —and then notice how those very words begin to pop up over and over again in your everyday reading. Let's try it.

Imagine that you found the words below in the following sentences. How well could you puzzle out the meanings of those you haven't seen before? Check what you consider the correct definition for each word, compare with the answers given at the end of the test, then continue with the explanations of these and related words.

1. malinger
2. acumen
3. enervated
4. gullible
5. vindictive

6. querulous
7. dipsomaniac
8. implacable
9. cacophony
10. obdurate

1. Prison doctors have learned to detect willful *malingering.*
   a—cowardice, b—pretense of illness, c—evasion of duty
2. Business executives are usually men of *acumen.*
   a—political power, b—wealth, c—mental quickness
3. His all-night vigil *enervated* him.
   a—exhausted, b—caused loss of sleep to, c—brought illness to
4. *Gullible* housewives fall easy prey to unscrupulous salesmen.
   a—stupid, b—easily fooled, c—overanxious
5. On hearing of such atrocities, one cannot help feeling *vindictive.*
   a—terrified, b—eager for revenge, c—depressed

6. *Querulous* wives wear their husbands' patience thin.
   a—complaining, b—frowsy-looking, c—selfish
7. To a *dipsomaniac*, "Schenley's" is a beautiful word.
   a—advertisement writer, b—tavern owner, c—person morbidly addicted to liquor
8. The hope of democracy lies in the *implacable* foes of totalitarianism.
   a—unyielding, b—honest, c—armed
9. To rustic visitors, the *cacophony* of a big city is often terrifying.
   a—rush, b—harsh noise, c—coldness
10. The condemned man's wife begged for a pardon, or at least a commutation of sentence; but the Governor was *obdurate*.
   a—unyielding, b—unimpressed, c—unfavorable

Key: 1-b, 2-c, 3-a, 4-b, 5-b, 6-a, 7-c, 8-a, 9-b, 10-a.

RELATED WORDS

1. malignant
2. malevolent
3. malign (vb.)
4. malediction
5. malaise
6. perspicacity
7. perspicuity
8. plaintive
9. pyromaniac
10. arsonist
11. incendiary (n.)
12. complacent
13. placate (vb.)
14. euphony
15. eugenics
16. adamant
17. inexorable

To *malinger* is to pretend illness, or some physical inability, for the purpose of shirking one's duty. A practitioner of the art is a *malingerer*. The word is indirectly derived from the Latin adverb *male*, badly, an etymological root which is also responsible for the English words *malignant*, "harmful"; *malevolent*, "wishing harm"; to *malign*, a verb meaning "to spread slander about someone"; *malediction*, "a curse"; and *malaise*, "a vague feeling of physical discomfort."

Acumen, which is mental keenness, comes from the same root as *acute*, which means "sharp." *Acumen* and *perspicacity* are close

159

synonyms. *Perspicacity* should not be confused with *perspicuity*, which is the quality of being clear, easy to understand. Thus, only people show *perspicacity*—that is, keen mental ability, sharp discernment; but people or things, if their meaning is readily grasped, possess *perspicuity*. When you call a writer *perspicacious*, you admire the keenness of his intellect; when you call him *perspicuous*, you are paying a compliment to his lucid style.

Querulous and *plaintive* are synonymous in the sense that both have a primary meaning of complaining. But *querulous*, a disparaging adjective, indicates habitual complaint, nagging, fretfulness; while *plaintive* is a much pleasanter word with the connotations of melancholy or mournfulness. There is a distinctly different emotional flavor in the two words.

A *dipsomaniac* is morbidly addicted to the consumption of alcohol, in any form that human beings can tolerate, and in quantities impossible to describe or even imagine. He is a sot, a continual imbiber, a slave to John Barleycorn. People who suffer under the burden of a different kind of psychic disturbance—namely the inability to resist setting fires—are called *pyromaniacs*. Do not confuse these unfortunates, for whom fire has a morbid and irresistible attraction, with *incendiaries*, or, to use the legal term, *arsonists*, who set fires maliciously and through a desire for illegal gain, as for example collecting on a fire insurance policy.

Two frequently encountered synonyms of *implacable* are *adamant* and *inexorable:* all three words mean virtually the same thing, incapable of being moved or made to change one's mind or decision. *Complacent* and the verb *placate* come from the same root as *implacable*, the Latin word *placeo*, "to please." A *complacent* person is smugly pleased with himself; to *placate* is to soothe, pacify.

Cacophony, harsh sound, is the opposite of *euphony*, pleasant sound. The same root, *eu*, from the Greek word for *good*, is found in *eugenics*, the science of good breeding.

When you are *enervated*, you are completely weakened or exhausted, or utterly fatigued, whether physically, mentally, or morally. The state of such weakness, exhaustion, or fatigue is *enervation*; the verb is to *enervate*, i.e., weaken, exhaust, or fatigue

160

(someone). One can feel *enervated* during illness, or after a stormy emotional encounter, or from unrelieved and monotonous work.

A *gullible* person is easily *gulled*, i.e., cheated, deceived, tricked, or fooled. Hence, if you are *gullible* you believe almost anything you hear, you are utterly without skepticism, you tend to be over-trusting and unsuspicious. The noun is *gullibility*.

The *vindictive* person harbors grudges and, usually maliciously, seeks to retaliate for real or fancied wrongs. The spirit of charity or forgiveness is unknown to him.

Although the words in this section have at best been discussed superficially, let us see how well you can do on a quick review test.

Test Your Learning

Directions: If two words are the same in meaning, check S; if they are opposite in meaning, check O.

S O 1. malinger; shirk
S O 2. acumen; stupidity
S O 3. enervated; tired
S O 4. gullible; skeptical
S O 5. vindictive; forgiving
S O 6. querulous; satisfied
S O 7. dipsomaniac; teeto-
taler
S O 8. implacable; inexora-
ble
S O 9. cacophony; euphony
S O 10. obdurate; adamant

S O 11. malignant; kind
S O 12. malevolent; charita-
ble
S O 13. malediction; curse
S O 14. malaise; exhilaration
S O 15. perspicuity; clearness
S O 16. perspicacity; stu-
pidity
S O 17. complacent; discon-
tented
S O 18. placate; pacify
S O 19. pyromaniac; fire-
bug

Key: 1—S, 2—O, 3—S, 4—O, 5—O, 6—O, 7—O, 8—S, 9—O, 10—S, 11—O, 12—O, 13—S, 14—O, 15—S, 16—O, 17—O, 18—S, 19—S.

Here, now, is the complete list of the 27 words in alphabetical order. Working with your dictionary, look each one up and take notes according to the instructions on page 149.

1. acumen
2. adamant

3. arsonist
4. cacophony

5. complacent
6. dipsomaniac
7. enervated
8. eulogy
9. euphony
10. gullible
11. implacable
12. incendiary
13. inexorable
14. malaise
15. malediction
16. malevolent
17. malign (vb.)
18. malignant
19. malinger
20. obdurate
21. perspicacity
22. perspicuity
23. placate
24. plaintive
25. pyromaniac
26. querulous
27. vindictive

Study your notes, and when you feel that you have command of these words, do the following exercise.

Test Your Learning

Referring to the list above, write the word that fits each of the following definitions. Make sure to supply the part of speech (i.e., the verb, noun, or adjective form) that is required.

1. unyielding
1. _____ or _____ or _____

2. one who pretends illness or disability to avoid work or duty
2. _____

3. mentally keen
3. _____

4. mental keenness
4. _____ or _____

5. the crime of setting fires
5. _____ or _____

6. one who has a compulsion to set fires
6. _____

7. revengeful
7. _____

8. a curse
8. _____

9. harsh-sounding
9. _____

10. not to be pleased
10. _____

11. one who sets fires maliciously
11. _____ or _____

12. feeling of physical discomfort
12. _____

13. to slander
13. _____

14. exhausted; weakened   14._____
15. pleasant in sound   15._____
16. to soothe   16._____
17. easily deceived   17._____
18. fretfully complaining   18._____
19. mournful; sad; unhappy and 19._____
    discontented
20. smug; self-satisfied   20._____
21. science of good breeding   21._____
22. hateful; wishing evil   22._____ or
                                _____
23. clear and understandable   23._____

Key: 1. adamant, inexorable, or obdurate, 2. malingerer, 3. perspicacious, 4. acumen, perspicacity, or perspicaciousness, 5. arson or incendiarism, 6. pyromaniac, 7. vindictive, 8. malediction, 9. cacophonous, 10. implacable, 11. incendiary or arsonist, 12. malaise, 13. malign, 14. enervated, 15. euphonious, 16. placate, 17. gullible, 18. querulous, 19. plaintive, 20. complacent, 21. eugenics, 22. malignant or malevolent, 23. perspicuous

A SECOND CHALLENGE TO YOUR READING HABITS

Toward the end of chapter 5, a point you reached some days ago, I challenged you to read a complete novel in a single evening. Have you met this challenge?

If you have (and I assume that as a serious student you are following every item of your training with scrupulous care), fill in the statistics required on the chart below.

First Novel Read in One Sitting

1. TITLE OF NOVEL: _____
2. AUTHOR: _____
3. TOTAL NUMBER OF PAGES: _____
4. TOTAL NUMBER OF HOURS AND MINUTES SPENT IN READING:
                _____ HRS. _____ MINS.
5. APPROXIMATE NUMBER OF WORDS IN THE NOVEL:_____
    To arrive at this statistic, turn to any full page in the book, compute

the average number of words per line, and multiply by the number of lines on the page. Then multiply your last figure by the number of pages in the book.

6. YOUR AVERAGE RATE OF READING: ＿＿＿＿＿＿＿＿＿ W.P.M.

To arrive at this statistic, reduce the figure in item 4 to minutes (for example 3 hours, 20 minutes would be 200 minutes), and divide this into the figure in item 5. Thus, if the novel contains approximately 100,000 words, you divide 200 into 100,000 and get as a result 500 w.p.m.

You are now ready for your second challenge. As you know, the guiding principle of this or any other training program is that as soon as you comfortably attain a certain degree of skill or excellence in your performance, the goals are set just a little higher, and you have to draw once again on your innate capacities, you have to strive once again for a new pinnacle.

To prepare you for your next pinnacle I ask you to fill out a second chart:

Novels Read and Unread

Fill in below the titles (and authors, if you remember them) of *five* novels you have completely read in the last six months. (If you have not read five novels in that period of time—and that averages out to less than one every four weeks—write down as many as you have read.)

1. ＿＿＿＿＿＿＿＿＿＿＿＿＿＿＿＿＿＿＿＿＿＿＿＿＿＿＿＿＿＿
2. ＿＿＿＿＿＿＿＿＿＿＿＿＿＿＿＿＿＿＿＿＿＿＿＿＿＿＿＿＿＿
3. ＿＿＿＿＿＿＿＿＿＿＿＿＿＿＿＿＿＿＿＿＿＿＿＿＿＿＿＿＿＿
4. ＿＿＿＿＿＿＿＿＿＿＿＿＿＿＿＿＿＿＿＿＿＿＿＿＿＿＿＿＿＿
5. ＿＿＿＿＿＿＿＿＿＿＿＿＿＿＿＿＿＿＿＿＿＿＿＿＿＿＿＿＿＿

Now fill in the names of *four* novels you have intended to read, or would like to read, but have somehow never got around to. (If you are not a novel-reader, and have never said to yourself, "That's a book I want to read," make a choice of four titles from the recommended list on page 359; or, if you prefer, ask your friends or your local librarian for suggestions of the sort of book you would probably enjoy.)

1. _____
2. _____
3. _____
4. _____

Of the four titles listed above, obtain any *two* from a convenient source—borrow them from a friend or from your library, buy them from a bookshop, or pick them up in inexpensive reprint editions at a stationery store or newsstand.

And then attempt to meet this second challenge to your reading habits: Within the next week, no more, read these two novels, *each in a single evening,* going fast enough to get through in three to five hours of concentrated reading, skimming or skipping wherever and whenever you wish, and aiming for a quick total picture of the plot. This should not be a difficult assignment for you at this point in your training—the only obstacle you are likely to encounter is that you may not find the time.

But one doesn't *find* time for leisure reading—one *makes* the time. (You will not learn to enjoy reading, you will not become a rapid and skillful reader, if you dip into books only occasionally or at odd moments or for a few minutes before you fall off to sleep at night. Some people use books and reading purely as a sedative, as a kind of harmless sleeping pill, when they get into bed—*this is not for you if you wish to become a better reader.*) And you *can* make the time during the next week, you *can* arrange your schedule in such a way that two evenings out of the next seven will be free for reading—you can if you really want to. Possibly you are working on this book in the evenings—if so, allocate two of the evenings you planned to devote to your training to the reading of novels.

Before you start each book, note the total number of pages and decide, from your previous experience with reading a novel in one sitting, approximately how long it will take you to get through. Then figure how many pages you should read every hour in order to meet your self-imposed deadline—*and see to it that you meet it.* (This discipline, which is known in the trade as "pacing oneself," is, all by itself, a remarkable and effective method of developing faster reading habits.) As before, keep a record of the number of hours and minutes spent in actual reading.

If you can meet this challenge successfully (and you can if you honestly try), think what it will mean. At the rate of two novels a week, you can cover (allowing some weeks for the reading of non-fiction or of magazines) *fifty to one hundred novels* in the next year, whereas, in sharp contrast, you may have been unable to fill in a simple list of only *five* novels read in the last six months.

You may wonder, now, whether good readers do in fact read two full books a week. They do, indeed—*at least two*. They make the time for books, because reading books is, for them, an extremely *pleasurable and relaxing activity*—and even the busiest person, if he is at all sensible, devotes some part of his twenty-four-hour day to pleasure and relaxation.

You too can enjoy reading two or more books a week—try it, and discover how right I am.

CHAPTER 7

HOW TO READ WITH
AGGRESSIVE COMPREHENSION

Preview

The aggressive reader pushes through material intent on total meaning, on main ideas; he senses the structure and organization of the writing; he does not get enmeshed in details, but instead sees them in their proper perspective—as a means of giving impact, convincingness, and solidity to the author's basic message. And it is this basic message, above all else, that the aggressive reader wants to understand as quickly and as clearly as he possibly can.

In this chapter you continue training the aggressiveness of your own comprehension. For this purpose you:

• Work on nine long, time-checked selections, driving always for the gist, the central ideas.

• Become more adept at recognizing an author's pattern of thinking, and at using this pattern to clarify your understanding of his main ideas.

• Learn more about how subordinate details serve to introduce, support, clarify, explain, or illustrate main ideas.

• Develop still further your ability to speed through words and get down efficiently to basic meaning.

> *Chapter 7* offers you additional practice in speeding up your comprehension; shows you how to use a new technique for increasing the usability for your peripheral vision; and asks you to make a detailed evaluation of your progress to date.

★ SESSION 14

RESPONDING TO TOTAL MEANING

To read aggressively, you must get into the unshakable habit of viewing material *as a whole,* instead of passively absorbing it thought by thought, sentence by sentence, or word by word.

You have probably made a good start at developing this valuable habit. In the four articles you worked on in chapter 2, and again in the twelve rapid comprehension exercises of chapter 5, you attempted to react to each selection as a complete unit by purposefully seeking out the answer to one dominating question—namely, *What, in total, is the author trying to say, What is the main idea of the piece, What is the final meaning that all the words and sentences add up to?* (And these are not, of course, three separate questions, but only three ways of framing the same question.)

This, no matter in what form we express it, is the important question you must force all material to answer—and you must learn to extract that answer quickly and skillfully from the mass of words and details.

But in order to find, and respond actively to, the central, final, and total meaning of material, you must be able, as you read, to "touch the mind of the writer in his writing" (as John Ciardi, one of the editors of the *Saturday Review,* has so well phrased it); you must be able to meet the writer at least halfway; you must be able to think along with the writer. When you can do all this, when you can accurately sense how a writer has organized his thinking and in what pattern he is presenting his thoughts to you, *then* you will be able—confidently, efficiently, and speedily—to strip a page down to its essentials; *then* you will be reading aggressively.

If you practice correctly and conscientiously on the nine long selections in this chapter you will find yourself moving a little closer to your goal of becoming an aggressive and rapid reader. Cover each selection with a slight, but conscious, pressure on your speed, with an awareness that you are going fast. Pay no attention to fixations or eye-movements, and make no attempt to inhibit inner speech—these factors will take care of themselves if you follow the other instructions carefully. Do, however, avoid unnecessary regressions—if a word or a phrase eludes you, keep plowing ahead notwithstanding.

Keep clearly in mind that your dominating aim, as you read, is to grasp total meaning. To do this rapidly and accurately, try to sense the broad structure of the writing; try to get a feeling for the pattern the author is using in presenting his material to you; try to realize how the details serve to highlight the main ideas, but don't let these details slow you up.

Skim or skip whenever you feel you can safely do so, i.e., when you are pretty sure you know what a sentence or paragraph will contain. One of the overriding values of detecting the pattern of a piece is that you don't have to read every single word, or every single sentence, or every single paragraph—you know, by thinking along with the author in the pattern he has set up, what is likely to come next, and whether it is important, less important, or completely unimportant to the final meaning of the selection.

You may not be able to follow these instructions with absolute success right away, even though you will try. But if you study carefully the discussion that follows each piece you will gradually learn more and more about structure and pattern, you will gradually develop a keener sense for what an author is doing and for how he is doing it.

With these selections we shall resume our time-checks on your reading so that you will again have statistical evidence of your continuing progress. As in the past, start your timing at the first black arrow; when you reach the second arrow, note, in the appropriate blank, the exact number of minutes and seconds you required to finish the selection. The table for computing your rate will follow each comprehension test.

Selection 7

PROFESSORS LEARN TO READ
by Esther J. McConihe

I

Start timing→ When the headline, "Profs Learn to Read," appeared over a story in the campus paper at Western Reserve University, it marked the beginning of considerable interest in a training program to improve reading efficiency that had been inaugurated after repeated requests from an interested faculty to "give us a chance to brush up on our reading techniques."

II

2. Early in the fall semester, 40 faculty members who had indicated an interest in reading training were organized into two sections on the basis of convenience in scheduling. The "students" included, among others, a dean of the liberal arts school and professor of English, author of many articles in professional journals, of two books, and of two workbooks on word study; a member of the Law School fac-

ulty; several research doctors in the School of Medicine; professors from the Frances Payne Bolton School of Nursing, some of whom have written extensively for publication; a university librarian; and a professor of geology and astronomy, also an author.

3. The academic status of the group indicated considerable expertness with the written word from extensive experience in both reading and writing. Needless to say, the challenge from a group of this calibre was great.

III

4. A 10-week program of weekly hour and a half sessions was started. At the opening session the members were introduced to the procedures. The "gadgets," i.e., the reading pacers, tachistoscope, and reading films, were demonstrated and their purpose in training explained. The group decided upon testing to determine the status of each member's reading skills; con-

From *Adult Education*. Reprinted by permission. Mrs. McConihe is Head of the Adult Reading Center, Western Reserve University.

sequently at the second session the Cooperative English Test, C2 Reading, Form T, and the Minnesota Speed of Reading Test, Form A, were administered. The zeal with which the groups applied themselves to this humdrum experience was inspiring to the writer and would have opened the eyes of many of the underclassmen of the university if they could have witnessed it.

5. Results of the tests were given to each member individually in a personal report. Group data on this testing will be discussed below under "Results."

6. The following eight sessions were devoted to training. Tachistoscopic practice with digits and phrases was one of the most popular devices, and the group was very quickly reading phrases of from 21 to 25 typewriter units of space in 1/100 of a second. Digit reading for such groups rarely equals phrase reading because the practice periods are too short and infrequent to develop the requisite skill in reproducing such an exacting presentation as a seven-digit number shown in 1/100 of a second. A second mechanical technique was the Harvard Reading Films, Series B, which have been explained in detail in many places so need not be discussed further here. For this group the films were of less value than my experience has shown them to be with most adult groups.

7. At each session a brief lecture-discussion period gave the instructor the opportunity to demonstrate something of the complex nature of reading and to present the various techniques which are useful to the able adult in bringing his reading skills up to the level of his reading needs. Since this was a group of very able readers, it was necessary only to stress various means of utilizing the already good language and logic skills of the members and to press for speed of comprehension. These orientation periods were also the time for individual members to air their problems. Many a "Yes, but —" put the leader to devising realistic suggestions for meeting the problems which were aired during these discussion periods. Frequently the group made its own suggestions, i.e., a problem by one member was met by a suggestion from another who had encountered the same problem.

8. Each session concluded with a timed reading test. Results of this test were plotted on individual graphs so that each member could watch his progress from week to week. This is a good motivating device because it presents progress in graphic form. Many times a reader needs this tangible proof of progress because at first he may not be aware of improved speed in day-by-day reading.

9. Between sessions each member came to the Center twice a week and read, using one of the several reading pacing devices with which many reading training centers are equipped. Each person was urged to bring a book of his own choosing but was advised to keep to easy-

flowing prose at first in an attempt to develop a rapid pace with rhythmic eye movements. The emphasis in programs like this is at first on improving the mechanics. Fewer and shorter fixations, or pauses, per line, a good return sweep to the next line with rhythmic progression across the line and down the page are some of these. Easy fiction furnishes the best practice because it offers no obstacles from unfamiliar vocabulary, complex organization of ideas, or unfamiliar content.

10. A third area of training was reading at home without benefit of coaching or machines. Selected articles, chosen for their suitability to the group's interests as well as for the particular techniques being developed, were given at every session. These were read at any time between sessions, timed, and the words per minute computed by the reader. The central thought of the article was written out and this material was discussed at the sessions. Such discussion was fruitful in revealing to the group the reading experiences of the several members as they experimented with the techniques they were practicing. Members were urged to read an hour a day, attempting to reproduce, unaided, the same smooth-flowing, rhythmic, rapid rate they were developing with the pacing machines.

IV

11. What were the results of such a course with such a group? As measured by standardized reading tests, the group as a whole made 76 per cent improvement in speed, with comprehension held constant. The greatest gain by a reader was 135 per cent, a gain of 285 words per minute over his entering speed. This reader had perfect attendance, used the reading pacing machine between sessions more times than any other member, and reported back on all intersessional material assigned. Another reader showed only 10 per cent gain in speed and with it a 10 per cent loss in comprehension. This member was, by observation, extremely ego-involved throughout the training, found the techniques disturbing, although challenging, and wrote at the close of the course, ". . . For a time during the course my pride suffered acutely and all kinds of blocks and distractions came between me and those timed readings you gave us. I am not yet over that, but I believe it is due to the fact that I do not yet feel the degree of security which I hope (and plan) to achieve." It may be expected that when this reader returns for a recheck in six months, more noticeable gains will be evident.

12. So much for formal gain, but what about subjective report and observation? Here the results are varied and interesting. This being a group of persons for whom good reading is as essential as good intelligence, they were in dead earnest about benefiting from the training. Here are some of their comments:

13. ". . . the ability to free oneself

(an on-going process still) from the feeling that *everything* must be read for complete and specific details."

14. ". . . one reads with variations in speed as is necessary. I find myself doing that with less thought about it—skimming here, reading rapidly now, then again more slowly as I may feel the need for meditating on some particular thought or enjoying some particular passage."

15. "Improvement in my mental outlook on reading. When I sit down now to a piece of reading, I realize I must concentrate, get rid of distractions, look for the sign-posts of organization, such as topic sentences, transitional words and summaries, and read with a flexible speed that depends on what I want to get out of the piece."

16. "Has given me a new method of attack on reading. I really ask myself, 'Why am I reading this?' I believe this has helped me increase my speed even in articles from which I need to get minute details."

17. "Has increased my ability to skim medical and nursing literature. This has been proven to me many times over. I can get what I want from an article by skimming in the right way."

18. "What I expected at the outset was to increase my speed, but what I have gained is an appreciation of how to read."

19. "I remember . . . my feeling of resentment about having so little time to read. Now I know I can read much more if I do not try to read everything at the same rate with which I read difficult clinical material."

20. "One technique that has been particularly useful to me has been the idea of getting a frame of reference for the material being read. Heretofore I think I had usually simply started at the beginning and read. I believe the 'previewing' aids in retention of the material read. It also eliminates unnecessary detail."

21. Needless to say, this course was a lively and illuminating experience for both the participants and the leader. Most of the members discovered to their surprise that this skill, which had always been a vital part of their stock-in-trade, could be considerably improved. Several showed up in the instructor's office requesting additional training. All put the techniques to use throughout the course and took active part in the discussion.

22. The "Yes, but—" responses mentioned above were the times when the instructor learned a good deal about how well-trained adults read. "Am I not insulting the author when I read at breakneck speed something which it took him days or weeks to write?" "What do I do when these transitional words don't really 'transish'?" (This from a Law School professor.) "Yes, but sometimes a specific word makes all the difference between understanding and not understanding, so am I not in danger of missing the meaning if I read by phrases?" "We've been trained to believe that every detail

173

is absolutely essential. What if I read a patient's chart like this?" (This being rapid overviewing and the comment being made by a member of the nursing school faculty.) Each objection was legitimate and each had to be answered within its own framework. The result was a lively atmosphere of mutual respect, understanding, and learning between leader and group which resulted in an experience that was rich and rewarding to this author and, it is to be hoped, to the 20 persons who successfully completed the course. ←End timing

RECORD HERE THE TIME REQUIRED ON THIS SELECTION: _____ MIN.

_____ SEC.

Test Your Comprehension

Which *one* of the following statements most accurately summarizes the *main idea* of the selection you have just finished? Check your choice without referring to the text.

1. There was great interest in a training program to improve the reading efficiency of professors at Western Reserve University. This program was started as a result of repeated requests from the faculty.

2. This program went on for ten weeks with hour-and-a-half sessions, and used a number of electrical "gadgets."

3. A group of professors who had had extensive experience with the written word were trained in specified ways to improve their reading—as a result, they increased their speed by 76 per cent on the average and learned with surprise that their skill could be considerably sharpened.

4. At each session of training, techniques for better reading were taught, problems were discussed, speed of comprehension was stressed, and timed tests were given.

Compute Your Rate

(Approximate number of words: 1800)

TIME	W.P.M.	TIME	W.P.M.
2 min., 30 sec.	720	4 min., 15 sec.	425
2 min., 45 sec.	655	4 min., 30 sec.	400
3 min.	600	4 min., 45 sec.	380
3 min., 15 sec.	555	5 min.	360
3 min., 30 sec.	515	5 min., 15 sec.	345
3 min., 45 sec.	480	5 min., 30 sec.	325
4 min.	450	6 min.	300

TIME	W.P.M.	TIME	W.P.M.
6 min., 30 sec.	275	8 min., 30 sec.	210
7 min.	260	9 min.	200
7 min., 30 sec.	240	10 min.	180
8 min.	225	11 min.	165

YOUR RATE ON SELECTION 7: _____W.P.M.

Discussion of the Selection

When this article is considered *in its entirety,* the organization is clear, simple, and completely logical, to wit:

Paragraph 1: Introduction.
Paragraphs 2 and 3: Kind of students in the course.
Paragraphs 4 through 10: Explanation of the training offered.
Paragraphs 11 through 22: Results of the training.

What parts of the selection you read carefully and what parts you skimmed depended on your purpose. As a student who himself is being trained to improve his skill and speed, you were no doubt particularly interested in paragraphs 6 through 10, in which the actual details of training are explained—the more general reader might have skimmed through this part of the article. (Possibly, despite your interest, you skimmed nevertheless, since these details are by now so familiar to you.) A teacher of reading would also be interested in the specific methods that Mrs. McConihe used, but would likely skim the section to discover whether it contained anything that was new to him. As a teacher, he might be especially alert to the implications of the last two paragraphs, in which the author explains her reaction to her students. And I think that any skillful reader would have largely skimmed paragraphs 12 through 20 as soon as he recognized that these were repetitive details of the students' subjective reactions to the training—unless, for private reasons of his own, he had some personal interest in these details as *details,* rather than in their total meaning.

What I am saying, then, is that the first purpose of reading any selection—a purpose common to all readers—is to get the central meaning of the *whole* and to recognize how the author organizes his facts and information to make this central idea most clear, most convincing, most effective. Thus the skillful reader, long habituated to concentrating on the *important* elements of material, would sense

175

at once that paragraphs 2 and 3 of this selection begin to develop the main idea. *Aha!* he will think to himself, consciously or otherwise, *these professors should already be good readers, they've had so much experience.* His mind is focused now on discovering whether there is still room for improvement, and so he is alert to the continued development of the main theme in paragraph 11 (*they increased their speed by 76 per cent*) and again in paragraph 21 (*they learned with surprise, etc.*). Although reading for the main idea, he does not *ignore* the details. However, instead of getting lost in them, he fits them into their proper place in the framework of the piece and notes how they contribute to the central theme—by this means he can skim through them whenever he wishes to.

Above and beyond this primary purpose of quickly finding the total meaning and general structure of writing, a skillful reader will react to material according to any individual purpose he may have. He will skim or read thoroughly, go faster or slow up, push aside details once he understands their function or concentrate on them carefully—all depending on what his purpose is.

Correct choice on the comprehension test is statement 3.

You are ready now to record your rate statistic for selection 7 on a new chart and graph, which you will find on page 393. First, however, turn to page 392, where you have recorded your average rate on the four timed selections of chapter 2, and copy that figure here:

AVERAGE RATE ON SELECTIONS 3–6: _____W.P.M.

Now locate this figure on the graph on page 393 and draw a straight line parallel to line AB, so that you will have a continuous basis for comparison with your rate of reading for the nine selections in this chapter. Fill in, also, line 1 on the chart on page 393.

At the end of each of the remaining timed selections in this chapter, you will be able to compute your speed in words per minute. Plot each speed on the graph, and connect the points by straight lines.

Keeping a careful record of your progress is one of the best incentives, in self-training, for maintaining your enthusiasm at a high pitch and your effort at a maximum. Such a record will tell you, at a glance, how well you are doing, how much success attends your efforts.

Selection 8

"MAKE ME A CHILD AGAIN,
JUST FOR TO-NIGHT"

by Milton R. Stern

Start timing→

> *"Backward, turn backward, O
> Time, in your flight,
> Make me a child again just for
> to-night."*

The lines above are from a poem called "Rock Me To Sleep, Mother," by Elizabeth Akers Allen, who was born in 1832 and died in 1911. By modern standards, this quotation is inexcusably sentimental and inaccurate. We moderns know better than to think of childhood as happy and carefree. We have gone to another, perhaps oversolemn, extreme. We hold that childhood is such a difficult time of life that we have child guidance associations and child study clinics and child psychologists and "child-centered" homes and a host of similar institutions in order to make childhood endurable for the infants who have to live through it.

2. But every age has its own kind of sentimentality, and we who have created the soap opera can scarcely afford to throw stones at the late Victorians.

3. Sentimental as it may be, the quotation from Miss Allen's poem is worth a moment of study by people in evening classes for what it suggests about the learning process—in children and in grown-ups. If we mature adults who are studying in evening classes could be children again—just for that time we spend in class—we might be considerably surprised at how much faster and more easily we would learn.

4. And if we cannot actually be children again, perhaps we can pick up a few helpful hints by turning backward ourselves, "just for tonight," and noticing some of the differences between the way children learn and the way grown-ups learn.

5. Whatever the subject matter— whether it is the dates of English kings or how to pick pockets, like Oliver Twist—when it comes to learning something new, children

From *Pleasures in Learning,* published by the Division of General Education, New York University. Reprinted by permission. Mr. Stern is Assistant to the Dean, Publications and Counseling, Division of General Education, New York University.

177

usually learn faster than adults. A child in an unhappy situation may quickly acquire the habit of lying as a defense mechanism. But his luckier contemporaries thirstily drink in useful information of all kinds. First- and second-graders delight in the discovery of new words, new ideas, or new places on the map, African animals or the Museum of Natural History. They keep their teachers wedded to the profession by their enthusiastic curiosity, and they give their parents moments of enormous pleasure by their sudden, unexpected grasp of things.

6. Adults, on the other hand, are by and large cautious learners. They are more timid than youngsters about asking questions. Adults have scar tissue—they are often afraid to ask questions for fear of seeming ridiculous. There are other ways in which grown-ups are handicapped as learners. They have many more demands on their time than children. They have more responsibilities—and these responsibilities cannot usually be lightly shrugged off.

7. Furthermore, adults have often gotten more or less unconsciously into bad habits. Some adults have almost a compulsion to be "experts" on practically every subject that comes up, and others have drifted unaware into the habit of accepting whatever the "experts" say. Adults also are handicapped as students by the fact that they have largely got out of the habit of *listening*. And where first-graders are whole-hearted scholars, warmly embracing the teacher as a learner, too, but equipped with more answers, the grown-ups have largely forgotten how to *use* their teachers, even as the bounce board of skeptical questioning.

8. Evening college administrators say that adult experience is a priceless commodity in the classroom—for both teacher and students. And so it is. But experience is not enough. Attitude is equally important, and mature men and women need something of the enthusiasm and unself-consciousness of the child if they are to capitalize fully in the classroom on their life experience. But can grown people reacquire these qualities? Make-me-a-child-again-just-for-tonight is all very well, but is it really possible for the mature student to recapture some of the spontaneity of the six- or seven-year-old?

9. I think it is.

10. Perhaps a key idea to keep in mind is that of *purpose*—what educators (and the Navy) call motivation in learning. With children, motivation is easy to understand. Children literally thirst after knowledge, because they must. They have a long way to grow, and a major part of growth is the development of that subtle instrument, the mind. Actually, children have a natural or built-in motivation. They want to communicate and to be communicated with. They want to be in touch. They want mastery and power. They want to understand and to be understood.

178

11. And children have sanction and approval for this almost instinctual drive. The whole society is organized to further it. Not only does the truant officer come after them if they stay away from school, but it is a rare parent who does not praise and take pride in the child's expanding knowledge.

12. But with the adult student in evening classes, purpose does not operate in such an automatic and instinctive fashion. Nor does the adult student always come in for such complete approval and sanction in his efforts. Children, in their world, cannot afford not to know. It makes them too helpless and powerless. But adults, in their world, too often persuade themselves they can afford to be ignorant. How easy it is to find a rationalization to avoid trying to understand anything difficult. We all know how little time there is, how difficult it is to win mastery over any subject, and the omnipresent "experts" are all too eager to give us escape through the cliché of "A little knowledge is a dangerous thing" or "You can't teach an old dog new tricks." There is, too, the reality of an anti-intellectual climate of opinion. Indeed, it seems sometimes that if an adult knows enough to come in out of the rain, he may run into a certain amount of silent or open mockery when he aspires to anything further.

13. Only when the purpose of evening study is very, very obvious can the adult student feel sure of social approval. If he does not speak English well and goes to an evening college to overcome this handicap or if he needs more education to get into a better paying job, then he may feel fairly sure that nobody will try to dissuade him from studying in the afterschool years of life. But if his goal is not going to pay off immediately in some highly visible way, like more money or higher social prestige, then he not only has to go to school, he has to defend himself for going. Let him! He can do so boldly.

14. "Does he propose to understand literature, music, art?"

15. "Yes. Is there a better use of a man's time?"

16. "Does he aspire to be an 'egghead,' then?"

17. Let him answer "Yes," enthusiastically. "There are thousands of us."

18. But whatever we study, and whether we seek to overcome an obvious handicap of communication or information or technical skill, or whether we are sparked by curiosity about philosophy or chemistry, we will find such study most enjoyable and fruitful if it is approached in the way first- and second-graders approach the birth of rabbits or the circumstance that r-o-u-g-h is not pronounced the same as b-o-u-g-h.

19. Make me a child again just for tonight? Each of us in the classroom or out, quizzing a teacher or reading a book, can be as active a learner as we were when we were six years old. We can take conscious account of our adult purposes and make them give us pleasure in

learning in the same way as did our early, less conscious drives. There is the child in each of us. We have but to be aware of the fact and have the sense and courage to acknowledge it. ←**End timing**

RECORD HERE THE TIME REQUIRED ON THIS SELECTION: _____ MIN. _____ SEC.

Test Your Comprehension

Which *one* of the following statements most accurately summarizes the *main idea* of the selection you have just finished? Check your choice without referring to the text.

1. Adults would be happier if they could be children again.
2. Children usually learn faster than adults.
3. Adults are cautious and timid learners and hesitate to ask questions.
4. Adults like to be experts on every subject that comes up.
5. Adults in evening classes would learn faster and more easily if they reacted the way children do.

Compute Your Rate

(*Approximate number of words: 1300*)

TIME	W.P.M.	TIME	W.P.M.
1 min., 30 sec.	865	3 min., 45 sec.	345
1 min., 45 sec.	745	4 min.	325
2 min.	650	4 min., 15 sec.	305
2 min., 15 sec.	580	4 min., 30 sec.	290
2 min., 30 sec.	520	5 min.	260
2 min., 45 sec.	480	5 min., 30 sec.	235
3 min.	435	6 min.	220
3 min., 15 sec.	400	6 min., 30 sec.	200
3 min., 30 sec.	370	7 min.	185

YOUR RATE ON SELECTION 8: _____W.P.M.

(*Record this statistic on the chart and graph on page 393.*)

Discussion of the Selection

Glance back at the article, now, and notice the pattern Mr. Stern has followed in presenting his thinking to the reader:

Paragraphs 1 and 2 and the beginning of paragraph 3: Two lines from a poem are used as a springboard to the central theme.

180

Paragraph 3: The central theme is explicitly stated—*adults in evening classes would learn faster and more easily if they reacted the way children do.*

Paragraph 4: Transition.

Paragraphs 5 through 8: First part of the development of the central theme—*contrast between the learning attitudes, habits, and characteristics of children and of adults.* The last sentence of paragraph 8, in the form of a question, and the answer to that question in paragraph 9, serve as transition to paragraph 10.

Paragraphs 10 through 17: The second part of the development of the central theme—*adults, if they wish to learn as effectively as children do, should have the same purpose and drive that motivated their learning earlier in life.*

Paragraphs 18 and 19: Summary—the central theme is restated in terms of the two parts of its development, namely (1) *attitudes,* etc., and (2) *purpose and drives.*

Correct choice on the comprehension test is statement 5.

Learning to sense structure as you read is not easy, and I am not for a moment pretending that it is. But with every selection you practice on, you will become a little surer, a little defter, in your technique. And as you study the discussion that follows each piece, you will learn to see a little more clearly how an author organizes his thinking, how he develops his theme, how he uses his details and subordinate points to elaborate on, clarify, and drive home his main idea—in short, how he skillfully shapes a mass of words into a unified and artistic *whole.* (The more skillful and lucid the writing, of course, the more clearly and easily will you be able to see all this.)

No doubt you realize that the selection you have just finished appears to contradict the paragraph on page 109, which claims that adults, not children, are the best learners. I suggest you reread that paragraph and decide whether it is possible to reconcile these seemingly opposed views. Or, if you find them unreconcilable, with which, from your own experience, do you agree?

Selection 9

TAKE IT EASY TO LEARN BETTER
by Donald A. Laird, ScD.

Start timing→ Spare-time learners are usually the best learners. Their rate of learning is helped, of course, by the fact that they want to learn and consequently try to learn. But they are also helped by circumstances—they are forced to take *their learning by easy stages*. Other work prevents them from applying themselves to learning for so long that they get dyspepsia of learning.

2. Edgar Burchell, the janitor who became a leading medical scientist and teacher, is an example. He was one of nine children, and he had to leave school and go to work before finishing the grades. At twenty-two he was scrubbing floors twelve hours a day at the New York Eye and Ear Infirmary.

3. But during his lunch hour he attended staff lectures, carefully pretending he was in the lecture amphitheater for janitor work, but drinking in every word that was said. When his twelve-hour stint was up he remained at the infirmary, watching the interns in the laboratory. "Teach me how you do these things," he said to them, "and I'll do them for you." Then, from his small savings, he bought a second-hand anatomy text which he studied in his other spare moments.

4. Picking up his education in this way, Burchell made himself one of the world's authorities on bacteriology and on the anatomy of the head. Surgeons from all over the country consulted this former janitor before performing puzzling head operations. He had never been a medical student, yet he was given one of those rare honorary degrees of Doctor of Science.

5. Such spare-time learning is especially efficient since there is time for it to soak in between learning periods. When learning complex things, there is an extra advantage in taking breathing spells. When beginning something new it also speeds up learning to have breathers. Most eager beginners push themselves too long at a time. Such crowded study or practice produces fatigue or boredom which hinders learning.

6. You can't gain wisdom quickly, but you can gain wisdom steadily by easy stages.

7. Instead of practicing at the typewriter, or piano, or behind the steering wheel, for two solid hours,

From *Your Life*. Reprinted with permission.

practice only one hour. Then take a breather before doing the second hour of practice or study. You will be fresher when you start the second lap. Such spaced practice or study is better for learning than is continuous practice of the same total length.

8. Spaced practice not only eliminates fatigue and boredom, but also some maturation of the nerve connections which have been exercised seems to take place during the space between practice periods. Whatever the reason, however, distributed practice is better than continuous practice. Long practice periods can be safely used only after one has acquired considerable skill.

9. The most efficient distribution of practice or study sessions varies with the kind of material being learned. Each person has to find the best distribution of practice that fits him and his task. Follow these two guides in spacing your learning periods:

1. Each practice should be long enough to warm you up and to allow the peak of your present skill to be reached.

2. It should be halted when fatigue, boredom, errors, or slowness appear.

II

10. Learning is more efficient when it is fun, less efficient when it is drudgery. Practice periods can safely be made longer if the learner is excited about learning. Learning is often more effective in a group, since individual progress then ac-quires some features of a game or contest. The clever teacher, or expert job trainer, has the knack of arousing the learner's interest to the point of actual excitement. The ambitious individual often lets his ambition provide the excitement.

11. Keeping score on oneself gives some of this game spirit to the lone learner. People usually master a sport such as golf or bowling quickly largely because they naturally keep tabs on how they're doing. Score keeping is easy for some kinds of learning, such as typing speed. These scores can be charted week after week to show one's learning curve, or rate of progress in mastering the subject.

12. Sometimes a numerical score is not possible, but there are other ways to find an indication of one's progress. The person who is trying to improve his handwriting, for example, can keep samples of his regular Saturday morning penmanship for a period of time, pasting them side by side to observe the improvement.

13. Don't guess at your progress if it is possible to figure some way to keep a week-by-week record. This record can give you the encouragement needed to break through a temporary slump in progress.

III

14. Most learning shows rapid progress for the first few days; then it tapers off. After six months of practice it may take a full month of practice to make as much progress as was made the first week.

This is often called the principle of diminishing returns, but that description is illusory. While the gain per week of practice may diminish, it is still a gain, bringing one closer to perfection. The jack-of-all-trades stops practice when the increases become small; so thus he never becomes king of any trade.

15. It is when the gains slow down that you must become excited over even a slight gain.

16. Extra practice is especially needed where the gains are small, or when the job seems to be mastered at last. Just-enough-to-learn is not enough to be satisfied. The extra practice after it is "just learned" makes the learning more permanent and easier to perform in daily life. Psychologists call this overlearning.

17. Taxi-drivers can weave their vehicles through congested traffic with breath-taking skill because they have overlearned through months and months of practice in actual driving. Their careenings may frighten bystanders, but these overpracticed drivers have the world's best safety records.

18. The job details which are not routinely used over and over so they become overlearned should be practiced in spare and slack times until they *are* overlearned.

19. For example, when Raymond L. Ditmars was sixteen his job did not give enough practice for him to overlearn his shorthand. Consequently he practiced it by taking down the sermon in church!

20. Much education is lost because it was not overlearned at school—and because learning stopped when school stopped. When children return to school in the fall they know about 20 per cent less than they did in June. A year after graduating from high school there is a learning loss of 50 per cent. This backsliding in learning is more marked among businessmen than among professional men.

21. Keep your learning useful by rehearsing it in spare moments. Keep it growing by expanding your reading, observation, and thinking. We are what we have learned. What we have let slip is what we used to be.

IV

22. The simplest learning is that of muscle control, as in learning to walk, swim, throw a ball, and in some of the simpler factory operations. A higher degree of motor skill also can be learned—such as that developed by the baseball pitcher.

23. Sensory-motor learning involves the cooperation of muscles and senses. Learning to play a musical instrument, to typewrite, and to handle many factory jobs are examples of sensory-motor learning.

24. Ideo-motor learning combines higher thought processes with muscular actions. Learning shorthand, bookkeeping, or a foreign language are examples.

25. Ideational learning is the highest type, in which muscular factors are not appreciably concerned. This learning is in the realm of ideas.

26. Such a classification from muscular to ideational learning is convenient, but somewhat artificial. In practical life learning is usually a mixture of several of these levels, although one is possibly more marked than the others.

27. The level of learning for one and the same job may also vary during the different stages of learning it. Laying bricks may be primarily a muscular task—in which case we have a "mechanical" bricklayer who is assigned to rough work. After the muscular parts of bricklaying are learned, however, ideational learning can be added— as Frank Gilbreth did when he learned to lay bricks with about one-third the conventional number of motions.

28. The motor or mechanical aspects of a job are likely to be learned first; then the sensory and ideational aspects. When these higher aspects are neglected, the individual is no more than a mechanical worker.

29. For individual advancement one should strive to learn not only the motions of a job, but also the sensory and ideational parts. In the practical world salary schedules run parallel to that classification of learning levels: jobs which call for mere motor learning have lowest pay scales, sensory-motor jobs a little higher pay, ideo-motor jobs still higher, and ideational the highest.

30. Learn to use your head along with your hands; then use your head more than your hands. The ideational part of learning removes one from the wage class and promotes one into the salary class— from a job into a position, from an occupation into a profession.

V

31. But whether simple motor learning or abstract ideational learning is involved, the laws for efficient learning are pretty much the same. The laws of efficient learning are as valuable for business as for the ambitious individual. It costs business around $100 to "break in" an employee on the simplest job; the average job has a break-in cost of $400 to $500; on some jobs the cost runs into the thousands.

32. To the individual inefficient learning means a low earning level —and discouragement. Speed up your learning. Make it stay with you longer. Do this by:

1. Wanting to learn.
2. Taking it by easy stages at the outset.
3. Pushing yourself—but not to the point of staleness.
4. Keeping a record of your progress.
5. Getting excited about learning.
6. Keeping up practice as increases become small.
7. Using your head.

Learners come to be earners.

←End timing

RECORD HERE THE TIME REQUIRED ON THIS SELECTION: _____ MIN.

_____ SEC.

Test Your Comprehension

Which *one* of the following statements most accurately summarizes the *main idea* of the selection you have just finished? Check your choice without referring to the text.

1. These are the main principles of efficient learning: space your practice; keep a record of your progress; overlearn; use your head along with, or more than, your hands. Apply these principles if you wish to get ahead.

2. Learning in spare time is better than full-time learning, because there is time for knowledge to sink in between practice periods.

3. Never break the rhythm of your learning. Keep at a learning task continuously, without interruption, for quickest and most permanent results.

4. Learning of physical skills is much more difficult than the acquisition of mental abilities.

5. Learning starts off slowly but gains momentum in later stages, with spectacular gains toward the end of the learning process.

Compute Your Rate
(Approximate number of words: 1825)

TIME	W.P.M.	TIME	W.P.M.
2 min.	913	4 min., 30 sec.	406
2 min., 15 sec.	812	5 min.	365
2 min., 30 sec.	730	5 min., 30 sec.	332
2 min., 45 sec.	664	6 min.	304
3 min.	608	6 min., 30 sec.	280
3 min., 15 sec.	560	7 min.	261
3 min., 30 sec.	522	7 min., 30 sec.	244
3 min., 45 sec.	488	8 min.	228
4 min.	456	9 min.	203

YOUR RATE ON SELECTION 9: _____W.P.M.

(Record this statistic on the chart and graph on page 393.)

Discussion of the Selection

"Here," Dr. Laird is saying to his readers, "are the principles of efficient learning. Apply them if you wish to get ahead." Nowhere in the piece is this *explicitly* stated—but it is clearly *implicit*, from beginning to end, in every sentence, in every example, in every exhortation.

186

In paragraphs 1 through 9, the author explains in elaborate detail the first of these principles—*for best results space your learning and practice,* i.e., take your learning in easy stages, etc. For the next four paragraphs (through 13), he offers and enlarges on his second suggestion—*keep a record of your progress.* In paragraphs 14 through 21, he calls for *overlearning;* then, through paragraph 30, he describes four broad types of learning and suggests that you *"use your head along with . . . [or] more than your hands."*

Finally, in the last two paragraphs, he sums up, under seven headings, the four major principles around which the article is built.

Correct choice on the comprehension test is statement 1.

Selection 10

WHAT IF I DON'T GET MARRIED?
by Virginia Hurray

Start timing→ They tell me I may never marry. It's a matter of cold fact that women are outnumbering men and that there just aren't enough unmarried men today for all the eligible women.

At 27, I am amply forewarned by statistics that my dreams of marriage may never come true. Nevertheless, I can face the prospect of middle-aged and old maidenhood with something like indifference.

II

I'm glad to have been exposed to the statistics: it's good to know what the score is. But I am convinced that the statistics are being presented with too much gloom and foreboding.

The authors of articles on the man shortage (have you noticed that they are invariably men?) are altogether too distressed and apprehensive about the unmarried female. They fear loneliness and frustration among unclaimed women will lead to wholesale snatching of other women's husbands.

Rubbish, I say to these worries! They insult the integrity of women and belittle all the efforts that parents, pastors and teachers made in our childhood to fill us with the determination to lead moral and useful lives. They are based on the

From *Look.* Reprinted with permission of the Cowles Syndicate. Miss Hurray is a feature writer for the Youngstown, Ohio, *Vindicator.*

old Freudian idea that sex is the one all-important fact of life—an idea with which most psychiatrists today do not agree.

Frankly, like most other members of my sex, I hope to marry. But I am not interested in getting a husband by hook or crook. Neither are most of the single girls of my acquaintance.

To insinuate that all unmarried women of mature age are frustrated is grossly unfair. The dictionary says "frustrate" means "to disappoint; to render null or ineffectual; to prevent from attaining a purpose."

Let's look at the first meaning. The very articles that warn us of a man shortage protect us from disappointment. For if we know that not all of us can marry, the mateless future will be less of a disappointment.

In the second meaning of the word—"to render null or ineffectual"—I find real reason to rebel. I could cite here the names of many famous unmarried women in the arts, sciences and professions. No one can call *them* "null or ineffectual."

However, most of the eight million women who must remain single are, like myself, not unusual. Some of us may have careers; most of us just have jobs. Some of us may possess brilliant talents; most of us merely show aptitudes. Some may become famous, but most will remain unknown. Nevertheless we can and do lead full, satisfying, effective lives.

I'm thinking of several dynamic school teachers I know who are past 40. I'm thinking of the elderly and charming hostess at a restaurant where I sometimes dine, and of the cheerful domestic whose dutiful performance of household chores is a great contribution to the smooth operation of her employer's home.

These women are all unmarried. Judging by the generally pleasing dispositions they display, I would say that they all lead lives which are far from "null or ineffectual."

But there is a third meaning for "frustrate"—to prevent from attaining a purpose.

Now, I ask, do I hope to get married just for the sake of being married? Is that my purpose? Or do I want to be married because I see that marriage is a means of attaining happiness and a full life?

The answer is, of course, that marriage is only one means of achieving my real purpose. It is, I agree, the most tried-and-true means, but it is not the only one.

III

What if I *don't* get married? I can perfect whatever work I earn my living by, and so become essential to my employer. (Isn't that, after all, a basic need for all of us —to be essential?) I can become fairly important to my relatives and friends too. Being unmarried need not deter me from exchanging visits.

Because a single woman has more leisure time than a married one, I can become a zealous volunteer worker whenever there is a campaign for some worthy purpose at my church or in my community.

As a single woman, I'll have more time for hobbies. The number of hours my married sister spends mending clothes for her husband and children I can conscientiously use to do fancy embroidery, watercolors or whatever else I like.

Will I be lonely? I don't think so. With all the contacts I'll have the opportunity to make at the office and in club and committee work, I certainly should find at least a few human beings with whom I share enough similar interest for friendship.

If you are going to compare the loneliness of married and unmarried women you must also remember that women live longer than men. Thus wifehood entails the risk of widowhood. And the woman who has given all her time to her husband may feel much more lonely after his death than the woman of the same age who has never experienced the close partnership of marriage.

If I should not marry, will the full blooming of my womanly personality be thwarted by my failure to experience motherhood? I certainly hope not. Motherhood, as I've seen it at best, is more than just the physical begetting of a child. It is also guiding and assisting the young to worthy adulthood.

I imagine there will always be a relative's child, or a kid in the neighborhood, or a youngster my pastor can tell me about who could do happily with more adult attention than he is getting. If my maternal instincts really want to come to the fore, I believe I'll have no difficulty finding baby-sitting employment.

How about sex? Will I not have missed something if I go to my grave without ever having known connubial bliss? Undoubtedly, yes! But just as a married woman woos disaster by constantly brooding about the independence she lost when she declared her wedding vows, so, too, am I inviting trouble by concentrating upon sex and what I'm likely to miss by not being wed.

IV

What if I *don't* get married? I'll get along all right—and so will most of the other eight million women who must remain single.

Stop worrying about us!

←**End timing**

RECORD HERE THE TIME REQUIRED ON THIS SELECTION: _____ MIN.

_____ SEC.

Test Your Comprehension

Which *one* of the following statements most accurately summarizes the *main idea* of the selection you have just finished? Check your choice without referring to the text.

1. Unmarried women are happier than married women—they live longer and have more interesting lives.
2. It's all right to get married, but it is foolish to become anxious about the unmarried state.
3. Married women can also be frustrated—this feeling is not restricted to spinsters.
4. Even if women do not marry, they can lead fruitful, happy, and full lives. The problem is not as bad as some people think.
5. There is no point in getting married just for the sake of being married.

Compute Your Rate

(Approximate number of words: 1060)

TIME	W.P.M.	TIME	W.P.M.
1 min., 15 sec.	848	2 min., 45 sec.	386
1 min., 30 sec.	707	3 min.	354
1 min., 45 sec.	606	3 min., 30 sec.	303
2 min.	530	4 min.	265
2 min., 15 sec.	472	4 min., 30 sec.	236
2 min., 30 sec.	424	5 min.	212

YOUR RATE ON SELECTION 10: _____W.P.M.

(Record this statistic on the chart and graph on page 393.)

Discussion of the Selection

Taking a second look at the article, notice the pattern around which the author presents her thinking:

Section I: Miss Hurray introduces the problem ("I may never marry"), tells why the problem exists ("aren't enough unmarried men"), and how she feels about it ("something like indifference").

Section II: Here the author begins to develop her main theme—she shows how an unmarried woman need not be frustrated in any of the dictionary meanings of the word, but can, on the contrary, lead a fruitful, effective, satisfying, and purposeful life.

Section III: Now the author pursues a second tack in developing her theme—she shows how, as a spinster, she will capitalize on the advantages of being unmarried while nevertheless, as far as she can, avoiding the disadvantages.

190

Section IV: And now she sums up, very briefly, the final message she wishes to leave with the reader.

Correct choice in the comprehension test is statement 4.

Selection 11

THE I.Q. AND SCHOOLING
by Benjamin Fine

Start timing→ For many years educators and psychologists have insisted that the I.Q. remains constant. Allowance was made for slight variations, perhaps five to ten points, but this was termed the "margin of error." Basically, the belief existed that a person retained the amount of brains that nature endowed him with, and that very little could be done about it. Most textbooks on the subject upheld that belief.

2. Now this position is seriously questioned. A twenty-year study, conducted by Dr. Irving Lorge, head of the educational research institute at Teachers College, Columbia University, presents evidence that the intelligence quotient fluctuates with the amount of education an individual attains. A report of that study is published in the May issue of the Teachers College Record.

3. Dr. Lorge set out to discover whether a group of individuals tested twenty years ago had the same intelligence quotients today. In doing so he tested not only the individuals but also the theory that a boy, say, who had an I.Q. of 110 at the age of 14, would have the same I.Q., with slight variation, at the age of 34.

4. It did not turn out that way. Those who had additional years of schooling had raised their I.Q.'s by as much as fifteen or twenty points —with due allowance for the margin of error.

5. Here is the way Dr. Lorge came to his far-reaching conclusions: he compared sets of boys who, twenty years ago, were matched at the same intelligence score, let us say at 105. But one of the boys had continued his schooling and completed a four-year college course. The other boy had stopped at the end of elementary school. This boy retained his 105 I.Q.—he did not go backward. The student who had gone to college had raised his to

From the *New York Times*, reprinted with permission. Dr. Fine is Education Editor of the *Times* and author of a series of articles on "The Crisis in American Education."

125. That was not according to the books.

6. Subsidized by the Carnegie Corporation, the study began in 1921, under the direction of Prof. Edward L. Thorndike, when a representative sampling of 863 boys in the eighth grade of New York City's public elementary schools received series of tests for abstract intelligence, mechanical adroitness and clerical ability.

7. In May, 1941, as the twentieth year of the experiment came to a close, Dr. Lorge, who by that time had succeeded Dr. Thorndike at Teachers College, invited the original group to come to the college for a retesting. In all, 131 responded, enough to provide a reliable cross-section of the original group, and thus of the larger student body.

8. In essence, the study showed that the men who had gone to college made higher ratings on their intelligence tests than those who had not. Strikingly enough, even as little as a year of schooling raised the I.Q. And the more education a person received, the higher his I.Q. became.

9. For example, a boy who at the age of 14 had an intelligence quotient of 100, raised that score to 115 or 120 by going to school. On the other hand, another boy who stopped going to school at the end of the eighth grade retained his 100 I.Q. While his intelligence score did not improve, neither did it go down.

10. According to Dr. Lorge, the mental ages of the men who completed three years or more of college are two full years higher than those of the men who completed less than two years of high school. Men who had equal intelligence at the age of 14 revealed striking differences at age 34, depending upon the amount of education received in the meantime.

11. In other words, while the intellectual ability of a person is not lost as he grows older even though he does not go to school, his full abilities are not realized. It is not true that a boy who comes up the "hard way" has the same advantages as the person who receives formal schooling. However, even though education makes a profound difference, Dr. Lorge warns that "it would be overly optimistic to expect it to change the least able into the most able."

12. "An adult's measured mental ability is related to his intelligence as a boy and to the extent of his subsequent schooling," Dr. Lorge comments. ←End timing

RECORD HERE THE TIME REQUIRED ON THIS SELECTION: _____ MIN.
_____ SEC.

Test Your Comprehension

Which *one* of the following statements most accurately summarizes the *main idea* of the selection you have just finished? Check your choice without referring to the text.

192

1. College graduates have higher I.Q.'s than uneducated people.
2. Very little can be done about a person's brain power—he has what nature endowed him with.
3. Education can change the least able into the most able.
4. The I.Q. can be increased by schooling, for through education a person's full abilities are realized.
5. A person's I.Q. remains fairly constant over a twenty-year period.

Compute Your Rate
(*Approximate number of words: 625*)

TIME	W.P.M.	TIME	W.P.M.
40 sec.	939	1 min., 50 sec.	342
50 sec.	750	2 min.	313
1 min.	625	2 min., 15 sec.	278
1 min., 10 sec.	517	2 min., 30 sec.	250
1 min., 20 sec.	470	2 min., 45 sec.	228
1 min., 30 sec.	418	3 min.	208
1 min., 40 sec.	375		

YOUR RATE OF SELECTION 11: _____W.P.M.
(*Record this statistic on the chart and graph on page 393.*)

Discussion of the Selection

Let us again look back at the material and examine the author's pattern of thinking.

Paragraph 1: What, essentially, is Dr. Fine saying here? Simply that we have long held the belief that the I.Q. remains constant. This is expressed in the first sentence and all the rest of the paragraph merely restates, explains, or clarifies the same point.

Paragraph 2: Now, says Dr. Fine, a new study presents contrary evidence. The words "intelligence quotient fluctuates with the amount of education" obviously are the first statement of the central theme.

Paragraphs 1–2, then, are the beginning, the introduction, the springboard, call it what you will, of the article. Old belief—constancy of I.Q.; new study—fluctuation of I.Q. with education.

Paragraph 3: Now Dr. Fine starts describing the study in detail.

Paragraph 4: Continuing description of the study and repetition of central theme—"additional . . . schooling . . . raised . . . I.Q.'s."

Paragraph 5: More details of the study, further restatement of central theme.

Paragraph 6: Still on the study.

Paragraph 7: Still on the study.

Paragraph 8: Results of the study and again a restatement of the central theme.

Paragraph 9: Still on the study, this time a specific example to support the central theme.

Paragraph 10: More examples from the study to support the central theme.

Paragraphs 3–10, then, describe the mechanics and the results of the study—this is the middle of the structure.

Paragraph 11: Summary—this, in short, Dr. Fine is saying, is what the study proves; and he adds, inferentially, that the reason for the results is that schooling helps a person realize his full abilities.

Paragraph 12: Continued summary in the form of a quotation from one of the directors of the study that again restates the central theme.

Paragraphs 11–12, then, are a kind of summary of all the rest of the article, the end part of the structure.

Dr. Fine's central theme is inescapable, pervading almost every paragraph. It can be expressed quite as starkly as *the I.Q. can be increased by schooling;* or if preferably we included the implication in paragraph 11, we might add *because through education a person's full abilities are realized.* (Correct choice in the comprehension test: statement 4.)

So what have we here when we boil it all down?

Introduction, paragraphs 1–2: A 20-year study shows that the I.Q. fluctuates with education.

Body, paragraphs 3–10: description of the study, and how it proves that schooling increases the I.Q.

Summary, paragraphs 11–12: Schooling increases the I.Q.

The efficient reader does all this boiling down as a matter of habit; his sensitivity to structure helps him see clearly and quickly how the twelve paragraphs of this piece are related to one another, and how the subordinate details provide background for, explain, and support the central theme.

In your work on this chapter you too are attempting to develop the indispensable habit of boiling down material through sensing the relationship of the parts, through realizing, even if only dimly, what pattern the author is following in presenting his thinking to you. The kind of practice and study you are now engaging in is immensely valuable in developing and strengthening this habit, and directly after a session of perception training and vocabulary study you will have a chance to continue your practice on four more selections.

★ SESSION 15

PERCEPTION TRAINING VI

Perception Exercise 20

Before you do this exercise, review the correct procedure as outlined on page 62. Keep a record of your errors, if any.

84727 ←_____	83720 ←_____	10392 ←_____
74820 ←_____	83720 ←_____	83720 ←_____
09287 ←_____	83920 ←_____	93820 ←_____
83721 ←_____	83720 ←_____	19382 ←_____
71819 ←_____	93827 ←_____	93820 ←_____
55267 ←_____	93821 ←_____	84721 ←_____
74629 ←_____	11029 ←_____	84720 ←_____
11029 ←_____	64527 ←_____	93827 ←_____
88377 ←_____	83720 ←_____	62539 ←_____

62539 ←_____	84762 ←_____	72604 ←_____
02928 ←_____	93802 ←_____	23487 ←_____
83726 ←_____	83762 ←_____	45731 ←_____
83728 ←_____	93802 ←_____	15293 ←_____
94850 ←_____	83762 ←_____	92745 ←_____
94840 ←_____	94894 ←_____	84723 ←_____
94804 ←_____	84796 ←_____	73986 ←_____
84793 ←_____	84785 ←_____	

NUMBER CORRECT OUT OF 50: _____

Perception Exercise 21

Continue as before.

81754 ←_____	53264 ←_____	20791 ←_____
29395 ←_____	10972 ←_____	58623 ←_____
21362 ←_____	27912 ←_____	09217 ←_____
54729 ←_____	38564 ←_____	19271 ←_____
32748 ←_____	84095 ←_____	46583 ←_____
26312 ←_____	67328 ←_____	05489 ←_____
32748 ←_____	91270 ←_____	23867 ←_____
62739 ←_____	58463 ←_____	89391 ←_____
68973 ←_____	83980 ←_____	16070 ←_____
84725 ←_____	76422 ←_____	79201 ←_____
93726 ←_____	84950 ←_____	34658 ←_____

50948	←_____	97466	←_____	32177	←_____
76328	←_____	26054	←_____	58317	←_____
43888	←_____	80576	←_____	56328	←_____
94370	←_____	31642	←_____	72931	←_____
58712	←_____	76489	←_____	05867	←_____
36918	←_____	58116	←_____		

NUMBER CORRECT OUT OF 50: _____

Perception Exercise 22

As preparation for a new kind of perception training that will follow in the next exercise, let us once again use the Flashmeter card on phrases. You will notice, as soon as you start to work, that these disconnected phrases are for the most part somewhat longer than the ones you have practiced on in the past—now you must, to be successful, rely more strongly on interpreting the somewhat indistinct peripheral images that your eyes will photograph in the fraction of a second in which each phrase is exposed. (To refresh your memory on peripheral and macular vision, see page 68.) Keep these exposures as brief as you possibly can so that you will gradually adjust to reacting, instantaneously, to the complete phrase in one single fixation. You may not, for a time, have any realization of seeing the outer extremities of the exposed line. Or perhaps you actually may not catch the extremities at all—what you don't see you will nevertheless be able to surmise, and probably with great accuracy.

This is not going to be child's play, but with effort and practice you will soon be doing better than you may expect.

→   a rosy-cheeked child   →   the lumbering elephant

→   the rosy-fingered dawn   →   a strong brew of coffee

→   with full speed ahead   →   a snowy landscape

→   a characteristic smile   →   his bulging muscles

197

→	a furiously speeding car	→	furiously revolving
→	his happily smiling face	→	slowly revolving
→	a mud-stained finger	→	articles of faith
→	an ink-stained face	→	his religious beliefs
→	an ink-stained wretch	→	principles of learning
→	mud-splattered fender	→	his military uniform
→	a grandstand seat	→	their unknown beliefs
→	mud-splattered window	→	their threatening gestures
→	two broken windows	→	her beautiful fingernails
→	a black telephone	→	our foolish fantasies
→	a rear-view mirror	→	a dreamlike sequence
→	that clammy feeling	→	in mob psychology
→	his depressed feelings	→	under other circumstances
→	our early ancestors	→	changing circumstances
→	his royal ancestors	→	waves of the ocean
→	many tall ancestors		

Perception Exercise 23

Now I have a different type of task for you. The preceding exercise, which challenged you to make greater use of your peripheral vision, was not particularly easy—this exercise, continuing the challenge, may at first be even more difficult. However, when you finally attain some degree of success in perception drills of this nature, the rewards in terms of comfortable speed will amply compensate you for any initial difficulty. So follow the instructions carefully.

You will find, below, three columns of print, slightly narrower than those previously used in the book. Fixate in line with the broad black arrow, which is located at approximately the center of each column (we shall not need the Flashmeter card in this and the following exercises), and read down as rapidly as you can without loss of comprehension. Concentrate on three things: (1) going very fast, (2) keeping your eyes focused in the center of each line so that you will not be tempted to make more than one fixation, and (3) understanding what you read.

The more rapidly you move, the more you will have to make use of your peripheral vision, a wholly involuntary process that can be refined and perfected only through constant and unremitting practice. Some of this practice you've already had in our previous phrase-perception training—now, in the present exercise, a wholly new and very effective approach is being made to the same goal.

LIFE INSURANCE

"Why did you buy life insurance?" I asked him.

"Well," he said, "it was because once I met a young person coming up the stairs of an apartment house with her arms full of packages, one of them dangling from a slender string. I didn't think she'd mind, so I offered to help her. At the door of her apartment, I saw that she was quite pretty. She still is.

"Because late one night, while she and I were waiting at a dimly lighted railway station for the Owl to take me home, I said, 'We could live on the money I'm spending for railroad fares! What do you say we try it?' We did, and it worked.

"Because one day I was offered a job by another company, and when I told my boss, he promised me ten dollars more a week if I'd stay. When I told her of the boss's generosity, she said, 'What do you mean, generous? If he knew you were worth that much to him, he should have paid it to you before he had to.' So I quit and took the new job.

"Because one night she woke me up and said, 'I think I'd better go.' We went, and the last I saw of her that night, she was being trundled down a long corridor in a wheelchair, in spite of her protests that she could walk. When I saw her the next morning she was lying very still and white and with the sweetish smell of ether on her breath. A nurse came in and asked, 'Wouldn't you like to

An advertisement of the Travelers Insurance Co. Reprinted with permission.

see him?" But I wasn't interested in babies just then—not even our own.

"Because one autumn evening, while we were driving leisurely along a country road, we came upon a small white cottage, its windows ablaze with the light of the setting sun. She said, 'What a place this would be for us!' Yes, what a place it has been for us!

"It's because of these memories, and many others that I wouldn't tell you and that wouldn't interest you even if I did, that I bought life insurance.

"And if the premiums could be paid in blood, instead of money, pernicious anemia would be a pleasure."

Did you understand what you read? Then check the reason why the man in the story bought life insurance.

1. Because life insurance is a safe investment.
2. Because he wished to protect someone he loved very dearly.
3. Because his conscience would give him no rest if he didn't.

Key: Subtract three from five to determine the number of the correct answer.

Perception Exercise 24

How was that? Hard? It will become easier and more comfortable as you go on. Here is a second selection, to be read in the same way. Remember—go as fast as you can without sacrificing comprehension; keep your eyes focused on the center of the line and let your peripheral vision bring you the two ends.

EFFICIENCY

by Paul F. Watkins

Like most little tin gods, Efficiency is all right in its place, in the shop, the factory, the store. The trouble with efficiency is that it is a jealous god; it wants to rule our play as well as our work; it won't be content to reign in the shop, it follows us home.

From the *Herald Progress*, Ashland, Virginia. Reprinted with permission.

↓ ↓ ↓

And so we streamline our leisure hours for higher production; live by the clock even when time doesn't matter; standardize and mechanize our homes; speed the machinery of living so that we can go the most places, do the most things in the shortest period of time possible. We even eat, sleep, and loaf efficiently. Even on holidays and Sundays, the efficient man relaxes on schedule with one eye on the clock and the other on an appointment sheet. To squeeze the most out of each shining hour we have streamlined the opera, condensed the classics, put energy in pellets and culture in pocket-sized packages. We make the busy bee look like an idler, the ant like a sluggard. We live sixty-miles a minute and the great God Efficiency smiles.

We wish we would return to that pleasant day when we considered time a friend instead of a competitor; when we did things spontaneously and because we wanted to; rather than because our schedule called for it. But that of course wouldn't be efficiency. And we Americans must be efficient.

Did you understand what you read? Then check the point that Mr. Watkins is making:

1. Americans are the most efficient people in the world, both at work and at play.

2. If we are efficient, we will squeeze the most work and pleasure out of every hour.

3. It is all right to be efficient and concerned with time on the job; but outside of our working hours we ought to be less a slave to a time schedule.

4. The trouble with us is that we consider time a competitor instead of a friend.

Key: Subtract eight from ten and add one to obtain the number of the correct answer.

Perception Exercise 25

Continue as before, making sure to follow the instructions exactly.

A CHILD'S VOCABULARY

by Anna Perrott Rose

It was through Jimmy John that I discovered that a vocabulary is an outgrowth of experience. As fast as he learned some activity, he acquired without effort the vocabulary that went with it. From the pony he learned saddle, bridle, stirrup, blacksmith, and so on, although to begin with he had hidden from our pet in terror, with absolutely no words to describe anything about him. After a summer of sailing he unconsciously acquired nautical terms as a matter of course. But when we tried to increase his vocabulary by making him memorize words arbitrarily, he became confused and mixed them all up and misused them amusingly. The first time he saw a funeral procession he asked, "What's dat?" and someone said, "It's a hearse." Now it happened that Jimmy John had not been looking at the hearse when this was said. His attention had focused on an Army officer in the procession. Some time later he announced that there was a hearse in front of our house and when we peered out, rather alarmed, we saw a soldier standing there talking calmly to someone. No hearse anywhere.

I then realized that you can't make a child merely memorize words; he has to live them, and therefore many experiences are vital to the growth of a child's vocabulary. I suppose all educators know this but, when I found it out for myself, I felt as if I had discovered a new continent. I dare say a good many parents do not realize this, nor do they know that by limiting their offsprings' activities they may, to say the least, be reducing their children's chances for a good showing in those "aptitude tests" which come later and depend so much on a good vocabulary. Jimmy John educated me, I think, more than I ever educated him!

From "Jimmy John," in the *Ladies' Home Journal*. Reprinted by permission of the author.

Did you understand what you read? Then check the central point of this selection.

1. A child with a poor vocabulary is not very intelligent.
2. A child's vocabulary comes from experience—he has to live the words he learns.

3. A child with a poor vocabulary will not pass "aptitude tests."
4. Children educate their parents more often than the other way around.

Key: Add four and one and subtract three to determine the number of the correct answer.

Perception Exercise 26

Continue as before.

TO BE FRANK
by Frank Kingdon

I would like to go on record as saying that I am sick and tired of the Aga Khan, Aly Khan, their Begums, their matrimonial flipperies, their weights, their horses, their jewels, and their whole kit and kaboodle. If I never saw another line about these refugees from responsibility who squander the gifts brought them by ignorant and superstitious people they have been at no pains to educate or enlighten I should not feel that anything of importance was missing from my life.

They represent the essence of vulgarity.

There is no vulgarity about poverty which has been forced on somebody by misfortune, ill-luck, or the circumstances of life; there is no vulgarity more complete than riches used for nothing but display and personal indulgence. There is nothing vulgar about illiteracy where opportunity for learning has been denied; there is an ultimate vulgarity about educated minds with no thoughts beyond their own sensual satisfactions.

Maybe I should run with my tongue hanging out to slobber over every titled pensioner of exploited

people who has run away from his duty and his office. I must report that I find nothing to honor in them. I want some distinction higher than descent from Fatima to command my respect. I do not thrill with the thought of a man who gave up his throne but still collects his income from the people he refused to serve. The sycophants of privilege who toady to these decadent sprouts of historic heritage I find nauseating.

When I read that a woman has been robbed of jewels I join with all who cry that the criminals must

From the New York *Post.* Reprinted with permission of the author.

be punished. When I go a little further and find that the estimated value of these gim-cracks in her bags varies from $450,000 to $800,000 I can only guess at what the paltry $350,000 difference means among such friends.

When I lay the story aside I am left with the question whether anybody has any right to own so much conspicuous waste, and whether the first antisocial feature is not here. I don't think people should be allowed to go around robbing begums, but I still wonder whether there ought to be begums to rob.

I hope nobody will dub me a killjoy, or think me a pompous ass, but I cannot read such stuff without my gorge rising at the injustice it represents. I do not believe this kind of wasteful wealth can be publicized without leaving a rancor in the minds of those who read it.

Human beings may be such snobs that they revel in descriptions of these fabulous wastrels, but I doubt it. I think these human jewel cases are symptoms of something rotten in the state of our society and I believe their antics will stir a resentment that will

some day happily eliminate them.

Winston Churchill once called Gandhi a "naked fakir." The phrase was intended to demolish the Mahatma. I would put the "naked fakir," who went back to his people and lived among them, in the scales against the berobed and bejewelled Aga, who lives as a voluptuary far from his people, and I will throw in with him all his possessions, and know with certainty that the scale with the prince will rise as though he were a sparrow's feather.

If any one can qualify for oblivion, the Aga can.

Did you understand what you read? Then check the statement that best summarizes the content of the piece.

1. Dr. Kingdon doesn't like titled nobility.

2. Dr. Kingdon does not cherish the memory of Gandhi.

3. Dr. Kingdon thinks that people who rob vast wealth should not be punished too severely.

4. Dr. Kingdon finds that people of vast wealth are antisocial.

5. Dr. Kingdon thinks that people of vast wealth who contribute nothing to society and fail of their duty to mankind are symptoms of something rotten in our society.

6. Dr. Kingdon believes that robbery of unproductive people of great wealth should be severely punished.

Key: Add two and four and subtract one.

204

VOCABULARY STUDY III

Here are 25 words selected at random from our master list of 500. Check off those with which you are partially or wholly unfamiliar.

1. abject	9. fetid	18. quixotic
2. abstruse	10. germane	19. raucous
3. baleful	11. halcyon	20. sanctimonious
4. blithe	12. insouciant	21. sanguine
5. carnivorous	13. libidinous	22. suave
6. corpulent	14. meretricious	23. taciturn
7. defunct	15. naïve	24. unwitting
8. effete	16. oblique	25. voluble
	17. pallid	

Now look up in your dictionary each of the words you have checked. Study its common or nontechnical meanings, note and practice its correct pronunciation, understand its derivation, and discover from preceding or following entries its related noun or verb forms, if any.

For best results, record all this information briefly in your vocabulary notebook or on a scratch pad. Then study your notes until you feel that you have pretty nearly mastered all the new words you looked up. An excellent idea, also, is to write a short sentence or phrase using each word so that your learning will take a more active turn. Finally, when you feel that you are ready, put away all your notes and take this series of short tests.

Test Your Learning

I. Match word to definition.

1. abject	a—meat-eating
2. blithe	b—malodorous
3. corpulent	c—peaceful
4. fetid	d—wretched
5. raucous	e—pale
6. defunct	f—fat
7. germane	g—hoarse
8. carnivorous	h—pertinent
9. halcyon	i—extinct
10. pallid	j—gay

II. Check a *yes* or *no* answer to each question.
1. Is *abstruse* language commonly understood? ☐yes ☐**no**
2. Does a *baleful* glance show love? ☐yes ☐no
3. Is an *effete* civilization young and vigorous? ☐yes ☐no
4. Does *insouciance* indicate anxiety? ☐yes ☐no
5. Are *libidinous* thoughts pure and innocent? ☐yes ☐no
6. Is *meretricious* display cheap and flashy? ☐yes ☐no
7. Does *naïveté* betoken a lack of experience? ☐yes ☐no
8. Are *oblique* answers evasive? ☐yes ☐no
9. Are *quixotic* people impractical? ☐yes ☐no
10. Is *sanctimony* sincere? ☐yes ☐no

III. Decide whether each pair of words is more nearly *similar* or *opposed* in meaning, and check the proper letter.

1. sanguine—hopeful	S or O?	6. blithe—despondent	S or O?
2. suave—discourteous	S or O?	7. germane—relevant	S or O?
3. unwitting—uncon- scious	S or O?	8. corpulent—slim	S or O?
4. taciturn—talkative	S or O?	9. naïve—sophisti- cated	S or O?
5. voluble—silent	S or O?	10. oblique—indirect	S or O?

IV. Choose from the list the word that best fits each definition.
1. carefree_____
2. absurdly chivalrous_____
3. harsh-sounding_____
4. hard to understand_____
5. smoothly gracious _____

6. hypocritically pious, holy, or religious _____
7. without realization of what one is doing_____
8. mean _____
9. stout_____
10. relevant_____
11. having lost vigor or energy _____
12. hoarse_____
13. peaceful_____
14. attractive or alluring in a cheap and showy way _____
15. indirect _____
16. full of malice_____
17. colorless _____
18. having an offensive smell_____
19. optimistic_____
20. no longer in existence_____
21. romantically impractical_____
22. lustful_____
23. unworldly _____
24. gay_____
25. pale_____
26. without anxiety_____
27. closely related_____
28. disinclined to conversation _____
29. subsisting mainly or wholly on meat_____
30. talking with great and easy fluency_____

Key:
I. 1—d, 2—j, 3—f, 4—b, 5—g, 6—i, 7—h, 8—a, 9—c, 10—e
II. 1–5, no; 6–9, yes; 10, no.
III. 1—S, 2—O, 3—S, 4—O, 5—O, 6—O, 7—S, 8—O, 9—O, 10—S.
IV. 1. insouciant, 2. quixotic, 3. raucous, 4. abstruse, 5. suave, 6. sanctimonious, 7. unwitting, 8. abject, 9. corpulent, 10. germane, 11. effete, 12. raucous, 13. halcyon, 14. meretricious, 15. oblique, 16. baleful, 17. pallid, 18. fetid, 19. sanguine, 20. defunct, 21. quixotic, 22. libidinous, 23. naïve, 24. blithe, 25. pallid, 26. insouciant, 27. germane, 28. taciturn, 29. carnivorous, 30. voluble.

HOW TO X-RAY MATERIAL

The discussion that follows each selection in this chapter is designed to show you *how to think along with the author* as you read; *how to X-ray a piece,* so to speak, in order to see clearly the inner framework that holds the ideas together; and *how to pursue the central theme* of material so that you can quickly, efficiently, and correctly distill out of a vast mass of words and sentences and paragraphs one final and total meaning.

When you have learned how to do all this, when you have learned and overlearned it so thoroughly that it has become an integral, reflexive, habitual pattern in your everyday performance, then you will be reading with aggressive comprehension, you will no longer be passively absorbing the ideas and details, one after another, as they appear on a page—instead, you will understand them as parts of a unified whole, you will see them as components of a total structure, you will recognize them as related factors that work together to produce upon you, the reader, the effect or the impact that the author is striving for.

Such learning and overlearning can come only from practice, from intelligent, persistent practice on selection after selection—this is not a technique that you can master overnight, or that you can immediately put into operation simply by understanding it. But with enough practice, mastery will be achieved. Slowly, gradually, little by little, you will become surer, more skillful, more efficient. And as this happens, you will find that you are also becoming much more deeply involved in material, that you are taking a much more active role in responding to an author's thinking, and that you are pushing through much more rapidly and purposefully in pursuit of his central meaning.

Not only that.

You will discover, also, that your concentration will be improved.

For concentration, in reading as in any other activity, consists of such deep, active, and purposeful involvement that inner distractions cannot occur, mind-wandering is eliminated, and the external world might as well, for the time being, be completely nonexistent.

(How often has it happened to you that you find yourself reading the *words* on a page with absolutely no response to their *meaning*—suddenly you stop and realize that you've been going through all the motions of reading with none of the effect, that your mind has, for the last few minutes, been wrestling with a totally irrelevant problem, or that you have in actuality been concentrating on the sounds around you, not on the thoughts contained in the lines of print. So you go back, perhaps angry or perhaps amused that you have become so scatterbrained, and start all over again. This kind of thing is unlikely to happen—unless, of course, you are undergoing some deep emotional stresses—if you are actively engaged in searching for the pattern and structure that underlie what a writer is saying.)

Deeper involvement in material, a more dynamic response to an author's thinking, faster and more purposeful pursuit of central meaning, better concentration—all these are rich and desirable dividends. They are dividends you can receive if your investment is great enough. And that is why, at this halfway mark in your work in this chapter, I ask for continued practice, for earnest study of the discussion of every selection, and for inspired effort in applying what you learn, from your work in any one selection, to each subsequent selection that you read.

Let us turn now to the remaining selections of the chapter; and keep in mind, as you read, five important rules that will be most helpful to you at this stage of your training:

1. Push ahead with conscious speed.
2. Try to sense the broad pattern of the author's thinking.
3. Purposefully pursue the central ideas so that when you have finished the last line you will have a clear and accurate understanding of the *gist* of the author's communication to you.
4. Avoid unnecessary regressions.
5. Skim whenever you wish to, if you feel that such skimming will not be detrimental to efficient grasp of total meaning.

Selection 12

BANGLING THE LANGUAGE
by Norman Cousins

Start timing→ For some years, the popular impression has prevailed that the English-American language has been steadily expanding in range, variety, and color. Every so often we see impressive lists of new words which, with the blessings of the lexicographers, have passed into the bloodstream of the general vocabulary. But very little is said about the fact that many useful words are dying out each year— not because they lack value or vitality but because of increasingly lazy habits of writing and speaking.

For the fact remains that our language may actually be shrinking —despite the highly publicized stream of new recruits drawn regularly from slang, sports, entertainment, new trades, and current events. This shrinkage is represented by the loss of thousands of pithy, precise, essential words— words which, in a sort of Gresham's law applied to vocabulary, have been driven out over the years by flat, juiceless expressions. A recent edition of Shakespeare, for example, provided explanations for twenty-four hundred words which had long since passed out of general usage. True, a large number of these words deserved to die, either because they were replaced by sharper, more satisfying words, or because they were strictly a product of their times. But this still leaves a fair number of words which are as indispensable to the language today as they were when Shakespeare used them.

Could anyone think of a better word for defining someone who steals house servants out from under the unsuspecting noses of his best friends than the word *slockster?* This is not slang but a lost word from standard Anglo-Saxon English. Is there a better verb to describe the act of pushing and poking about in a crowd than the verb *to prog?* Is there any excuse for using the expression "petty liar" when the correct but forgotten word for it is *fibster?* Is there any single word in use today than can express more readily the ability of the fingers to enable the brain to recognize objects through touch alone than the lost word *felth?* And what a shorter way of referring to

Reprinted from the *Saturday Review* with permission. Mr. Cousins is the editor of the *Saturday Review* and author of *Modern Man Is Obsolete.*

an unweaned infant than the old word *suckerel*? Or *taverner* for tavern-keeper? Or *nappy* for midday sleepiness?

If economy of expression is a virtue, then we have injured the language through the loss through disuse of such words as *flinders* (combining fragments and splinters); *janglesome* (combining nerve-wracking and quarrelsome); *lanken* (combining leanness and lankiness); *keek* (combining peeping with slyness); *maffle* (combining stammering and blundering); *sloomy* (combining dullness, laziness, heaviness, and sleepiness all at once).

Only sloominess in our thinking could be responsible for the fact that although we use the word "smattering" we have neglected the much more useful noun from which it is derived, *smatters*, to describe small matters or trifles. Similarly, we use the trite expression "smash it to smithereens," but overlook the word *smither*, an excellent way of describing a tiny fragment. The word "ungainly" is in common usage today but not so its affirmative opposite, *gainly*, a handy way of describing someone who is shapely, elegant, provocative. The word "same" has an equally useful variant, *samely*, which can be used instead of the phrase "always the same." We use "bereave," but what about *reave*? ("To *reave* the orphan of his patrimony"—Shakespeare's "Henry VI.")

In the matter of precision, is there any one word that describes an attitude not so strong as the word dislike but stronger than the word indifferent? Yes; the word is *mislike*. Incidentally, there is a long list of other words which, combined with the prefix *mis,* make for an effective and lucid use of English. *Misproud*—proud for the wrong reason; *misgo*—arrive at the wrong place; *misexpense*—using money for the wrong purposes; *misbelieve*—to acquire mistaken convictions; *mislive*—to lead a wasted life; *misfare*—to have things turn out poorly; etc.

If one of the proofs of a virile language is its ability to generate verbs with striking power and pithiness, then we have been enfeebling English by neglecting such trenchant verbs as *to tolter*—move with slowness and heaviness; *to strome* —walk up and down while pondering some decision; *to rax*—reach and stretch at the same time; *to bangle*—fritter away an inheritance by carelessness and stupidity; *to gowl*—weep in anger rather than sorrow; *to spuddle*—assume pompous airs in the execution of a minor mission; *to stodge*—overstuff grotesquely; *to thrump*—bump into people in a crowd; *to slorp*—eat gluttonously and with monstrous sound effects.

Picturesque, time-saving expressions we have bangled over the years would include *barrel-fever* or *jug-bitten* to describe the disease of alcoholism, or, even more directly, the noun *bouse*, which combines souse and booze. *Knee-crooking* is

211

probably the etymological ancestor of the expression "brown-nosing," so commonly used in the recent war to describe self-debasement in honeying up to a superior. *Forswat and forswunk* is a good phrase to describe someone who is grimy and sweaty after he emerges from a long day's toil in the coal pits. The word *fluttersome* could hardly be improved upon for a picture of someone gadding about at a party talking with much emotion and little sense. The victims of such flutters would aptly be termed *tirelings*. Those who can converse only by arguing and snapping and by exhibiting their tempers would be described as *toitish*.

In no branch of language is there greater need for endless reinforcements than the uncomplimentary reference. Consider these lost gems: *gowk*—an open-mouthed fool; *jabbernowle*—a slow thinker and a bore; *chuff*—a Shakespearian favorite to describe someone who converts his extra wealth into extra chins; *mome*—someone not quite arrived at, but well on his way to, the status of a blockhead; *sumph*—the same man upon becoming a blockhead; *scroil*—a slick, mean fellow; *bummel*—a small-time tramp; *dumble*—short for dumbbell.

Is it too much to hope that words such as these may be restored to the language? Far from it; we have only to consider that a large number of words which had virtually disappeared towards the end of the nineteenth century have been since rediscovered and are in common use today: *deft, blurt, gab, kindle, glower, glamor, hotfoot, grub, grip, malodorous, forbear, foreword, afterword, lush, reek, pixie, quash, runt, sheen, sag, sleuth, slick, snack, uncanny, tinsel, snarl, bolt, imp, tryste, sliver, slogan, kink, dump, croon, cleave, mole, monger.*

The value of new or rediscovered words is not that they add to the language but that they enlarge one's choice in speaking or writing with greater precision, suppleness, color. Certainly no one wants to be *word-ridden*, a lost but handy word describing a slave to words for words' sake. They used to tell the story, incidentally, about the English fishwife who looked on blandly when Daniel O'Connor accused her in court of being a perjurer, thief, strumpet, and procurer, but who put her foot down when he called her a parallelogram. ←End timing

RECORD HERE THE TIME REQUIRED ON THIS SELECTION: _____ MIN.
_____ SEC.

Test Your Comprehension

Which *one* of the following statements most accurately summarizes the *main idea* of the selection you have just finished? Check your choice without referring to the text.

1. We don't have enough words in our language.
2. New words don't have the impact of old ones.
3. High school students cannot understand Shakespeare because we have lost so many Shakespearean terms from the language.
4. Our language may be shrinking and losing some of its force because of the thousands of old words that are no longer used; but perhaps we will rediscover some of them and thereby be able to add precision, suppleness, and color to our speaking and writing.

Compute Your Rate

(Approximate number of words: 1275)

TIME	W.P.M.	TIME	W.P.M.
1 min., 30 sec.	850	3 min., 30 sec.	364
1 min., 45 sec.	730	4 min.	319
2 min.	638	4 min., 30 sec.	284
2 min., 15 sec.	567	5 min.	255
2 min., 30 sec.	510	5 min., 30 sec.	232
3 min.	425	6 min.	213

YOUR RATE ON SELECTION 12: _____W.P.M.
(Record this statistic on the chart and graph on page 393.)

Discussion of the Selection

The central theme of this piece is explicitly stated in *the last sentence of the first paragraph and the first sentence of the second paragraph;* and again, after rich and elaborate supporting details, in *the summarizing sentence at the beginning of the final paragraph.*

Mr. Cousins' pattern of presentation is admirably clear-cut:

1. It has been popularly thought that our language is expanding in range, variety, and color. (Introduction.)

2. Instead, the opposite may be happening because we are lazily neglecting the older words. (Central theme.)

3. Look at all these excellent, economical, precise, striking, pithy, and picturesque words that are now obsolete. (Development of the theme with specific examples.)

4. But we are rediscovering many of these useful words, whose value is that they add precision, suppleness, and color to our written and spoken expression. (Recapitulation of central theme.)

Correct choice on the comprehension test is statement 4.

Selection 13

IT AIN'T THE LENGTH, IT'S THE OBSCURITY

Start timing→ We hear from a friend to the following effect: "In your editorial column, you guys have now and then expressed great scorn of windy language, big $7 words, and other methods of concealing thought or lack of thought. Well, browsing through recent editorials of yours, I have come across such things as 'intolerable,' 'incompatibility,' 'vulnerable,' 'genocide,' and several other biggies. Ain't going highhat on us, be ye?"

2. Nope, we ain't; at least, not intentionally. If now and then we let an overstuffed word fall into this column, maybe it's because our inborn culchaw and refeenment just overcome us from time to time.

3. We do think, though, that this aspect of the use of language is not as simple as the mere difference in length between a word of four letters and one of 12, 15 or 18.

4. For illustration, here are some shorties which we'd call real $7 words, and wouldn't use here at this time without explanation: adit, erg, ergo, ohm, gloze, cozen, griff, modal, mure, snash, viable.

5. Those are all perfectly good English or Scotch words (except ergo—it's Latin, meaning therefore); likewise clean. But they're $7 words or worse, as we figure it, because so few people know what they mean. When you're writing for the general public, the main object is to use language which that public can understand at a glance, without having to go grubbing into a dictionary to find out what in the blue blazes you are trying to say.

6. But there are plenty of big, long, many-syllable words which almost everybody who can read understands. We submit that three of the four specimens listed above by our pal and critic are widely understood.

7. Breathes there a reader who doesn't know that "intolerable" means "unbearable"?—though we must admit we prefer the latter.

8. "Incompatibility" is a widely familiar word because of the many divorce suits brought on grounds of incompatibility—meaning two married persons just can't get along together. Bridge is a tremendously popular card game; hence "vulnerable" is a well-known word to millions of people.

9. "Genocide" is something else again, and we'll admit we muffed a ball when we dropped that one into this column without explaining what it meant. Sorry, and we'll try

An editorial in the New York *News*. Reprinted with permission.

214

not to let such a thing happen again. Here's the dope on "genocide." It's a new word, of Latin derivation, and it means murder of a whole racial or other human group. It originated, to the best of our information, at the Nurnberg trials of the German war criminals.

10. There are whole battalions of words in common use nowadays which wouldn't have meant much, if anything, to Samuel Johnson and Noah Webster, two famous dictionary makers of generations gone by —only they called themselves lexicographers.

11. Among these are "fission," used in connection with the atom; "blooper," when you're discussing baseball; "airborne," which is what a plane is when it gets safely off the ground; "chairborne," which is a popular word in modern wars to describe officers who never hear a shot fired in anger from start to finish of the fracas.

12. In the gobbledygook of diplomats and bureaucrats, there are any number of big, fat blimps of words. Among these, the three that make us maddest are "quadripartite," "unilateral" and "directive." Why the boys can't just say "four-party," "onesided" and "order" is beyond us—unless, as some suspect, most present-day diplomats and bureaucrats aim with malice aforethought to confuse and befuddle the general public.

13. To make this subject of big and little words still more fascinating, there is the fact that most people are well aware of the meaning and historical background of the very longest non-scientific word of all in current dictionaries. That one, of course, is "antidisestablishmentarianism"—and most of us know what it means simply because it has been so widely hailed as the champ. Huge though old anti-etc. is, he is in no way a $7 word.

14. So we'd say, about this part of the technic of using the English language, that it isn't the size of a word which should rule it out of newspapers, but its obscurity. If most people know what it means, go ahead and use it, no matter how big it is; otherwise, blackball it, or be polite enough to the readers to dub in an explanation in parentheses if you feel you've got to use it.

15. This answer the question?

←End timing

RECORD HERE THE TIME REQUIRED ON THIS SELECTION: _____ MIN. _____ SEC.

Test Your Comprehension

Which *one* of the following statements most accurately summarizes the *main idea* of the selection you have just finished? Check your choice without referring to the text.

1. The editors are sorry that they have used long words in the past and will not do so in the future.

2. A word may be long and still fully comprehensible to the readers of the paper; or it may be short and difficult to understand. Size by itself is no criterion of obscurity.

3. If a word is English or Scotch, rather than Latin, it may be used in the paper's editorial columns no matter how long it is.

4. Diplomats use long and obscure words to confuse the general public.

Compute Your Rate

(Approximate number of words: 770)

TIME	W.P.M.	TIME	W.P.M.
1 min.	770	2 min., 15 sec.	344
1 min., 10 sec.	660	2 min., 30 sec.	308
1 min., 20 sec.	579	2 min., 45 sec.	280
1 min., 30 sec.	514	3 min.	257
1 min., 40 sec.	462	3 min., 30 sec.	220
1 min., 50 sec.	420	4 min.	193
2 min.	385		

YOUR RATE ON SELECTION 13: _____W.P.M.

(Record this statistic on the chart and graph on page 393.)

Discussion of the Selection

This editorial, like Mr. Cousins' article, follows a four-point organization:

1. Introduction—Paragraphs 1–2: We've been asked whether, contrary to our own expressed sentiments, we're going high-hat by using $7 words. We're not.

2. Central Theme—Paragraphs 3–6: A word may be short and difficult to understand; or it may be long and still fully comprehensible to the general public. (A few illustrations to support the theme are included.)

3. Development of central theme, with further illustrations— Paragraphs 7–13: Consider these examples of big words, some commonly understood, some not.

4. Recapitulation—Paragraphs 14–15: Size by itself is no criterion of understandability.

Correct choice on the comprehension test is statement 2.

Selection 14

GREEN LIGHT MEANS DANGER
by William S. Dutton

Start timing→ She had the green light. Confidently she drove her black sedan out onto the six-lane highway to cross. It never occurred to her to look to the left, the most likely point of danger.

2. On the main highway a speeding driver saw, too late, the red light commanding him to stop. He jammed on his brakes, and his tires shrieked as if in horror at the impending crash. The woman was killed instantly. He died that night.

3. Indignant witnesses blamed the man alone; he had broken a law. In grim reality she was equally to blame, for if she had but looked to the left, there would have been no accident. She had placed too much trust in a green light and in her fellow drivers.

4. That fault today, common to most of us, is one of the largest contributors to our mounting motor casualty lists, according to two of the newest studies of how and where fatal accidents happen. The message of these studies is that a green light means not safety, but: *Beware of death!*

5. Wilmington, Delaware, made the initial study. It embraced 15 years, 1,606 intersections and revealed that the danger ratio at light-controlled crossings, in terms of deaths, was 8.65 times higher than at unmarked and unguarded crossings in that city.

6. Moreover, both the number and severity of accidents grew as the traffic controls moved up from none to slow signs, to stop signs, to lights. For every one death at unmarked crossings, 2.27 occurred at crossings marked slow. At stop streets, 3.51.

7. The amazed Wilmington engineers asked the Philadelphia Bureau of Traffic Engineering to make a similar study as a check. The larger survey covered one year and 9,294 intersections of all kinds. The death ratio at light-controlled crossings as compared to those unmarked was slightly *higher* than Wilmington's.

8. In Texas, records of the state police show that more than 80 per cent of its highway deaths there are the result of motorists or others violating some traffic law or control.

9. Only rarely are these violations deliberate. They happen every day

in every community. And because to err is human, all the controls and police in the land can't put a stop to them. Each of us who drives becomes, by the law of averages, a potential if unwilling killer.

10. What to do about it?

11. "When you reach a corner and another car is approaching fast from a crossroad, let him cross first even if you have the right of way," warns the National Safety Council of Chicago.

12. "We (and this means all of us) must change our thinking on traffic controls," says E. F. Koester, Wilmington's chief engineer. "Controls don't end danger. They proclaim it."

13. No control is put up without strong reason. That reason is usually a record of previous accidents at that crossing. Lights, the most arbitrary control, proclaim the greatest need for caution. The turn from yellow to green means to proceed with eyes open and wits alert, for here people have been killed and maimed—or they may be.

14. The exact opposite attitude is assumed by most drivers toward controls, Mr. Koester says.

15. Our mistaken notion of controls is reflected in neighborhood agitations for traffic lights as soon as a few bad accidents happen at a local corner. Mothers especially seem to think that their children will be safe if they "wait for the green light." Schools teach pupils this fallacy. The teaching is good only in part. Its emphasis is wrong, creating a false sense of security that makes the child, and later the adult, the easy victim of the first driver who didn't see that the red light was against him until too late.

16. The feeling of safety, now induced by lights and other controls that are actually warnings, is our greatest traffic hazard of all, and it will continue to be until we change our views.   ←End timing

RECORD HERE THE TIME REQUIRED ON THIS SELECTION: _____ MIN.
_____ SEC.

Test Your Comprehension

Which *one* of the following statements most accurately summarizes the *main idea* of the selection you have just finished? Check your choice without referring to the text.

1. It is safer to cross *against* the green light than *with* the green light.

2. The green light gives us a false sense of security. We should be just as careful when the green light is in our favor as we are when no traffic signal governs an intersection.

3. There are more deaths at traffic-light intersections than at uncontrolled intersections.

4. Schools and parents teach children wrong concepts about traffic.

Compute Your Rate
(Approximate number of words: 670)

TIME	W.P.M.	TIME	W.P.M.
50 sec.	804	2 min., 15 sec.	300
1 min.	670	2 min., 30 sec.	268
1 min., 15 sec.	536	2 min., 45 sec.	244
1 min., 30 sec.	448	3 min.	224
1 min., 45 sec.	384	3 min., 15 sec.	210
2 min.	335	3 min., 30 sec.	198

YOUR RATE ON SELECTION 14: _____W.P.M.

(Record this statistic on the chart and graph on page 393.)

Discussion of the Selection

Reading aggressively, as you now realize, is simply a matter of quickly and efficiently grasping total meaning by understanding, and reacting to, the relationship between the parts of material. I say "simply" because it's that and no more, but do not therefore infer that this is a simple technique, or one that is simple to apply. Seeing relationships is after all the very basis of intelligence and thinking; it is also the foundation of all comprehension. And training in aggressive reading demands of you a deeper and more active recognition of, and response to, the components of a piece of writing than you have perhaps been in the habit of using; *it demands that you think while you read.*

How clearly did you sense the pattern of Mr. Dutton's article, how successfully did you grasp his total meaning?

Let us go back to the selection and examine the relationship between the parts.

Paragraphs 1–3: Narrative introduction leading up to an interpretation that foreshadows the central theme—". . . too much trust in a green light. . . ."

Paragraph 4: More elaborate expression of the central theme, with transition to the detailed support (". . . according to two of the newest studies. . . .")

Paragraphs 5–9: Support of the central theme by a description of the studies made in Wilmington and Philadelphia, plus facts from Texas.

Paragraphs 10–13: Pounding home of the central theme—how we should react to a green light.

219

Paragraphs 14–16: Further variations on the theme—how most of us mistakenly react to the green light, with the last paragraph concisely summing up all that has gone before.

Correct choice on the comprehension test is statement 2.

Note how the author uses paragraphs 4, 10, and 14 as transition from one section to the next:

Paragraph 4: "That fault" refers to the error of the woman who proceeded confidently when she saw the green light (paragraphs 1–3); "according to . . . studies" leads us to the content of the following five paragraphs.

Paragraph 10: "What to do" tells us what's coming in paragraphs 11–13; "about it" links those paragraphs up with the preceding information.

Paragraph 14: "The exact opposite" will be discussed in paragraph 15. The exact opposite of what? Of what was described as ideal behavior in the preceding paragraphs.

Selection 15

IS TRAFFIC-COURT JUSTICE BLIND?
by Albert Q. Maisel

Start timing→ It was 2 a.m. on a hot August night. In a San Francisco suburb, a man lurched out of a bar and into his car, and roared northward at 80 miles an hour.

2. Before police could stop the drink-crazed driver he had crashed into another car and sent six persons to the hospital. At the police station he was examined by a doctor who confirmed, by chemical test, what everyone already knew. Six people had been maimed because a madman, too drunk even to walk, had gotten behind the wheel.

3. Is that driver now in jail? Hardly. Police charged the man with felony drunken driving (which carries a penitentiary penalty in California), reckless driving and driving on the wrong side of the highway. When he was taken to court, the felony charge was dismissed. The injured were there, ready to testify, but they weren't even called to the stand. The two lesser charges brought a fine of only $200 and a slap-on-the-wrist license suspension of 90 days.

From *Reader's Digest.* Reprinted with permission of the author and of *Reader's Digest.*

4. Move up the coast now to Portland, Ore., where a motorized maniac was brought into court after killing his victim and running from the scene. Did he end in the penitentiary? Not at all. A charge of negligent homicide was substituted for the original indictment and the killer, after paying a $75 fine, walked out of court a free man.

5. These cases are not exceptional. New York City's magistrates last year discharged nearly two-thirds of all the defendants who were tried before them for drunken driving. Of those they convicted, 91 per cent were let off with either a suspended sentence or a small fine. Not a single one of the five—that's right, only five—who received jail sentences served more than 30 days.

6. Records such as these go a long way toward explaining why we still kill some 32,000 people on our highways every year and maim 1,100,000 others. In most cities, serious offenses are all too easily written off the books in a flood of continuances, dismissals, and ridiculously small fines.

7. But there is another shocking side to the traffic-court picture. In city after city, police and the courts have ganged up on the least dangerous of motor-law offenders—the harried salesman and the busy housewife who violate parking ordinances. These motorists, guilty of little more than trying to go about their business, are being pursued with single-minded efficiency. Police are taken off their motorcycles and squad cars to spend their days ticketing parked cars.

8. How far this has gone is demonstrated by St. Paul, Minn. In 1940 that city had 31,747 traffic cases. Last year the load on its courts had almost doubled: 63,266 cases. The entire increase is accounted for by the drive against parkers. Overtime parking cases rose from less than 22,000 in 1940 to nearly 55,000 last year.

9. In Detroit, between 1940 and 1948, police complaints against parkers increased 65 per cent while complaints against nonparking violators increased less than two per cent.

10. In Syracuse, N. Y., convictions for moving violations increased less than ten per cent between 1936 and 1948 while convictions for parking violators increased more than 450 per cent.

11. Behind this urge to penalize parking lies the discovery by many tax-hungry municipal officials that there is a gold mine in parking-law enforcement. Cleveland's income from traffic fines last year was six times as great as in 1940. In Charleston, S. C., Salt Lake City, Utah, and Kalamazoo, Mich., traffic-fine revenues have jumped more than 400 per cent. In Los Angeles, traffic fines and forfeitures pay the cost of operating all municipal courts and yield the city a profit of $3,200,000 besides.

12. Throughout the country, the campaign to soak the parker has more than doubled the already

overwhelming burden of traffic cases that have clogged our court machinery for years. Judges are so busy mechanically repeating the routine of "Five dollars and costs" in trivial cases that they have no time to deal properly with serious violators.

13. As the number of trivial traffic cases has grown, city after city has resorted to a new device—the cash-register or cafeteria court. More than 70 per cent of all traffic tickets served by the police are now answerable in such Violations Bureaus. All the overtime parker has to do is to plead guilty—whether guilty or not—swallow his perhaps valid mitigating explanations and answer "Yes" to the clerk's refrain of "Yawanna pay?"

14. True, the ticketed citizen still has the right to demand his day in court. But when he tries to exercise that right, he finds numerous pressures exerted to induce a guilty plea. I have sat in 40 courtrooms during the last six months watching this parody of justice. Typical was the performance I witnessed in a New York court last summer.

15. The judge arrived more than an hour late while nearly 200 accused motorists sweated and fumed. First he had his clerk call up all who were ready to plead guilty. Anyone offering a not-guilty plea or an explanation was gruffly ordered back to his seat. One woman approached the bench with a baby in her arms, to ask for special consideration. The magistrate cut her short with "Lady, if you hadn't

done wrong you wouldn't be here. Now get back to your seat and take your turn like everyone else."

16. The vast majority of the "guilty" were overtime parkers or those caught parking in restricted areas. Without discernible rhyme or reason they drew fines of from four to ten dollars.

17. Next—an hour later—came the "guilty with an explanation" group. Many were speeders. If their stories were glib, they got off with fines which were sometimes less than those of the parkers who had pleaded guilty before them.

18. Those who pleaded not guilty had to wait till noon before they were even called before the bench. Then the vast majority were held over for a trial at a later date. Confronted with further loss of time from work, many offered to change their pleas to guilty.

19. Small wonder that the attitude of the average motorist tagged with a parking ticket is one of utter cynicism. As my neighbor in court, a burly truck driver, put it: "Don't be a dope. Plead guilty and get it over with."

20. Drives against the parker do not contribute to traffic safety; often they work against it. For the last year and a half, New York City's police have been conducting a savage drive against parkers. Last year they ticketed 83,806 more parking-ordinance violators than the year before. But to accomplish this prodigy of law enforcement they had to let up elsewhere. They caught 8,270 fewer speeders, 6,807

fewer drivers who ran through red lights.

21. As a result, New York—which has always been below the national average in street safety—has fallen into last place among the largest cities of the country. Accidents, injuries, and deaths have all increased in 1949 over the previous year.

22. Chicago has had a different experience. Long at the bottom of the heap in traffic safety, Chicago finally called upon the Northwestern University Traffic Institute and the International Association of Chiefs of Police for a plan to cure its difficulties. Studies made early in 1948 showed that 80 per cent of all traffic tickets being issued in Chicago were for nonmoving violations. In the month of February, only three speeding tickets were issued.

23. A new policy of selective enforcement was developed. Men were called away from the fruitless job of tagging parked cars. The number of motorcycle policemen was trebled and 54 special traffic-control autos were added. Police were instructed to give priority to violations connected with traffic accidents. Reckless and drunken driving were placed at the top of the enforcement list.

24. The pay-off has been dramatic. In the year ending June 30, 1948 (the year before the reform), Chicago had 529 traffic deaths. In the year since, traffic deaths dropped to 435. Ninety-four lives were saved and thousands of injuries avoided.

25. But Chicago knows this is only the first step. The process of driving shoppers and businessmen out of town by the parking-ticket route has been halted. Now the city is planning to invite more cars than ever before to park in its busiest districts—not on the streets but in municipally owned lots and garages. Nearly 30,000 parking meters are to be installed in the Loop and on outlying arteries. The revenue from these meters will finance new off-street parking spaces.

26. Outstanding in this respect has been the achievement of White Plains, N. Y., a large shopping center, which set up the first Parking Authority in the United States in 1947. Instead of chasing parkers away with punitive fines, the city put meters on its main streets and dedicated their revenue to the improvement of parking facilities. Meter revenues have soared and the money is used by the Parking Authority.

27. San Francisco, with one large underground municipal garage already paying for itself, is planning $19,000,000 worth of new projects to house 15,000 cars. Pittsburgh has set up a Parking Authority and is issuing $34,000,000 in bonds to be liquidated by the income from 32 big public lots and garages. Denver has a $4,500,000 program under way.

28. These plans are impressive. Yet, there are still far too many cities which still think of parking as merely a matter for police action. Until these cities wake up, our

traffic courts will continue to be
swamped with petty violators and
real law enforcement for safety will
continue to be sacrificed.

RECORD HERE THE TIME REQUIRED
ON THIS SELECTION: _____ MIN.
_____ SEC.

←End timing

Test Your Comprehension

Which *one* of the following statements most accurately summarizes the *main idea* of the selection you have just finished? Check your choice without referring to the text.

1. Parking meters are the best and simplest method of solving traffic problems.

2. Traffic courts are generally abusive and discourteous to the motoring public—and the traffic court setup is the chief cause of present-day traffic problems.

3. Traffic accidents will decrease when our cities concentrate on enforcing the law against serious traffic offenses, and on providing more parking space, rather than on detecting parking violations.

4. Because our traffic courts are inefficient, perpetrators of serious traffic violations usually escape with light and inadequate punishment.

5. Experience proves that whether you are guilty or innocent, you can save time and trouble in traffic courts if you plead guilty.

Compute Your Rate

(*Approximate number of words: 1600*)

TIME	W.P.M.	TIME	W.P.M.
2 min.	800	4 min., 15 sec.	376
2 min., 10 sec.	738	4 min., 30 sec.	356
2 min., 15 sec.	692	4 min., 45 sec.	336
2 min., 30 sec.	640	5 min.	320
2 min., 45 sec.	580	5 min., 15 sec.	306
3 min.	533	5 min., 30 sec.	292
3 min., 15 sec.	492	5 min., 45 sec.	278
3 min., 30 sec.	457	6 min.	267
3 min., 45 sec.	428	6 min., 30 sec.	247
4 min.	400	7 min.	229

YOUR RATE ON SELECTION 15: _____W.P.M.

(*Record this statistic on the chart and graph on page 393.*)

Discussion of the Selection

Mr. Maisel is making three important points in his article: (a) police and courts are cracking down on parking violations, rather than on serious traffic offenses; (b) as a result, safety on the road is as bad as, or worse than, ever, and shoppers and businessmen are being driven out of town; and (c) the sensible solution, followed by many cities, is to provide ample, usually off-street, parking space.

Note the clear-cut pattern of the author's presentation:

Paragraphs 1–5: Introduction, with narrative incidents to illustrate how lightly the traffic courts are punishing serious offenders.

Paragraphs 6–7: First part of the central theme—*how this attitude explains the poor safety record on our highways; and how police and courts are going after the illegal parker, rather than the reckless driver.*

Paragraphs 8–21: Statistical, illustrative, and supporting details that elaborate upon, and clarify, this part of central theme. (Paragraphs 11 and 12 contain significant details that explain the causes of the problem—the desire for revenue on the part of municipalities, and the fact that the courts are so clogged with parking cases that there is no time to deal properly with serious violations.)

Paragraphs 22–27: The second part of the central theme is elaborated upon—*the way to solve the problem is to provide more parking space.*

Paragraph 28: Recapitulation of the complete central theme.

Correct choice on the comprehension test is statement 3.

All right. With this selection we conclude the comprehension training of the chapter, and we are ready to recapitulate your rate statistics.

Copy, from the chart on page 393, your rates on selections 7–15:

SELECTION 7 (PROFESSORS READ):	_____W.P.M.
SELECTION 8 (ADULT LEARNING):	_____W.P.M.
SELECTION 9 (LEARNING PRINCIPLES):	_____W.P.M.
SELECTION 10 (MARRIAGE):	_____W.P.M.
SELECTION 11 (I.Q. AND SCHOOLING):	_____W.P.M.
SELECTION 12 (OLD WORDS):	_____W.P.M.
SELECTION 13 (LONG WORDS):	_____W.P.M.
SELECTION 14 (GREEN LIGHT):	_____W.P.M.
SELECTION 15 (TRAFFIC-COURT JUSTICE):	_____W.P.M.

Add these figures, divide by 9 to find your average rate, and record the result in the first line below.

(1) AVERAGE RATE IN CHAPTER 7:   _____W.P.M.
(2) INITIAL RATE: _____W.P.M.
(3) AVERAGE GAIN: _____W.P.M.
(4) PERCENTAGE GAIN: _____ %
(5) PERCENTAGE GAIN IN CHAPTER 2: _____ %
(6) GAIN IN PERCENTAGE: _____ %

To complete line 2 of the chart, copy the rate at which you read the first selection in the book, which you recorded on page 11. Then subtract line 2 from line 1 and write the answer on line 3. Now divide your average gain (line 3) by your initial rate (line 2), carry the result to two decimal places, and fill in line 4. Next copy from page 392 your percentage gain in chapter 2 to fill in line 5, and complete the chart by subtracting line 5 from line 4. Now you have a graphic picture of your progress to date.

Let us do two more things with these statistics.

(1) Use the figures from lines 1, 3, and 4, and fill in the appropriate spaces on the chart on page 393.

(2) Take your average rate on the nine selections of this chapter (line 1), locate that figure on the graph on page 393, and draw a straight line parallel to line AB. Label this line "average, phase 2."

The completed graph (assuming, of course, entirely hypothetical statistics) may look something like this:

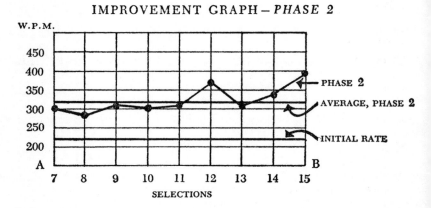

IMPROVEMENT GRAPH — *PHASE 2*

PERCEPTION TRAINING VII

Perception Exercise 27

Using the Flashmeter card, expose the numbers for a fraction of a second, getting a *visual* impression. Do not say the digits to yourself. Reproduce each number in the blank to the right and then check your result.

23487	←_____	62739	←_____	20739	←_____
45731	←_____	68973	←_____	43872	←_____
15293	←_____	84725	←_____	63416	←_____
81754	←_____	93726	←_____	50743	←_____
29395	←_____	53264	←_____	60739	←_____
21362	←_____	53842	←_____	60842	←_____
54729	←_____	96476	←_____	91647	←_____
32748	←_____	10873	←_____	30805	←_____
26312	←_____	92856	←_____	76412	←_____
92745	←_____	73214	←_____	13468	←_____
84723	←_____	91376	←_____	21467	←_____
73986	←_____	80768	←_____	86410	←_____
32748	←_____	04396	←_____	05708	←_____

64662 ←_____ 42137 ←_____ 39872 ←_____

47318 ←_____ 06421 ←_____ 20643 ←_____

02146 ←_____ 70764 ←_____ 31846 ←_____

94210 ←_____ 77737 ←_____

NUMBER CORRECT OUT OF 50: _____

Perception Exercise 28

Proceed as before.

10793 ←_____ 86420 ←_____ 94057 ←_____

20586 ←_____ 30641 ←_____ 70856 ←_____

43218 ←_____ 15846 ←_____ 05708 ←_____

97624 ←_____ 54564 ←_____ 53910 ←_____

38413 ←_____ 80832 ←_____ 86581 ←_____

57641 ← _____ 30846 ←_____ 38462 ←_____

18765 ←_____ 74321 ←_____ 43865 ←_____

68430 ←_____ 39874 ←_____ 90308 ←_____

90468 ←_____ 46852 ←_____ 21643 ←_____

20578 ←_____ 38597 ←_____ 90468 ←_____

91087 ←_____ 48765 ←_____ 30431 ←_____

64062 ←_____ 98543 ←_____ 46213 ←_____

30984 ←_____ 32167 ←_____ 68432 ←_____

43786 ←_____ 43856 ←_____ 25979 ←_____

73210 ←_____ 73218 ←_____ 50755 ←_____

93042   ←_____   60646   ←_____   30707   ←_____

40434   ←_____   40646   ←_____

NUMBER CORRECT OUT OF 50: _____

Perception Exercise 29

Using the Flashmeter card, attempt to recognize each phrase in one exceedingly brief exposure. Avoid, if possible, saying the phrase to yourself.

→ a fashionable audience

→ the evening performance

→ frame of reference

→ tens of thousands

→ one of Germany's

→ two or three friends

→ small band of scholars

→ big commercial debt

→ all the earmarks of

→ why this play has

→ believe in hard work

→ much greater understanding

→ few, if any, differences

→ more conservative in action

→ his many needy relatives

→ softness of flesh

→ preparation for disaster

→ yearns to re-establish

→ insists on his privileges

→ fraught with urgency

→ might start producing

→ conspirators in larceny

→ large combustion chamber

→ one million Japanese

→ hundred million Chinese

→ Union of South Africa

→ have fascinating histories

→ history of the affair

→ end of the long night

→ heart of the matter

→ working on a shoestring

→ tied to her apron strings

→ this series of words	→ found to his dismay
→ brief period of exposure	→ return of the good life
→ this briefest synopsis	→ for better or for worse
→ her optional accessories	→ will run for office
→ high-octane gasoline	→ found to his dismay
→ many reclining figures	→ Greeks bearing gifts
→ those damn Yankees	→ sat down for supper
→ easily won the pennant	

Perception Exercise 30

Now, dispensing with the Flashmeter card, attempt to sweep down each column of print with only one fixation to the line and relying, if possible, more on visual responses than on inner speech. The material in this exercise is reprinted, with permission, from *Publishers' Weekly*.

↓ ↓ ↓

Edgar Rice Burroughs,	About 36,000,000	was Mr. Burroughs'
creator of Tarzan,	copies	first published book;
a fictional Caspar	of his 23	it was written
Hauser	Tarzan books	while the author was
or ape-man,	have been sold,	a department manager
whose jungle exploits	and his income	at Sears Roebuck,
are known	from the sale	and was based
to people	of his books,	on extensive research
in the four corners	the Tarzan movies	which Mr. Burroughs
of the globe,	and cartoons	did
died on March 19	is estimated at	in his spare time
at the age	$10,000,000.	at the Chicago
of 74.	"Tarzan of the Apes"	Public Library.

He first sent
the manuscript
to a number of
Eastern publishers
but they all
turned it down
as being
too fantastic.
He then sent it
to *Argosy Magazine*
which promptly
accepted it
for serial publication.
After a few installments
had appeared,
the late Herbert A.
Gould,
then director
of McClurg's
retail store
on Wabash Avenue,
discovered there was
a demand
for a book
that would contain
the complete story.
Mr. Gould
talked it over
with the late
Joseph Bray,
then head of
McClurg's
publishing department,
who immediately saw
its tremendous
possibilities.
McClurg published it
in 1914
and it was
an instant success.
Mr. Burroughs
found himself famous
overnight.
Succeeding Tarzan
books
became best sellers,
too,
as soon as
they were published.
The last
Tarzan book,
"Tarzan and the
Foreign Legion,"
was published
three years ago.
Mr. Burroughs
was the author
of thirty-five
other books
of adventure stories,
and hundreds of
short stories.
He set up
his own
publishing company
in southern California
some years ago;
it is located in a town
called Tarzana.

How was your comprehension? ☐good ☐fair ☐poor

Perception Exercise 31

Continue as before.

THE IMPROVEMENT OF EYE MOVEMENTS
by Ruth Strang

↓ ↓ ↓

Good eye movements	or the violin.	and so on
underlie	In order to understand	until they reach
efficient reading.	how to train the eyes,	the end of the line.
Poor eye movements	it is first necessary	The movement of the
are signs of	to learn how	eyes along the lines
lack of skill	they are used	of print
in reading.	in reading.	is somewhat like
Accordingly,	As you read	the movement
we should understand	a line of print,	of an automobile
how the eyes work	your eyes	down a street
and how to make them	are not moving smoothly	with traffic lights—
work better.	and steadily	with many
The eyes	across the page.	stops and starts
can be trained.	Rather,	in its progress.
With the right kind	they move	During the movement
of training,	"by fits and starts"—	from one pause to
they become	they make	another, no words
more efficient	a swift movement,	are recognized.
just as the fingers	pause,	The printed line
become more skillful	make another	is a blur
with practice	swift movement,	because the eye moves
on the piano	pause again,	like a flash

From *Study Type of Reading Exercises*. Reprinted with permission. Dr. Strang is Professor of Education at Teachers College, Columbia University, and Director of the High School and College Reading Center of Teachers College. She is the author of numerous books and articles on reading improvement.

232

↓

between stops.
There is not time
to see the words clearly.
Only about 6 per cent
of the total time
of reading
is spent in movement.
It is
during the pauses
that we comprehend
the meaning
of the printed words.
Even the pauses
are only about
one-fourth of a second
in length,
but that is long enough
to take in
an "eyeful" of words.
A good reader may pause
only four times
in reading a line
on which a poor reader
may make nine pauses.
The more pauses,
of course,
the slower is the rate
of reading.
The good reader
may be able
to recognize
four or five words

↓

in a single pause;
the poor reader only one.
The number of pauses
per line
also depends
on the difficulty
of the material
and the purpose
for which
we are reading it.
Stories and other
easy material
which we read
just for pleasure
can be understood
with very few pauses
per line, while
mathematics problems
and other
difficult material
which we must study
require a larger number
of pauses per line.
These facts about
eye movements
were discovered
by taking
moving pictures
of the eyes of people
who were reading.
The pictures
show clearly

↓

how many pauses
each person's eyes made
as he read,
and whether his eyes
often moved backward
along the line of print.
You can see for yourself
how one's eyes work
when he reads,
by making
the following
experiment:
Punch a small hole
in the center
of a separate page
of print.
Then ask your friend
to hold the sheet
at a comfortable
reading distance
from his eyes.
Put one eye
to the little hole
in the sheet
and watch his eyes
as he reads.
Count the number
of times
his eyes pause
on each line.
See whether his eyes
sometimes move back

↓   ↓   ↓

across the line
and how quickly
and accurately
his eyes sweep
from the end of one line
to the beginning
of the next line.
Few pauses,
no backward
movements,
and an accurate jump
from one line
to the next
are signs
of efficient reading.
Eye movements
cannot be improved
by thinking too much
about them.
To do so
might put us
in the state
of the centipede
that got mixed up
as soon as it began
to think about
which leg
to move first.
The best way
to improve
eye movements
is to read

a good deal
of interesting material
with keen attention.
Such reading,
with no attention
to the mechanics
of eye movements,
trains the eyes.
For example,
in reading a paragraph,
it is better to think
of its meaning
than to wonder
how many pauses
our eyes are making.
If we eagerly
read material
that is not
too difficult for us
our eyes
naturally take in
a group of words
at each pause.
The eyes are not checked
in their
forward movement
by lack of
comprehension.
Nor do they
have to go back
over the line
to pick up the meaning

of some of the words.
Reading many easy
interesting books
is the best way
to improve
eye movements.
A second way
of increasing
the number of words
we can take in
at a single pause
of the eyes
is to use
the daily newspaper
for practice material.
The newspaper column
is so narrow
that good readers
can get the meaning
of a line
by letting their eyes
rest on it
only once.
An attempt to grasp
the meaning
of this short line
by means of
only one pause
gives excellent practice
in increasing the number
of words recognized
at each stop.

↓　　　　　　　　↓　　　　　　　　↓

A third way of learning
to take in the meaning
of a phrase or clause
rather than
of single words
is to use
practice cards
which we can make
ourselves.
These cards may be
three by five inches
in size.
In the center
of each card
we may either type
one or more words
or paste words
cut from magazines.
The first set of cards
may have one word
on each;

the second set,
two words;
and so on up to
five or six words.
We may ask someone
to hold the cards
at a comfortable distance
from our eyes
and uncover each card
for about one-fourth
of a second.
In that short time,
we should try
to recognize
the words on it.
At first,
we may be able
to recognize
only one or two words
in a quick glance.
Some students

like to use
a small notebook
for this kind of drill.
They type
a group of words
on each page
and practice getting
the meaning
of the words
as they quickly turn
each page.
If we can get the meaning
of three or four words
together,
quick as a flash,
we can take in
a line of print
rapidly
and are well on our way
toward becoming
good readers.

How was your comprehension? □good □fair □poor

Perception Exercise 32

And now, finally, practice on reading narrow columns of solid text by going as rapidly as you can without loss of comprehension. Fixate at the broad black arrow as you sweep down each column, depending on your peripheral vision to bring you the extremities of each line. (For full instructions, see page 230.)

ON A MAGAZINE COVER

by Bennett Cerf

Have you ever entertained the notion that editing a magazine would be just your dish? If so, this little piece is intended to give you pause. No job in the world offers a surer and quicker promise of a first-class case of stomach ulcers, and if you don't believe me, you have only to take a canvass of all the dyspeptic specimens now extant.

Finding new writers and artists, and then holding onto them, avoiding libel and plagiarism suits, fighting the inroads of eager beavers in the advertising department, and getting copy to the printer on time for every issue are only part of their problem. They must also live under the perpetual fear that something is going to happen while a number is on press or about to hit the stands that will make one of their leading articles —perhaps the one featured on the cover —look ridiculous.

Especially vulnerable, of course, are the news magazines— not to mention the motion picture "fan" periodicals, which often come out with rapturous descriptions of the idyllic home life of two famous Hollywood love-birds a day or so after said love-birds have hit the front page with a super-colossal free-for-all in a night club, and marched off to the divorce courts.

The day after the Jap raid on Pearl Harbor, one of our best-known magazines appeared with a lead article designed to prove that Hawaii never could be attacked successfully. And just when our unprepared and pitifully inadequate forces were being knocked silly by Japanese aviators, another periodical was featuring a piece of an "expert" who proved conclusively that the Japs were worthless as air fighters because their planes were antiquated puddle-jumpers, their pilots were cock-eyed, and their bombs were duds.

Some years ago, an enterprising editor bagged a piece by a noted octogenarian which gave in details his secrets of longevity. Unfortunately, the day before the article appeared the octogenarian dropped dead. Another editor lined up eight pages of colored photographs of the accession to the throne of King Edward VIII, and a description of same by the highest-paid journalist in Britain. The editor was correcting proofs

From *Shake Well Before Using,* Simon and Schuster, New York. Reprinted with permission.

236

when his wife called out, "Hurry up if you want to hear Edward abdicate over the radio."

In August, 1914, a magazine featured an article about the Kaiser, calling it "The World's Greatest Peace Advocate." When it appeared, German soldiers were already tramping through the towns of Belgium. In October, 1929, a big financial digest devoted most of an issue to a widely bullish interpretation of the market. It reached the stands during the greatest Wall Street crash in history. In April, 1947, another periodical printed Leo Durocher's picture on its cover, and hailed him as one of baseball's indispensables. Manager Durocher, unfortunately, had just been suspended from his job as manager of the Brooklyn Dodgers for the entire season. These were in no sense "boners" on the part of the editors involved; they simply were tough breaks, and there are dozens more like them on the records.

The great newspaper cartoonist, Jay Darling ("Ding"), made a drawing in 1935 labeled "The Fates Are Funny That Way," depicting a whole series of national calamities; earthquakes, floods, and train wrecks— but in the concluding panel he showed Mr. Public complaining to his wife, "Yet nothing ever seems to happen to Huey Long!" Three days later, Long was assassinated. One Western paper, in fact, received Ding's cartoon a bit late, and ran it and the story of Long's death in adjoining columns.

During the war, edition after edition of the big news weeklies had to be ripped apart at the last moment because of some sudden and spectacular happening. Even now, the editors of these weeklies spend the twenty-four hours before press time praying that nothing will occur to necessitate a complete reshuffling of an issue's contents. Their wives see them, if at all, by television. One of them hasn't spent a

week-end away from his office since he came down with pneumonia trying to catch pictures of a fight between a flounder and a soft shell crab.

Do you still yearn to be a magazine editor? Or maybe you'd like to try your hand as a circulation manager! Listen to the sad tale of one of them.

At enormous expense, he installed a complicated machine that isolated all the index plates of patrons whose subscriptions were going to run out in five or six weeks. It automatically printed their names and addresses at the tops of one of those irresistible form letters that begin "Surely you are not going to allow yourself to miss a single issue, etc., etc.," sealed and stamped the envelopes, and dropped them in a chute without human hands even so much as touching them. The circulation manager was so proud of this machine that he wrote a long article about it and hailed the company that built it as

↓ ↓ ↓

a benefactor of humanity.

Unfortunately, the machine went out of kilter one day this summer, and before the slip-up was discovered, a baffled rancher in Montana received 11,834 letters telling him his subscription was about to expire. The local postmaster had to hire a special truck to deliver them all. When the ranger succeeded in digging himself out from under, he wrote to the magazine, "I give up! A check for five dollars, renewing my subscription, is enclosed herewith."

With or without their editors, the magazines march on!

Did you follow the thinking of this selection? Then check the main idea.

1. Magazine editors are a rather scatter-brained lot.
2. Magazine editors have special and peculiar problems (largely in relation to "timing") that make their lives particularly trying.
3. A magazine editor's problems are harder than those of a circulation manager.
4. Despite the editors, magazines still manage to survive.
5. Don't become an editor.

Key: Subtract seven from eight, add one.

Perception Exercise 33

Proceed as before.

WHAT? YOU A QUIZ CLANSMAN?
by Murray Robinson

↓ ↓ ↓

A customer walked into a neighborhood candy store in Brooklyn and said: "I want a pint of coffee ice cream."

The proprietor, a party named Max, deftly cracked a pistachio nut, spat out the shell, chewed, swallowed, and replied: "If I had coffee flavor, wouldn't I give *you?* What am I in business for?"

The customer, who could take a hint,

From the New York *World-Telegram and Sun.* Reprinted with permission. Mr. Robinson is a staff writer for the *World-Telegram and Sun.*

said: "All right, butter pecan'll do."

Max cracked another pistachio and looked dolefully at the customer.

"Does anybody around this here neighborhood ever want butter pecan?" he answered. "Why should I keep butter pecan if I couldn't sell a pint, even, in a whole month?"

The customer reared. "Who wants to hear your troubles?" he demanded. "Don't you think I have troubles of my own?"

Max looked at him with sudden interest and respect. The customer was now speaking his language—questions, nothing but questions.

"You think you got troubles?" Max asked heatedly, but with evident relish. "Did you ever try THIS lousy business? Do customers want something I got in stock? Why do they always want something I ain't got?"

Max's wife, who had been arranging halvah on the counter, cracked a pistachio loudly for attention.

"Max," she said, "are you forgetting what the doctor said? Why do you have to get so excited?"

The customer departed, and, as he walked away, he tallied the score. Max had spoken three times. Nothing but questions. His wife had spoken once—and had asked two. And the customer himself had fallen into the question habit after two affirmative statements.

Max and his wife are but two members of a strange cult spread all over New York City—the Quiz Clan. They're the people who answer questions with other questions. Under peril of losing their franchise, they never make a flat statement.

This phenomenon makes strangers blow their gaskets, but the clan members consider it a test of wit, a delicate fencing game.

Take two sportsmen of the Quiz Clan who meet at the races. Their conversation goes like this:

First Sportsman: You woikin'?

Second Sportsman: Me woikin'? **You** woikin'?

First Sportsman: Doin' yourself **any** good?

Second Sportsman: Who does any good **in** this here swindle?

First Sportsman: You comin' out tomorrow?

Second Sportsman: How else can I get even?

The all-quiz, no-answer system is used effectively by the girls. Here's a recent sample conversation between two subway riders who apparently hadn't seen each other in some time:

"You take the express?"

"Why should I take the express and get suffocated? The local isn't fast enough?"

"Don't you have to get in by nine?"

"Does HE get in by nine? So how will he know if I don't? Where you working now?"

"Did you forget already?"

"In the same place?"

"Is it so unusual for a girl to hold a situation for a year?"

They were still matching questions

↓ ↓ ↓

when the local's clatter drowned out the quiz bee.

Every bus rider has met the driver with a card in the Quiz Clan, whose coat of arms is a large angry-red question mark rampant on a field of smaller bilious green question marks.

This driver always has a bus whose signs are coated with a month's grime. "Does this bus go to 42nd St.?" you ask him, peering futilely at the illegible sign.

And he always says: "Whatsamatter, Mac, can't you read?"

Cops guarding a parade route usually qualify for membership in the clan. Some old lady always totters up to one of them and asks: "Is there a parade?"

The cop looks at her steadily and answers: "What do YOU think, lady?"

Did you follow the thinking of this selection? Then check the main idea.

1. Some people never answer any questions.
2. In New York, members of the Quiz Clan always answer questions with other questions.
3. There is something wrong with people who never make an affirmative statement.
4. People in New York are cranky and difficult to get information from.

Key: Add one and three, subtract two, to determine the number of the correct answer.

★ SESSION 19

VOCABULARY STUDY IV

Words for Today

1. ameliorate
2. cajole
3. castigate
4. cavil
5. cogitate
6. condone
7. emulate
8. eschew
9. expostulate (with)
10. extirpate
11. fulminate (against)
12. harass

240

13. immolate
14. impugn
15. inure (to)
16. militate (against)

17. mulct
18. preclude
19. presage
20. propitiate

First, check those words with which you are completely or partially unfamiliar. Look these up in your dictionary, taking notes on (a) meaning, (b) part of speech, (c) related forms, (d) derivation, and (e) sample phrases where these are given. Pronounce each word aloud, and write your own illustrative phrase or sentence.

Next, study your notes in preparation for the following tests.

Test Your Learning

I. From the list above choose the word that most closely fits each of the following definitions. Write your answer in the space provided for that purpose.

1. avoid; stay away from _____
2. punish in order to correct _____
3. condemn loudly and vehemently _____
4. call into doubt; challenge as untrue _____
5. think deeply _____
6. work (against) _____
7. cheat (of) by trickery _____
8. reason seriously with in order to dissuade _____
9. persuade by flattery _____
10. prevent from happening _____
11. attempt to equal _____
12. foreshadow _____
13. overlook (an error or offense) _____
14. make more friendly or favorable _____
15. torment; persecute pettily _____
16. criticize slashingly _____
17. sacrifice; offer or kill as a sacrifice _____
18. make impossible _____
19. predict _____
20. find fault over trifles _____
21. accustom (to something unpleasant) _____
22. imitate in order to equal _____
23. improve; make better _____
24. remove or destroy completely _____
25. coax _____

II. Write the noun form of each verb.

1. ameliorate _____   11. fulminate _____
2. cajole _____   12. harass _____
3. castigate _____   13. immolate _____
4. cavil _____   14. impugn _____
5. cogitate _____   15. inure _____
6. condone _____   16. militate _____
7. emulate _____   17. preclude _____
8. eschew _____   18. presage _____
9. expostulate _____   19. propitiate _____
10. extirpate _____

Key:

I. 1. eschew, 2. castigate, 3. fulminate, 4. impugn, 5. cogitate, 6. militate, 7. mulct, 8. expostulate, 9. cajole, 10. preclude, 11. emulate, 12. presage, 13. condone, 14. propitiate, 15. harass, 16. castigate, 17. immolate, 18. preclude, 19. presage, 20. cavil, 21. inure, 22. emulate, 23. ameliorate, 24. extirpate, 25. cajole

II. 1. amelioration, 2. cajolery, 3. castigation, 4. cavil, 5. cogitation, 6. condonation, 7. emulation, 8. eschewal, 9. expostulation, 10. extirpation, 11. fulmination, 12. harassment, 13. immolation, 14. impugnment, or impugnation, 15. inurement, 16. militation, 17. preclusion, 18. presage, 19. propitiation

AN ANALYSIS OF YOUR ACCOMPLISHMENTS

The many-faceted training offered in this book involves a tremendous amount of learning, of very difficult learning. It demands the acquisition and refinement of a great number of new and complex skills. It continuously challenges you to exploit your innate, but perhaps dormant, talents. It sets ever higher (but always attainable) goals. It requires the sloughing off of inefficient, but wonderfully comfortable and long-familiar, habits of response, and the gradual development of new and more efficient responses that will, for a brief period, be somewhat uncomfortable. And, finally, it draws heavily on your time, your energy, and your capacity for self-discipline.

This is, indeed, as arduous and intensive—but also as rewarding and fruitful—a learning experience as you are ever likely to undergo.

And so, now that your formal training is more than half over, let us pause to draw up a kind of balance sheet of your progress to date, of what you have accomplished and have not yet accomplished, of your successes and your failures.

In column I of the chart below you will find a fairly complete list of the goals you have been attempting to reach during your training. In column II are pertinent and searching questions that explore how successfully you have reached them—answer these questions in writing, and as honestly and objectively as you can. And in column III check the word that fairly assesses your accomplishment to date. Then, when you have filled out this chart, you will have a graphic appraisal of your progress so far—you will be able to tell at a glance where your weaknesses and strengths lie, in what areas you must invest more time and practice, where you need to devote more effort, and in what aspects of reading you have made the most improvement.

GOAL	QUESTIONS	YOUR EVALUATION OF ACCOMPLISHMENT
1. Increase in general speed	Do you now consciously and deliberately move faster through material than you were formerly in the habit of doing? ☐*yes* ☐*no* How much faster do you now read than you did on selection 1? _____w.p.m. (*See page 11.*) What is the percentage of your gain? _____%	☐Poor ☐Fair ☐Good ☐Spectacular
2. Greater efficiency of comprehension	Do you actively distinguish supporting, clarifying, etc., details from main concepts as you read? ☐*yes* ☐*no* Do you alertly follow an author's central theme? ☐*yes* ☐*no* Do you quickly sense the framework of thinking that shapes an author's presentation? ☐*yes* ☐*no*	☐Poor ☐Fair ☐Good ☐Spectacular

GOAL	QUESTIONS	YOUR EVALUATION OF ACCOMPLISHMENT
3. Decrease of fixation time	Do you feel any greater skill in reacting instantaneously to four- and five-digit combinations? □yes □no What score do you generally make out of 100 tries: on four-digit numbers? _____ on five-digit numbers? _____ on individual words? _____	□Poor □Fair □Good □Spectacular
4. Enlargement of recognition span	Do you respond accurately to disconnected phrase-units in single Flashmeter exposures? □yes □no Do you feel that you can run down a column of connected phrases in single fixations and with good comprehension? □yes □no	□Poor □Fair □Good □Spectacular
5. Greater use of your peripheral vision	Can you fixate at the center of a narrow column of continuous text and read down with good comprehension? □yes □no	□Poor □Fair □Good □Spectacular
6. Decreased reliance on inner speech	Can you read through a selection rapidly with less awareness of the individual words than of the ideas and thoughts they add up to? □yes □no Can you do the digit exercises without repeating the numbers you see? □yes □no	□Poor □Fair □Good □Spectacular
7. Elimination of lip movements, whispering, and other vocal or motor responses	Are your lips absolutely motionless when you read? □yes □no Are all other parts of your vocal apparatus completely quiet? □yes □no Do you ever feel hoarse after a	□Poor □Fair □Good □Spectacular

GOAL	QUESTIONS	

long stretch of reading? ☐*yes* ☐*no*

8. Elimination of unnecessary regressions and by this means the improvement of the smooth flow of meaning	Do you have enough faith in your comprehension to read always forward even if you occasionally miss an unimportant point, word, or phrase? ☐*yes* ☐*no* Do you have to go back frequently to check on figures, punctuation, or words? ☐*yes* ☐*no*	☐Poor ☐Fair ☐Good ☐Spectacular
9. Deeper and more immediate concentration	Can you jump right into material in pursuit of central meaning? ☐*yes* ☐*no* Do you think along with the author, actively and directly participating in the ideas he presents to you? ☐*yes* ☐*no*	☐Poor ☐Fair ☐Good ☐Spectacular
10. Better retention	Have you made a creditable score on the two retention tests (pages 48 and 123)? ☐*yes* ☐*no* Is your understanding of most of what you read strong enough for you to hold it in your mind and recall it when asked to? ☐*yes* ☐*no*	☐Poor ☐Fair ☐Good ☐Spectacular
11. More time, especially longer blocks of continuous time, spent on reading	Have you attempted to read a full novel in a single sitting? ☐*yes* ☐*no* Do you, when you sit down with a novel, set yourself a high but reasonable goal of so many pages an hour, so many hours for the complete book? ☐*yes* ☐*no*	☐Poor ☐Fair ☐Good ☐Spectacular

245

GOAL	QUESTIONS	
	Have you been able to meet such goals? ☐*yes* ☐*no* Have you read at least three novels in this way since you started your training? ☐*yes* ☐*no* What are the titles of these novels? 1) _____ ; 2) _____ ; 3) _____ ;	
12. Improvement of reading vocabulary	Have you directly studied a large number of new words by actual reference to the dictionary? ☐*yes* ☐*no* Name of your dictionary: _____	☐Poor ☐Fair ☐Good ☐Spectacular
	Can you, without referring to previous pages, think of ten new words you've learned? (1) _____ (2) _____ (3) _____ (4) _____ (5) _____ (6) _____ (7) _____ (8) _____ (9) _____ (10) _____	
13. Self-discipline (The more you develop this ability, the more time you will be able to spend on reading after your training is over.)	Have you spent a half-hour to an hour most days of the week, or, alternatively, one to two hours twice or three times a week, on your training? ☐*yes* ☐*no* Do you methodically continue your training with no wide gaps, or do you pick this book up only sporadically? ☐*methodically* ☐*sporadically*	☐Poor ☐Fair ☐Good ☐Spectacular

246

14. Pleasure in reading	Are you beginning to find greater enjoyment in the printed page? □yes □no Do you get more stimulation from reading than you used to? □yes □no	□Poor □Fair □Good □Spectacular

As you glance over your appraisals in column III you should, if you are at all like the typical adult who embarks on a long and intensive learning program, find that you have checked off a few "Poors," a slightly larger number of "Fairs," a still larger number of "Goods," and an occasional "Spectacular." Let's make a graph of your self-evaluations so that we can see the results in a continuous profile:

SELF-EVALUATION GRAPH

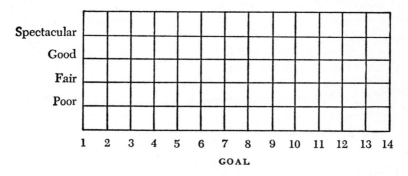

If you compare your performance six months or a year from now with your performance before you picked up this book, the over-all, long-run change will be tremendous. But don't expect a revolution overnight. If you set for yourself such goals as are easily attainable, you will, on the one hand, avoid a feeling of frustration or discouragement; and, on the other, you will receive a growing sense of satisfaction, assurance, and success. Don't, for example, try to double your speed immediately; don't expect to stretch your perception span from four digits to five digits in one quick session; don't try to eliminate *all* vocalization, lip movements, regressions, and inner speech at one big jump; don't, in short, aim to become an expert reader in five easy lessons. Take it easy, give yourself enough time

247

and practice, and get there by short stages. When you achieve your final goal by these short, sure steps, your achievement will be permanent and efficient; rapid reading will finally be habitual and effortless.

Take your time and work for the long pull. It is impossible for a person of normal intelligence, no matter what his age, *not* to show improvement in a skill if he keeps practicing regularly under guidance. It is impossible for you *not* to increase your reading efficiency and speed if you apply the guiding principles in this book regularly and patiently. Be a sufficiently strict taskmaster to keep yourself at your training sessions every day, or nearly every day; but do not be so unreasonable a taskmaster as to demand immediate success.

Be satisfied with a 25 to 50 per cent increase in speed at this point in your work; be elated if you have decreased any tendencies to vocalization, motor responses, or regressions; feel triumphant if you have begun to look for main ideas and to sense structure in much of the reading you do; and so on, right down the line.

So let us catalogue the general progress you can reasonably expect to have made up to this point:

1. A new attitude to the main ideas and structure of material.

2. A decrease in regressions, vocalization, lip movements, and dependence on inner speech.

3. A 25–50 per cent gain in speed of general reading.

4. Greater ease in perceiving full phrases in single fixations.

5. The development of regular habits of work and practice.

6. The ability to cover an average-length novel in an evening of concentrated reading.

7. Freedom from word-by-word reading, from enslavement to the unimportant words and minor points of material.

8. More immediate concentration and improved retention.

9. And, finally, a growing realization that your *potential* reading ability is far better than your performance before training may have indicated.

One more point, now, before you resume your training. Occasionally, during your work, you will find yourself on what we might call a "performance plateau." That is, you will continue to apply yourself to a problem (say speed, digit- or phrase-perception, use of peripheral vision, pursuit of central theme, response to structure, etc.) as earnestly and as enthusiastically as ever, but your performance will apparently not improve to any measurable degree. These plateaus are temporary—they almost invariably occur in every extended learning process—they are no cause for discouragement—and they usually vanish as suddenly as they appeared. During a plateau, you are refining and integrating new learning, or are consolidating your previous gains—your mind is not quite ready to translate what it has absorbed into actual performance. It is as if you were filling your tanks with fuel while the motor idles, or as if your body were digesting the food you have eaten before transforming it into energy or assimilating it into the blood supply for growth and repair of tissues. When the fuel is all aboard (to continue the analogy), the wheels will start to turn again; when the food is broken down into its nutrients, your body will start distributing it to the proper organs; when the learning is integrated and refined, the performance plateau will disappear. And since refinement and integration of learning and consolidation of gains are largely an unconscious process, the only thing you can do to hurry the ending of a plateau is continue intelligent and purposeful practice while maintaining your enthusiasm and desire at a high pitch.

CHAPTER 8

HOW TO SKIM

Some material must be read more or less thoroughly, some only for the over-all ideas; and some can, and should be, skimmed. In this chapter:

• You get intensive instruction in skimming.

• You learn how the technique is applied to specific selections, in various circumstances, and to suit certain needs and purposes.

• You are challenged to read a complete issue of your favorite magazine in a single evening.

Almost all reading can be skimmed here and there; *chapter 8* tells you when and where, shows you how.

★ SESSION 20

REASONS FOR SKIMMING

You have now come far enough in your training, you have now sufficiently sharpened your comprehension and perception skills, to be ready to use one of the most effective weapons in the arsenal of the rapid, efficient reader.

That weapon is *skimming*.

Why should one skim? When is skimming necessary? When is it useful? When is it, on the other hand, undesirable? What does one gain, and what does one lose, by skimming? Are there various degrees or extents of skimming?

These questions are worth exploring.

To begin with, let us understand that the trained reader *always skims to a slight degree*. He does this by paying very little attention to, by practically ignoring, unimportant, linking words—words like *the, a, for, with, to, on, it, and, is, was,* etc. You yourself, if you have increased your speed by 25 per cent or more, and if you now read over 300 w.p.m., more or less engage in this kind of skimming without, perhaps, even being aware of it.

For example, let me present to you a few sentences that will sound familiar, sentences from which the unimportant, linking words have been omitted:

> . . . 2 a.m. hot August night. San Francisco suburb, man lurched out of bar, into car, roared northward 80 miles hour. Before police stop drink-crazed driver, crashed another car, sent six persons hospital.

(These sentences look familiar because they are the opening lines of material you've already read—selection 15, page 220.)

Now this sentence-structure may look peculiar, because ideas are not usually expressed in such telegraphic style—but you cannot deny that there is exactly as much meaning in these lines as you would get from them if the unimportant, almost meaningless words were restored:

> *It was* 2 a.m. *on a* hot August night. *In a* San Francisco suburb, *a* man lurched out of *a* bar *and* into *his* car, *and* roared northward *at* 80 miles *an* hour. Before police *could* stop *the* drink-crazed driver *he had* crashed *into* another car *and* sent six persons *to the* hospital.

Yet 21 words out of the 54, approximately 40 per cent of the content, have been eliminated! The percentage of unimportant words varies considerably, of course, from sentence to sentence and line to line in all material, but such is the nature of our language that it is rarely less than 20 to 30 per cent. (In Latin, on the contrary, there are no words to correspond to *the, a,* or *an,* pronouns are almost always omitted, and most other linking elements are indicated by the endings of the major words.)

So, if you read efficiently and rapidly, you skim at least 20 per cent of all material without thinking further about it. In all your phrase-perception exercises you are forced to ignore unimportant words in order to respond to the meaning of a phrase in a single, split-second fixation. And in those exercises in which you attempt to train your peripheral vision, you again, without perhaps realizing it, skim through rapidly, concentrating your mental responses only on the meaningful terms, on the words that actually express thoughts and ideas.

Slight skimming, then, is no stranger to you—you've been doing it for weeks during your training, perhaps for years if you were a fairly efficient reader before you started this course. You are slightly skimming right now if you are reading this page with any skill.

But there are two other degrees of skimming—*partial skimming,* in which you go through a selection picking up mainly the central theme, the significant details that develop and clarify the theme, and only as much additional material as you want or need; and *complete skimming,* in which you read *only* for the gist or final meaning, skipping all details, all clarification and development, all illustrations, examples, and statistics, and restricting yourself largely to the opening lines and, occasionally, the closing sentence, of each paragraph.

Slight skimming is reflexive, almost automatic. Partial and complete skimming, however, are conscious and deliberate—each type is used if it suits your purpose and if the material lends itself to such skimming.

Should you skim? I cannot imagine any efficient reader going through a long article or story, or a complete novel or book of nonfiction, who does not, at least occasionally, partially skim a page, a section, or a chapter. He does not do this in all articles or stories (although he does in most books), for sometimes the style is so delightful or the details so essential to his needs that he does not wish, or cannot afford, to skip a single meaningful word. (The unimportant, linking, words, as I have said, are skipped reflexively, except, perhaps, in the fine print of a contract or other legal document, or by a copy editor or proofreader.) And any person who efficiently

252

and skillfully does a good deal of reading, who (as I expect it will eventually be true of you) goes through several magazines and books a week, in addition to one or more daily newspapers, or whose profession requires him to read material most of his working day, frequently does a great deal of partial skimming—and finds that he misses nothing of crucial value.

Should you skim? By all means. You should partially skim whenever you feel that the dictates of time, the structure of the material, and the needs that you are satisfying by reading make such skimming valuable, useful, or necessary. And you should skim with a clear conscience, for skillful skimming does not in any way deprive you of the total, final meaning that all your reading aims at. Indeed, there are times when partial skimming may aid comprehension. If material is so long-drawn-out, or so overfull of minor details, illustrations, and background information, that the author's main idea is becoming obscured and you are in danger of losing the essence of his communication, then partial skimming is useful, even necessary, for an accurate grasp and retention of the significant points.

Complete skimming, on the other hand, is a valuable tool only under certain special circumstances. If time is absolutely of the essence, if you have no more than a few minutes to devote to a long article, story, report, or other piece of writing from which you wish to extract only the final meaning, the bare plot, or the main points, then you necessarily skim it completely. You lose the flavor, the atmosphere, the details, the explanations, the background, and many other things—but these are things you either do not want or need, or are willing, under the circumstances, to sacrifice.

Such skimming is useful also as a means of reviewing. When your recollection of the main points or gist of material must be refreshed some time after an original reading—perhaps for a test or for an oral report—complete skimming can produce efficient recall in minimum time and with minimum effort and maximum success.

As a person training to develop the greatest degree of reading skill that your capacities permit, you will want to learn how to skim successfully so that you can use this technique whenever the exigencies of time or circumstances require it, or whenever your own needs or desires dictate its use.

Possibly you will have to revise your attitudes about writing before you can happily adjust to doing a certain amount of skimming whenever you read. Do you feel guilty if you do not read *every* word an author has written? Do you consider every author such a consummate stylist, or so economical and concise in his presentation, that every sentence, every thought, every paragraph is indispensable, supremely important? Or are you so diffident about your ability to comprehend that you don't trust your competence in sorting an author's chaff from his wheat? Or, finally, are you too conservative in your approach to material to take short cuts or to rely on time- and work-saving devices? I doubt that you would still answer any of these questions in the affirmative after the extensive practice you have had in stripping a page down to its essentials—but if you would, some successful experiences with skimming should change your feelings.

PRINCIPLES OF SKIMMING

What is skimming?

To skim milk, you take the cream, the richest part, off the top of the bottle.

To skim reading material, you extract the important parts—that is, the main points and the significant details; but you have to extract these where you find them, which is not necessarily at the top.

Skimming, then, is getting the essence of material without reading all of it—it involves judicious and selective skipping of nonessential, or of less essential, matter.

You have been invited throughout this book to do a certain amount of skimming whenever you felt so inclined; you have been asked to skim a little in novels and in a book of nonfiction in order to meet a time schedule. If you have already attempted to skim on your own, without detailed guidance or instruction (and I hope that you have), you are psychologically and intellectually well prepared to start using the technique more extensively.

Let us go back to the article on traffic-court justice in chapter 7 and see how it might have been skimmed efficiently and successfully. Refer to selection 15, page 220, and follow along with me as we skim through the piece.

Paragraphs 1–4 contain narrative incidents showing how lightly the traffic courts are punishing serious offenders. How much of this do you actually read? Comparatively little. You know that narrative details in a nonfiction piece are not important for themselves, but serve only to illustrate a point, so you skim rapidly through the details of the crash, the arrest, the medical examination, etc., in the first two paragraphs. You pick up the important question and answer that open paragraph 3 (*Is that driver now in jail? Hardly.*) and then skip down to the last line (*slap-on-the-wrist license suspension*) to realize what point is being illustrated (light punishment). The beginning of paragraph 4 indicates further incidents, so again you skip down to the final line or two (*$75 fine, walked out . . . a free man*) to realize that the same point is being reiterated. The beginning of paragraph 5 tells you that nothing new will be added here, so you drop down to paragraph 6, where you soon recognize that the central theme is being expressed. You read this entire paragraph, and also all of paragraph 7, where you recognize further central theme material.

Now, by full reading of only two paragraphs out of seven, you have the central theme as far as it has been expressed. Paragraph 8 opens with *How far this has gone is demonstrated . . .* , so you know that this paragraph will contain further supporting details. You skip down to paragraph 9, recognize from the first two words (*In Detroit . . .*) that support is continuing, and skip the rest of that paragraph. In paragraph 10, a similar opening (*In Syracuse . . .*) shows more support, so you drop down to paragraph 11, where the first few words (*Behind this urge to penalize parking lies . . .*) indicate a shift in pattern from *examples* to *causes.* You read paragraphs 11 and 12 fairly fully to pick up the causes of the problem, and then continue skimming, by reading only the opening lines or sentences, through paragraph 21, for you recognize quickly, from the beginning of each of these paragraphs, that this whole section of the material will only add support to, or substantiation of, what you have already learned.

In paragraph 22, the comprehension clue is the word *different.* If *Chicago has had a different experience* you know that something new is coming. So you read most of paragraphs 22 through 25, picking up the rest of the central theme—*the way Chicago has solved the problem.*

Paragraphs 26 and 27 are quickly recognized, from the opening lines, as elaboration on the Chicago solution, so you skip down to the last paragraph, which of course you read fully, since it is a recapitulation, in brief, of the entire article.

How much of the total piece have you read? Out of the 28 paragraphs you've given a more or less thorough reading to only 9 (paragraphs 1, 2, 11, 12, 22–25, and 28)—the rest you've skimmed, reading only the opening (or, occasionally, the closing) lines or sentences.

This was fairly complete skimming, yet you've extracted all the significant information—the problem, the causes of the problem, the solutions that have worked.

When you can readily distinguish main ideas from details, and when you can accurately sense the pattern of an author's presentation, you can successfully skim, to whatever extent you wish, any piece of writing that is readily skimmable.

The extent to which you skim, how much you leave out and how much you read, you yourself will determine according to what the writing contains and what you wish to get out of it. And whether or not you skim also depends on the nature, style, and content of the material and on what your purpose is in reading it. Some writing is so meaty, so complex, so difficult, or so pleasurable that there is no point in doing any skimming at all (other than the slight, reflexive, skimming that I have mentioned). Some material, on the contrary, has so little to say, and says it so lengthily, that it is a sheer waste not to skim. And some material can, and should, be skimmed in certain parts, but read thoroughly, even leisurely, even somewhat slowly and carefully, in other parts. Sometimes you will feel in the mood to skim partially or fairly completely; at other times, you will prefer, out of either need or desire, to read quite thoroughly.

Skimming, then, is a tool you use with discretion. You use it when you want to, when you have to, or when the limitation of time or the character of the material suggests it. Skimming, in short, is a kind of reserve high gear that you shift into whenever circumstances make it useful.

When you decide to skim, these are the principles you follow:

1. Read only as much of each paragraph as you have to in order to discover whether it contains details or a main idea. This may mean reading one or more of the opening sentences or possibly no further than the first few words.

2. If the opening line or lines indicate that a paragraph will express or extend a main idea, or that it will contain other material of importance to you, read it completely.

3. If it appears, on the contrary, that a paragraph is made up only of details that illustrate, clarify, support, or elaborate on what you already know, skim it.

4. Sometimes the main idea of a piece is expressed at the *end* of one of the opening paragraphs, all the details leading up to it. So it may be necessary, at the beginning, to read also the *last* sentence or two of each paragraph.

5. Try to sense the author's pattern of thinking. What you are doing in skimming is clearing away all the padding, all the superstructure, and getting down to the basic framework—you are, in a manner of speaking, pulling off all the flesh and laying bare the skeleton. It is only the basic framework, the skeleton, that you're interested in when you do complete skimming. When you do partial skimming, you read in addition any details you consider significant and anything else that interests you.

6. When you skim to any extent you often do not read complete sentences. If you are pretty sure, from your total involvement in, and accurate understanding of, what an author has been saying, that you know what the tag end of a sentence will contain, skip along to the next sentence.

7. Read thoroughly all paragraphs containing expressions of the main idea. The first few paragraphs usually (but not always) either set up, or lead to, the central theme, and the closing paragraphs often recapitulate the main points that the author has been making, so pay particular attention to these. And, of course, any number of paragraphs in the middle of material may be important—if you stay alert to the author's pattern you will have no difficulty in discovering *these*.

8. Follow comprehension clues to discover whether material is continuing in the same vein or whether a change of pattern is occurring. Do the first few words indicate that more of the previous is coming? Then skip down to the next paragraph. Do the opening words suggest, on the contrary, that the author is about to express, repeat, or extend his main idea? Or that he is about to shift from introduction to development, or from development to recapitulation, or from facts to conclusions, or from narrative to interpreta-

257

tion? Or that he is beginning a whole new section, moving, say, from the cause of the problem to the solution, or from a description of a study or experiment to the results or findings? Then you will read thoroughly, skimming and skipping again when you come to paragraphs of details or of unessential information.

Skimming, I have said, is getting the essence of material without reading all of it. To decide what parts to read and what parts to skip, you rely on two things: your ability to sense the pattern of a writer's presentation; and, through this, your recognition of what is important to the writer's basic message and what is considerably less important.

PRACTICE IN SKIMMING

Let us apply our eight principles of skimming to a number of selections.

You will notice that somewhat less than half of the material in Exercise 1 is printed in boldface (heavy black) type. *Read only the boldface print—skip all the rest.*

Skimming Exercise 1

"BENEFITS" FOR BIG BOYS
by Sylvia F. Porter

R.A. is one of the policy-making vice presidents of a nationally-known corporation which has made a lot of money in the last few years. If you saw his monthly paycheck, though, you would be surprised; you would expect the check to be much bigger considering the name of the company, the industry and his key job.

2. But R.A.'s paycheck would give you a badly distorted view of the actual financial setup. For in addition to a cash salary, R.A.'s company has just in the last five years given him:

3. A handsome expense account which covers virtually all his entertain-

---

(Reprinted, by permission, from the *New York Post*. Copyright 1956, The Hall Syndicate, Inc. Miss Porter is the financial columnist of the *Post*.)

ing, travel costs, etc. It also provides him with a new car every year and a beautiful vacation haven.

4. **A retirement program** under which he's already guaranteed $21,000 a year for life and his retirement benefits are steadily increasing.

5. **A special contract** retaining him as a "consultant" at $14,000 a year **for ten years** beginning when he's 65.

6. **A privilege to buy a big chunk of the company's stock** at a specified price at any time between now and 1965. The stock is now quoted at $40 above the price at which R.A. can buy (or has bought) the stock and his paper profits on the stock top a quarter-million dollars.

7. **So, if you added to R.A.'s cash salary all his "fringe benefits,"** you would find that in this era of stiff taxes on high incomes R.A. is not only building a major estate for his family; he also is in a position to move easily and comfortably in the so-called million-dollar circles of our land.

8. **Am I making this report on R.A. because he is so exceptional? Oh no!** The point is that R.A. is becoming less and less the exception.

9. **In corporation after corporation key officers are getting contracts and pay deals that rival or surpass the one R.A. has. As an illustration,** the magazine "Sales Management" made a survey of 50 leading corporations a short while ago, found only one in which the chief sales executive is compensated by salary alone.

10. **In corporation after corporation, top management men are being tied to their jobs for life by a "golden cord" of fringe benefits. The deals make the executives all but immune to offers from the companies' competitors** because the men would have to give up their impressively attractive benefits if they quit.

11. **What are some of the ways corporations are compensating key men —outside of cash? These:**

12. **A stock option deal.** Under this plan, a key employee gets the option to buy a specified total of the company's stock at a specified price during a specified period of years. If the stock soars during the period, he still can exercise his option at the fixed price; when and as he sells his shares, his gain will be taxed only at the capital gains rate, meaning at a top of 25 per cent. The profits of some men who have stock option deals run into millions of dollars!

13. **A deferred bonus arrangement.** Under this, the company votes the officer a bonus payable in installments over a number of years, thereby cutting his year-to-year tax liability. In some cases, the executive prefers (and will get) payment of his bonus after he retires.

14. **Handsome retirement programs.** Some contracts I've seen give executives really eye-popping incomes for life. In addition, many have contracts to remain as consultants at impressive salaries after 65.

259

15. **Rich insurance policies and fat expense accounts,** special health programs, profit-sharing arrangements, many other variations of benefits.

16. **The publicized statistics on the rate of rise in executives' salaries are meaningless unless the fringe benefits also are included.** It's becoming commonplace for top men to turn down flatly hikes in cash pay in favor of pay in forms which are subject to only moderate taxes.

17. **The cash paycheck of an American executive is less and less the yardstick of his financial well-being and it'll continue to be less and less so as his fringe benefits multiply.**

Let us see how we apply our skimming principles to this material.

The monthly pay check of a key executive, says Miss Porter in paragraphs 1 and 2, *is surprisingly small—but his cash salary is no indication of the actual financial setup.* All this is clearly central theme material, and you read most of it.

Then, from paragraphs 3 through 7, you skim by reading only opening lines, for this section of the article contains corroborating and illustrative details that support the statements made in the first two paragraphs.

The opening lines of paragraphs 8 and 9 state that R.A. is no exception; you skip to paragraph 10, in which the central theme is extended—*the fringe benefits, rather than the cash remuneration, keep executives tied to a corporation.*

Paragraph 11 is a guidepost that alerts you to coming explanatory details, and these you pick up by skimming paragraphs 12 through 15, realizing, as you read, that these details for the most part are a repetition of those found in paragraphs 3–7.

In paragraphs 16 and 17 you recognize a recapitulation of the total piece, including a restatement of the central theme, and so you read more or less fully.

Thus, having read, in full, only paragraphs 1, 2, 10, 11, 16, and 17 —six paragraphs out of seventeen—you have a clear understanding of what the author has said and of the pattern in which she has said it. *Fringe benefits, such as expense accounts, retirement programs, stock options, deferred bonuses, etc., are more the yardstick of remuneration to executives than their actual pay checks; and these keep the executives all but immune to offers from competitive corporations*—this is the gist of the piece. *Central theme; supporting details; extension of the theme; more details; recapitulation—*

this is the structure of the author's presentation, a structure to which you are keenly alert as you skim through the content.

What have you lost by partial skimming? A certain richness of detail and explanation, mainly, which you must expect to sacrifice whenever you skim—and very little else. If this richness were important to you, or if you had some special interest in every bit of information, no matter how minor, that the selection contained—why, then, of course, you would not skim it.

Skimming Exercise 2

Directions: Read, again, only the boldface print, analyzing, as you move along, why certain paragraphs are to be read more or less thoroughly, the rest only skimmed.

HOW TO CONCENTRATE BETTER
by T. E. Cochran, Ph.D.

Most of us realize the importance of concentration—that is, the giving of close attention to anything. But do we know how to improve ourselves in this connection? Also, are we willing to pay the price for this kind of improvement?

2. There can be no doubt that concentration helps us to remember more accurately, more fully, and more permanently. We have all learned from experience that when we give close attention to a sermon, a lecture, or anything we read, we can recall a rather large part of it, whereas without close attention we are able to recall but very little of what we have heard or read.

3. Most assuredly, it increases both the accuracy and speed of our movements. In reading or writing, for instance, we can do either more accurately and more rapidly by increasing the degree of our concentration.

4. Also, concentration begets interest in, and appreciation of, the finer things of life, such as music, painting, and literature. Without it one would never be interested in and enjoy the great music of such composers as Bach, Chopin, and Mozart, or the famous paintings of such artists as Rembrandt, Michelangelo, and Leonardo da Vinci, or the classical literature of such writers as Browning, Pope, and Shakespeare.

5. In fact, close attention increases our efficiency and enjoyment in

everything we do. It matters not what the activity is, whether it be reading a book, watching a sunset, listening to grand opera, learning a poem, writing an article, shooting at a target, playing golf, or making out our income tax report; if we are to do it well, and find enjoyment in it, we must give it close attention. Without close attention, we would not only waste much time and energy but would be only partially successful and by no means happy.

6. **"But how," you ask, "can I improve myself in attentive ability?" A good question, and here are a few suggestions.**

7. First, *avoid thinking of concentration, or attentive ability, as something beyond control.* To be sure, it is to some extent due to inheritance, but for the most part it is due to learning and training. For example, the artist will see things in a picture that the untrained person will miss, and the musician will notice features in a symphony that the untutored listener will overlook. If you are poor in attentive ability, it is not because you were born that way, but because you have not learned to concentrate.

8. Second, *try to rate as well as you can your ability to concentrate.* If you should find yourself somewhat lacking in this ability, this would probably serve as a stimulus to improvement.

9. **The degree of your power of concentration can be determined fairly well by the following test,** which consists of ten simple problems based upon familiar material, but of sufficient complexity to require continuous attention for quick solutions. If you can solve more than five of these correctly in eight minutes, you are above the average in concentration. Have someone time you so that you can give yourself fully to your work. Here are the problems:

1. Two different letters occur only once in the following proverb: "Be not wise in thy own eyes." Which is the second letter to occur?   ——

2. Four different letters occur only once in the following proverb: "A drowning man will grasp at straws." Which is the third letter to occur?   ——

3. Six different letters occur only once in this proverb: "No wind can do him good who steers for no port." Which is the fourth letter to occur?   ——

4. Seven different letters occur only once in this proverb: "Make hay while the sun shines." Which is the middle letter to occur?   ——

5. Write the letter that occurs the greatest number of times in this proverb: "A good name is rather to be chosen than great riches."   ——

6. Find the number of different letters that occur only once in this proverb: "Don't judge a book by its cover."   ——

7. What letter in *Constantinople* occurs just as far to the right of *C* as it does to the right of *a* in the alphabet?   ——

8. Write the letter that is the third letter to the right of the letter that is midway beween *N* and *R* in the alphabet. ____

9. Suppose the first and second letters of the alphabet were interchanged, also the third and fourth, the fifth and sixth, and so on. What would then be the nineteenth letter of the alphabet so formed? ____

10. A certain letter is the fourth letter to the left of another letter. This other letter is the seventh letter to the right of *N*. What is the *certain letter* first mentioned? ____

(The answers are as follows: 1-h; 2-m; 3-g; 4-w; 5-e; 6-12; 7-i; 8-S; 9-T; 10-Q.)

10. Third, *be sure you really desire to improve.* "Quite simple," you say. No, not at all.

11. To illustrate, take the case of the young woman who said that she wanted to reduce her waistline. Whenever she thought of how much better she would look and how many more dates she would probably have if her waistline were considerably reduced, she could very easily say, "Why, to be sure, I want to reduce my waistline." But whenever she thought of the many bending and stretching exercises to which she had to subject herself, and also the tempting foods and soft drinks she had to avoid, she could just as easily say, "I don't think I want to reduce my waistline."

12. What does she do? Well, it depends solely on whether she finds it more pleasant to be more attractive with a suitably reduced waistline or to keep to her accustomed method of eating.

13. So it is with your improvement in any trait, whether it be concentration, memory, imagination, reasoning or what not. You have to consider both the pros and the cons. If you will do this in regard to concentration, I think you will be able to say with some enthusiasm, "Of course I want to improve myself in attentive ability," and this desire is imperative if you are to improve yourself in this connection.

14. Fourth, *form the habit of having a definite purpose in whatever you plan to do.* Without a purpose, your mind is like a ship without a rudder, drifting hither and thither. Hence, in everything you do, try to see its value in reference to your own life.

15. To most of us, I dare say, geography was a rather uninteresting subject when we were in school. But there was a vast transformation in our attitude toward it during World War II when certain of our allies and our enemies were people of whom we had learned but little, and battles were being fought in places of which we had never heard.

16. Similarly the encyclopedia or the study of economics or a foreign language were uninteresting until we found some immediate need for them. In fact, the most boring material will become fascinating when it begins to serve some impelling purpose, and this makes concentration easy.

17. Fifth, *keep a record of your daily improvement in concentration.* It has been said that "nothing succeeds like success," which is indeed true. Without such a record, you will not always be conscious of any improvement; but if you keep a record, you will be stimulated to continue trying to improve. This record should include at least two things: (1) noting the ease with which you learned to eliminate or ignore distractions; and (2) keeping track of the time that it takes you to do certain things, such as the reading of a 1,000-word passage or the typing of 100 words without an error.

18. Many other suggestions could be given for improving your attentive ability. But if you follow these five suggestions, you will be surprised how quickly and how well they work.

Some kinds of material, as I have indicated, can be skimmed much more readily and successfully than others; similarly, some purposes are much better served by skimming than are others.

If you decided to skim an article with the title "How to Concentrate Better," what would you want to get out of it? Generally, of course, you want a quick and accurate understanding of the *essence* of material when you skim it. In this case, specifically, you want to know just how to go about concentrating better. With this in mind, you start to skim, clearly aware of what you expect to extract from the material.

The first paragraph, which you read completely, tells you that the article will provide what you want. The question, *But do we know how to improve ourselves in this connection?* implies a promise that the author will tell you how to concentrate better; and the following question, *Also, are we willing . . . ?* reinforces the promise, while adding that you'll have to pay a price for improvement.

Now you read the first sentence of paragraph 2 and realize that the author has begun to enlarge on the *value* of concentration, and that this ties up with the first sentence of paragraph 1.

You next skip to paragraph 3, where the opening sentence offers further information on *value;* thence to the first sentences of paragraphs 4 and 5, where still further *values* are given.

Paragraph 6 you read fully, recognizing it as a transition from *values* to *means*—a new section of the structure is starting, a section containing the real meat of the material.

Paragraph 7 starts off with *First* . . . ; this, then, you know, is the *first rule* for better concentration. You read the rule, skip the explanation and details, and drop to paragraph 8 for the *second rule,* reading only the first sentence. Now you go to paragraph 9, where the opening lines indicate further details on the second rule; skipping this mass of details in the form of a test (if you were not skimming you might be tempted to take the test), you push along to paragraph 10 for the *third rule.*

Paragraphs 11, 12, and 13 you recognize immediately as elaboration on the third rule, so you skip to the opening sentence of paragraph 14 for the *fourth rule,* omit the explanation in the rest of this paragraph and in paragraphs 15 and 16, and read the *fifth rule* in the opening sentence of paragraph 17.

Now you skip to the final paragraph, which you read completely, and in which you find a sort of recapitulation of the body of the article.

All right. By reading only three full paragraphs out of eighteen (the first, the sixth, and the last) and the opening words or sentences of the others, you have successfully skimmed the piece, extracting from it: (a) the values of concentration, and (b) five rules for better concentration. And this is all, except for details and explanations, that the article contains.

By skimming you have lost the details and explanations—but these I assume you were willing to do without, else, of course, you would not have decided to skim. You have not lost the main points, the essence of the material—and it is for the purpose of extracting the essence with a minimum of time and effort that skimming is used.

Skimming Exercise 3

In the following piece I shall again indicate, by the use of bold-face print, the lines that must be read so that the bare essence can be quickly extracted. Read these lines plus just as much additional material as you need in order to come away with a feeling that you understand what the author is saying.

HOW TO MAKE A MILLION
by Joseph T. Nolan

The late man-about-resorts, Alexander Phillips, bemoaning the decline of moneyed society in the United States, once complained: "The '400' has been marked down to $3.98." Now the Internal Revenue Service has come along with a further markdown—to 148. That, say the revenue officials in a report just published, is all we have left in the way of real millionaires; that is, men and women with incomes of $1,000,000 or more a year. In 1950 there were 219 in the million-dollar-a-year class, and back in 1929 before Wall Street's graphs went though the floor there were 513.
2. Millionaires, of course, come in all shapes and sizes. There are the little ones who, perhaps after almost a lifetime of labor, have just barely managed to amass a million dollars worth of property, stocks and bonds, and cash. They are big wheels only in their local communities, and for them life is often a race to keep up with the Vanderbilts. Then there are those with net assets of five-to-ten million, many of whom have inherited money and invested prudently. They can live comfortably these days provided they don't splurge on things like overly fancy yachts. (J. P. Morgan told an acquaintance who inquired about the upkeep on a yacht: "If you have to ask, you can't afford one.")
3. Then, there are those with an annual income above a million. Some get into this select bracket only now and then, possibly in a year when they sell an oil well or a uranium mine; others have a million dollars coming in every year and these are the big rich. It is the million-a-year group that the Internal Revenue report discusses, statistically but namelessly, and says is getting smaller all the time.
4. However, this situation is not quite so alarming as it might appear on the surface, according to financiers, investment counselors and tax specialists. Styles change, they point out, in millionaires as in millinery. The massive fortunes of the "Pittsburgh millionaires" of the nineteenth century and the "Detroit millionaires" of the Twenties are a phenomenon not likely to be repeated. But, say the authorities, a fellow with energy, imagination and luck can still scrape together a modest million or so in the course of a lifetime if he knows the ground rules and takes advantage of them.

Reprinted, by permission, from the *New York Times Magazine*. Mr. Nolan is a staff member of the Sunday *Times*.

5. Financial experts do not see eye to eye on many things these days, but they do agree generally on these three points:

6. Point 1. *It is harder to make a million now than it was forty or fifty years ago.*

7. Five times as hard, in the opinion of Bernard M. Baruch, who certainly qualifies as an authority. Baruch, who made his first million before he was 30, amassed a fortune once estimated at $25 million. Now 84, he has quietly given away the bulk of his money, though he told a friend not long ago that "right up to the day they put the coffin lid on me, I'll always have a dollar more than I need."

8. Laurance S. Rockefeller, chairman of the board of Rockefeller Center and a grandson of the first John D., once remarked: "We just don't have money the way people used to have it." Actually, not many people ever had money the way Grandfather John D. used to have it. Guesses on the size of his wealth ran up to $2 billion, and one statistician figured at the turn of the century that if his money were left to accumulate at the going rate for thirty years, it would amount to $90 trillion.

9. Statistical support for the theory that it is tougher to make a million these days is provided in a study just completed by the Tax Foundation, a private, non-profit research organization. It is a hypothetical case history of two men going into the same kind of business, with the same capital ($150,000), and the same rate of return (33 1/3 per cent), at two different periods. Mr. A started in 1920, Mr. B in 1955. After the first year their books looked like this:

	Mr. A.	Mr. B.
Original Investment	$150,000	$150,000
Return on Investment	50,000	50,000
Net Income (after 10 per cent deduction for expenses)	45,000	45,000
Federal Taxes	7,680	16,648
Income After Taxes	37,320	28,352
Living Expenses	15,000	24,000
Profit Reinvested	22,320	4,352
Added to Original Investment Makes	172,320	154,352

10. At this rate, Mr. A, the 1920 man, would have run up his original stake to $1,000,000 in just eleven years. Lower tax rates and a lower cost of living would have permitted him to plow back into his business a sizable portion of each year's income.

11. On the other hand, Mr. B, the 1955 man, would have found that at the end of eleven years he had increased his investment to only $239,933. It would have taken him thirty-four years altogether, taxes and living costs being what they are, to make his million.

12. **Point 2.** *Chances are strongly against anybody's making a million in his lifetime by depending on salary alone.*

13. In 1900 when Andrew Carnegie earned $23,000,000 from his vast steel enterprises, he paid his chief lieutenant and golfing partner, Charles M. Schwab, a salary of $1,000,000. Not only did Schwab have no Federal income tax to pay, but his dollar went about three times as far then as it would now.

14. "Today," says comedian Bob Hope, "the dollar goes a long way, too— all the way to Washington, D. C. But in the old days you were allowed to feel it, see it, even to use it." In the higher-income brackets the tax collector now takes up to 87 cents out of every dollar. So no companies are paying million-dollar salaries any more. Industry's highest-paid executive is Harlow H. Curtice, president of General Motors, who collected $686,000 in salary and bonuses last year. Though actual income tax returns are confidential, it is possible to figure out very roughly from a tax rate schedule that the Federal Government's claim on Curtice's income would amount to something like $595,000.

15. A further indication of the futility of depending on salary alone to make a million is found in the Internal Revenue report on the 148 million-dollar-a-year men and women. Salaries accounted for less than 2 per cent of their total incomes. They got almost half their money from dividends and another quarter from the sale of assets at a profit.

16. **Point 3.** *A person's best bet for making a million is to take advantage of some of the "gimmicks" that are available.*

17. There are dozens of these "gimmicks," but here are three that the experts say have been responsible for making many of the "new" millionaires.

18. *Capital Gains Deals.* Capital gains are the profits a person gets by selling stocks, bonds, land, houses or other property not a part of his stock-in-trade for more than they cost him. Suppose a man, reading that burlesque is on its way back to New York, invests his money in a theatre. Burlesque proves to be such a hit that the man finds he can sell out six months later at a profit of $100,000. If this profit were taxed as ordinary income he would have to pay the Federal Government $66,798. But by taking advantage of the capital gains tax he can get off by paying only $25,000.

19. This tax concession, under which assets held for at least six months can be sold and the profits taxed only 25 per cent, was put on the books to induce people to risk their capital. The result has been to give many an enterprising fellow a few dollars he can call his own. For instance, Vernon Pick, the first of the successful "amateur" uranium prospectors, became a millionaire on the strength of this "gimmick." He sold his Utah

uranium mine last year to an investment company called Atlas Corporation for $9,370,000 and was able to keep 75 per cent of his take.

20. *Depletion Allowances.* These have been called "capital gains with a Texas twist." Because of the risks involved in drilling for oil—$100,000 or more to sink a well that often will turn out to be dry—the Government allows oil men to pocket 27½ per cent of their gross income before paying a cent of taxes. They can continue these deductions for the life of their oil wells and can also write off large sums as "intangible development" costs.

21. This tax bonanza has produced a fabulous number of Texas millionaires (fifty, it is said, from Henderson County alone) and equally fabulous stories of their antics. Like the one about the Houston oil man who, glancing over his new six-car garage and seeing only five pairs of fishtails sticking out of the stalls, told his chauffeur matter-of-factly: "Buy me another Cadillac to plug that hole." Not long ago, one Texan brushed off a rival with the crack, "That guy never had more than forty or fifty million to his name."

22. Texas' best known oil millionaires are Sid Richardson and Clint Murchison. (Of his fortune, Murchison says: "I don't know how big it is; I try to have fun out of business, make it a hobby instead of drudgery.") Reputedly wealthier than either of them, though, is 66-year-old Haroldson Lafayette Hunt, whose estimated million-dollar-a-week income makes him, in many an expert's book, "the richest man in the United States."

23. *Stock Option Plans.* The story is told of a board meeting at which the president of a large corporation was being badgered about a poor performance in one of the company's divisions. Someone suggested that the vice president in charge of the division be called on the carpet. "Hell," said the president, "I can't chew that guy out. He became a millionaire last week." During the past five or six years of the bull market, dozens of vice presidents have become millionaires—through stock option plans.

24. The plans work like this: To give a key man some additional reward that will not be grabbed up by the tax collector, a company offers him an option to buy 10,000 shares of stock at $50 a share. That is 5 per cent below the market price of the stock. The executive has, say, five years to make up his mind whether he wants to buy.

25. A year later, the stock has gone up to $75 a share so the executive borrows money and buys it. He pays not the regular price of $75 a share but the originally agreed on price of $50. So he already has a "paper profit" of $250,000. Two years later, the stock is up to $150 a share. The company decides on a stock split of two shares for one. The executive now has 20,000 shares, each worth $75 on the market after the split.

26. In another year, the stock is up to $125, so the executive decides to

sell his 20,000 shares at this price. All told, he gets $2,500,000. Allowing for his original stake of $500,000, he has a profit of $2,000,000. On this he pays a capital gains tax of 25 per cent. That leaves him $1,500,000 in the clear.

27. These and other "gimmicks" are helping many today to realize the American dream and ambition of "making a million." Most of them don't make it—or keep it—in a single year, but they get it eventually. Few of them are wealthy enough to be mentioned in the same breath with the Fords or the Woolworths or the Astors. But if they are just plain, garden-variety millionaires and not the super-millionaires of yesterday, they can perhaps take some consolation from old John Jacob Astor, who used to say: "A man who has a million dollars is as well off as if he were rich."

Before skimming Mr. Nolan's article you decided, from the title, just what you might expect from it—*suggestions, obviously, on how to make a million dollars.*

The first paragraph, which you read fully, points out that there are fewer millionaires than there used to be. You skim paragraphs 2 and 3, since these hold out little promise of anything new, the final sentence of paragraph 3 reiterating the point of paragraph 1. The first and final sentences of paragraph 4, and the single sentence of paragraph 5, prepare you for main points to come; the first of these appears in paragraph 6, followed by several paragraphs of explanation. Point 2 occurs in paragraph 12, followed by more explanation; and point 3 occurs in paragraph 16.

Having skimmed more than half the material so far, you have found and extracted three important points—*harder now to make a million; chances are against making it out of salary; and the best bet is to take advantage of available "gimmicks."*

You are now, you realize, right at the core of the author's communication—he is going to tell you how to make your million.

Paragraph 17, which you read fully, alerts you to the three "gimmicks" that are most effective; and skimming through you pick up the three from paragraphs 18, 20, and 24—*capital gains, depletion allowances, and stock options.* How much of the details and explanations you read depends on what you want from the material— if you need only the bare essence, you've just about finished reading, except for the opening sentence of paragraph 27, which summarizes the second half of the article.

Skimming, then, gave you the pure gist of the piece—the three points in the first part of the material and the three popular "gimmicks" described in the final part.

WHEN TO SKIM

We are clear, now, on how the technique of skimming operates, when it is most useful, and what advantages and disadvantages it entails. As you have discovered, you can cover, when you skim fairly completely, a tremendous amount of material in a very short time without missing anything of crucial importance—you can strip a page right down to its essence, its final meaning, without wading through paragraphs of details, support, explanation, or examples.

On the other hand, complete skimming does involve some loss, a loss you expect and are resigned to before you start. Skimmed material is deprived of a certain amount of richness, flavor, and convincingness—with everything but the main idea stripped away, a piece of writing is usually robbed of much of its sparkle and pleasurableness, the personality of the author often fails to shine through, and the reader must be content with unornamented and unclothed final meaning. And it is certainly not possible to feel a strong and satisfying emotional response to an article, a story, or a book from which only the key ideas and salient points are picked out.

So I do not, obviously, recommend that you skim everything you read—*complete skimming* is a technique to be applied when time and circumstances demand it, when the sole purpose of your reading is to pull out the essence as quickly as possible.

However, I do recommend that you engage in *occasional and partial skimming* whenever you feel so inclined, or whenever your needs are best met by such skimming. Is there a longish book you have to get through within the next few days? Decide which are the most important chapters, read those, and skim the rest. Does a long article offer more explanation and illustration than you want or need? Skim the parts you can do without. Do you have a rough idea of what the next few paragraphs of a piece of writing are likely to say, and are you impatient to get on into new territory? Skim those paragraphs—the author might have been better advised to leave them out in the first place. Does an otherwise excellent novel seem to be getting bogged down in superfluous detail and description? Skim along until the plot thickens again. (You'd be surprised at how longwinded some writers are, and at how immeasurably their work improves with occasional skimming!)

In doing any kind of reading you sustain no loss of any significance if you skim intelligently here and there. And you suffer no loss whatever if you skip the tail end of a sentence or paragraph which is only repeating what you have already learned and understood.

So, to become repetitious myself, by all means skim when you read. Skim occasionally, partially, judiciously; or, at times, skim completely, if it suits your requirements; skim, in short, according to your needs and desires of the moment.

Skimming cuts the excess fat off the frame of an author's work. With the large amount of reading that you should expect to do in the next months and years (and which a later chapter will discuss with you in detail), intelligent and skillful skimming will prove a valuable cutting instrument.

★ SESSION 21

PERCEPTION TRAINING VIII

Perception Exercise 34

Using the Flashmeter card, expose the numbers for a fraction of a second, getting a *visual* impression. Do not say the digits to yourself. Reproduce each number in the blank to the right and then check your result.

15862	←_____	42935	←_____	30941	←_____
93764	←_____	67381	←_____	60641	←_____
08731	←_____	03164	←_____	71328	←_____
15986	←_____	98765	←_____	94390	←_____

19640	←_____	67381	←_____	06641	←_____
05962	←_____	05786	←_____	07777	←_____
36947	←_____	05687	←_____	39816	←_____
64385	←_____	50678	←_____	52152	←_____
46872	←_____	30167	←_____	67047	←_____
86542	←_____	34642	←_____	85058	←_____
10879	←_____	25879	←_____	37037	←_____
68436	←_____	38564	←_____	51876	←_____
59321	←_____	43871	←_____	90391	←_____
18764	←_____	17834	←_____	43987	←_____
39860	←_____	11814	←_____	56821	←_____
10739	←_____	44187	←_____	18764	←_____
40692	←_____	66238	←_____		

NUMBER CORRECT OUT OF 50: _____

Perception Exercise 35

Sweep down each column, making only one fixation to the line. Go as fast as adequate comprehension permits, and be more aware of the ideas than of inner speech.

273

THE INTERVAL IN LEARNING
by Bruno Furst

↓

The interval between
learning and repetition
is much more important
than people
usually assume,
and it is one
of the factors
regrettably neglected
in our school education.
Almost every good book
on psychology
and learning
stresses the importance
of these intervals,
but I have not yet seen
a single schoolbook
that takes advantage
of these findings.
Ebbinghaus,
a German professor,
devoted much time
to experiments
in this particular line,
and his tests

↓

have been checked
and double-checked
in almost every country.
You know
as well as I do
that it is entirely wrong
to assume
that any subject matter
which we once learned
and mastered
will remain
our mental property
forever.
You know
that a person
may have spoken
a foreign language
rather fluently
but,
by not using it
for several years,
may have lost
the ability
completely

↓

and be forced
to admit
that he can neither
speak it
nor understand it
any more.
Of course,
that cannot happen
if he uses the language
constantly.
Use is repetition,
and repetition
is necessary
for everything
which we wish
to keep alive
in our minds.
So far,
the facts are known
to everyone.
What is not
so well known
is that
the spacing

From *Stop Forgetting*, Greenberg: Publisher, New York. Reprinted with permission of the author. Dr. Furst is Director of The School of Memory and Concentration in New York.

↓

of repetition
plays a very important
role
in time-saving.
Ebbinghaus
has found
that a subject
which requires
68 repetitions
if learned in one day
requires only
38 repetitions
if they are
spread out
over three days.
A more complex subject
which required
504 repetitions
in one day
could be mastered
by repeating it
158 times
the first day,
109 times
the second day,
and 75 times
the third day.
Thus repetitions
for all three
consecutive days
add up to 342,
effecting a saving

↓

of time
amounting to
approximately
30 per cent
if compared
with the 504 repetitions
on a single day.
Since time is,
or should be,
of great value
to all of us,
nobody should fail
to make use of
such a
time-saving device,
especially if it is
so easy to apply
as the proper spacing
of learning
and repetition.
Whenever
you have to learn
something new,
do not try
to master it
completely
on the first day.
Be satisfied
if you acquire
a fair knowledge
of it,
allow it to

275

↓

sink into your memory,
and then repeat it
on the two following days
and you will see
that you can master it
better
with less effort.
It is one of
the strange phenomena
of the human mind
that memory
continues to work
even when
the actual task
of learning
has ceased
and even when
we are asleep.
It is the same
peculiar occurrence
which helps us
to solve a problem
while we are dreaming,
especially a problem
on which
we focused our attention
before going to sleep
and which proved
too tough
for solution.
The only explanation
which is possible

↓

for both phenomena
is the fact that
our subconscious mind
continues working
and thinking
while our conscious mind
is asleep.
The same mental power
which produces dreams
must be able to work
on problems
and to solve them.
It is evidently wrong
to think

↓

of our conscious
and our subconscious
functioning
as two mental activities
which are
eternally divided.
It is much better
to think of them
as two rooms
whose separating wall
is flexible
and easily removable.
It is
figuratively accurate
to speak

↓

of the "threshold"
between the conscious
and the
subconscious mind,
for every thought
can easily lapse
from the conscious
to the subconscious,
and we are
sometimes able
to draw a thought
from the subconscious
over this threshold
into the conscious mind.

How was your comprehension? ☐good ☐fair ☐poor
Were you comparatively unaware of inner speech? ☐yes ☐no

Perception Exercise 36

Sweep down the narrow columns of text, reading as fast as you can for good comprehension, and fixating at the broad black arrow in the center of the column.

The following material is excerpted from a column in the *New York Herald Tribune* of March 3, 1957, by Don Ross, feature writer for the drama section of that newspaper. Copyright 1957 by the New York Herald Tribune, Inc. Reprinted with permission.

↓

The other night we
climbed up to Ten-
nessee Williams'
second-floor two-room
apartment in E. 58th
St. and had a little

↓

talk about several
subjects, such as why
he writes plays, what
kind of people he
writes about, does he
try to shock his audi-

↓

ence, is he an optimist
or a pessimist, and
does he consider him-
self a moralist.

He has a home in
Key West where he

spends much of his time and does his best work. He was at his New York apartment because his new play, "Orpheus Descending," opens at the Martin Beck March 21, and he had to be close by during rehearsals.

A pleasant-faced short man a little on the plump side, Mr. Williams fixed vodka on the rocks for his guest and himself, and settled himself comfortably on the sofa and waited for the first question.

Some people accuse you of filling your plays with sordid characters. Are they right?

Mr. Williams took a long pull on the vodka and answered the question with a somewhat indignant inflection to his voice, which is an unusual blend of Dixie-British. He was born in Mississippi but has spent much time abroad.

"I don't think Blanche DuBois was sordid," he said, hissing the word *sordid* in a way that indicated he didn't think much of it. "I think she was rather noble. I don't think deeply troubled people are sordid. She was troubled. Miss Alma in 'Summer and Smoke' was almost a puritan. Is that sordid? Tell me who was sordid in 'The Glass Menagerie'? In 'The Rose Tattoo' Serafina was earthy and sensual. These things can be very beautiful, I have always thought."

It was clear that the more Mr. Williams thought of the word sordid as applied to his people, the more preposterous it became.

"Coming to 'Cat on a Hot Tin Roof,' I don't think either Maggie or Brick was sordid. Brick was troubled. Maggie was desperate. I thought both were admirable people in different ways. I thought Big Daddy had a certain stature and bigness, almost a nobility, in his crude ways.

"I can't think of any of my main characters who have been sordid. I think pettiness and meanness are sordid. I would never choose a person of that sort for a main protagonist because they don't interest me."

Perception Exercise 37

Continue as before.

The following is an excerpt from "The Origins of *Peter Pan*," by Marietta Karpe, and is reprinted, with permission, from the *Psychoanalytic Review* of January, 1956.

Recently, those of us who have access to a television set were witnesses to a surprising spectacle. One of the well-known ac-

tresses of Broadway starred in a fairy tale, playing the part of a

277

little boy. This in itself would not be too surprising if it had been on one of the usual children's programs, but this play was broadcast at night, for a period of two hours, for an audience of many millions of viewers, adults as well as children, from coast to coast. I am referring to the play, "Peter Pan," by Sir James Matthew Barrie. This was a complete Broadway production, televised nationally at a cost of approximately $400,-000, and the next day it was hailed by the critics as "the most polished, finished, and delightful show" that ever appeared on television.

This is certainly an unusual honor bestowed on a simple whimsical fairy tale, and a phenomenon worth investigating. What makes all these sophisticated, mature adults take this play so seriously? How is it possible that all audiences during the Broadway run, not only at children's matinees but also in the evenings always answered with a rousing "Yes!" to the question: "Do you believe in fairies?" What special magic does this play have that would cause adults to revert willingly and cheerfully back to childhood? The theme of this play must touch on a basic and universal need, shared by everybody, which has made audiences react that way for the period of half a century.

The play "Peter Pan" was first produced in 1904 and has been revived six times since then, and each time the part of Peter Pan was played by a prominent actress of that generation. From the first production in 1904 in London and in 1905 and 1906 on Broadway with Maude Adams in the title role, through another revival with Miss Adams in 1912 and 1913, a revival in 1924 with Marilyn Miller and in 1928 with Eva Le Galienne, another revival in 1950 with Jean Arthur, and finally the recent brilliant revival with Mary Martin, the play had a total of over 700 performances on Broadway alone. Furthermore, there were many more performances in England, on tour all over the United States, and also a French production in Paris and an Italian production in Turin. In addition to that the story also was very successful in book form, as a movie, and on records.

This would be a very remarkable success for any play, but it is especially astonishing if we consider the childlike simplicity and unsophistication of its plot. However, if we examine the story more closely, we find that it deals with the basic problems of life: with the problem of aging and death versus eternal youth and immortality. The author of Peter Pan, Sir James Matthew Barrie, is concerned with these problems from his earliest works on and seems to struggle with them all his life.

One fact becomes immediately obvious: children who fly through the air at night in their night-

278

gowns are obviously dead children. The only way that a child can accomplish the feat of never growing up is by dying at an early age. In the play, the only indication that Peter is not made from the same substance as ordinary children is given in his refusal to be touched by Wendy. This was an afterthought of Barrie's, after the show had already gone into rehearsal, and it posed quite a problem for the stage direction because during rehearsals, up to that point, Wendy had tousled Peter's hair and had fondled him like a mother would caress a little boy. But Barrie remained adamant on that detail against all arguments from actors and director. Other stage directors and critics demanded other changes in the play, but Barrie refused to make concessions in his conception of the "careless boy." His ideas on the subject seem to be beyond critical argument and logical surveillance and seem to have a deeply personal meaning for him.

Perception Exercise 38

Proceed as before with the following material, which is excerpted, with permission, from "Improving Rate of Comprehension," by Lester R. Wheeler and Viola D. Wheeler, in the *High School Journal*. The Wheelers are directors of the Reading Clinic at the University of Miami, Coral Gables, Florida.

Slow readers, even with good comprehension, haven't time for the extensive reading required both in and out of school. Many jobs are jeopardized by slow reading habits, and academic success is difficult unless students can compete with classmates in quantity as well as quality. Furthermore, slow reading is tedious, replete with boredom, fatigue and daydreaming. Mature readers control speed. They differentiate rates to accommodate not only material and purpose but also the various comprehension needs within a selection by varying speed from line to line, sentence to sentence, paragraph to paragraph, and chapter to chapter. Slow reading, sometimes the result and sometimes the cause of deficiencies in other reading skills, is affected by ability to (1) read by thought units, (2) see relationships, (3) determine author-reader purpose, (4) use key ideas, (5) develop adequate sight and meaning vocabulary, and (6) eliminate inner speech. Improvement in these skills should improve rate, but such is not always the case; slow reading may be a mental habit of long standing, a carry-over from earlier training. Overemphasis on word analysis, pronunciation, phonics and oral reading tend to establish habit patterns more closely related to oral than to silent reading. Many slow readers in high-school and college have not made adequate transition from oral to silent reading.

Relation of Rate to Comprehension. There is no merit in rapid or slow reading except that it meets comprehension needs. By and large, more comprehension difficulties stem from too slow, rather than from too fast, a reading rate. Theoretically, efficient reading rate should correspond to an individual's rate of thinking. Only then does the reader give full attention to the context and overcome the arch enemy of comprehension — reverie reading. Obviously, vocabulary difficulties and other deficiencies in mechanics affect concentration; however, with easy-reading materials, a reading speed which approaches thinking rate improves comprehension.

Recognizing Key Ideas. Not every word in a reading selection is important. Usually two-thirds of a sentence, paragraph or chapter is illustrative, explanatory or repetitious. Slow readers tend to (1) confuse supplemental material with main ideas, (2) give equal emphasis to important and unimportant words, and (3) comprehend isolated ideas rather than related wholes. In slow reading, key ideas become so widely separated by intervening connectives and supplemental materials that continuity of thought is often lost.

Mature readers detect key ideas rapidly and subordinate nonessential details. Efficient rapid readers see relationships more clearly, and the induced concentration sharpens their wits for better comprehension and retention. In reporting on a selection which he has read, the slow reader tends to recount isolated details and incidents rather than to summarize key thoughts. To some extent, this may be due to over-conscientiousness; through past experience the reader may have developed a distorted idea of careful reading. A slow reader, already lost among details, is only further confused when a teacher admonishes, "Read this again, CAREFULLY!" Rapid reading discourages the kind of "careful" reading that contributes to fragmentary thinking.

VOCABULARY STUDY V

Words for Today

Do the usual dictionary research on those words that are unfamiliar to you, then study your notes in preparation for the following tests.

1. aberration	6. omnipresent	12. sepulchral
2. duplicity	7. omniscient	13. taciturn
3. insidious	8. omnivorous	14. trenchant
4. loquacious	9. prodigal	15. ubiquitous
5. omnipotent	10. prolix	16. verbose
	11. ribald	

Test Your Learning

I. If two words are *similar* in meaning, write S in the preceding blank; if they are essentially *opposed*, write O.

1._____aberration—deviation
2._____duplicity—double-dealing
3._____insidious—wily
4._____loquacious—talkative
5._____omnipotent—weak
6._____omnipresent—nonexistent
7._____omniscient—ignorant
8._____omnivorous—selective
9._____prodigal—economical
10._____prolix—wordy
11._____ribald—humorless
12._____sepulchral—tomblike
13._____taciturn—talkative
14._____trenchant—sharp
15._____ubiquitous—prevalent
16._____verbose—laconic

II. Write the noun form, other than one ending in *-ness*, for each of the following adjectives.

1. loquacious_____
2. omnipotent_____
3. omnipresent_____
4. omniscient_____

281

5. prodigal_____   9. trenchant_____
6. prolix_____   10. ubiquitous_____
7. ribald_____   11. verbose_____
8. taciturn_____

Key:

I. 1—S, 2—S, 3—S, 4—S, 5—O, 6—O, 7—O, 8—O, 9—O, 10—S, 11—O, 12—S, 13—O, 14—S, 15—S, 16—O.

II. 1. loquacity, 2. omnipotence, 3. omnipresence, 4. omniscience, 5. prodigality, 6. prolixity, 7. ribaldry, 8. taciturnity, 9. trenchancy, 10. ubiquity, 11. verbosity

A THIRD CHALLENGE TO YOUR READING HABITS

You have already attempted, probably with reasonable success, to cover three not-too-heavy novels, each in a single stretch of continuous reading, and pacing yourself to finish within a few hours. (Possibly, if you were delighted with the efficiency of this type of reading, you decided to go through more than the two books required by the assignment in chapter 6, and now find that you pick up a novel whenever you have a free evening, cruising and skimming right through from beginning to end before you put it down.)

Here, now, is another challenge for you to meet.

Within the next few days, find an evening in which you will have an hour or two at your disposal, and sit down with an issue of any magazine that you generally read—a new issue that you have not yet looked at.

Before the evening is over, finish that magazine from cover to cover.

This does not mean reading every word, nor every page, nor even every article and story.

Read those things in the magazine which interest you—it may be a total of a third, a half, three quarters, or any fraction of the issue that appeals to you. Skim whenever you feel so inclined, skip whatever you like, but stay with the magazine until you've got out of it what you want, until you've reached the point where that particular issue holds nothing else for you, and you're ready to add it to your collection for the Salvation Army, or to pass it on to other members of the family.

Read, of course, as always, in rapid pursuit of the central theme of each article, for the general framework of the plot of each story. Have an awareness, if you can, of the structure of thinking and planning used by the author—and think along with him as you read.

Try to make it a habit to read magazines through, in this way, in one sitting. If success attends your efforts, either immediately or eventually, you will discover that you can get twice as much magazine reading done as you used to—and in the same time and probably with greater enjoyment!

CHAPTER 9

PRACTICE IN DRIVING
FOR THE GIST

Preview

Now, as a warm-up to a third round of timed reading, you work on a number of shorter selections, practicing to:
• Increase your skill and speed in driving through details to get a total picture.
• Understand more clearly how details contribute to, or reinforce, a main idea.
• Sharpen your response to main ideas by trying to answer, in your own words, questions on the central meaning of what you have read.

> *Chapter* 9 challenges you to read a selection through quickly and then tell what it says.

CONCENTRATE ON THE GIST!

All the parts of any artistic whole are intimately related; the artist consciously and deliberately uses his details in such a way as to achieve a maximum total effect.

When you look at a painting, a piece of sculpture, a building, a dress, or a beautifully furnished room—and all these are artistic compositions—what strikes you first and with the greatest impact is the over-all design. The details are there, for without them there would be no design, but the painter, the sculptor, the architect, the fashion artist, or the interior decorator has so arranged and disposed the details that although each may be comparatively inconspicuous by itself, it nevertheless contributes, in one way or another, to the final result.

Indeed, if any detail is so prominent that it catches and holds the eye, thus weakening the effect of the whole, we say that the composition lacks unity and is an artistic failure. In a landscape, for example, the artist may have a palm tree at the edge of a desert; or in a still life he may have painted some spots on a banana; but it's not the tree or the spots he wants you to see as much as the whole sweep of the desert or the whole bowl of fruit. Similarly, the sculptor carves a nose and a mouth on the face of a statue, the architect strategically locates windows and doors in a structure, the designer places buttons and bows in a garment, the decorator hangs drapes and pictures in a room—but it's the effect of the *whole* statue, the *whole* building, the *whole* dress, or the *whole* room that the artist is striving for.

So also in a piece of writing. Like any other creative artist, the author arranges his details to achieve a total effect, a final meaning, a lasting impression, and he no more wants you to concentrate on

285

isolated details than does the painter, the sculptor, the architect, the dress designer, or the interior decorator.

Unfortunately, unlike most other artistic creations, a piece of writing cannot be comprehended in a single glance. The reader has to plow through the individual details, he has to fit these details together in his own mind, he has to do a certain amount of thinking about the details, before he can fully appreciate the author's final and total meaning. The reader, as you have already discovered from your own experience, has to work at seeing and understanding the over-all meaning. He has to translate words into ideas, he has to weigh the relative importance of these ideas; he has to understand details not as independent elements but as steppingstones to, or support for, or as explanation or clarification of, the gist of what a writer is trying to say to him. And, if he is a skillful reader, he does all this rapidly, accurately, and intelligently. Rapidly, so that the words and details do not get in the way of his total understanding. Accurately, so that he comes away with the final meaning the author is aiming at, rather than some entirely different and incorrect meaning. And intelligently, so that he can either accept the author's thinking as logical, well-based, and in accord with truth and reality, or reject it as illogical, unfounded, or untrue.

Again I ask you, as I did in chapter 5, to read a group of short selections, purposefully aiming for an efficient grasp of the main ideas. Needless to say, you are not to revert to any old habits of slow, dawdling comprehension; instead, understand each selection quickly, look for the main thought, find it, and get out.

I need no longer remind you to "read fast"; by now you have matured in your reading attitudes to the point where you are aware that there is no such objective phenomenon as "fast reading." There are "fast perception" and "fast comprehension"; and when you combine the two you have all the circumstances that make efficient reading possible, if not inevitable. So you need not keep telling yourself as you read: "I must go fast, fast, fast. . . ." Such self-urging may lead to tension and thus reduce the ease and smoothness of your comprehension.

Instead, keep training your new habit of pushing through to the gist of the author's ideas rapidly, without waste motion or time lag. Get the main thought; get it as quickly as you *comfortably* can. If you follow this technique properly you'll be aware, not that you're *reading* fast, but that you're *understanding* fast. You'll be avoiding tendencies to vocal responses, motor responses, word-by-word responses, regression responses, excessive auditory responses—in fine, you'll avoid consciousness of all responses but the one vital response: the intellectual and psychological response to the author's main ideas.

After each selection there will be a number of comprehension questions. *Answer these without, for the moment, further reference to the material.*

The first question, in each case, will test your understanding of, and your ability to recall, the *gist* of what you have read; next will come one or more questions on the important contributing elements that explain or clarify the author's main point.

Write out all your answers. Be brief, and use your own words— do not be concerned with style or grammar, just express your thoughts in a way that is clear to yourself. (Answer all comprehension questions on the first *five* selections before checking with the key that follows exercise 16.)

Rapid Comprehension Exercise 13

SELF-RESPECT AND SELF-CONFIDENCE
by Douglas Remsen, M.D.

No one can live with himself comfortably without self-respect; without self-confidence no one can enjoy the sense of satisfaction in accomplishment. Self-respect depends upon an emotional equilibrium in which anger, resentment, fear, and love are supports to the person's efforts and activities, not whips which drive and lacerate. Self-confidence depends upon ability, upon the adequacy to meet a situation, or to do something successfully. It incorporates also a capacity to take stock, to be honest in self-appraisal, so that one doesn't shoot at the moon and torture oneself for missing it. It means knowing what one knows—and more important— knowing what one doesn't know and not being ashamed to say so.

The standards we set unconsciously—social, puritanical, intellectual, perfectionistic—we rarely meet perfectly; but too many of us dwell upon

From *Talk*. Reprinted with permission.

the things we *didn't* do, the questions we *didn't* answer, to the point where the things done well are insufficient to support our self-respect and nurture our self-confidence. Then there follows self-abasement, inferiority feelings, inhibitions, and depression.

This quirk of human nature frequently has its roots in the home and environmental settings. As a small child, little Willie is subjected to a constant barrage of: Don't!, Quit!, Stop it!, Why did you do that?—the equivalent of "You stupid little idiot." The parent forgets that he or she is Olympian authority in the small one's eyes. This constant equivalent of "you stupid little idiot" chokes the childish struggle for being important and for building self-confidence. There is no thought of giving any praise or approval to the fumbling successes of the child. And the final lethal dose of poison to budding self-respect and self-confidence is "Aren't you ashamed of yourself?" administered so frequently with no thought of its stultifying effect. In later years, the fear of being shamed throws the stutterer into a dither, sends the alcoholic to have another drink, and the neurotic to hide in the cave of his inhibitions.

Mr. X, a stutterer, never stutters when he issues commands as a drill sergeant at the armory. He is confident and sure. But when he meets any person who symbolizes authority, he stutters miserably. He first stuttered when he faced uniformed authority five years ago to take a test and failed. You will not be surprised to learn that his stern father, the symbol of authority, never offered him as a child a word of approval for his accomplishments, but only the belittling condemnation of "Aren't you ashamed?"

It's time for an inventory. Take stock, but with excitement; not with the doubts of an inhibited soul! What you have done and experienced can be the foundation for self-respect and self-confidence.

Comprehension Test

1. What, in brief, makes for self-respect and self-confidence?

_____

_____

2. In what way do childhood relationships frequently play a role in failing to support an adult's self-respect and self-confidence?

_____

_____

SPEECH PATTERNS

Literally putting out his tongue at his audience, Dr. Cyril Darlington, a fellow of the Royal Society, a geneticist, declared that language and dialect and speech characteristics depended on heredity.

He said that it now had been well established by work on blood groups —as a result of blood transfusion work in the war more than 4,000,000 persons in Britain alone had been grouped—that there was a definite connection between genetic characteristics and language. Different human groups have different tongue and throat formations that he said are transmitted by parents.

To demonstrate this, he pushed out his tongue in the form of a cylinder and challenged his audience to try it. He said half of them would be able to do it and the other half would not.

To support his claim of the relation of language to genetics, he took the sound "th" and showed that, far from being an Anglo-Saxon characteristic as generally supposed, it extended from Iceland through Norway, Denmark, Britain, Spain, Greece, the Levant, South Arabia, South India, Burma and Siam into China. In fact, he declared, it corresponds accurately with the geographic distribution of the O blood group.

Dr. Darlington also asserted that in families, the children in learning to speak had characteristic impediments that represented individual expression of a genotype and could be identified with the parental genes.

Dialects, he added, are not just acquired habits of locality but a definite expression of local or regional characteristics arising from hereditary types produced by intermarriage. Heredity, as much as local loyalties, resists the pressure of dialect change, he maintained, saying that continuing work on blood group distribution would definitely establish a connection between heredity and the character of language.

Excerpted from a news item in the *New York Times*. Reprinted with permission of the *Times*.

Comprehension Test

1. According to Dr. Darlington, what is the determining causative factor of people's speech patterns? _____

_____

2. By what means did Dr. Darlington arrive at his conclusion?

Rapid Comprehension Exercise 15

RETALIATION REACTION
by James Sonnett Greene, M.D.

An old precept admonishes us to count ten before acting in anger. I thought of that recently when someone I had liked and trusted took advantage of that trust to advance himself personally, at my expense. My first reaction was to retaliate, but having learned from sad experience the folly of acting destructively when in an emotional state, I turned my mobilized energies into a quite different channel and accomplished a task I had been trying to get to for several days.

This is a type of experience that everyone goes through many times in his life, and the typical first reaction is one of retaliation. If we analyze this reaction, we find that the only thing we are really seeking at the moment, and the only thing we accomplish for ourselves by retaliation, is release of the tension that the situation has built up in us. But we accomplish this usually at the expense of erasing any feelings of guilt or remorse the other fellow may have, and thus our retaliatory reaction, far from "paying him back," actually plays into the other person's hands.

We can release tension just as well by other types of action and with real reward to ourselves. The best way is to utilize the energy that has been mobilized by our anger to counteract, by some constructive action, the harm that the other person has done us. If this is impossible, the energy should be drained off in some other useful activity. But for many reasons—and if for no other, then for purely selfish ones—we should not react destructively.

The important thing is to realize in our moment of anger that our adrenal glands have flooded us with energy which demands an "out," and that to play safe we should release it immediately into some constructive channel. By immediately drawing off the "charge," we avoid the danger

From *Talk*. Reprinted by permission. The late Dr. Greene was Medical Director of the National Hospital for Speech Disorders, New York, and editor of its official publication, *Talk*.

of explosion with all its potentialities for harmful consequences to ourselves and others.

In brief, when angry emotion is aroused act quickly—but not in retaliation. *War never pays!*

Comprehension Test

1. What, according to Dr. Greene, are the best ways to react when angry? _____

_____

2. What are we really seeking when we react with retaliation?

_____

3. In what way does such a reaction play into the hands of the object of our anger? _____

4. What is the physiological result of anger? _____

_____

Rapid Comprehension Exercise 16

CHINESE, JAPANESE, AND POLYNESIAN
by Bjorn Karlsen

Of the countries in Asia whose written languages do not utilize the Roman alphabet, China has the most unusual language of them all. The teaching of reading in China, therefore, presents some unique problems. The written language consists of "characters," each of which has one sound functioning more or less like an English syllable. Many of these characters sound alike but look different and have different meanings. This situation exists to a slight degree in English, too. The sound "too" can be spelled "to," "two," or "too," and has six different meanings. In Chinese, however, there are only about 600 different word sounds, but they cover more than 50,000 meanings. These meanings are revealed only by the characters. These characters are usually combined, forming nearly

Excerpt from a lecture delivered at the Claremont College Reading Conference, Claremont, California, 1955. Reprinted by permission. Dr. Karlsen is Professor of Education, San Diego State College, San Diego, California.

six times as many polysyllabic words as monosyllabic. Each character retains its original pronunciation, but the word itself takes on an entirely different meaning. (For example, the Chinese character "Tung" means east, the character "Hsi" means west, but the two characters combined mean "a thing.")

It is quite obvious that this language is a very difficult one to learn to read. One Chinese scholar, Fang Chao-ying, is of the opinion that China will never become literate with this system of writing, and most Chinese will agree that the written language is one of their biggest educational problems. Three solutions for this problem have been suggested. First of all, much effort has been exerted to reduce the number of characters. These attempts have been quite successful, partly because of the existence of a great number of obsolete characters. Twenty five years ago, a Chinese unabridged dictionary could contain 45,000 characters. This number has recently been reduced to 10,000. It has been estimated by one Chinese authority that a minimum knowledge of 5000 characters is necessary for a person to manage his own affairs. The average student in China will know 5000 characters by the time he reaches twelfth grade. His word vocabulary is three times as large, however, because of his knowledge of polysyllabic words.

An expert on the Chinese language, Jimmy Yen, has determined which 1000 characters are most commonly used, and has developed reading materials using nothing but these characters. Although this does simplify the processes involved in learning to read, a person is only partially literate after having learned these characters.

A second approach to this problem has been the development of 37 phonetic symbols (Juyin Fuhau), which are relatively easy to learn. Few books are printed using these symbols and they are, by most people, considered merely as stepping stones to the learning of the characters.

Finally, several systems have been devised to Romanize the Chinese languages, using 22 letters. However, one syllable might have 100 meanings so that a word written with phonetic symbols or letters would not convey its exact meaning. This problem does not exist with the use of characters.

The problem is a difficult one, one that is affecting many millions of people. So far, none of the solutions suggested seems to be satisfactory.

Similar problems exist in Japan. Dr. Frank Freeman, who was a member of the U. S. Education Mission to Japan shortly after World War II, wrote:

> "Another difficulty lies in the cumbersome written language which makes it impossible for children in the elementary school to learn to read and write more than the rudiments of the language. They spend half their time in acquiring this meager command of writing and

reading. They are therefore unable to learn more than a modicum of the content subjects. The mission recommended a simplification of the written language which would overcome these difficulties."

There are, at the other extreme, some languages that are easy to learn. One of these is Polynesian which consists of a group of dialects spoken on the Polynesian Islands. The missionaries working on these islands have developed a written language which is probably the simplest in the world. The alphabet has only 12 letters, 5 vowels and 7 consonants. Each letter stands for one sound, making the language 100 per cent phonetic. In using this system, reading can be learned in a very short time, in most instances in a couple of hours. The simplicity of this language has resulted in, except for Europe and North America, the highest literacy rate in the world today. This is a quite remarkable fact considering that many of the people on these islands were cannibals only a century ago.

Comprehension Test

1. How does Dr. Karlsen account for the low literacy rate in China and Japan, and the high literacy rate in the Polynesian Islands? _____

_____

2. What makes Chinese so difficult to read? _____

_____

3. What makes Polynesian so easy to read? _____

Key to Exercises 13–16

(Your language will of course differ from that used in the answers below, but the thoughts should be similar. Refer to each selection when you study the discussions.)

Exercise 13 (*page 287*): 1. Ability, adequacy, and successes; not setting perfectionist goals that are unachievable; not constantly dwelling on one's failures; etc. 2. Criticism and abasement of the child by parents instead of approval and praise for accomplishments.

Discussion: The main idea is explicitly expressed in the last half of the first paragraph, and repeated, in the form of a personal exhortation to the reader, in the final paragraph—all else in the piece is elaboration and illustrative details. The third paragraph contains important material, since it offers an explanation of the cause for self-doubts.

Exercise 14 (page 289): 1. Heredity, i.e., the different tongue and throat formations transmitted from parents to offspring. 2. By classifying people into blood groups.

Discussion: As you would expect in any news item, the "lead," or main point, occurs right at the beginning, with elaboration and illustration rounding out the "story." An important detail explains by what means the conclusion was reached (paragraph 2).

Exercise 15 (page 290): 1. By counteracting damage through constructive action, or by engaging in some useful activity. 2. Release of the tension (or draining off of the excess energy) produced by anger. 3. Relieves his guilt or remorse. 4. Flooding of the body with energy by the adrenal glands.

Discussion: After some introductory material, Dr. Greene foreshadows his main point toward the end of paragraph 1, expresses it completely in paragraph 3, and pounds it home again in the final paragraph. The three important details queried in the test (what we seek when we retaliate, how retaliation affects the other person, and what anger does to our physiology) all explain the reasoning behind the author's central thought.

Exercise 16 (page 291): 1. The difficulties of learning to read the complicated Chinese and Japanese written languages, and the ease of learning to read the simple Polynesian written language. 2. The large number of characters and the fact that the different word sounds combine to make up so many diverse meanings. 3. The small number of characters and the fact that the language is completely phonetic.

Discussion: Here is a more complicated selection, one containing a whole mass of details that the reader must sort in his mind in order to arrive neatly, efficiently, and accurately at the central point —namely the relationship between literacy and the structure of the written language. Note how closely the important details (why Chinese is hard, and Polynesian easy, to read) tie in with the main idea.

A piece of writing, we have decided, differs from true forms of visual art in that you cannot respond to the effect of the whole in a single glance. In reading, the "viewer" has to work at seeing and understanding, for a page of print, though at first apprehended by the eye, is fundamentally grasped by the mind through the powers of interpretation, reasoning, and analysis.

But just as your vision can be educated so that you respond more intelligently to a work of art, so your powers of interpretation, reasoning, and analysis can be refined so that you respond more efficiently and more rapidly to what a writer offers you on a page of print.

This process of refinement started years ago—when you first learned to read at the age of six or seven. It continued through elementary and high school and into your late adolescence. And then, possibly, it stopped, though there was still much room for improvement.

However, the training you have been receiving has aimed at further refinement of all the visual and comprehension skills that efficient reading demands; and by now these skills should be sufficiently sharpened to enable you to jump into a selection and react so quickly to the gist of an author's thinking that it might almost seem—to exaggerate a bit—as if you are comprehending the essence of a paragraph almost at a glance.

Let us continue, now, the immensely valuable practice in which you attempt to respond quickly and accurately to the main point of a short selection. As before, drive straight for the gist, confident that you need not get entangled in the minor details, and aware, as you read, how the important details provide the necessary foundation for clear and full understanding.

Rapid Comprehension Exercise 17

LENGTHENING LONGEVITY
by William C. FitzGibbon

Although man has often been in doubt as to how life should be lived, he has never doubted that it should be—and for as long as possible. His efforts to prolong life (occasional lapses into wholesale homicide notwithstanding), have succeeded. Since 1900 in America, for example, he has stretched his life expectancy from 48 years to the recently announced figure of 69.8 years, an unprecedented gain of more than twenty years in little more than half a century. Thus a child born today in the United

From *The New York Times Magazine*. Reprinted by permission.

States has the bright prospect of living out the legendary (though heretofore uncommon), three score and ten.

The newborn child, according to the Metropolitan Life statisticians, never had it so good. In the Bronze Age—so studies of unearthed bones reveal—an infant had a life expectancy of 18 years. Two thousand years ago a Roman urchin could count on 22 years. In the Middle Ages the figure rose to 35, with no change from then until 1838 when, in England and Wales, the expectancy hit 40.

Today's increase in life expectancy is common to most Western countries. Norway, the Netherlands, Sweden, Denmark and England have rates much the same as the United States, with other European nations close behind. Lowest life expectancy among countries on which figures are available is in India, where the rate is 32. (India is the only country where life expectancy of males is higher than that of females.) Other low rates: Egypt: 35; Mexico: 39; Puerto Rico: 46. No recent figures are available on Russia. (Scientists doubt, incidentally, that anyone has lived beyond 150 years—or that medical technique can ever extend life expectancy much over 100.)

Life expectancy tables had their start in the middle of the seventeenth century, one of the early innovators being the English astronomer Halley, of comet fame. Since life expectancy is a figure arrived at by averaging a population's death ages, the biggest single reason for longer expectancy has been the drop in infant mortality.

When an American wakes to find that he has reached the life expectancy figure of 69.8 years, he shouldn't expect to perish before the day is up. He is one of the lucky ones who probably will live out the years at the farther end of the average. A man reaching 69.8 may expect to live 10 to 12 more years; at 75 he has about eight years; at 80 he has six. This does not, however, go on ad infinitum. Sorry.

Comprehension Test *

1. What has happened to life expectancy in most Western countries since 1900? _____

_____

2. What is a main reason for the increase in life expectancy? ____

_____

* Do exercises 17–20 before checking your answers against the key on page 301.

Rapid Comprehension Exercise 18

LIGHTNING AND SAFETY
by Dr. Theodore R. Van Dellen

A flash of lightning and a deafening crash of thunder are enough to make a child scream and a dog scoot under the bed, his tail between his legs. Some adults also are frightened, particularly those who have had a close call with nature's fireworks.

The child who is frightened by thunder and lightning needs comfort rather than ridicule. At night, stay in the bedroom if necessary. The majority can be calmed by a story or song. Older tots are helped by watching and discussing the flashes and roars provided the parents show no evidence of alarm.

The experiments of Benjamin Franklin 200 years ago helped dispel superstitions and primitive ideas about this natural phenomenon.

If a church instead of a nearby gambling joint is struck by lightning, the people no longer are amazed that a good rather than a bad place should bear the brunt. They realize the church was struck because its steeple is the highest point in the vicinity.

Lightning represents a discharge of atmospheric electricity from one cloud to another or from a cloud to the earth. The best targets here below are projections of some height. This makes the church spire more vulnerable than a low building protected by a grove of trees.

On the other hand a single tree, shack, fence pole or human being becomes the best target on a prairie, more so when representing the only inlet for a bolt of lightning within a radius of miles.

When an electrical charge strikes a hollow object, such as a tin box, the charge runs down the outside, not the inside. This means that when a house, metal auto or steel freight car is struck the occupants need not worry provided they are not near an open window or door.

Electricity also is conducted easier through wet objects than dry. Consequently, it is poor policy to be in an open boat in the middle of a lake or under a lone wet tree on the golf course during a storm. When fishing on a lake, at the first sign of a storm, row for shore pronto. Swimmers should leave the water and seek protection.

Reprinted from the *New York Sunday News* by permission of the author and of the Chicago-Tribune—New York News Syndicate, Inc.

Stay indoors during a thunderstorm but if caught outside, choose a safe shelter, preferably a large metal building or a dwelling protected against lightning.

If these are not available look for a cave, depression in the ground, valley, the foot of an overhanging cliff, or dense woods. Keep away from small exposed sheds, isolated trees, wire fences, hilltops and open spaces.

Comprehension Test

1. What should you do during a lightning storm? _____

_____

2. How should you react to a child's fright over lightning? _____

_____

3. What kind of structures does lightning generally strike? _____

_____

4. What makes indoors safe? _____

_____

5. Why is water unsafe? _____

_____

Rapid Comprehension Exercise 19

IMPROVING TEACHER QUALITY
by Benjamin Fine

In the frantic search for more teachers, quality is taking a back seat. Hard-won professional standards are losing ground in many of the nation's schools. Unqualified teachers are being recruited into the classrooms in all grade levels.

These sentiments are being voiced with increasing frequency at educational gatherings. The subject of teacher quality has been singled out for special study by the forthcoming White House Conference on Education. Educators have become outspokenly alarmed over the gradual lowering of admission standards to the teaching profession.

Many educators contend that the current emphasis on quantity, while helping to alleviate the teacher shortage, creates an even worse problem when quality is ignored. The ultimate sufferers, they point out, are the children, the community and the nation.

Reprinted by permission from the Sunday edition of *The New York Times*.

If children are adversely affected by unqualified teachers, the damage is even more lasting and serious where younger children in the nursery, kindergarten and primary grades are concerned. This belief was underscored at the four-day biennial conference of the National Association for Nursery Education which ended in Boston yesterday.

Miss Amy Hostler, president of the Mills College of Education in New York City, told a session of the conference that "by forsaking quality for quantity, we are intensifying the very problem we are trying to solve."

"Focusing our sights on mere numbers," she said, "could be a short-sighted way of solving the teacher shortage. If we do not improve teacher education by providing a broader scope of studies and a more scholarly approach to science, the arts and humanities; if we do not seek quality to an even greater degree than quantity, then the outlook is indeed grave."

The Boston conference was attended by 1,500 members representing the fields of early childhood education, psychiatry, medicine, child development, social work and teacher education. President Hostler spoke as chairman of a session on maintaining the quality of teacher education.

"Let us send into the nation's classrooms men and women who are teachers rather than custodians, educators rather than caretakers," she pleaded. "It is time to combat the assault on the dignity of our profession."

President Hostler represents a college that specializes in the preparation of teachers of young children. In her remarks, however, she voiced the concern that is shared by an increasing number of spokesmen for educational institutions that prepare teachers for all age levels.

Comprehension Test

What is the result of our frantic search for more teachers? _____

_____

_____

Rapid Comprehension Exercise 20

QUIZ KID
by Katherine V. Bishop

Recently, while driving from one school to another, I heard part of a quiz program over the car radio. The MC introduced an eleven year old

---
Excerpted from an address delivered at the Claremont College Reading Conference,

boy as a contestant. The youngster was well poised, and established his need for a bicycle in an admirable manner.

The first question was put to the boy. The MC asked him to give a six letter word ending in *it*, the name of an animal. After a second or so of heavy silence the MC said, "Think, now, I'm asking for the name of an animal, a six letter word ending in *it*, this is the name of an animal we think of at Easter." Still no answer from the boy and the MC said, "Maybe it will help you to know that the word begins with the letter *r*."

"BUNNY!" shouted the boy.

The studio audience roared with laughter and the boy was given full credit for a correct answer.

"The next question," said the MC, "asks you to name three things we learn to do in school. In the words of a song each of these begins with the letter *r*." Since no response was forthcoming the MC said, "Give me the name of just one of the three." There was no response. In desperation, for time was running out, the MC said, "Tell me, what do you do when you open a book?"

There was no hesitation now as the eleven year old boy answered, "Look at the pictures." Hilarious laughter followed this answer and the boy was awarded the prize he sought, money enough to buy a bicycle.

What can this boy read from this experience with adults other than that it *is funny and lucrative to be ignorant?*

To me this episode is far from laughable and far from unimportant. It is an example of the unreality that characterizes adult-child relations at home, at school, and in the community at large. In this case, I believe that the boy should have been told that he had failed to answer the questions correctly and that for that reason he had not won the money; but, that because his need was urgent the money would be loaned to him on terms that he could meet.

Through such action the boy would have gained two things more important, in my estimation, than money. He would have gained respect for the fairness of the adults in charge of the quiz, and ultimately by fulfilling his obligation, *self-respect.*

Claremont, California. Reprinted, by permission, from the Claremont College Reading Conference Yearbook for 1954. Dr. Bishop is Professor of Education at San Francisco State College.

Comprehension Test

1. What, in Dr. Bishop's opinion, does this episode illustrate?

2. What has the child learned from his experience? _____

_____

3. How does Dr. Bishop think the problem might better have been handled? _____

_____

4. What would have been the result of this preferable method?

_____

Key to Exercises 17–20

(Your language will of course differ from that used below, but the thoughts should be similar. Refer to each selection when you study the discussions.)

Exercise 17 (page 295): 1. It has increased considerably—more than 20 years. 2. Drop in infant deaths.

Discussion: We have here a mass of interesting details on life expectancy. Clearly, what the author is pointing out in total is that life expectancy has increased tremendously in recent years and that the biggest single reason is a drop in infant mortality.

Exercise 18 (page 297): 1. During a lightning storm stay indoors or in a safe shelter. 2. Be comforting, soothing, calm, show no alarm, etc. 3. High, projecting, isolated, etc. 4. Lightning charge runs down the outside of a hollow object. 5. Wet objects are better conductors for electricity than dry.

Discussion: Dr. Van Dellen is obviously telling his readers how to avoid being struck by lightning. Though using a large number of details and scientific facts, he is cautioning us, in essence, to remain indoors or in a safe shelter during a lightning storm, and to avoid places usually struck by lightning.

Exercise 19 (page 298): We are sacrificing quality to quantity in order to alleviate the teacher shortage, thus creating worse problems, causing damage to children, community, and nation, etc.

Discussion: The gist of Dr. Fine's article is stated, as you might expect in a news item, in the first paragraph. The main idea is repeated and extended throughout the piece, and is supported and explained by a wealth of detail.

Exercise 20 (page 299): 1. The unreality of relations between adults and children. 2. That it pays to be ignorant. 3. The money loaned, rather than given to him, since he failed to answer the questions. 4. Respect by the boy for adults' fairness and for himself.

Discussion: Most of this excerpt is devoted to a narrative description of the radio quiz, the MC's questions, and the child's naïve answers. Then comes an important detail (". . . it is funny and lucrative to be ignorant.") that prepares the reader for Dr. Bishop's main idea, that adult-child relations are, as this episode shows, unrealistic. Dr. Bishop then clarifies her position with two further important details—how the boy might have been treated more realistically, and how this realistic approach would have served him better.

The training in this chapter has given you excellent practice in finding and following main ideas, in reacting quickly, efficiently, and accurately to the gist of what an author is saying, and in using the important details of material to round out your understanding.

Your next step is to apply what you have learned to a third round of longer selections in which we shall measure your performance in terms of speed and over-all comprehension. First, however, let us devote a session to perception and vocabulary improvement.

★ SESSION 24

PERCEPTION TRAINING IX

Perception Exercise 39

To help you prepare for training in six-digit perception, this exercise in "jumping digits" is presented. The span occupied by the following three-, four-, and five-digit numbers is equal to that occupied by six-digit numbers, but one or more digits are omitted in each instance. When you can do this and the next exercise comfortably, you will be prepared for complete six-digit training.

3 9 9	←_____	3 2 9	←_____	8 0 71	←_____
78 2	←_____	0 64	←_____	0 9 65	←_____
9 87	←_____	87 5	←_____	17 9 4	←_____ .
9 0 6	←_____	1 62	←_____	54 28	←_____
65 2	←_____	3 2 5	←_____	390 1	←_____
4 4 3	←_____	1 0 4	←_____	2 407	←_____
6 63	←_____	29 7	←_____	39 16	←_____
42 6	←_____	0 3 7	←_____	703 1	←_____
63 2	←_____	42 9	←_____	68 73	←_____
76 7	←_____	5 68	←_____	0 1 90	←_____
7 78	←_____	66 89	←_____	302 1	←_____
6 2 4	←_____	96 0 0	←_____	19 64	←_____
90 2	←_____	53 2 7	←_____	107 2	←_____
8 7 8	←_____	91 98	←_____	3 50 9	←_____
3 2 5	←_____	55 87	←_____	53 2 7	←_____
2 79	←_____	74 6 4	←_____	4 35 0	←_____
51 4	←_____	39 1 2	←_____		

NUMBER CORRECT OUT OF 50: _____

Perception Exercise 40

As further preparation for six-digit training, here is an exercise combining five digits with a letter.

5L4382	←_____	2P7643	←_____	64S421	←_____
9R7641	←_____	598R72	←_____	75T953	←_____

86B847	←_____	82Q951	←_____	413P92	←_____
546A91	←_____	51Q860	←_____	518P67	←_____
753B82	←_____	84M912	←_____	719S22	←_____
854C94	←_____	39N518	←_____	423S43	←_____
62D593	←_____	46T107	←_____	8P9134	←_____
84D871	←_____	50312R	←_____	9R4178	←_____
99L506	←_____	V54318	←_____	8S9188	←_____
38G518	←_____	51P684	←_____	6R9881	←_____
94H913	←_____	8Q9538	←_____	5R8916	←_____
22H516	←_____	4P7861	←_____	2R8712	←_____
33J617	←_____	5G8432	←_____	5S2132	←_____
43K519	←_____	9P1234	←_____	4T1078	←_____
77K622	←_____	8Q7041	←_____	9G6712	←_____
84K418	←_____	94K492	←_____	1R4114	←_____
954U86	←_____	62L599	←_____		

NUMBER CORRECT OUT OF 50: _____

Perception Exercise 41

You are now ready to start your training in six-digit perception.

Using the Flashmeter card, expose the numbers for a fraction of a second, getting a *visual* impression. Do not say the digits to yourself. Reproduce each number in the blank to the right and then check your result.

| 824793 | ←_____ | 679154 | ←_____ | 912345 | ←_____ |
| 796531 | ←_____ | 563978 | ←_____ | 435689 | ←_____ |

135697 ←_____	943762 ←_____	903416 ←_____
397428 ←_____	472747 ←_____	037513 ←_____
479231 ←_____	329682 ←_____	827364 ←_____
246815 ←_____	484263 ←_____	928732 ←_____
814563 ←_____	836425 ←_____	837290 ←_____
683159 ←_____	983682 ←_____	983110 ←_____
632748 ←_____	839402 ←_____	119820 ←_____
763894 ←_____	790432 ←_____	198112 ←_____
782379 ←_____	749382 ←_____	836453 ←_____
364717 ←_____	714902 ←_____	700080 ←_____
134762 ←_____	854819 ←_____	839190 ←_____
376987 ←_____	736291 ←_____	837283 ←_____
725368 ←_____	954032 ←_____	754637 ←_____
197426 ←_____	841390 ←_____	736457 ←_____
274379 ←_____	738572 ←_____	

NUMBER CORRECT OUT OF 50: _____

Perception Exercise 42

Sweep down each column, making only one fixation to the line. Go as fast as adequate comprehension permits, and be more aware of the ideas than of inner speech.

Your eyes are muscles, and correct use of those muscles	cannot injure them. If you make sure to do	most of your reading in daylight, or in artificial light

↓

↓

↓

so placed	in a shaded lamp—	overhead lights
that no shadow falls	preferably	in your home;
on the page,	from a frosted bulb—	use a lamp,
and of sufficient strength	coming over	placed to your left
so that the act	your left shoulder,	whenever practicable,
of reading	produces ideal,	and see that the bulbs
causes no strain,	shadowless reading	are no weaker
you can,	conditions.	than 75 watts.
under these	Try to avoid doing	The important things
ideal conditions,	any considerable amount	are:
go on reading	of reading	a sufficient intensity
for hours	in a moving train,	of light
without feeling	especially at night.	for your type of eyes,
the slightest fatigue.	Avoid also	and the
It is generally agreed	doing any great amount	complete absence
that 75 to 100 watts	of reading	of shadows.
of electricity,	by means of	

Perception Exercise 43

Continue as before.

THE BEST TIME FOR LEARNING

↓

↓

↓

Did you ever notice	the morning hours?	not disturbed
when your sleep	Some people sleep	by a noise
is deeper;	so much deeper	that would wake
is it at night	at night	them up
or during	that they are	in the morning.

From "You *Can* Remember," A Home Study Course in Memory and Concentration, by Dr. Bruno Furst and Lotte Furst. Reprinted by permission.

↓ ↓ ↓

The opposite holds true for the morning sleeper. That fact in itself should not concern us in a memory course, but there is a very interesting connection between the depth of your sleep and the best time for you to learn and memorize. Many tests have proven that the person who sleeps easily and deeply during the early hours of the night is alert and full of life the moment he wakes up in the morning. Therefore his best learning time is the hour immediately after awaking. On the other hand, people who sleep deeper in the morning usually need several hours after breakfast to reach the peak of their mental ability. Their best learning time is the late afternoon and evening. Whether or not your job permits you to make use of your "best time" for such work as a memory course is another question. Frequently your business may require you to spend your "best time for learning" on some kind of mechanical work. If your "best time" is in the evening, you may be too tired after a full day's work to devote the evening hours to mental work. All this can happen in everyday life, but it is still important for you to be aware of your best learning time. Some day it may be possible for you to adjust your working hours and to do mental work at such times as are best for you. Doing so will save much effort and will considerably shorten the time you need to devote to repetition.

VOCABULARY STUDY VI

Words for Today

1. acerbity
2. altruism
3. bathos
4. bromide
5. claustrophobia
6. debauchery
7. ebullience
8. fracas
9. hauteur
10. iniquity
11. jingoism
12. kleptomania
13. limbo
14. malefactor
15. nostalgia
16. opulence
17. persiflage
18. quintessence
19. sadism
20. tedium

Do the usual dictionary study on those words that are not completely familiar to you, recording the essential information on meaning, pronunciation, derivation, related forms, and usage in your notebook, and writing a brief illustrative phrase or sentence for each word. Review your notes, then take the following test.

Test Your Learning

I. Write the adjective form for each of the following:

1. acerbity _____
2. altruism _____
3. bathos _____
4. bromide _____
5. claustrophobia _____
6. debauchery _____
7. ebullience _____
8. iniquity _____
9. jingoism _____
10. kleptomania _____
11. nostalgia _____
12. opulence _____
13. quintessence _____
14. sadism _____
15. tedium _____

II. Referring to the list on this page, choose the word that best fits each definition. _____

1. fear of enclosed places _____
2. seduction from virtue _____
3. great injustice _____
4. sourness of taste _____

5. pathological cruelty _____
6. advocacy of a warlike foreign policy _____
7. great noise or disturbance _____
8. great wealth _____
9. sudden falling off in dignity or importance _____
10. condition or state of being forgotten _____
11. perfect embodiment _____
12. overweening haughtiness _____
13. tiresome cliché _____
14. compulsive and pathological thievery _____
15. wrongdoer _____
16. bantering, witty talk _____
17. greater interest in the welfare of others than in one's own welfare _____
18. state of being boringly wearisome _____
19. bubbling enthusiasm _____
20. homesickness _____
21. excessive indulgence in sensual activity _____
22. great abundance _____
23. wickedness _____
24. harshness of temper or attitude _____
25. concentrated essence _____

Key:
I. 1. acerb, 2. altruistic, 3. bathetic, 4. bromidic, 5. claustrophobic, 6. debauched, 7. ebullient, 8. iniquitous, 9. jingoistic, 10. kleptomaniacal, 11. nostalgic, 12. opulent, 13. quintessential, 14. sadistic, 15. tedious.

II. 1. claustrophobia, 2. debauchery, 3. iniquity, 4. acerbity, 5. sadism, 6. jingoism, 7. fracas, 8. opulence, 9. bathos, 10. limbo, 11. quintessence, 12. hauteur, 13. bromide, 14. kleptomania, 15. malefactor, 16. persiflage, 17. altruism, 18. tedium, 19. ebullience, 20. nostalgia, 21. debauchery, 22. opulence, 23. iniquity, 24. acerbity, 25. quintessence.

HOW TO WHIP THROUGH MATERIAL WITH GOOD COMPREHENSION

Preview

Your training is winding up to a close now, and in this chapter you:
* Tackle a third round of timed reading selections.
* Practice to keep up your new speed even though the material will be somewhat more difficult.
* Try to increase your responsiveness to an author's pattern of thinking.
* Sharpen your skill in stripping a page down to its essential meaning.
* Are confronted with a fourth challenge to your reading habits.

> *Chapter 10* gives you added training in aggressive and rapid comprehension.

BREAKING THROUGH THE SPEED BARRIER

For many weeks you have been training to increase the efficiency of your reading habits by intensive practice:

1. In consciously moving faster through material—
2. In speedily pursuing the central theme of a selection while sensing the structure of the author's thinking—
3. In reducing regressions, eliminating any tendency to vocalization, and decreasing your dependency on inner speech—
4. In enlarging your recognition span, shortening your fixation time, and making greater use of your peripheral vision—
5. In covering a complete novel or magazine in one evening—
6. In improving your reading vocabulary—
7. In skimming the less important parts of material—

And, in general, in learning to employ all the aggressive techniques that help you strip a page down to its essential meaning in the least possible time—techniques which, in a manner of speaking, permit you to break through the speed barrier that stands in the way of the inexperienced and unskillful reader.

We are now approaching the final phases of your training program. There is still a good deal of practice ahead of you—practice in refining and perfecting all the techniques of rapid and efficient comprehension that you have already learned; practice in still further speeding up your perception and in enlarging your span of recognition; practice in adding still more words to your reading vocabulary; and practice in covering a complete book of nonfiction in two or three evenings.

In these final stages of your work, you will continue to extend your horizons. Are you ready to branch out some more, to spread your wings, so to speak, and fly off into new territory? Are you ready to read new magazines, new authors, new categories of books? (We cover this question in the second part of chapter 11.) Are you ready to react more skeptically to what you read? (We work on this in the first part of chapter 11.) Have you developed enough faith in your comprehension to do a certain amount of skimming?

And have you, by now, sufficiently sharpened your general reading skill to cruise through somewhat more complex selections with at least the same speed and accuracy of comprehension that you have shown on previous, easier, selections?

This is the question we shall answer in the present chapter.

As a basis for comparison with your performance on the four selections in this chapter we shall use two figures—your initial rate on selection 1, which you recorded on page 11, and your average rate on the nine selections of chapter 7, which you recorded on the chart on page 393. Find these statistics, and copy them below.

INITIAL RATE IN CHAPTER 1 (*Page 11*): _____W.P.M.

AVERAGE RATE IN CHAPTER 7 (*Page 393*): _____W.P.M.

On your third-phase progress graph (page 394), draw a straight line parallel to the base line AB to correspond to each of these figures you have just copied. Label one line "initial rate," and the other "average rate, phase 2." Again, as in chapter 7, keep a careful record of your rates, completing the chart and graph as you go along.

By now, whenever you read, you should have the feeling that you are moving along at a rapid clip, understanding rapidly, thinking rapidly, responding rapidly. But you do more than that. You aim for a quick grasp of the main idea, the central theme, the gist, the total meaning (call it what you will) of the material. You see the minor details as background, the important details as support, clarification, elaboration, or extension of the main idea. You sense the pattern of the author's thinking, and you think along with him in that pattern. You skim, without guilt or anxiety, whenever the content of the page and your purpose in reading call for, or admit of, skimming. In short, you use every technique you possess to understand quickly, accurately, and intelligently.

Now sometimes, of course, you may slow up, you may reduce your rate, depending on the nature of the material and on what you want to get out of it. You will probably not be able to read all the selections of this chapter at the same, identical, unvarying speed, but will vary your pace to suit the varying content. However, you

will probably never again, if your training has been at all successful, read as slowly as you did before you started working in this
book.

A brief discussion following each comprehension test will consider the pattern and framework of the author's thinking. Study
these discussions carefully, referring to the selections as you do so,
in order to continue refining your awareness and understanding of
the structure of writing.

Selection 16

"CURES" FOR THE COMMON COLD
by Harold S. Diehl, M.D.

Start timing→ Despite general
skepticism about cures for the common cold, millions of dollars'
worth of commercial remedies are
still sold in this country every year.
Old-fashioned cures like asafetida
and camphor are no longer in
vogue, but in their place has come
a whole new arsenal of popular
remedies—vitamins, vaccines, nasal
medications and other drugs. Yet
careful investigation shows that
many of the most widely advertised
remedies now on the market are
utterly worthless. Some of them, in
fact, may be definitely harmful.

I

In an effort to discover an effective cold remedy, a series of investigations was begun ten years ago at
the University of Minnesota. The
studies grew out of a chance obser-

vation which had led me to believe
that morphine might be of value in
relieving acute head colds. Extensive tests corroborated this observation; but morphine, because of its
toxicity and the danger of habituation to it, was obviously unsuited
for general use. The scope of the
investigation was consequently
broadened in the hope of finding a
remedy that would be equally effective but less harmful. In this way,
many of the most widely used cold
preparations came under close
study.

The investigations were carried
out by the Students' Health Service
of the University. Each study was
specifically planned to avoid prejudice for or against any particular
medication. Physicians wrote prescriptions merely for "cold medication." The pharmacist filling them

From *The American Mercury*. Reprinted with permission.

used in sequence the medications being studied at the time. Neither physician nor patient knew what medication had been given. After forty-eight hours of treatment, the patients reported the results on cards prepared for this purpose. Upon the basis of these reports the effectiveness of the medication in each case was estimated. Finally, the pharmacist's record was obtained and the results tabulated according to the various medications used.

In each of these studies some of the tablets and capsules given out contained only milk sugar. These were included so that we might know what proportion of patients would recover without treatment in the forty-eight-hour period for which results were reported. In other words, the group who received sugar tablets, thinking that they contained medication, served as a "control group" for the rest of the study.

The importance of having this control was clearly shown in the very first investigations. Approximately 35 per cent of the students who got the sugar tablets reported "definite improvement" or "complete cure" of their colds within forty-eight hours. Some of them experienced such prompt and remarkable improvement, in fact, that they went out of their way to praise the tablets as the most effective treatments they had ever taken. Apart from the humor of the situation, this control group showed that ap-

proximately 35 per cent of patients would have recovered quickly regardless of any medication. For the purposes of our studies, therefore, we put down as of little or no value all cold medications from which less than 50 per cent of our subjects reported benefit.

Virtually all of the most commonly used medications proved, on this basis, to be almost valueless. This group of remedies included aspirin, calcium and iodine, halibut liver oil (which is vitamin A), amytal, ephedrine, atropine, an aspirin-phenacetin-caffeine compound (which is sold under various names) and soda.

Although aspirin ranks at the top of this group, the results from it are very little better than from the sugar tablets. This is true regardless of the brand of aspirin used, "genuine" or otherwise.

Even less valuable were the results obtained from soda, another widely recommended cold remedy. Advertisers have emphasized the importance of "alkalization" in the treatment of colds. In this study we gave sufficient dosages of soda to produce much more alkalization than is possible from any of the commercial preparations sold in drug stores. Yet the results of this alkalization were exactly the same as those reported from the sugar tablets.

Perhaps the most commonly used of all cold remedies are the preparations to be dropped or sprayed into the nose. In our studies we selected

314

the most extensively advertised and widely sold brand of "nose drops."

It was transferred to unlabeled bottles, and then dispensed to the students with the directions given by the manufacturer. Only 31 per cent reported benefit from it, about the same as those who used sugar tablets.

Nasal preparations not only have little value, but may do harm by interfering with the body's natural defenses. Medical research has shown that the common cold is usually initiated by a virus or by bacteria which gain entry through the upper respiratory tract. A primary stage of infection follows, whose symptoms are stuffiness of the nose, sneezing, watery nasal discharge, dryness of the throat, occasionally mild headaches, and often mild general symptoms—but with no elevation of temperature and a usual duration of four to five days. This stage may be followed by secondary infections caused by other germs that happen to be present in the nose and throat. The secondary stage is accompanied by a thick, yellow discharge, and runs a typical subacute course of two or three weeks.

Nature has provided man with remarkable local defenses against these bacterial invaders. At the entrance to the nasal passages are tiny hairs, called vibrissae, which filter out the larger particles of foreign material in the air. Next in the defense system are numerous glands located throughout the membranes of the nose. These glands constantly produce a moist, slightly sticky secretion which covers the surfaces of the membranes with a mucous film. The film is in constant movement toward the pharynx, and is renewed approximately every ten minutes. It has been estimated that 75 per cent of the dust and germs present in the air are removed in this manner.

The mucous film also protects the delicate membranes of the nose from mechanical injury by particles of dust. It is extremely difficult for bacteria to find their way through this mucous covering as long as it remains intact. On the other hand, injury to this mucous coat and exposure of the underlying membranes opens a portal of entry for infection.

Last of nature's defenses are the cilia. These are microscopic, hairlike projections covering most of the mucous membranes in the nose. They are in constant wave-like motion, much like fields of grain. They pick up cells and particles of foreign matter and carry these to the pharynx, from which they are discharged or swallowed.

Nasal preparations may be harmful precisely because they can destroy or interfere with this defense system. Drying and medicated oils first slow and eventually stop the action of the cilia. Their constant use may even destroy respiratory epithelium. More important, nasal sprays or oils, though they may give temporary relief of congestion

315

and stuffiness, frequently produce a distinct irritation of the nasal mucous membranes, in this way facilitating the path of secondary bacterial infection.

Finally, there is always the danger of a specific type of pneumonia that may result from the inhalation of oily substances into the lungs. For all of these reasons, nose and throat specialists warn against the introduction of medicinal preparations into the nose. It should be done only when definitely indicated and recommended by a physician for the treatment of some specific condition.

Equally useless are the mouth washes, gargles and antiseptics urged by advertisers upon the public. These preparations may destroy germs in test tubes if given sufficient time. But none of them acts instantaneously, nor are they effective in the weak solutions which can be tolerated by the membranes of the nose and throat. Furthermore, only a very small proportion of the membranes of the nose and throat can possibly be reached by sprays and gargles.

Several other more or less universal home remedies proved valueless in our studies. Cathartics of various kinds, for example, have long figured in home treatment of colds, and are included in many of the advertised remedies. Actually, two recent studies both show that cathartics are of no value in colds, and that patients who take them lose more time from work than those who do not.

Another popular belief stresses the value of large quantities of liquids, in the form of water, lemonade, orange juice and other drinks. The purpose of the liquids is to increase excretion. Presumably, this aids in the elimination of the supposedly toxic products produced by the infection. This sounds plausible, but unfortunately there is no evidence that it actually occurs.

Alcohol, in the form of whiskey, brandy and "hot toddies," is still another popular remedy of dubious value. Fear of increasing that popularity prevented us from using it in our series of studies. Scientifically, there may be some basis, or perhaps excuse, for the use of alcohol in colds. It causes an increase in the blood flow to the skin, with a resultant feeling of warmth if one is wet and chilled. On the other hand. alcohol itself causes nasal congestion in some people; and many reliable studies have shown that its continuous or excessive use lowers resistance to pneumonia, the most serious complication of colds.

II

Considerable effort has been made in recent years to discover possible measures for the *prevention* of colds. Two types of treatment have received particular notice. One of them is the use of dietary measures, including the taking of vitamins. The other employs the various kinds of cold vaccines.

A complete, adequate and balanced diet is necessary for the maintenance of health. But beyond this general truth, no special diet has value for either the prevention or the cure of colds. The same is true of vitamins, which have been particularly exploited as a preventive method. Studies have shown that both animals and man have a decreased resistance to infections of various kinds when suffering from vitamin deficiencies; and apparently this may be true for each of the better known vitamins. But it has not been shown that use of particular vitamins has any value for the prevention of colds. Although cod-liver oil, which contains vitamins A and D, has been reported by a number of authors to reduce the severity and the frequency of colds, most of these reports are based upon inadequately controlled studies.

To determine the value of cold vaccines, studies were made over a period of several years. These vaccines—not "cold serums" as they are commonly called—contain various mixtures of the bacteria most commonly found in the nose and throat of persons infected with colds. Our studies included two bacterial vaccines. One was administered hypodermically and the other by mouth.

Here again, we took special precautions to ensure maximum reliability. The students who volunteered for the study were assigned alternately and without selection to control groups and experimental groups. The control group received blanks instead of vaccines; but all students thought they were receiving vaccine, and so had the same attitude toward the study. Each student reported to the Health Service whenever a cold developed, and kept a record of each cold of more than twenty-four hours' duration. But even the physicians who saw these patients did not know which group they represented. The number and severity of colds experienced by these students were then tabulated according to the group—control or vaccine—to which they belonged.

First, here are the results obtained from injected bacterial vaccine, or "cold shots"—the oldest and most widely used vaccine. The students vaccinated with it reported that during the previous year they had averaged 4.7 colds per person. During the year that they were taking the vaccine they averaged only 2.1 colds per person. This is a reduction of 55 per cent—apparently an excellent result. In fact, this reduction was the same as has been reported in other studies, indicating that these vaccines are of value.

Unfortunately, this report was completely neutralized by the control students who reported an average of 4.9 colds during the previous year. During the year of the study, they had only 1.9 colds, a reduction of 61 per cent. In other words, the control group, which got nothing of any possible value for the prevention of colds, reported just as good results as did the group which got the vaccine. It is thus easy to see how enthusiastic recommendations may be made in good faith for particular cold remedies, and still be entirely without scientific justification.

Our results with the oral vaccine were astonishingly similar. This oral vaccine consists essentially of the same organisms contained in the vaccines for subcutaneous use. They are killed by heat and administered in capsules or tablets. In our study, the students of the experimental group received capsules containing vaccine. The control group received capsules filled only with sugar.

The reports from the vaccinated group showed a reduction of approximately 70 per cent in the average number of colds per person in the year of study. This looked like an excellent result, and was again approximately the same reduction as had been reported by other investigators. But the control group, as in the previous study, also reported the same reduction in the average number of colds. Moreover, during the year of the study the vaccinated group had an average of 2.1 colds per person, which was virtually the same as the 2.0 average reported by the control group. To make the parallel even more striking, the average number of days lost per person from school work was exactly the same for the two groups!

III

Is there any remedy, then, of value in the treatment of colds?

There is no measure that is uniformly effective for the prevention of the common cold. Our studies,

however, did reveal one group of medications which seemed to have distinct benefit. I have already stated that morphine, which is a derivative of opium, showed excellent results but was discarded because of its dangers. But several other derivatives of opium, which are less toxic and carry no practical danger of habituation, proved to be definitely valuable. In our first studies, codeine and papaverine both gave evidence of value in the treatment of acute colds. Neither was so effective as morphine, however, and since both are quite different chemically it was decided to try them in combination.

The codeine-papaverine mixture proved to be, after morphine, the most valuable of all cold medications. A preparation consisting of one-quarter grain of codeine and one-quarter grain of papaverine was finally selected as the most effective dosage. Of 1,500 students who were given this preparation for the treatment of acute head colds, 72 per cent reported definite improvement or complete relief within twenty-four to forty-eight hours. The chief beneficial effect was a marked decrease or complete disappearance of nasal congestion and discharge. With the relief of these symptoms, in many cases, the progress of the cold seemed to be arrested and the secondary stage of protracted nasal discharge avoided.

While taking this medication, most of the students were up and about, attending classes. Had they remained in bed while using it, it

318

is probable that even better results might have been obtained. The earlier in the course of the cold that this preparation is used, the larger the proportion of good results. This preparation, commonly called Copavin, is not advertised to the public. But it is available through physicians, who should decide when and in what dosage it should be used.

Since these studies were made, confirmatory reports have been published by several other investigators. Dr. Russell Cecil of New York, and Dr. Fritz Hutter of Vienna, both found that the codeine-papaverine mixture was particularly beneficial if used by their patients at the very beginning of the infection. In this connection, too, it is of interest to recall the statement that opium users rarely have colds. De Quincey, in his *Confessions,* wrote that during the years in which he had taken opium he "never once caught cold, as the phrase is, nor even the slightest cough. But after discontinuing the use of opium, a violent cold attacked me, and a cough soon after." In a similar vein writes Cocteau, in his *Diary of an Addict.* "Opium," he says, "is a season. The smoker no longer suffers from changes in the weather. He never catches cold."

Less effective, but still of moderate value, were several other opium derivatives. In addition to codeine alone and papaverine alone, it was found that powdered opium and the old-fashioned Dover's powder (a combination of powdered opium and powdered ipecac) were bene-ficial. Quinine also came to be included in this group of moderately valuable medications. The proportion of individuals who reported "complete relief" or "definite improvement" after the use of these preparations ranged from 57 per cent for powdered opium down to 50 per cent for quinine.

Finally, certain general hygienic measures are helpful in the treatment of colds. Going to bed and remaining there until recovery is good advice. The value of bed rest lies in protecting others from exposure, in increasing general resistance, and in keeping the body warm. Bed rest during the acute stages of colds, supplemented by such other treatment as is indicated, would diminish their severity, limit their spread and reduce the frequency of complications.

Hot baths for the treatment of colds may consist of hot water, hot air or steam. The effect of these baths is to dilate the blood vessels of the skin and to increase blood flow through them. As a result, nasal congestion and stuffiness are reduced. Similar effects may be obtained with massage or other forms of physiotherapy, with hot or cold compresses, mustard plasters and certain medicated ointments. If such treatments are followed by rest in bed with sufficient covers to prevent cooling, the effect is prolonged and the possibility of their being of more than temporary benefit is increased. Exercise, frequently utilized by athletes to "sweat out" a cold, has a similar effect. But usu-

319

ally the symptoms return when the body gets chilled, and then the cold may become even more severe than before.   ←**End timing**

Test Your Comprehension

Of the following eight statements, three are main points. Check the *three* main points.

1. These investigations were carried on at the University of Minnesota.
2. Many widely advertised cold cures and home remedies are worthless or harmful.
3. Students treated with sugar tablets showed little or no improvement.
4. Neither vaccines, nor vitamins and other dietary measures, prevent colds.
5. Only a codeine-papaverine mixture, quinine, or certain hygienic measures were found to provide any relief or improvement in the treatment of colds.
6. Nasal oils and sprays were found to be dangerous.
7. The first type of cold remedy experimented with was hot baths.
8. Staying in bed for the duration of a cold was the only remedy that showed any results.

Compute Your Rate

(*Approximate number of words: 3000*)

TIME	W.P.M.	TIME	W.P.M.
4 min.	750	9 min.	333
5 min.	600	10 min.	300
6 min.	500	11 min.	272
7 min.	429	12 min.	250
8 min.	375	13 min.	231

YOUR RATE ON SELECTION 16: _____W.P.M.
(*Record this statistic on the chart and graph on page 394.*)

Discussion of the Selection

Paragraph 1: Dr. Diehl has three main points he wishes to make, and he states one of them at the end of his first paragraph—*many widely advertised remedies are worthless; some may be harmful.*

Section I: Here the author explains why these remedies are worthless or harmful, supporting his first point with the results of the experiment at the University of Minnesota, and with medical facts.

Section II: Now Dr. Diehl develops his second point—*colds apparently cannot be prevented either by dietary measures (including vitamins) or by vaccines.* Again he supports his statements by results of the experimental study.

Section III: Developing his third point, Dr. Diehl explains how he found a *codeine-papaverine mixture* effective in providing relief or improvement; comments on the values of *morphine* and of *quinine;* and suggests such *hygienic measures* as bed-rest, massage, etc. as having some benefit in the treatment of colds.

If, as you were reading, you were able to sense the three-part structure of this article, you realized clearly that the author's final meaning was somewhat as follows: *Many advertised cold cures and home remedies are worthless or harmful; vaccines, vitamins, and dietary measures do not prevent colds; only a codeine-papaverine mixture, quinine, or certain hygienic measures were found to provide any relief or improvement.*

The statements you should have checked in the comprehension test were numbers 2, 4, and 5.

Selection 17

GIVE YOUNG DOCTORS A BREAK
by J. D. Ratcliff

Start timing→ It is axiomatic that the future of medicine lies in the hands of highly trained young physicians. Yet in a shockingly high percentage of communities these gifted young men are being systematically barred from practice by older men—medical monopolists.

It works this way. Young Dr. Smith completes his long, arduous and expensive medical training. He then passes the examinations which qualify him as a specialist. He finds a town that needs a man of his talents. He then applies to the local hospital for admission to the staff—

From the *Woman's Home Companion*, copyright 1948 by Crowell-Collier Publishing Co. Reprinted with permission of the author.

which will permit him to take patients to that hospital.

The older physicians he talks to are friendly. But what about the hospital appointment, he asks? Here he runs head on into the ugly facts of medical economics.

In a great many communities older doctors do not want aggressive competition. In this respect they are like others involved in making a living. Yet there is a difference. A lawyer would find it difficult to keep another lawyer from opening an office. A filling station operator would find it impossible to keep a competitor off an attractive corner. Physicians *do* have the power to squelch potentially dangerous competition—by denying hospital staff appointments.

Dr. Smith is told he must serve a "probationary period." How long this probationary period is to last is left up in the air. Dr. Smith can treat sniffles and boils and children's leg aches. But if any of his patients require hospital care, he must refer them to a man already on the staff—probably never to see them again. Patients conclude that there must be something wrong with Dr. Smith—otherwise he would be admitted to the hospital. Therefore, why go back to him?

Of course there are a good many established doctors who make a point of helping the young Dr. Smiths of America. But they are comparatively few. There are cases where Dr. Smiths have waited one to five years for hospital appointments; and cases where appoint-

ments have never been granted. Dean Willard C. Rappleye of Columbia University's College of Physicians and Surgeons considers this "the greatest waste in our present system of medical service." It is accentuating the drift to the cities, where there is too much medical practice to be controlled by any small group of monopolists. It is robbing smaller communities of the bright young men who might revitalize the whole practice of medicine.

War gave one rapidly growing southern city dozens of new industries—each required one or more doctors. Young physicians saw this as an easy means of getting into practice in the town. But the hospital staff moved swiftly. They decreed that these men would have to wait a minimum of five years for a hospital appointment. The same sort of action was also taken in many west coast cities.

In another town in the midwest the hospital staff required interns to sign agreements not to practice in the town for at least ten years after their training!

In other situations young physicians receive hospital appointments —but have no patients referred to them by older doctors. This happened to a young surgeon in a Pennsylvania town. Other physicians were quick to detect his remarkable skill. In his first year he performed only eight operations. Each patient was the wife of a physician! The doctors wanted their wives to have the best. At the end of a year the young man gave up. A question naturally arises. Isn't surgery an art which is acquired only after years of practice? Many professors in teaching hospitals answer this with an emphatic *no*. The young men turned out today are, they say, the most highly qualified in the profession. To be sure, they will continue to learn in practice. Strong emphasis should be placed on another point: we aren't speaking here of graduates from Grade B medical schools. We are speaking of the really well-trained young physicians—who face the same difficulties as the most poorly trained.

Let's take a specific case of what a well-trained young man goes through before he is ready to hang out his shingle. In premedical college Jim S. was a brilliant student—straight A's. He knew he had to be good to get into the medical college he had selected, one of the finest in the world. When he completed this preliminary training there were twenty-five hundred applications for one hundred places in the freshman class of this medical college. He managed to make it.

Even though he cut expenses to the bone, Jim was a big drain on his family, which was none too well off. Tuition, books and lab fees, room, board, clothing, trips home (on a bus) and other expenses brought the total per year to two thousand dollars.

Jim graduated in 1939. By this time he had decided to specialize in surgery. He had fine manual dexterity and ability to reason calmly under stress—qualifications for a good surgeon. The problem facing him now was to get an internship.

It was simple enough, Jim knew, to get an internship if one weren't too choosy. But in many hospitals an internship is little better than a form of slave labor. Such hospitals offer meager opportunities to learn.

So Jim applied for internship in the great teaching hospital associated with the medical college from which he had been graduated. There were hundreds of applications for the nine internships open in general surgery at Metropolis Hospital. Grave-faced physicians prodded him with questions. His past life was investigated, his class records and grades scrutinized. Finally Jim was accepted for one of the nine places.

During his eighteen months' internship Jim still had to rely on his family for help. Bed and board were free and there were no tuition or lab fees. Still, he had to have some money—fifty dollars a month.

In most hospitals Jim would have had little surgical practice. But in his eighteen months at Metropolis he did a number of major operations—always, of course, with an older, more experienced man at his side.

At the end of his internship Jim might have gone into private practice. But he still felt he wasn't ready. He wanted more graduate training as a resident, a residency

323

being the main avenue toward a specialty.

At this point competition had become really fierce. Only five interns would be selected for junior assistant residencies (fifty dollars per month) in surgery. Again Jim was fortunate—thanks to his readily recognized talents. Then the Japs struck, on December 7, 1941. Jim was in uniform by February, 1942, commissioned a captain.

When the invasion did come, Jim moved into Holland. It was hard, grinding work. Jim realized that war was the greatest of all laboratories in which to learn surgery. In weeks or months a man could accumulate experience he would spend years getting in civilian practice.

Jim wound up his army service in November, 1945, came back to student life—and to a degree of not-so-genteel poverty. As assistant resident his salary was seventy-five dollars a month. Thus the grind went on—the grind that is required today of any man who wishes to become a really skilled practitioner of a medical specialty.

By 1946 Jim had gone through his junior assistant residency and his assistant residency. He was now ready for his senior residency (one hundred dollars a month)—if he could get it. In the United States there are probably no more than a hundred and twenty-five senior residencies in surgery—and Jim had picked one of the most difficult of all spots to apply, world-famous Metropolis Hospital.

Jim got the appointment. He did great and difficult pieces of surgery during this year—removal of lungs, kidney surgery, exploration of the common bile duct for tiny stones that cause blockage.

At this point the reader would conclude that any hospital in the country would welcome Jim. The fact is that Jim knew he would be barred from practice in hundreds of communities by men with a fraction of his skill. He might have to wait one to five years before he could perform the types of major surgery for which he has unusual talent.

Furthermore, he knew that he would not have access to hospital libraries with the books and journals which he could not afford. Nor would he have the elaborate equipment and diagnostic aids which he had been taught to rely on. Jim had some rather sour thoughts about his wisdom in selecting medicine as a career. When the medical college from which he was graduated offered him a job as instructor in surgery, Jim jumped at it. The salary: thirty-six hundred dollars a year.

The objection will be raised that Jim is hardly typical of the young physician entering practice. This is true. He isn't. He is representative of the best. But the hundreds of Jims among the five thousand-odd physicians who will enter practice this year will face the same barriers that confront the most poorly trained. Religious and racial prejudices further complicate the picture. Thus hundreds of communities are denied the superior type of medical and surgical service which these young physicians might provide. There are many towns of fifty thousand people with not a single modernly trained surgeon.

The solution? There is no easy one. The best medical minds are troubled by the situation. One group suggests that once a student has passed his specialty board examinations—which screen out all but the most highly qualified—he should be admitted to any hospital staff automatically.

Another group contends this would produce ruinous competition which would tend to lower medical standards. As an alternative they see group or clinic practice as the answer—where an orthopedist, internist, pediatrician and other specialists go together to give a community a miniature Mayo or Lahey clinic. Whatever the answer, the problem is there—an ugly stumbling block on the road to better medical care. It is one requiring thought and action, for as long as it exists, many communities will continue to get 1920 medicine for 1948 ills.   ←End timing

RECORD HERE THE TIME REQUIRED ON THIS SELECTION: _____ MIN.
_____ SEC.

Test Your Comprehension

Check the main idea:

1. Young doctors need more practice before they should be permitted to attempt difficult surgical cases.

2. Older doctors do not want aggressive competition, because they feel that the public will suffer.

3. Young doctors should be permitted to gain skill by practicing on patients, even if it is not for the patients' ultimate good.

4. Many older doctors who don't want competition bar brilliant young doctors from using their talents by refusing them hospital appointments (or by making it most difficult for them to get such appointments); this is a stumbling block to better medical care.

Compute Your Rate

(*Approximate number of words: 1685*)

TIME	W.P.M.	TIME	W.P.M.
2 min.	843	3 min., 30 sec.	482
2 min., 15 sec.	749	4 min.	422
2 min., 30 sec.	674	4 min., 30 sec.	374
2 min., 45 sec.	613	5 min.	337
3 min.	562	5 min., 30 sec.	306

TIME	W.P.M.	TIME	W.P.M.
6 min.	281	8 min.	211
7 min.	241		

YOUR RATE ON SELECTION 17: _____W.P.M.
(*Record this statistic on the chart and graph on page 394.*)

Discussion of the Selection

Mr. Ratcliff hammers home one major point throughout this piece (statement no. 4 in the comprehension test), expressing it completely and explicitly by the end of the fourth paragraph (specifically in paragraphs 1 and 4). From then on, he piles supporting details upon details, repetition of the theme upon repetition, right down to the last word in the last sentence of the final paragraph.

The last two paragraphs, as you doubtless realized, contained two possible solutions; and the author makes it clear that we must find *some* solution if we are to have better medical care.

Selection 18

DIET AND DIE
by Carlton Fredericks

I

Start timing→ Most Americans love to diet. Men and women, old and young, plump and fat, rich and poor, sooner or later are tempted to try some "miracle diet" that promises to shed weight easily, quickly, and painlessly. Yet in their eagerness to outwit the laws of nature and medicine, they forget that improper dieting can lead to grim and inexorable death.

2. But wait a minute, you protest. Isn't that statement about death extreme? Intelligent people don't go in for lethal diets and deadly food fads. They cut out fats and starches, to be sure; perhaps they try mineral-oil salad dressings or some of the other widely publicized tricks. But can such dietary shortcuts lead directly to the grave?

3. Well, it is true that death certificates never read "Reducing Diet." Yet science has taught us that a

From *Coronet*, April, 1947, copyright 1947 by Esquire, Inc. Reprinted with permission of *Coronet* and of the author. Mr. Fredericks is a nationally known nutrition research consultant.

human body lacking in a full ration of proteins and vitamins stands little chance in a fight against disease. So no matter how the certificates may read, if death comes on the heels of a reducing diet, who is the real culprit? The disease germ itself, or the inadequate diet that weakened the body?

4. First, let's glance at some case histories in Hollywood, where the camera makes everyone look ten pounds heavier. Thanks to this phenomenon of the lens, the calory is the god of movie stars. And because the waistline is the lifeline of film society, the calory has driven some studio notables to gastronomic suicide.

5. Remember Laird Cregar, brilliant but bulky screen villain? Villains don't make romantic stars, so he decided to reduce. In a few months he starved away 100 pounds. As delighted as his tailor, he looked forward to more glamorous roles.

6. The end of the story was no beat of publicity drums for the "new" Cregar, but a muffled roll for his death. Actually it occurred on the operating table, yet everyone knows that operations are more often successful if the patient is strong and in good condition. Was this precipitous loss of weight and the untimely loss of life merely a strange coincidence?

7. And how about bent-nosed, beloved Louis Wolheim? Months and pounds passed away as he dieted. Then the wire services flashed the stark words: "Louis Wolheim, ex-professor of mathematics, star of *What Price Glory*, died suddenly tonight." Wolheim's death certificate didn't read "starvation." But did he decide to juggle calories with waistline and forget to hold on to health? . . .

8. Now for the case of a third Hollywood star. By the grace of her physician's intervention she is still on the screen, so let's call her plain Mary. She was another who found herself losing in the endless fight against the fattening camera, so she condemned herself to breakfasts of black coffee and butterless toast, luncheons of skimpy salads and almost vitamin-free Melba toast, dinners of one lamb chop, vegetable and coffee. Yet even this diet, pittance for a hard-working body, failed to bring her weight down.

9. Whereupon Mary shifted from skimpiness to starvation. This did the trick—yet scarcely had she remodeled her wardrobe when she was rushed to a sanitarium.

10. The studio said: "Mary has been overworking. She must guard against a nervous breakdown."

11. The truth was, Mary's reducing diet lacked everything the human body needs to sustain life. *Everything:* proteins, calories, fats, vitamins, minerals, and bulk.

12. Unfortunately, you don't have to be a movie star to find the die in diet. Furthermore, for the unknown ordinary thousands who learn too late, there are countless others who escape the grave, only to fall victim to influenza, pneumo-

nia, insanity, prolonged invalidism, and pregnancy complications.

13. If you embark on a dolt's diet —which they all are unless tailored by an expert to your own specifications—any of these disasters can occur. According to the Mayo Clinic, a group of volunteer subjects traveled to the edge of insanity on what seemed to be a nourishing diet. It was adequate indeed, as to calories, but far below the danger point in a vitamin essential to the nervous system. After a few months every "guinea pig" reported insomnia, forgetfulness, confusion, apathy, and "an inescapable sense" that some misfortune awaited him.

14. Further proof that proper nutrition involves far more than a minimum number of calories is offered by the case of Miss S.R. Proud of her figure, this young Manhattan woman fought the battle of the bulge successfully until she underwent an operation. Then inactivity and a forced diet caused her to gain twenty pounds. Her doctor wisely refused to help, saying: "Plenty of time for that when you're completely well again."

15. So S.R. walked out on him and into the hands of a "specialist"— "naturopath," to be precise. This gentleman was happy to take her currency in return for placing her on a two-month diet of nothing but mashed potatoes and fruit juices. As the pounds slipped away, S.R. was happy too. Delighted, in fact—until they began slipping too fast.

16. Fright then set in, changing to terror when her face erupted with boils, her ankles swelled, her nails grew dry and brittle, and her hair fell out by the handful. Sensibly she dropped the diet. But it was too late; the symptoms continued. So back to her doctor she went— pale, sallow, anemic.

17. He found her deficient in everything essential to minimum nutrition. Like many people, she didn't realize that nutritional deficiencies can become irreversible. In other words, human cells too long deprived of essential substances reach a point where they cannot assimilate these substances, no matter how the concentrations are administered.

18. S.R. happened to be lucky. A high protein diet, ample in calories, rich in vitamins and minerals, brought her slowly back to normal. And today she has a stock reply to everyone who mentions the subject of reducing: "Narrow coffins cost as much as wide ones."

19. Because we are civilized people, we like our meat "fractionated" —that is, the muscle meats separated from the organ meats, just as we prefer grains stripped of the vitamin-rich bran and germ. While we attempt partially to replace natural vitamins lost in baker's bread with synthetic ones, we do not replace the food values lost in eating muscle meats without the organs.

20. The Eskimos forestall this danger intuitively. They gobble their animals from nose to tail, including bone marrow, with the result that pernicious anemia and prematurely

328

gray hair are rare in the Arctic. When white explorers contract scurvy up there, the Eskimos cure them with animals' adrenal glands containing high concentrations of vitamin C.

21. Suppose your "common sense" low-starch muscle-meat diet happens to lack pantothenic acid, the vitamin which affects the endocrine gland. Dogs deficient in it look well and even eat well, right up to the moment when, without warning, they drop dead.

22. We have much to learn about the effects of pantothenic acid on human beings, yet we know that a lack of it produces an unhealthy mouth and tongue. It also slows down peristalsis of the colon, a phenomenon which contributes to the $100,000,000-a-year laxative business—and to nothing else.

23. Yes—the fact that people don't die from their diets is a testimonial not to the diet but to the adaptability of the human body. For example, the wiseacres who substitute mineral oil for salad dressings are making, in one step, more mistakes than their instinct for error should permit.

24. Mineral oil hinders the body in absorbing the fat-soluble vitamins A, D, E and K. Vitamin A prevents colds and skin trouble; D helps the skin to assimilate oxygen; E wards off miscarriage and other pregnancy complications; K is the blood-clotting vitamin that slows down or averts hemorrhages. Mineral oil also interferes with the absorption of C, the anti-tooth-decay vitamin. I have

actually seen scurvy in children fed plenty of orange juice—and too much mineral oil. The oil washes the vitamin out of the body.

25. But there's still more to the grim story. Mineral oil forms a coating in the digestive tract which sneers at the vitally important vitamin-B complex—the B complex which serves many functions, such as helping digestion. Americans who contracted heart weakness as prisoners of war and were released before the muscle failure had become irreversible responded successfully to B complex treatment.

26. Some scientists suspect that the human embryo itself is affected by B complex deficiency. We know it causes harelips, cleft palates, and bone derangements in animals. It has not yet been proved that human harelips are similarly caused, but the implication is enough to warn against toying with vitamin-B complex.

II

27. If I have persuaded you that there is a die in diet, so much the better. Yet reducing *can* be safe and successful. All you need do is follow a few simple rules.

28. First, if you are too fat you must discover the cause. It may be plain overeating, a glandular defect, or even nerves.

29. Actually, a neurotic frustration is a common cause, as in the case of T. W., a 35-year-old Brooklyn housewife. Five feet six inches tall, she weighed 245 pounds—all of it acquired on a diet of penny candy,

coffee, meat, cigarettes, laxatives and indigestion remedies. She complained that the skimpy meals merely added more weight. Her dietitian soon discovered she had never been popular with men, and that food proved a happy substitute. Even her small amount was always there, always pleasing and soothing.

30. The dietitian persuaded her to toss the candy overboard, while the skimpy meals were replaced by three balanced ones, low only in calories. She felt she was eating more, but she lost 115 pounds in 18 months.

31. When she reached her proper weight she became pregnant for the first time in seven years of married life. Her grateful glands had finally responded, a frequent result once fatness has been overcome by a balanced diet.

32. Glandular obesity is as rare as a hen's tooth. Only one case of overweight in a thousand, say the specialists, can be traced to the glands. Yet glands serve as scapegoats for droves of fat females.

33. Of course thyroid and pituitary obesity do exist. But the rare case of thyroid overweight is not necessarily corrected by administering extract, for the gland may have become underactive for quite another reason: a deficiency of vitamin B_1 or thiamine.

34. Hydrated individuals, people whose tissues store abnormal quantities of water, sometimes lose weight under a diet of restricted salt and fluids. And occasionally effective treatment is given for pituitary disturbance. But whether obesity is normal or otherwise, diet is the first step that must be taken. Everything else is secondary.

35. Once you have discovered why you are fat, it is time to start shedding the pounds. And a good way to begin is to get rid of all your food superstitions.

36. No phase of nutrition has provoked more folklore than reducing. Often you hear people say: "Don't eat that. It's fattening." Just ignore them. No food is fattening in itself, any more than an extra shovel of coal is necessarily too much for the furnace.

37. Like coal, food makes energy. Like the furnace, your body needs food to burn into energy. Without knowing how much fuel has already been fed to the furnace, how do you know which shovelful is too much? The same thing is true of food. The kind and quantity must be determined in exact relation to the body's needs.

38. A particularly vicious superstition is the one which says, "Don't take vitamins when reducing. They make you gain." Only calories make you gain. Vitamins have no calories. They do, however, perform the vital job of protecting you against the deficiencies of a reducing diet. That is why nutritionists supplement diets with vitamin prescriptions.

39. In addition to getting rid of superstitions and guarding against nutritional deficiencies, avoid drugs. The magic road to sylphdom was never traveled with a suitcase of pills and potions. At best they are

330

useless. At worst they pack a terrible wallop of misery. Let those who tried excess doses of various phenol products show you the cataracts on their eyes.

40. Psyllium-seed laxatives, touted because they form bulk and thus create an illusion of fullness in the stomach, are of no value unless taken under careful medical guidance. Most other "reducing aids" are merely powerful laxatives—and nothing more. Concocted of salts, leaves or herbs, they rush foods through the system so fast that the calories vanish along with the food. So do the vitamins, minerals, and proteins. If this is your choice of how to lose weight, why bother to eat at all?

41. But you still think there is a magic road to reducing? Exercise, for example, or massage or nine-day diets? Exercise will not do it. Look at the charts to see how many miles of walking is necessary to dispose of the calories in one lamb chop and an apple.

42. Massage is a wonderful reducer —for the massager. Try to pound the fat out of a piece of meat. Even a sledge hammer won't do it, and surely you are not going to put that kind of a weapon in the hefty arms of your masseur.

43. As to most of the nine-day wonder diets, the wonder is that you survive. Many nutrition specialists warn against them because their caloric restrictions are too severe or because they lack vitamins. Yet this imbalance is a minor drawback compared to the one they share with all mass-production diets. Whether a reducing regimen includes starvation, drugs, psychoanalysis, deficiencies, and nine- or even 90-day schedules, it is never suitable for all cases of obesity. Every diet must be individually planned.

44. A physician may order a 1,200-calory diet to take 40 pounds off a 160-pounder, and he may prescribe the same number of calories from a totally different diet to remove the same weight from a 200-pounder. This is because the two people have different requirements, and indulge in different activities. These and other variables must be carefully considered when one is prescribing a diet tailored precisely to each individual's needs.

45. C.K. found this out to her eventual joy. At 16, she carried 178 pounds on a five-foot chassis. Yet she, a growing girl, lived on a cruel diet of 800 calories a day, supplemented by baneful drugs and thyroid tablets. And to make matters worse, she kept gaining!

46. Vitamin-B complex, multiple vitamin and mineral capsules were substituted for the drugs she had been taking, and a 1,200-calory diet was ordered, well balanced but not too high in proteins. For the first ten days she was restricted in salt and fluid intake. The youngster proceeded to lose 12 pounds in 40 days. Today she weighs 110 pounds. Her complexion, hair and nails are proof enough of her excellent health.

47. Whoever you are and whatever your individual requirements, remember that a reducing diet should not be fantastic, distorted, unbalanced, or deficient in anything essential to health. It should be supplemented with the calory-free elements it lacks. Except that it is low in calories, it should be a miniature of an unrestricted diet.

48. The acid test of a perfect reducing diet is this: *Can you expand the size of the portions and live happily ever after?* If not, think of those deceptive death certificates and, with the help of a competent doctor, work out a diet which will meet every nutritional test.

←End timing

RECORD HERE THE TIME REQUIRED ON THIS SELECTION: _____ MIN.

_____ SEC.

Test Your Comprehension

Check the main idea:

1. Unwise dieting will mean a sure and quick trip to the cemetery.
2. The advice of a physician is not necessary in selecting a proper diet if we just use common sense.
3. Improper dieting can be extremely harmful or even fatal; the safe and successful diet is made by a physician to fit your individual needs, is low in total calories, and is nutritionally balanced.
4. A number of well-known Hollywood stars died because the strain of dieting as well as acting proved too much for their constitutions.
5. Nutritional deficiencies, if unduly prolonged, can always be overcome by skillful doctoring.
6. In preparing a diet, the expert nutritionist mainly has to select fattening foods to be avoided.

Compute Your Rate

(*Approximate number of words: 2850*)

TIME	W.P.M.	TIME	W.P.M.
3 min.	950	7 min.	407
3 min., 30 sec.	814	7 min., 30 sec.	380
4 min.	706	8 min.	353
4 min., 30 sec.	634	8 min., 30 sec.	336
5 min.	570	9 min.	317
5 min., 30 sec.	518	10 min.	285
6 min.	475	11 min.	259
6 min., 30 sec.	436	12 min.	238

YOUR RATE ON SELECTION 18: _____W.P.M.

(*Record this statistic on the chart and graph on page 394.*)

Discussion of the Selection

As you read this long selection, you may have been aware that Mr. Fredericks has organized his presentation into three divisions. Let's look at the piece together to see what these divisions are and what each contains.

PART 1

Paragraph 1: First part of central theme—*improper dieting can be fatal.*

Paragraphs 2–26: Elaborate development of this part of the theme, full of examples, illustrations, case histories, and explanations of how bad diets can be extremely harmful, even indirectly causing death.

PART 2

Paragraph 27: Transition from part 1 ("a die in diet") to part 2 ("simple rules" for "safe and successful" dieting).

Paragraphs 28–34: The rules for safe and successful dieting. First, discover the cause of stoutness—is it neurotic, glandular (rare), or plain overeating?

Paragraphs 35–38: Next, get rid of food superstitions, and guard against nutritional deficiencies.

Paragraphs 39–40: Avoid drugs.

Paragraphs 41–43: No magic road—not exercise, nor massage, nor wonder diets.

Paragraphs 43 (last sentence)–46: Diets must be individually planned.

PART 3

Paragraphs 47–48: Summary—expression of the second part of the central theme as detailed and supported in part 2, plus recapitulation of first part (diets can be fatal).

Part 1, then, elaborated on the main point that *improper dieting can be harmful or fatal;* part 2 gave the *rules for safe and successful dieting;* and part 3 summarized the entire article. Correct choice on the comprehension test is statement 3.

Selection 19

COEXISTING WITH TEEN-AGERS
by Eda J. LeShan

I

Start timing→ In any discussion among parents of adolescents, sooner or later one question is almost certain to arise: What shall we do when we know our children are doing things we don't approve of? Shall we voice our objections? Or shall we accept the behavior on the theory that in this way at least we avoid secrecy and deceit?

Do we, because a 16-year-old insists that "it's done," serve cocktails to youngsters at a birthday dance? ("Otherwise," the adolescent may insist, "somebody's liable to spike the punch!") Do we buy cigarettes for a 12-year-old and sit by while he smokes them? ("I can get them for 2 cents apiece from a guy at school. You wouldn't want me smoking in the street, would you?") Do we, to prove our broad-mindedness, laugh at—and thus encourage—the 14-year-old's off-color stories or ignore his locker-room language just because we know it is commonplace among other youngsters his age?

For many parents the course is never in doubt. No child of theirs will do thus and so! Others, however, may have been confused by warnings against "indoctrinating" their children with their own thinking, or attempting to "mold them in their own image." These are the ones who suffer doubts when questions like the above arise.

Methods of control that worked in earlier years are useless now. (The 12-year-old who wants to try smoking will not be "distracted" for long by a lollipop!) By this time, too, youngsters have learned to hide what they are doing. Or they may not even resort to subterfuge but will announce, "If I can't do this in front of you, I'll just do it behind your back!"

Parents who want urgently to keep their youngsters' confidence by acting as "pals" might consider the experience reported recently by a young social worker. On his first job as recreation leader in a community center, wanting very much to be accepted by the neighborhood adolescents, he decided to gain their confidence by "meeting them at their level."

From *The New York Times Magazine*. Reprinted by permission. Mrs. LeShan, a clinical and child psychologist, is educational director of the New Rochelle, N.Y., Guidance Center.

He began spending a good deal of time at their local hang-outs. Then after several months, thinking he had been accepted almost as a member of the gang, he joined a crap game one night and rolled the dice like a veteran. He noticed a stiffening in the group around him, an uneasiness later as they all walked home. Finally, one boy said: "You know, Doc, you get more and more like *us* instead of us getting more like you!"

In their attempts to be "modern" some mothers and fathers may run the risk of a reaction similar to the social worker's experience. Yet parents want to keep up-to-date. They've been cautioned against making their youngsters "different" from their friends. The adult wish to get a clear picture of the youngster's social scene today has prompted an increasing number of surveys among parents and students of various schools on such matters as clothing considered appropriate for school and parties, use of make-up, smoking, dating behavior. (One recent survey included a question on whether or not lights should be left on during parties.)

II

Interestingly enough, the results of a recent questionnaire given to 2,000 parents and students in a big city junior high school indicated that the students were just as uncertain about standards and limits as their parents. While the youngsters demonstrated a wish for many signs of increasing freedom (such as being permitted to earn money and have full responsibility for handling allowances), they also showed a strong desire for parental controls in matters where they seemed aware that their own impulses might get the best of them.

These youngsters said they thought parties should be planned, should have adult supervision; felt their parents should know where they were and with whom. Two-thirds of the students thought they ought to be home by midnight on week-ends and holidays, and seemed to want help in scheduling homework and keeping to a reasonable bedtime during the week.

The results of such a questionnaire suggest that, useful as such surveys may be in giving parents a picture of the social scene today, youngsters in the complicated business of growing up need more than the statistical analysis of a questionnaire to guide them. It is important for children of all ages to have direct guidance and a clear understanding of what their parents expect of them, even though they cannot live up to parental standards all the time.

Often mothers and fathers can help youngsters understand what behavior is appropriate and acceptable merely by their own steady example of maturity and good judgment. At other times they may have to point out in no uncertain terms the hazards of certain conduct, and suggest more acceptable ways of doing.

But growing up is slow. Even

with the best of adult guidance, youngsters will experiment with new forms of behavior in ways that parents may not like. There will be times when their self-control will fail, when they will feel they must challenge parental authority, when they must satisfy special needs whether their conduct has parental approval or not. Adult sanction for inappropriate behavior, however, may just add to adolescent confusion.

It is certainly true that young people must learn to think for themselves. In a time of rapid social change they will inevitably face situations requiring new judgments that we cannot make for them. But it is quite possible to encourage individual thinking, while still keeping in mind the inexperience and immaturity of youngsters which make them need a strong foundation from which to move forward. We must give them both "roots and wings."

Young people gain strength in controlling their impulses when we hold to our point of view with firmness, accepting the fact that behind-the-back experimentation may be the price we will pay occasionally for sticking to the validity and worth of our standards.

←End timing

RECORD HERE THE TIME REQUIRED ON THIS SELECTION: _____ MIN. _____ SEC.

Test Your Comprehension

Check the main idea.

1. Parents of adolescents are constantly beset with the problem of the best way to handle their children, and should learn to find out what the adolescents themselves want.

2. Those parents who insist on rigid discipline and see that their standards are lived up to will produce the most secure adolescents.

3. Parents who act as "pals" to their youngsters will help adolescents fit into the community pattern.

4. Adolescents want parental control in certain areas; they need guidance and clear understanding of parental expectations, although they may not always be able to live up to these expectations.

5. Adolescence is a period of conflict and insecurity, for parents as well as children. The best rule to follow in this troublesome period is to teach young people to think for themselves.

Compute Your Rate
(*Approximate number of words: 1010*)

TIME	W.P.M.	TIME	W.P.M.
1 min., 15 sec.	810	2 min., 30 sec.	405
1 min., 20 sec.	760	2 min., 45 sec.	370
1 min., 30 sec.	675	3 min.	340
1 min., 40 sec.	605	3 min., 15 sec.	310
1 min., 50 sec.	550	3 min., 30 sec.	290
2 min.	505	4 min.	255
2 min., 15 sec.	450	4 min., 30 sec.	225

YOUR RATE ON SELECTION 19: _____W.P.M.
(*Record this statistic on the chart and graph on page 394.*)

Discussion of the Selection

This piece divides nicely into two parts:

SECTION I—The Problem

The first paragraph expresses the problem: How should parents react when adolescents do things parents don't approve of—with acceptance or with objections? The rest of the section then elaborates on the problem, with emphasis on the doubts of parents who fear to be too controlling and on the possible negative results of being too accepting.

SECTION II—The Solution

Now the central idea of the piece, as summarized in statement 4 of the comprehension test, is developed, with a kind of recapitulation in the final paragraph.

The selection first poses the problem; next shows why it is so complex; finally indicates a solution that arises out of the adolescents' own desires and needs.

Now let us consider your performance on the four selections of this chapter.

Copy, from the chart on page 394, your rates on the following pieces:

SELECTION 16 (COMMON COLD): _____W.P.M.
SELECTION 17 (YOUNG DOCTORS): _____W.P.M.
SELECTION 18 (DIETS): _____W.P.M.
SELECTION 19 (TEEN-AGERS): _____W.P.M.

337

Add these figures, divide by 4 to find your average rate in this chapter, and write the result in the first line below.

(1) AVERAGE RATE IN CHAPTER 10: _____W.P.M.
(2) INITIAL RATE: _____W.P.M.
(3) AVERAGE GAIN: _____W.P.M.
(4) PERCENTAGE GAIN: _____%
(5) PERCENTAGE GAIN MADE IN CHAPTER 7: _____%
(6) GAIN IN PERCENTAGE OVER CHAPTER 7: _____%

To complete line 2 of the chart, copy the rate at which you read the first selection in the book, which you recorded on page 11. Then subtract line 2 from line 1 and write the answer on line 3. Now divide your average gain (line 3) by your initial rate (line 2), carry the result to two decimal places, and fill in line 4. Next copy from page 393 your percentage gain in chapter 7 to fill in line 5, and complete the chart by subtracting line 5 from line 4. Now you have a graphic picture of your progress to date.

Let us do two more things with these statistics.

(1) Use the figures from lines 1, 3, and 4, and fill in the appropriate spaces on the chart on page 394.

(2) Take your average rate on the four selections of this chapter (line 1), locate that figure on the graph on page 394, and draw a straight line parallel to line AB. Label this line "average rate, phase 3."

You may possibly have made no appreciable percentage gain over your average rate on chapter 7; or your gain may be small; or, possibly, you may show a 10 to 20 per cent gain or more.

This will depend on how great an increase in speed chapter 7 represented over chapter 2—normally, the biggest jump is expected in the second series of timed selections (chapter 7), with relatively smaller increases showing up after that, as the new skills become integrated and refined, much greater comfort is achieved, and the habits and techniques become less self-conscious, more nearly reflexive or automatic.

On the other hand, it is possible that you had so well integrated your new skills of comprehension, perception, and use of peripheral vision before you started working on the selections of this chapter that your speed has taken another healthy jump. If this is so, your self-training has been signally successful; and while future gains may for a time be small, there is no reason why you cannot eventually still further improve the skill and speed of your comprehension. The important thing, at this point, is for you to feel—subjectively—that you naturally move along much faster, much more competently, much more self-confidently than you used to in the past—that you are no longer intimidated by a page, an article, a chapter, or even an entire book—that you look forward to every reading experience as a pleasure, as something you cannot wait to enjoy—that you find you have much more time for reading because you willingly, indeed eagerly, make the time.

A FOURTH CHALLENGE TO YOUR READING HABITS

Which brings us to the fourth challenge to your reading habits. You have already tried, I expect with some measure of success, to read novels through at one sitting and to cover a complete magazine in one evening. Now let us see how successfully you can read a whole book of nonfiction in a strictly limited time.

The secret of meeting this challenge lies in your choice of the book to be read, and the determining factor in that choice is your field of interest.

What area of human knowledge, information, or living can you get most excited about? Science, art, music, psychology, mathematics, history, religion, economics, politics, sports, criminology? In which of these, or any other, subjects can a book most easily, most successfully stimulate you, hold your attention and interest, keep you engrossed?

Your first step, then, is to choose a book to which you will be able to make a rapid and happy emotional adjustment. Find a book that is not overly long, that is written for popular consumption rather than for specialists or experts, that is simple, readable, and interesting. Ask for a recommendation at your local library, from your friends, or at a bookstore. (These days, incidentally, many excellent nonfiction titles are published in inexpensive paper-covered editions.) Or make your choice from the books suggested on page 354. Or, if you are a college student, choose a title in some field that you are currently studying, a field in which you are, preferably, vitally interested.

Once you have the physical book in hand, sit down with it when you have two to three hours at your disposal. Read the table of contents carefully so that you can make a quick orientation to the type of material you will be reading. Then arbitrarily divide the book into either two or three approximately equal parts depending on how long a book you are tackling, and determine that you are going to finish *one* of those parts before you stop reading.

Now start reading—and read rapidly, for an over-all perspective. *Do not study.* Do not read every sentence, nor every paragraph, nor every page. Skim a little here and there, even if at times the knowledge you gain from the chapters is somewhat superficial. Read largely for central theme, for main ideas, for final meaning, without becoming unduly concerned about the masses of details (which, of course, every book possesses in abundance). And go through either one half or one third of the material in a single sitting of no more than three hours. (If you happen to get more than one part done in that time, so much the better.)

If you become really absorbed in what you're reading (and if your choice of title is a wise one, you'll become absorbed quickly), you will have no trouble staying with the book at least until you have finished the first portion that you decided to cover.

Your next step, of course, is to return to the book as soon as possible within the following days in order to complete the remaining portion or portions. In any case, determine to turn the last page of the book within no more than a week from the day you started it, and in no more than three sessions of continuous reading. That allows you up to nine hours, in total—no book of less than five or six hundred pages, if you skim judiciously, should take any longer.

This challenge, if you can meet it with any degree of success, may open for you a whole new approach to nonfiction reading— may make it possible for you to say three months from now, "In the last few months I have read almost a dozen solid, informative books that I would not have wanted to miss!"

And let's keep a record of your accomplishment with the book you're going to work on this week.

1. TITLE: _____
2. AUTHOR: _____
3. AREA OF KNOWLEDGE, INFORMATION, ETC. _____
4. NUMBER OF PAGES: _____

5. NUMBER OF SITTINGS: ☐2 ☐3
6. DATE BEGUN: _____; DATE FINISHED: _____
7. NUMBER OF HOURS SPENT: _____
8. APPROXIMATE NUMBER OF PAGES READ PER HOUR: _____
9. APPROXIMATE NUMBER OF WORDS PER PAGE: _____
10. AVERAGE RATE OF READING: _____W.P.M.

★ SESSION 26

PERCEPTION TRAINING X

Perception Exercise 44

Using the Flashmeter card, expose the numbers for a fraction of a second, getting a *visual* impression. Do not say the digits to yourself. Reproduce each number in the blank to the right and then check your result.

835820	←_____	847002	←_____	112911	←_____
748029	←_____	847833	←_____	938882	←_____
857263	←_____	847654	←_____	837920	←_____
784672	←_____	847992	←_____	948762	←_____
837458	←_____	783092	←_____	948702	←_____
857639	←_____	837625	←_____	837130	←_____
847110	←_____	837190	←_____	948762	←_____
110390	←_____	836873	←_____	635382	←_____
100983	←_____	847662	←_____	759285	←_____
993372	←_____	938810	←_____	745680	←_____

002988 ←_____	847302 ←_____	834499 ←_____
830012 ←_____	837257 ←_____	627302 ←_____
857031 ←_____	837013 ←_____	728011 ←_____
846726 ←_____	524389 ←_____	928331 ←_____
467930 ←_____	928312 ←_____	823399 ←_____
746293 ←_____	039281 ←_____	563855 ←_____
736523 ←_____	847291 ←_____	

NUMBER CORRECT OUT OF 50: _____

Perception Exercise 45

Sweep down each column, feeling that you are making only one fixation to the line. Go as fast as adequate comprehension permits, and be more aware of ideas than of inner speech.

The following material is excerpted from *Mind, Medicine, and Man,* by Gregory Zilboorg, M.D. Reprinted by permission of the publishers, Harcourt, Brace and Co., New York.

↓ ↓ ↓

The oral trends may, and they usually do, manifest themselves in a manner that has outwardly nothing to do with the mouth at all. Instead, they may, and they usually do, appear in the form of the individual's being rather a

sociable person who does not like to be and does not tolerate being alone, even as the little baby when awake is never left alone. Such people are not only very sociable, but some of them do not like to work alone;

they either always have collaborators or, if they do independent work, they concentrate best when there are people around and when there is even a little noise. Such people are frequently admired for their extraordinary powers of concentration

↓ | ↓ | ↓

despite the rattle
and din around them.
Yet it is
exactly this rattle
and din
that makes it possible
for them to concentrate;
as soon as
quiet sets in
and there is
a real chance
to concentrate
without interference,
such people are apt
to become restless,
and they either
drop their work

or turn on
the radio.
Such individuals
may concentrate so well
that they can write
with utmost
concentration
literally in the middle
of the street—
like Marcel Proust,
who wrote a part
of his
*Remembrance of
Things Past*
in the glass-covered
booth
of the porter
of the Ritz Hotel

in Paris.
Such people are also
given to moods,
mostly depressive
in nature,
but they may
just as easily
swing into a state
of great cheer.
They are self-centered
in a charming way,
and they are apt
to procrastinate
a great deal
despite the apparent
push and powers
of concentration.

Perception Exercise 46

Continue as before.

The following is excerpted from *Remedial Reading at the College and Adult Levels,* by G. T. Buswell, Professor of Educational Psychology, The University of Chicago. Reprinted by permission of the publishers, The University of Chicago Press, Chicago. Copyright 1939 by the University of Chicago.

↓ | ↓ | ↓

By calling attention
to the importance
of larger
perceptual units
in reading,

psychology has
contributed
a new methodology
to its teaching.
Under the old

word method,
for which oral reading
was largely responsible,
children developed
an ability

↓   ↓   ↓

to pronounce words	objectively	of recognition
but often failed	and are well known.	becomes a permanent
to develop	Good readers	characteristic.
equal ability	have attained	A narrow span
to understand meanings.	a broad span	not only necessitates
Present methods	of recognition	slow reading
of teaching reading	by the end of	but emphasizes
attempt to produce	the sixth grade	attention
as wide a span	of the elementary	to the form of words
of recognition	school;	and sentences,
as possible.	other readers	a rapid acquisition
The curves of growth	let their reading habits	of meaning
for this factor	crystallize at a point	being thereby blocked.
have been plotted	where a narrow span	

Perception Exercise 47

Continue as before.

The following is excerpted from "Measurement and Improvement in Reading," an article in the *Baltimore Bulletin of Education*, by Arthur E. Traxler, executive director of the Educational Records Bureau, New York. Reprinted with permission.

↓   ↓   ↓

It would seem correct	differ	in another environment.
to say	a great deal,	We know that
that *an individual*	a reading level	this is true
has a reading disability	that would represent	in connection with
whenever he is not able	a disability in	vocational adjustment
to read well enough	one environment	where an individual
to meet the	might be	with,
requirements	entirely satisfactory	let us say,
of his environment.	for successful	sixth-grade reading
Since environments	adjustment	ability

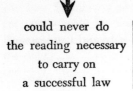

could never do	practice,	to the reading
the reading necessary	while he might	requirements
to carry on	be able to adjust	of a skilled trade.
a successful law	very well	

VOCABULARY STUDY VII

Words for Today

1. austere
2. convivial
3. esoteric
4. histrionic
5. mordant
6. obsequious
7. posthumous
8. risqué
9. solicitous
10. tacit
11. tenuous
12. translucent
13. urbane
14. vacuous
15. vitriolic

Look up in your dictionary those words with which you are partially or totally unfamiliar, writing, in your notebook or on your scratch pad, information as to meaning, pronunciation, use, derivation, and related forms. Compose, for each word, an illustrative phrase or sentence. After studying your notes, take the following tests.

Test Your Learning

I. Pair words and definitions.

1. austere
2. convivial
3. esoteric
4. histrionic
5. mordant
6. obsequious
7. posthumous
8. risqué
9. tacit
10. translucent

a—unspoken; not expressed in words
b—known only to a few
c—excessively polite
d—severely simple; severe in self-discipline
e—off-color or almost off-color or indelicate
f—occurring, published, born, etc., after the death of its creator, author, father, etc.
g—festive; fond of eating and drinking in company
h—admitting light
i—pertaining to acting; affected
j—caustic; sarcastic; biting (in speech, etc.)

345

II. Check *yes* or *no* to each question.

1. Are parents often *solicitous* of their children's welfare? YES; NO
2. Is a *tenuous* relationship clear and obvious? YES; NO
3. Do *urbane* people express themselves coarsely and use uncouth or vulgar expressions? YES; NO
4. Do intelligent, informed people have *vacuous* minds? YES; NO
5. Do gentle, kind people generally use *vitriolic* language?

   YES; NO
6. Is poverty sometimes the cause of *austere* living? YES; NO
7. Do puritanical people often tell *risqué* jokes? YES; NO
8. Are antisocial people usually *convivial?* YES; NO
9. Are servants often required to act *obsequiously?* YES; NO
10. Is *esoteric* knowledge widely disseminated? YES; NO

Key:

I. 1—d, 2—g, 3—b, 4—i, 5—j, 6—c, 7—f, 8—e, 9—a, 10—h.

II. 1—yes, 2—no, 3—no, 4—no, 5—no, 6—yes, 7—no, 8—no, 9—yes, 10—no.

HOW TO READ WITH A QUESTIONING MIND

Preview

Now, as we near the end of the course, we discuss the importance of:

• Reading critically.
• Resisting the "mesmerism which is resident in print."
• Traveling widely among books in order to form "a background for opinion and a touchstone for judgment."

> Chapter 11 offers you a list of lively books in 25 different fields of nonfiction, half a hundred novels, and a number of challenging magazines to guide your future reading; and asks you to follow a long-range plan that will help you become an alert, well-rounded reader.

THE IMPORTANCE OF SKEPTICISM

Whatever you read—a book, an article, a poem, a short story, a news item, an editorial, a column of opinion, criticism, or comment, even a road sign—tries to tell you something, tries to get a message across to you, tries to make you believe. Every author, no matter what his medium of communication, aims to convince you, his reader, that what he has to say is true and should be accepted as truth. Even a novelist or short-story writer attempts, consciously or otherwise, to persuade you that his characters could conceivably exist, that their conflicts are real and important, and that their behavior makes sense within the framework of time and place that he sets up. If he succeeds, he gets you to accept and even to share— at least momentarily—his philosophy of life, his attitude to people and events, and the point of view from which he looks at the world. In a broad sense, then, even though he is writing fiction, he is a special pleader.

And, of course, it is almost impossible to pick up a magazine or newspaper today without being bombarded by special pleading. As you turn the pages, almost every writer is saying to you, directly or by implication, "This is what I think; or, This is how I feel; or, This is how I interpret a situation; or, These are the conclusions I draw from the (selected) facts; or, This is how to solve a problem; or, This is how to do the job; or, This is how I react to what has happened; or, This is how you should react; or, This is the furniture, clothing, perfume, cereal, book, soap, cigarette, automobile, or liquor you should buy, the transportation you should use, the play or motion picture you should see, the vacation you should take, or the charity you should contribute to"; and so on and on, in endless, infinite variety. And in every case the writer uses all his skill and

348

knowledge to convince you of the truth and validity of what he is saying.

Even this book is a special pleader, and I, as the author, bend every effort to make you believe, and believe in, what I say. I strive constantly, by every means at my command, to persuade you to do certain things and do them in certain ways—I promise, I cajole, I threaten, I appeal to reason or emotion, I present evidence, and I draw on other authorities in the field, all for the purpose of eliciting as strong a positive response from you as I can possibly get.

And most, if not all, of the selections that we have used as reading exercises also ask you to believe. Mr. Maisel ("Traffic Court Justice"), for example, wants you to believe that most communities are handling the traffic problem all wrong, and that a better solution is being tried by Chicago, San Francisco, White Plains, etc.; Dr. Diehl ("Common Cold"), that most advertised remedies are valueless; Mr. Ratcliff ("Young Doctors"), that the attitude of older doctors is a stumbling block to better medical care; Mr. Fredericks ("Diet"), that some methods of dieting are dangerous, others safe and successful; Mrs. LeShan ("Teen-agers"), that there is an effective way to handle adolescents; and so on, selection after selection.

If you come right down to it, only a mathematical equation, a chemical formula, a page in the telephone directory, or something equally neutral, can be considered as totally free of every vestige of attempt by an author to gain the reader's acceptance and/or belief.

Most of your work in this program has been devoted to developing greater skill and efficiency in *understanding* what a page of print has to say. But understanding, no matter how skillful, how clear, or how accurate, is not, manifestly, enough. To be a mature and intelligent reader, you must be able to go beyond mere understanding; you must also be sufficiently skeptical to be in the habit of questioning, and sufficiently informed, knowledgeable, experienced, and alert to be able to decide, whether the conclusions of a piece of writing are valid and soundly reasoned, whether the interpretations are trustworthy, whether the selection of facts or so-called facts is honest, whether the author is unbiased, whether the publication in which it appears is known to be fair in its search for truth, and therefore whether the final meaning is, or is not, deserving of belief.

The person who reads intelligently approaches all material with a

349

questioning, even a skeptical, mind. He reads critically as well as accurately, he evaluates what the author says, he tests the truth of writing against his own knowledge and experience of reality, he does not accept statements and conclusions simply because they appear in print. As J. Donald Adams wrote in *The New York Times Book Review:*

> All our lives most of us, and perhaps most of all those in whom the habit of reading is ingrained, have to guard and fight against that strange mesmerism which is resident in print. Statements that have the peculiar sanction of type, and which, if orally made, we would brush away like a buzzing fly, often receive our respectful attention merely because they have achieved the spurious dignity of print. Sometimes I think the best we can get from a formal education is the inflexible habit of examining every new fact and every new conclusion drawn from fact, warily from top to toe. An education, however conducted, that neglects the skeptical approach is no education at all. And if the wisdom of the world is in books, so, too, is a vast amount of nonsense.

The ability to approach material critically can best be developed through wide reading. To judge, you must have a touchstone for judgment. To be skeptical of opinions expressed in writing, you must have tentative opinions of your own on a subject, opinions based either on personal experience or on knowledge. Few people can be directly experienced in more than a very limited number of areas, but anyone who knows how to read can acquire as much of the world's knowledge as he is willing to absorb. In one of the best books in its field, *Teaching Every Child to Read,** Kathleen B. Hester makes somewhat the same point:

> The type of reading required for critical evaluation is a complex form of comprehension in which the reader develops the habit of appraising the material against certain criteria. It is evident that the broader and richer the background of the reader, the more able he will be to judge the reasonableness, the worth-whileness, the relevancy, and the accuracy of what is read; the more tolerant he will be of material about which he possesses insufficient background. He will criticize in light of what he knows about the subject.

To gain the broad and rich background of which Miss Hester speaks you cannot, of course, restrict your reading to just one daily newspaper, a few light magazines, and an occasional novel.

---

* Harper and Brothers, 1955. Reprinted by permission.

How long have you been reading a single newspaper, and how much of an influence does this periodical exercise on your political and social thinking? If a paper of a different political or social complexion is available in your town, or can be bought by mail, try changing for a period—you may discover that some of your beliefs are prejudiced, that some of your attitudes come from not having heard both sides of the story.

Do you keep up with the outside world by reading the more or less conservative periodicals such as *Time, Newsweek, Life, U.S. News and World Report?* Fine. But to get a more or less liberal slant on changing events and to develop a broader base on which to form your opinions, vary your reading occasionally with such magazines as the *Saturday Review, Harper's,* the *Atlantic Monthly,* the *Reporter.* Or, vice versa, if much of your viewpoint is liberal, open your mind to what the conservative press has to say. We are privileged, in the United States, to be able to hear not only opposing sides but all shades of opinion in between—to sharpen your critical faculties, to develop habits of reacting skeptically to what you read, take advantage of this privilege.

Do you tend to accept most advertising with implicit faith? Read *Consumers Reports* or *Consumers Research Bulletin* for a few months if you want to adopt a less credulous attitude.

To broaden and enrich your background of knowledge, *read widely.* Read books in fields with which you are at present unacquainted; read newspapers with differing political and social viewpoints; read as great a variety of magazines as you can lay your hands on.

Go out of your way to hear, and to understand, the other side of the story. Read opinion, lots of it, that is opposed to your own instinctive prejudices, fears, likes, and dislikes. But *read.*

And when you read, keep an open mind. Do not accept passively or blindly; demand evidence, insist on all the facts, test whatever an author is saying against what you know, against what you have read in other sources.

Above all, don't succumb to the "mesmerism which is resident in print." Be alert to detect the "vast amount of nonsense," much of it probably sincere, but nonsense nonetheless, that you will find in many books, magazines, and newspapers.

351

WHAT TO READ

You have come a long way since the first day you started your training. If you have worked hard and faithfully, you have not only developed considerable skill as a reader, you have also begun to build habits that will help you *increase* your skill every time you tackle a page of print.

Learning to read, as you know, is a continuous, never-ending process. If, after you finish this book, you do very little additional reading, or if you read only material that offers no challenge to your comprehension, your training will be of little use to you.

Too many adults, once they reach a certain age, or once their formal schooling is completed, become so restricted in their choice of reading that they shy away from any new type of reading experience. They are reluctant to try anything beyond the level of a detective story or light novel, as if no other kind of book ever published could possibly interest them. Or they read only books in their professional or business field. Or only inspirational books. Or only their one favorite newspaper every morning. Or only one magazine for which they have developed a liking.

It is the *only* which causes the trouble. You do not read for entertainment *only*, nor for information *only*. You read also for intellectual growth, for mental stimulation, for enriching your background of knowledge, for increased wisdom, and for a broader outlook and a maturer understanding.

Let me quote from an editorial printed over twenty years ago in the *Saturday Review* (it was then called the *Saturday Review of Literature*) to impress upon you the importance of reading as an influence on intellectual growth. The editors were addressing the new graduates of the nation's colleges in the year 1935, but what they had to say is as pertinent and as true today as it was then:*

> At this moment, when the universities are again sending forth their eager thousands into a world distraught by gigantic problems, a fresh tide of energy is about to be let loose upon the country. The country, heaven knows, has need of all that it can get of vigor and idealism and ideas. But what it needs not at all is half-baked theorists and ill-buttressed opinions. It needs a youth full of generous enthu-

* Reprinted with permission.

siasm and ranging curiosity, versatile in its interests but not over-weening in its self-reliance, a youth that spurns, as is its prerogative, those mistakes of the past which the present has thrown into focus, but that has sufficient balance not to cry anathema on all that is because part of it is bad. It needs a youth that is versatile in the sense that it has aptitude for new tasks, but whose versatility smacks nothing of superficiality. It demands young men and young women who do not believe that education ends with college, but who carry away from the university an abiding delight in books as the source of entertainment and invigoration and guidance.

For the man who reads well is the man who thinks well, who has a background for opinion and a touchstone for judgment. He may be a Lincoln who derives wisdom from a few books or a Roosevelt who ranges from Icelandic sagas to "Penrod." But reading makes him a full man, and out of his fullness he draws that example and precept which stand him in good stead when confronted with the problems which beset a chaotic universe. Mere reading, of course, is nothing. It is but the veneer of education. But wise reading is a help to action. American versatility is too frequently dilettantism, but reinforced by knowledge it becomes motive power. "Learning," as Mr. James L. Mursell, writing of it in a current periodical, remarks, "cashes the blank check of native versatility." And learning is a process not to be concluded with the formal teaching of college days or to be enriched only by the active experience of later years, but to be broadened and deepened by persistent and judicious reading. "The true University of these days is a Collection of Books," said Carlyle. If that is not the whole of the truth it is enough of it for every graduate to hug to his bosom.

What kind of books should you read to continue your intellectual growth, to gain "a background for opinion and a touchstone for judgment"? The answer is a simple one: *Read books in fields you have little or no acquaintance with, books that will open for you new horizons of learning, books that will help you explore new areas of knowledge and experience, books that will make the world and people more understandable to you, books you can really sink your teeth into.*

Below you will find a wide choice of books of just such a type. Every one of them is eminently readable; each will be an exciting adventure in learning, a challenging and broadening experience.

I have, as you will see, divided these books into a number of general categories, and while I have certainly not included all the categories in which you may now be, or can become, interested, nor all the important books in any particular category, nevertheless I have suggested enough titles to get you well started on a comprehensive, long-range reading program.

Glance through the list now, checking off the fields you think you may enjoy exploring and a few books in each category that sound especially appealing.

RECOMMENDED NONFICTION

I. ANTHROPOLOGY
1. *Male and Female,* by Margaret Mead
2. *Patterns of Culture,* by Ruth Benedict
3. *The Study of Man,* by Ralph Linton
4. *Mankind So Far,* by William Howells

II. ARCHAEOLOGY
5. *Gods, Graves, and Scholars,* by C. W. Ceram
6. *Testimony of the Spade,* by Geoffrey Bibby
7. *Man, Time, and Fossils,* by Ruth Moore

III. ART
8. *The Arts,* by Hendrik Willem Van Loon
9. *Art Through the Ages,* by Helen Gardner
10. *A World History of Art,* by Sheldon Cheney
11. *The Meaning of Art,* by A. Philip MacMahon
12. *Art for Art's Sake,* by Albert Guérard
13. *The Art of Enjoying Art,* by A. Philip MacMahon

IV. ASTRONOMY
14. *Astronomy for Everyman,* edited by Martin Davidson

V. BIOGRAPHY AND AUTOBIOGRAPHY
(The starred titles are autobiographical.)
15. *The Peabody Sisters of Salem,* by Louise Hall Tharp
16. *Lust for Life,* by Irving Stone (Vincent Van Gogh)
17. *Moulin Rouge,* by Pierre La Mure (Toulouse-Lautrec)
18. *The Life of Mahatma Gandhi,* by Louis Fischer
19. *°Boswell's London Journal,* edited by Frederick Pottle
20. *Yankee from Olympus,* by Catherine Drinker Bowen (Oliver Wendell Holmes)
21. *John Adams and the American Revolution,* by Catherine Drinker Bowen
22. *The Legend of Henry Ford,* by Keith Sward
23. *Captain Sam Grant,* by Lloyd Lewis

130. *People in Quandaries,* by Wendell Johnson
XXV. SOCIOLOGY
131. *Middletown,* by Robert S. and Helen M. Lynd
132. *Middletown in Transition,* by Robert S. and Helen M. Lynd
133. *An American Dilemma,* by Gunnar Myrdal and others
134. *Street Corner Society,* by William F. Whyte

Not all of these books are in print, though most of them are as of this writing; those in print today may not be so when you read this. But any well-stocked public library will have most of them, and a surprisingly large number are in inexpensive paperback editions.

Any bookstore can determine for you whether the book you want is available for purchase; if you have no bookstore in your town write to *Doubleday Bookshops, Inc.,* 575 Madison Ave., *Brentano's, Inc.,* 586 Fifth Ave., or *Barnes and Noble, Inc.,* Fifth Avenue at 18th Street, all in New York City. Barnes and Noble can often supply used copies of books that are no longer in print.

To determine whether a book is available in a paper-covered edition, write to *The Paper Editions Book Club,* 2233 El Camino Real, Palo Alto, California, for a catalogue. If you live anywhere in or near New York City you will find an amazingly large collection of paperback books at Liggett's Drug Store, 42nd Street and Park Avenue, or at the National Book Store, 11 University Place, near 8th Street.

The list of valuable and stimulating books catalogued in this section makes no pretense at completeness, but if you spend the next year or two reading most of them you will be taking a long step forward in becoming an informed, well-rounded reader. If you have not had a liberal college education, these books will provide you with its equivalent; if you are a college graduate, they will continue and extend your education.

But do not completely restrict yourself either to the suggested categories or to the recommended individual titles. Between the time this is written and the time you read it, many new and excellent books will be published in a wide variety of fields, and once you develop a broad range of interests you will want to keep up with the latest thinking and discoveries in many areas of life, you will want to keep abreast of what's new in the world.

The two periodicals that will be most helpful to you in this respect are the *Saturday Review* and *The New York Times Book Review*, both of which can be obtained by mail. And *Harper's*, the *Atlantic Monthly*, *The New Yorker*, *Time*, and *Newsweek* contain excellent book review sections. Book clubs too, such as *The Book-of-the-Month Club*, *The Book Find Club*, or *The Literary Guild*, offer you expert guidance in selecting from among the best of current publications, as well as great convenience in purchasing your books by mail.

In addition to keeping up with the present, you will want to dip occasionally into the vital writing of the past, into the classics and semiclassics of world literature. The Modern Library publishes, at $1.65 each, as complete a selection of these as you will find anywhere. For a catalogue, write to Random House, Inc., 457 Madison Ave., New York 22, New York.

Good Reading, published by The New American Library of World Literature, 501 Madison Ave., New York 22, New York, at fifty cents, is an indispensable guide to the best of both current and older books, including inexpensive paper-bound reprints, and is available in most stationery stores or direct from the publisher. In its 284 pages you will find suggestions and recommendations for a whole lifetime of reading.

You will not, of course, want to neglect good novels in your plans for future reading. Any of the sources previously mentioned will keep you informed on the best in current and recent fiction, and I should like, also, to offer a number of recommendations of my own. Taste in novels is a highly personal thing, but I think you will find most of the suggestions below exciting experiences you will be glad not to have missed.

RECOMMENDED NOVELS

1. *Success*, by Lion Feuchtwanger
2. *Of Human Bondage*, by W. Somerset Maugham
3. *Crime and Punishment*, by Feodor Dostoevski
4. *South Wind*, by Norman Douglas
5. *The Store*, by T. S. Stribling
6. *Captain Horatio Hornblower*, by C. S. Forester
7. *Hold Autumn in Your Hand*, by George Sessions Perry
8. *Hunger*, by Knut Hamsun
9. *Giants in the Earth*, by O. E. Rölvaag

10. *Arrival and Departure,* by Arthur Koestler
11. *H. M. Pulham, Esq.,* by John P. Marquand
12. *Home Before Dark,* by Eileen Bassing
13. *Compulsion,* by Meyer Levin
14. *The Caine Mutiny,* by Herman Wouk
15. *Mottke the Thief,* by Sholem Asch
16. *The Disenchanted,* by Budd Schulberg
17. *Two Adolescents,* by Alberto Moravia
18. *Cry, The Beloved Country,* by Alan Paton
19. *Whistle Stop,* by Maritta M. Wolf
20. *The Lost Weekend,* by Charles Jackson
21. *The Grapes of Wrath,* by John Steinbeck
22. *The Good Earth,* by Pearl Buck
23. *Top of the World,* by Hans Ruesch
24. *Night and the City, Song of the Flea,* or *The Thousand Deaths of Mr. Small,* by Gerald Kersh
25. *Butterfield 8, Appointment in Samarra,* or *A Rage to Live,* by John O'Hara
26. *I Can Get It For You Wholesale,* by Jerome Weidman
27. *From Here to Eternity,* by James Jones
28. *The Postman Always Rings Twice,* by James M. Cain
29. *A Tree Grows in Brooklyn,* by Betty Smith
30. *The Fountainhead,* by Ayn Rand
31. *Gone With the Wind,* by Margaret Mitchell
32. *Tales of the South Pacific,* by James Michener
33. *Mine Own Executioner,* or *A Way Through the Woods,* by Nigel Balchin
34. *Animal Farm,* or *1984,* by George Orwell
35. *Reprisal,* by Arthur Gordon

You may perhaps wish to season your reading with an occasional mystery or detective story. The following, I think, are among the best of their type.

36. *The Maltese Falcon* or *The Glass Key,* by Dashiell Hammett
37. *Farewell My Lovely* or *Lady in the Lake,* by Raymond Chandler
38. *The Man with My Face,* by Samuel A. Taylor
39. *Background to Danger* or *Journey into Fear,* by Eric Ambler
40. *Before the Fact,* by Francis Iles
41. *Verdict of Twelve,* by Raymond Postgate
42. *Blood upon the Snow,* by Hilda Lawrence

Or, finally, you may thoroughly enjoy humorous biographical or autobiographical novels. Try any, or all, of these:

43. *Roughly Speaking,* by Louise Randall Pierson
44. *Cheaper by the Dozen,* by Frank Gilbreth and Ernestine Gilbreth Carey
45. *The Egg and I,* by Betty MacDonald
46. *My Sister Eileen,* by Ruth McKenney
47. *Anything Can Happen,* by George and Helen Papashvily
48. *Chicken Every Sunday,* by Rosemary Taylor
49. *Room for One More,* by Anna Perrott Rose
50. *Auntie Mame,* by Patrick Dennis

Not all of the foregoing are "great" novels, necessarily, but every one is superbly enjoyable, many are deeply moving, quite a few will vastly increase your understanding of people, and some of them will provide you with the richest kind of emotional experience. And these, after all, are the reasons for reading novels—to enjoy, to be moved, to develop a mature understanding, to experience vicariously.

This list, too, like the previous list of nonfiction titles, is far from complete, and is intended to provide only a point of departure, a jumping-off place, a sample of the kind of pleasure and excitement you can get from reading. Soon you will learn to make your own choices among both novels and nonfiction, you will discover the type of book that can delight and stimulate you; you will find authors to whom you make such an immediate and strong attachment that you will search out, and gobble up, everything they have written. When this happens, you will have no problem making time for reading, and you will wonder how you ever survived on a slim diet of half a dozen or so books a year.

MAKE A LONG-RANGE READING PROGRAM

Now is the time to make some definite plans for wide and continuous reading of as many types of books as you can become interested in. Decide on a *minimum* program of fifty books in the next year, at least one book a week. Once you have started, you will find that this goal is laughably easy to reach, that you can probably double or triple it without really trying.

You have already checked off a number of nonfiction titles in fields that appeal to you; now pick some titles from among the recommended novels, and make yourself a little list of the books you intend to read in the next few months.

You will be surprised what psychological motivation there is in having *physical possession* of the books you plan to read. Take your list to the public library, your local bookstore, or, if you wish to start working on paper-covered reprints, any stationery or drug store. Get the books you want, or reasonable substitutes for them, into your home and onto your living room or bedside table. Then decide which of the books you're going to start your reading program with, and *exactly when* you're going to get started. Make a date with one of the books on your list, and *keep your date*—keep it as faithfully as if you had purchased tickets to the theater or to a concert.

If you decide to start with a book of nonfiction, follow the procedure outlined in the *Fourth Challenge to Your Reading Habits*, page 339. Read rapidly, skim when you wish to, skip chapters or parts that are repetitive or that do not interest you, and get an over-all view of the subject matter of the book.

If you decide to start with a work of fiction, bear in mind that only a very long novel should require more than one or two evenings of continuous reading. With the training you have had, indeed, you are prepared to cover a comparatively short novel in a few hours if you push yourself a bit.

However you start, keep reading—complete at least one book a week, preferably two or three. Vary your diet with occasional magazines of the more challenging types. And, to avoid losing momentum, always have a few unread books around the house—books you plan to get to, and do get to, as soon as you've finished whatever book you're working on.

If you have been laboring under the delusion that you aren't the type of person who can do much leisure reading, let me disabuse you. I have found that most adults restrict their reading unnecessarily. They claim a lack of time, the wrong kind of temperament, or an inability to relate to, or enjoy, books, but, as a matter of fact, what holds them back is that they don't know *what* to read; or they

362

haven't yet discovered the *kind of reading* they can thoroughly enjoy; or they just don't keep enough good books at hand to get into the habit of spending their leisure time in the pleasant and stimulating relaxation that continuous reading provides more cheaply, more easily, and more satisfyingly than perhaps any other activity.

The success of your own future reading program will depend on your discovering, either from the list I have provided or from any of the other sources I have indicated, what kind of book you personally will find enjoyable and rewarding; on going out and getting those books; and on actually reading them, at a rate of no less than one a week, starting either immediately or as soon as you can after you finish your training with this book.

Once you get started, the pleasure and stimulation you derive will provide all the motivation you'll need. *If you put this plan into effect, and keep to it, you will find that the amount and range of your reading over the next twelve months may well dwarf your accomplishments of the last five, even ten, years.*

★ SESSION 28

PERCEPTION TRAINING XI

Perception Exercise 48

Using the Flashmeter card, expose each number for a fraction of a second, getting a *visual* impression. Do not say the digits to yourself. Reproduce each number in the blank to the right and then check your result.

738203	←_____	113382	←_____	820331	←_____
732957	←_____	827013	←_____	820178	←_____
920311	←_____	130495	←_____	938201	←_____
730293	←_____	920315	←_____	832203	←_____

882013 ←____	003911 ←____	473627 ←____
938273 ←____	938001 ←____	627397 ←____
003110 ←____	736229 ←____	135468 ←____
829031 ←____	837465 ←____	213574 ←____
829304 ←____	746583 ←____	921687 ←____
930211 ←____	029384 ←____	985621 ←____
452793 ←____	928374 ←____	632183 ←____
327392 ←____	726354 ←____	329857 ←____
382991 ←____	049586 ←____	937168 ←____
335283 ←____	029374 ←____	671954 ←____
350294 ←____	968702 ←____	534126 ←____
726389 ←____	143762 ←____	875262 ←____
736220 ←____	726253 ←____	

NUMBER CORRECT OUT OF 50: ____

Perception Exercise 49

Continue as before.

369134 ←____	126947 ←____	965248 ←____
518932 ←____	826913 ←____	319637 ←____
843561 ←____	359472 ←____	649619 ←____
427396 ←____	169468 ←____	824193 ←____
635129 ←____	914284 ←____	695631 ←____
563192 ←____	365967 ←____	425695 ←____

129378 ←_____	332013 ←_____	201138 ←_____
927384 ←_____	823402 ←_____	293312 ←_____
941027 ←_____	231112 ←_____	302116 ←_____
413920 ←_____	820163 ←_____	293113 ←_____
476592 ←_____	800213 ←_____	203382 ←_____
046281 ←_____	702911 ←_____	203319 ←_____
030920 ←_____	837201 ←_____	233190 ←_____
490193 ←_____	028375 ←_____	839221 ←_____
382913 ←_____	909293 ←_____	266372 ←_____
382938 ←_____	360182 ←_____	627655 ←_____
742093 ←_____	203188 ←_____	

NUMBER CORRECT OUT OF 50: _____

Perception Exercise 50

Sweep down each column, making only one fixation to the line. Go as fast as adequate comprehension permits, and be more aware of the ideas than of inner speech.

The material below is extracted from an address delivered at the Thirty-Fourth Annual Education Conference, University of Delaware, by J. Conrad Seegers, President of Muhlenberg College, Allentown, Penna. Reprinted by permission.

↓ | ↓ | ↓

It is a truism	must be critical.	with the type
to state that	The degree	and purpose,
if reading is	to which it	but if reading
to be productive,	must be critical	is to serve
that reading	varies, of course,	a purpose

365

the reader
must react to
what he reads,
and that reaction
is part and parcel
of what we call
critical reading.

*

Mastery of
the sheer mechanics
of reading
is not enough.
That in itself
is a major problem,
which by no means
ends with
the elementary school.
But critical reading,
reading for
complete
understanding,
reading in
the most complete sense
of that expression,
begins only after
mastery of mechanics
has been achieved.

*

Books are written
with varying purposes
and consequently
varying motives.

Some books
are written purely
for transmitting
information.
That is the typical
textbook approach.
In reading
such a book
we should ask
what qualifications
the author has.
We should investigate
the extent to which
he has consulted
sources of information
bearing upon the
subject,
particularly whether
he has recognized
conflicting views
which may exist
in that field.
We should ask
whether he presents
evidence for statements
which he makes.
In other words
we should ask
if the writer
has a right to say
what he said.
I believe

in my list of "musts"
in critical reading
this would rank first,
and it is not
by accident
that it heads
the list.
In college,
in high school,
and in
the elementary school,
we should
make people
understand
that we may not believe
all that we read.
One difficulty
which all teachers
have met
is the fact
that people
are too prone
to accept something
simply because
it has been written.
Especially are they
prone to accept
what has been written
by a writer
who occupies
an important position,
or whose name

↓ | ↓ | ↓

carries some weight.
Perhaps if pupils
could be taught
to read
with more attention
to evidence
and substantiation
we would be

less likely
to succumb
to specious argument.
Of course, propaganda,
in these days,
depends upon more
than the written word
for its persuasiveness,

and critical reading
alone
will not supply
all of the results
we should attempt
to achieve.
But we can start
with that.

Perception Exercise 51

Continue as before.

The following material is extracted from *Teaching Every Child to Read*, by Kathleen B. Hester, Professor of Education at Michigan State Normal College. Copyright 1955 by Harper and Brothers, publishers. Reprinted with permission.

↓ | ↓ | ↓

Critical reading
includes
ability to determine
the relevancy
of material
to a given topic;
the understanding that,
although a statement
may be important,
it may not be relevant
for the purpose;
the ability to check
the validity of a
statement
against other statements
in the same book;

the ability to check
the validity of a
statement
against other statements
by different authors;
the ability to detect
the difference between
a statement of fact
and a statement of
opinion;
the ability to use
the copyright date
as a means of checking
the validity of the
material;
the understanding that

a printed statement
is not always
a true statement;
the ability to check
the competence of the
author;
the ability to detect
a bias of the author;
and the ability to use
one's own experience
in appraising what
he has read.
To be able
to do these things
requires reading skill
of a high order.

↓ | ↓ | ↓

It requires the ability to retain | the ideas read until they can be evaluated | through further reading and through experience.

Perception Exercise 52

Continue as before.

The following material is extracted from *Emotional Difficulties in Reading*, by Beulah Kanter Ephron, published by The Julian Press, Inc. Reprinted with permission.

↓ | ↓ | ↓

The reader who reads "word-by-word" gives equal stress, time and value to every word. He cannot omit a single word without a nagging feeling that something important has been missed, and he retraces his steps to pick up the missing word. It is chiefly because of the word-by-word reading that the Harvard Films * | are used in the Improvement-of-Reading course. There is no magic in a mechanical stimulus, but the films do lead the students to make an important observation about themselves. Phrases flash by, never to return. The students groan. They have not had time to look long and thoroughly at every word, to go back and make sure | they have missed nothing, and they are certain they will not be able to recall much of the material. However, when they are tested on their retention of the article, they are pleasantly surprised to discover that most of it has been absorbed. They learn, therefore, that they are capable of observing a great deal without conscious awareness

* A tachistoscopic device by which phrases are flashed in sequence on a movie screen.

368

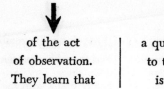

of the act	a quick exposure	that lingering and
of observation.	to the material	re-reading
They learn that	is sufficient,	is unnecessary.

Perception Exercise 53

We turn again, now, to exercises in training your peripheral vision.

Fixating at the broad arrow, speed down each column as rapidly as you can without loss of comprehension, making, as far as possible, only one fixation to the line.

The following material is from a television column by Harriet Van Horne which appeared in the March 13, 1957 issue of the *New York World-Telegram and The Sun*. Copyright 1957 by the *New York World-Telegram and The Sun*. Reprinted with permission.

$64,000 QUIZ NOW INFLATED $256,000
by Harriet Van Horne

↓ ↓ ↓

I may be out of step with the good, golden times but I sense something unhealthy in last night's announcement that the $64,000 Question had been inflated to $256,-000.

It's a staggering sum of money to most of us. That it should become the stake in a television parlor game is not only vulgar, it's faintly corrupt. I don't mean to say that the shows are fixed. I am reasonably sure they are not. But the producers of these Roman circuses have confessed that they are—it's their word—"controlled." The sum of $256,000, I beg to submit, should be *administered* by a trust, not controlled by a TV packaging company.

"Be not greedy to add money to money," says the Bible. It's a text the producers of all give-away programs might pursue with profit. And I do mean profit to their immortal souls, saith the preacher.

Why did the producers of the $64,000 Question suddenly quadruple the grand prize? Well, the first word that comes to mind is desperation. Ratings have declined in recent months. And look at the size of the winner's jackpot on that other show on that other network.

369

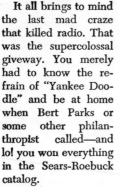

It all brings to mind the last mad craze that killed radio. That was the supercolossal giveway. You merely had to know the refrain of "Yankee Doodle" and be at home when Bert Parks or some other philanthropist called—and lo! you won everything in the Sears-Roebuck catalog.

At the outset the prizes stayed within the reasonable, or $64,000 limit. Then came the day when an innocent contestant won an old war surplus B-29. Another show, in a fit of whimsy, gave away its announcer. Madness set in. Contestants who'd hoped for a washing machine were stunned to receive an abandoned railway station, an old bus, not to mention lifetime supplies of cement, fertilizer, or hairpins. Anguished housewives began calling the Boy Scouts and the Salvation Army to please come and get the bulldozer or the nice brown horse that was kicking the porch in.

Inevitably, there were lawsuits. Inevitably, there was also boredom and distaste. The giant jackpot radio show vanished for the same reason the dinosaur vanished. And he vanished because he was too big, too stupid and too vicious to endure.

If the destruction of the poor is their poverty, then the destruction of the greedy will surely be their greed. People who besiege quiz shows are primarily drunk with the fantasy of quick, easy riches. They may have heads like junk shops, crammed with thousands of odd, unsorted facts. But they are not, as a rule, persons of achievement or creative talent. Most of them are awarded their prizes for freakish feats of memory. And now that the prizes have gotten completely out of hand, I suppose a goodly segment of the country will leave off delving and spinning for the memorizing of fact books. Television will be teeming with people who know everything . . . while wisdom crieth without in the streets.

★ SESSION 29

VOCABULARY STUDY VIII

Words for Today

1. ambiguous
2. autonomous
3. bucolic
4. contentious
5. dormant
6. fractious

7. inane	10. polyglot	13. stolid
8. mercurial	11. prolific	14. supercilious
9. occult	12. risible	15. unctuous

Do the usual dictionary study on those words that are not completely familiar to you, recording the essential information on meaning, pronunciation, derivation, related forms, and usage in your notebook, and writing a brief illustrative phrase or sentence for each word. Review your notes, then take the following test.

Test Your Learning

I. Write the letter of the proper definition before the number of each word in column 1.

1. WORDS	2. DEFINITIONS
——— 1. ambiguous	a—able to be understood in two or more ways
——— 2. autonomous	
——— 3. dormant	b—laughable; inclined to laugh
——— 4. inane	c—speaking many languages
——— 5. occult	d—haughty; contemptuous
——— 6. polyglot	e—fertile; producing much, especially figuratively
——— 7. prolific	
——— 8. risible	f—silly; senseless
——— 9. stolid	g—not easily moved; impassive
———10. supercilious	h—self-governing; independent
	i—mysterious; secret; known only to the initiated
	j—inactive; as if asleep

II. Check TRUE or FALSE for each of the following statements.

1. A shepherd's life can properly be called *bucolic*. TRUE; FALSE
2. *Contentious* people rarely argue. TRUE; FALSE
3. *Fractious* children are happy and well-behaved. TRUE; FALSE
4. A person of *mercurial* temper is often fickle and changeable.

TRUE; FALSE

5. *Unctuous* people are generally brutally frank. TRUE; FALSE

Key:
I. 1—a, 2—h, 3—j, 4—f, 5—i, 6—c, 7—e, 8—b, 9—g, 10—d.
II. 1—true, 2—false, 3—false, 4—true, 5—false.

More Words for Today
1. affluence
2. argot
3. chauvinism
4. dexterity
5. diffidence
6. equanimity
7. hypochondria
8. iconoclasm
9. lechery
10. mendacity
11. nuance
12. obloquy
13. propinquity
14. retribution
15. sagacity

Do the usual dictionary study on those words that are not completely familiar to you, recording the essential information on meaning, pronunciation, derivation, related forms, and usage in your notebook, and writing a brief illustrative phrase or sentence for each word. Review your notes, then take the following test.

Test Your Learning
I. Write the letter of the proper definition before the number of each word in column 1.

1. WORDS	2. DEFINITIONS
_____ 1. affluence	a—manual or mental skill of a high order
_____ 2. argot	b—lewdness; active indulgence in lust
_____ 3. chauvinism	c—mental composure; calmness of mind or temper
_____ 4. dexterity	
_____ 5. diffidence	d—contempt for tradition, cherished beliefs, etc.
_____ 6. equanimity	e—untruthfulness
_____ 7. hypochondria	f—great wealth
_____ 8. iconoclasm	g—delusions of ill health
_____ 9. lechery	h—excessive or blatant patriotism
_____10. mendacity	i—lack of self-confidence; timidity
	j—special language of a group or class

II. Check TRUE or FALSE for each of the following statements.
1. A *nuance* is a fine or subtle shade of meaning.　TRUE; FALSE
2. Persons to whose names *obloquy* is attached are generally well respected.　TRUE; FALSE
3. *Propinquity* refers to great distances.　TRUE; FALSE
4. One who is wronged often seeks *retribution*.　TRUE; FALSE
5. *Sagacity* is sometimes a product of age and education.
　TRUE; FALSE

Key:
　I. 1—f, 2—j, 3—h, 4—a, 5—i, 6—c, 7—g, 8—d, 9—b, 10—e.
　II. 1—true, 2—false, 3—false, 4—true, 5—true.

FINAL TRAINING IN RAPID COMPREHENSION

Preview

In this chapter, you:
• Tackle a final round of three long and fairly complex timed selections.
• Continue to aim for a quick and accurate grasp of main ideas by responding aggressively to the structure of writing.
• Evaluate your total progress to date by making a fourth chart and graph of your present reading speed.

> *Chapter 12* reminds you, as the course comes to a close, that this need not be the end of your training, and that you can go on by yourself making still further gains; for learning to read is a continuous, never-ending process.

FINAL PRACTICE TESTS IN FASTER READING

You are now coming to the end of weeks or months of hard practice in the techniques of rapid and efficient reading. During this time you have gradually increased your speed of comprehension, you have developed greater competence in attacking a page of print, you have begun to form habits of cruising through material with sharper awareness not only of *total meaning* but also of the *pattern* in which this meaning is presented. In short, if your training has been at all successful, you have become a better and much faster reader than you were when you started your work.

Now you will have your last chance (in this book, but of course not in your outside reading) to measure the speed of your performance. In reading the long and fairly difficult selections in this chapter, observe all the rules that have constantly been emphasized and re-emphasized throughout your training: push yourself a bit so that you have a feeling of comprehending rapidly; sense the broad outlines of structure; find and follow the main ideas without losing time on unimportant details; and skim or skip without guilt if your mood, your understanding, and the character of the material make this approach desirable and useful.

Time your reading of each piece, and keep a record of your statistics on the new chart and graph on page 395.

Ready for your final test?

Selection 20

YOU CAN'T SAY THAT!
by Jesse Zunser

I

Start timing→ Censorship is nothing new. From the first time a cave man had an idea different from his neighbor's, and tried to settle that difference with physical persuasion, argument by compulsion has been a familiar human activity. The wielded club and the censoring scissors are separated in history only by time. Both state, flatly, unequivocally and finally: "You can't say that!"

Almost from the day movies first flickered across the screen they have been an easy target for do-gooders, Mrs. Grundys, politicians, clergymen, propagandists, and all sorts of special censorial pleaders. In 1896 clergymen reared up in righteous wrath and roared "Scandalous!" at an innocuous little four-minute film clip that pictured a gentleman imprinting a prim little kiss upon a lady's cheek. Fifty-nine years later it's still going on—the kissing and the wrath.

II

Latest inciter, or victim, of man's incessant urge to compel cinematic conformity is the movie made from John van Druten's play "I Am a Camera," based on Christopher Isherwood's "Berlin Stories," which opens next week at the Little Carnegie. With Julie Harris starred, it won the New York Critics Circle award in 1952, and is an almost line-for-line reproduction of the play: a candid, sophisticated and uninhibited treatment of sex and "life among the artists," dealing with unwed pregnancy and abortion as it unfolds the frenetic story of Sally Bowles, a British girl living in Berlin in 1931. Her rather amoral behavior is discussed and pictured against the background and turmoil of the Nazi-dominated German capital—in a time and place much like the distraught, disillusioned, ex-patriate-filled Paris of the 1920's, that served so well for stories by Hemingway, Scott Fitzgerald, John Dos Passos, and others.

The movie's producers, Distributors Corporation of America, have clashed with the Motion Picture Association's Production Code on the propriety and acceptability of this picture, and with the Catholic Legion of Decency which is certain to condemn it. Distributors contend that sex—in and outside the frame-

From *Cue*. Reprinted by permission. Mr. Zunser is the motion picture editor of *Cue*.

work of our behavior and convention patterns—is a part of life; and as such is a legitimate subject for adult dramatic discussion, which purports to picture life.

For years people have complained that movies are infantile, asking "When will they grow up?" Distributors—and others—feel that movies will never grow up until they face the facts of life and recognize that no area of human activity is outside the province of intelligent cinematic dramatization. Books passed this point years ago, the theatre is at the edge of it, and the movies must reach it if they are ever to become a mature and significant art and communication medium.

Aside from the amoral behavior of its heroine Sally, opposition to the film has developed to the use in it of words like "virgin," "chaste" and "pregnant." These are no new bogeys in the movies.

The word "pregnancy" has been *verboten* in films for years, as though it were a dirty word. The first time I can recall hearing it spoken in a movie was in 1948, in "Apartment for Peggy," when Jeanne Crain told her husband, quite simply, "I'm pregnant." In Pennsylvania it was a long-time Censor Board rule that "women informing men about pregnancies are out—because it is offensive, indecent and obscene to womanhood as well as all right-thinking men." And one producer had to "cut out all full-length views of pregnant women."

In the movie lexicon, "bastard" too is a dirty word. U. S. censors threatened to clip it from Shakespeare's (and Laurence Olivier's) "Henry V," until they were persuaded that it was a fact rather than fiction. And Warner Bros. more recently had a hard time winning permission to use "The Virgin Queen" as a title for their forthcoming drama about Queen Elizabeth I of England.

Censors are shocked by beds. Nobody, they believe, ever sleeps in them. In Ohio they stopped a boarding-school teacher from saying, "My girls are in bed every night at nine o'clock." And although New York passed a scene where a man carries a girl into a bedroom, it balked when he shut the door. New York censors also cut a view of an indented pillow "showing hairpins on it." It was "too suggestive." They completed the job by cutting "all sounds of a yawn, indicating that the woman had been in bed shortly before."

Sometimes the omniscient censors presume to speak for God. Maryland's lady censor deleted Joan of Arc's anguished cry at the stake, "O Lord, why hast Thou forsaken me!" She explained that this "implied God would forsake any one, and this is simply not so." The lady forgot these were Jesus' words, too.

Compulsory censorship is the favorite last word of politicians. As recently as 1934 Tammany Hall tried to pass legislation forbidding movies "that tend to undermine confidence in officials and their conduct in of-

376

fice." The officials, of course, to be the judges.

Some municipalities, too, are extremely shy. Chicago's policeman censor systematically eliminated all reference to gangsters ever coming from there (including a movie about mobster Al Capone). Jersey City cut a film in which a plane pilot remarked, "We're approaching Jersey City—I can smell it." And Kansas banned a movie in which a teletype flashed: "The criminals were last seen in Kansas City." One public-spirited scissorman clipped a sequence in which a counterfeiter boasted, "My bills are as good as the originals."

It got so hard to please everybody that Samuel Goldwyn remarked, "I'd like to make a movie of 'Beverly of Graustark' if I could only be sure some mythical kingdom wouldn't complain!"

Many have tried to get into the censoring act—for personal, prideful, patriotic, political, propagandistic, moral, social, racial or theological reasons. Almost everybody believes he is specially qualified to advise, revise and edit movies—not only for himself and his group, but for the public as well.

Spain's church-dominated censor banned "Gentleman's Agreement" because "It is poison [to say that] a Christian is not superior to a Jew." And Jewish organizations tried to ban "Oliver Twist" because the villainous Fagin was a Jew (no mention of murderer Bill Sykes, who was not a Jew). Church groups condemned H. G. Wells' "Shape of Things to Come" because God was not mentioned in it. Catholic pressure banned "Martin Luther" in most of Canada and many other countries, and tinkered with history in "The Three Musketeers." In this film the wily Richelieu was pictured not as a Cardinal, prince of the Church, but as an unscrupulous civilian politician.

It has even come to a point where censoring the unseen is now an actuality. In "Seven Year Itch" Tom Ewell peeks into a photographic magazine and sees (what the audience *never* sees but is led to believe is) a nude photo of Marilyn Monroe. At Legion insistence after the film's release, 20th Century-Fox inserted a fast flash showing a photo of Miss Monroe clad in a proper bathing suit.

Thus the censors reached beyond the picture and censored the audience.

Producers and exhibitors frankly fear to run counter to Legion demands. They risk the loss not only of patronage of millions of Catholics who have taken the Legion pledge, but also "punishment" in the form of picketing and/or boycott of their theatres for periods of from one week to a year. Most big movie companies have contracts with producers guaranteeing that film product delivered will receive at least a Legion "B" rating.

III

The opposition to censorship is rooted in the belief that it would be a dangerous opening wedge for

377

the destruction of new ideas. And that it is too short a step from political and clerical censorship to regimentation of all independent thinking into a fixed pattern of conformity.

Producers believe that present laws are adequate to punish obscenity in motion pictures. And that therefore, pre-censorship is, by its very nature, not only restrictive and dangerous—but unnecessary.

Anti-censors feel that an "adult" approach to the movies, as to other arts, is not only more intelligent, but is far healthier; and that a continued and conspiratorial policy of "hush-hush" leads to more evils than a psychiatrist can ever get off a couch. As to dirt—the feeling is that such pictures, if unheralded and unadvertised by the censoring opposition, would soon die of their own accord. The censorial mind, they believe, seriously under-estimates the intelligence, the taste and decency of the public.

Progress flourishes only in an atmosphere of freedom. That freedom is its own best guardian against license.   ←End timing

RECORD HERE THE TIME REQUIRED ON THIS SELECTION: _____ MIN.
_____ SEC.

Test Your Comprehension

Which one of the following statements best summarizes the total and final meaning of this selection?

1. Film censorship is absurd, unhealthy, dangerous, and unnecessary.
2. Censorship is not new—it existed in the time of the cave man; and film censorship is just one symptom of a desire to force others to accept one's ideas and attitudes.
3. Movies will never grow up until producers are willing to accept the idea that no area of human activity is outside the province of cinematic dramatization.
4. Producers and exhibitors fear the power of censorship groups.

Compute Your Rate

(Approximate number of words: 1475)

TIME	W.P.M.	TIME	W.P.M.
2 min.	738	3 min.	492
2 min., 10 sec.	684	3 min., 15 sec.	456
2 min., 15 sec.	656	3 min., 30 sec.	422
2 min., 20 sec.	633	3 min., 45 sec.	392
2 min., 30 sec.	590	4 min.	369
2 min., 45 sec.	536	4 min., 15 sec.	348

YOUR RATE ON SELECTION 20: _____W.P.M.

(Record this statistic on the chart and graph on page 395.)

Discussion of the Selection

The body, and largest part, of this article is taken up with detailed, specific examples, all contributing to the conclusions that are expressed in the last five paragraphs, and foreshadowed by the tone of the first two, introductory, paragraphs.

Let's look at the material together.

Section I: Introduction, which points out that censorship is nothing new and which, in tone, sets the stage for both the coming examples and the conclusions.

Section II: Body of the article, containing examples of successful and unsuccessful attempts at motion picture censorship, the tone and style clearly showing the author's position and feeling.

Section III: Conclusions: the opposition to censorship is based on danger of destruction of new ideas, regimentation of thinking, present laws against obscenity sufficient, evils resulting from "hush-hush," stifling of progress, etc. In short, according to Mr. Zunser, film censorship is absurd, unhealthy, dangerous, and unnecessary. (Statement 1 on the comprehension test is the correct choice.)

Selection 21

BEWARE THE PSYCHOS

by Fred Dickenson

Start timing→ That pretty girl who just sold you the wrong pack of cigarets; that rude man who shoved ahead of you to grab the subway seat; the smiling fellow in the office who "forgot" to pay back the loan as he had promised so faithfully to do—watch out for them!

From the *New York Mirror*, reprinted with permission. Copyright 1956, King Features Syndicate, Inc.

2. They're psychopathic personalities and they're as dangerous as a package of dynamite with fuse attached and ready to go.

3. Scandal, disgrace, grief and even death await the unwary who are drawn too deeply into their erratic orbit. They walk the streets by the millions, sit beside you in the gay glitter of the theatre and in the calm sanctity of the church. They're at the wheel of the car bearing down on you.

4. Are they insane? Not in a legal sense. Nor do they exhibit any of the common symptoms we have come to associate with "crazy" people. They do not babble or burst into bizarre song, effect weird costumes or think they are Napoleon.

5. Because to the casual eye they can appear as normal as the sturdiest, they pack a double peril. When their unstable world collapses, they pull down with them anyone within reach. It can be you.

6. Police officers come into contact daily with psychopathic personalities, who are born "trouble makers." To guide officers in this work, The National Association for Mental Health has issued a manual called "How to Recognize and Handle Abnormal People," by Robert A. Matthews, M.D., head of the Department of Psychiatry and Neurology, Louisiana State University School of Medicine, and Lloyd W. Rowland, Ph.D., director of the Louisiana Association for Mental Health.

7. Their tips also form a valuable guide for the average person who may unwittingly become involved with a psychopathic personality unless he can spot and interpret flying danger signals.

8. Since the disorder shows up in many forms and degrees, one or several of the warning signs may be seen in a person by a trained observer. Crediting Hervey Cleckly's book, "The Mask of Sanity," as their source, Drs. Matthews and Rowland list in modified form the characteristic points which can alert you to the possibility that a person is a psychopath. They are:

1. Shallow, on the surface charm, often seems rather bright.

2. Lack of symptoms one would observe in a person who is mentally ill.

3. Lack of nervousness of the sort commonly seen in a neurotic patient.

4. Unreliability—you can't depend on him.

5. Untruthfulness and insincerity.

6. Selfishness—thinks only in terms of how things affect him personally; has no capacity to really love another person.

7. Antisocial behavior.

8. Poor judgment and failure to learn from experience.

9. Lack of any feeling of shame, after he has done something wrong.

10. Lack of feeling for the rights of others.

11. Lack of realization that there is something wrong with him. It is always somebody else's fault.

12. Callousness and lack of abil-

ity to work harmoniously or in a team with others.

13. Foolish behavior with drink or even without it.

14. Threats of suicide when in trouble—seldom carried out.

15. Sex life—superficial, often promiscuous.

16. Failure to follow a life plan.

9. "It is easy to see how persons with such character traits become vagrants and try all sorts of schemes to make money," say Drs. Matthews and Rowland. "They do foolhardy things that endanger their own lives and the lives of others, and they may eventually drift into crime.

10. "Many drug addicts are psychopaths and a large proportion of our criminal population belongs in this category. Sometimes the psychopath does well in a wartime army but is a troublemaker in a peacetime military unit when he cannot find a way to get rid of his hostile impulses."

11. The psychopath (unlike the truly insane) is held responsible by society for his behavior and is punished for his misdemeanors and crimes. Invariably, the doctors say, this punishment does no good but makes the person worse.

12. "He makes solemn promises to turn over a new leaf only to repeat some wrong act immediately upon release from custody. It almost seems that he feels a need to be punished because he lacks a conscience that will punish him."

13. What makes a psychopath— these persons whom an English physician long ago called "moral imbeciles" because they are often intelligent but have no sense of right or wrong?

14. Drs. Matthews and Rowland state that the psychiatric concensus today is that most persons with character defects get that way because of unfortunate childhood experiences. "As children, nobody wanted them or loved them. Many came from broken homes or homes where there were no sturdy parents to provide a pattern for growth.

15. "Sometimes they come from wealthy homes which are long on comfort but short on love. Feeling insecure, unwanted, even hated as a child, they can hardly have much faith in their future."

16. The psychopathic personality, they add, is angry at the world and gets even by doing things which are wrong. He feels he must seize his pleasure at the moment, and does so regardless of consequences. Punishment usually follows, and the cycle proceeds relentlessly until a delinquent or a criminal is created.

17. Since punishment does not seem to help, can anything else be done for them? In a London hospital today, a hundred persons with various character disorders are being treated in what is called a "therapeutic community." A sincere attempt is made to understand the psychopath, and with medical help the patients try to understand one another.

18. The feeling that people are for them and not against them seems to aid about half of the patients,

381

doctors report. Why the treatment does not work with the other 50 percent is still a mystery.

19. The fact that medical science cannot yet straighten the character kinks of so many psychopathic personalities is added warning to the layman to avoid their clutches. Giving children genuine love to prevent creation of new cases is the duty and responsibility of every parent. In the presence of a full-blown character disorder, however, the layman's wisest course to protect himself and society is to try to get the afflicted person to see a doctor.

20. How many psychopathic personalities are there? How many people steal, skip out on debts, start unfounded and malicious gossip, repeatedly walk out on jobs, wreak deliberate mischief, are constantly getting injured, or take physical revenge to the point of murder?

21. Their numbers dwarf the 750,000 persons now under the care of mental hospitals in this country. Of the latter, suffering recognized mental disorders such as schizophrenia, manic depression, involutional melancholia, etc., relatively few come from the ranks of the psychopathic personality.

22. Occasionally, a judge will recommend psychiatric care for an habitual thief and a person will cross the bridge between the two groups. A drug addict may wind up in a hospital and do the same thing. But all too often, say officials of the Mental Health Association, the psychopathic personality merely goes his weird way taking a frightful toll in blighted lives, and costing the public untold millions for the upkeep of jails, reformatories and various other institutions.

23. The enormity of the problem can be highlighted by the fact that already there are more people hospitalized in this country for *recognized mental illness* than for polio, cancer, heart disease and all other diseases combined. The chance of your being hospitalized for a severe mental illness today is one in 10, whereas in 1934 it was one in 20.

24. Of the $180,000,000 spent each year on all medical research, only about $6,000,000—or 3 percent—goes toward conquering the more than 100 different kinds of mental disorders.

25. Thus, the community must still grapple, somehow, with the vast number of psychopathic personalities about us who are not being treated and for whose problem virtually no research is being carried on.

26. They must wait until the more recognizable forms of mental illness are brought under control. Then, doctors say, the truly Herculean task of salvaging psychopathic personalities can begin. Meanwhile, the best the average citizen can do is be on his guard among them.

←End timing

RECORD HERE THE TIME REQUIRED ON THIS SELECTION: _____ MIN. _____ SEC.

Test Your Comprehension

Which one of the following statements best summarizes the total and final meaning of this selection?

1. Psychopathic personalities are not insane, in the legal sense of the word.

2. Be on guard against psychopathic personalities—they are dangerous.

3. Psychopathic personalities are charming, intelligent, and unusually calm.

4. Punishment does not cure the psychopathic personality.

Compute Your Rate

(Approximate number of words: 1520)

TIME	W.P.M.	TIME	W.P.M.
2 min.	760	3 min., 45 sec.	405
2 min., 10 sec.	700	4 min.	380
2 min., 15 sec.	675	4 min., 15 sec.	360
2 min., 20 sec.	660	4 min., 30 sec.	340
2 min., 30 sec.	610	4 min., 45 sec.	320
2 min., 40 sec.	570	5 min.	305
2 min., 45 sec.	550	5 min., 30 sec.	275
3 min.	505	6 min.	255
3 min., 15 sec.	470	6 min., 30 sec.	235
3 min., 30 sec.	435	7 min.	220

YOUR RATE ON SELECTION 21: _____W.P.M.

(Record this statistic on the chart and graph on page 395.)

Discussion of the Selection

Mr. Dickenson is saying one main thing to his readers. This point is mentioned in the title, is expressed clearly in paragraphs 1 and 2, and is fully developed and often repeated throughout the selection. He is saying, in brief: *Watch out for psychopathic personalities—they're dangerous.*

Let us examine together the pattern Mr. Dickenson follows in developing his central theme.

Paragraphs 1–2: Expression of central theme.

Paragraphs 3–5: Explanation of the danger.

Paragraphs 6–12: Description of the psychopathic personality.

Paragraphs 13–16: Causes of the psychopathic personality (lack of love in childhood, hence angry at the world).

Paragraphs 17–19: Treatment and prevention of the psychopathic personality—show people are not against him (works for 50 per cent of those treated); give love to children; get the afflicted person to see a doctor.

Paragraphs 20–26: Further description of the psychopathic personality, statistics as to his prevalence, etc., supporting the author's theme that the best thing we can do at present is be on our guard against him.

Mr. Dickenson uses every detail in his piece to bolster his main idea. *Watch out*, he says, *for psychopathic personalities—they're dangerous.* Then he goes on, point by point:

1. This is the danger they present.
2. This is how to recognize them.
3. This is what causes their affliction.
4. This is how to treat them, but treatment is effective in only half the cases.
5. Their numbers are vast, most of them are not treated, and there is virtually no research on their illness. So be on your guard!

Correct choice on the comprehension test is statement 2.

Selection 22

WHY DO ACCIDENTS HAPPEN?

Start timing→ Before we can develop a really effective program to prevent auto accidents, we will have to learn far more than we now know about why such accidents happen.

2. The National Safety Council, while pointing out that most accidents result from a combination of causes, and that "few accidents are investigated carefully enough to determine exactly what their underlying causes were," estimates that in about 80% of accidents, the most important single factor is the driver himself.

3. Bad weather, poor road conditions, and defects in cars do cause

From *Consumer Reports*, published by Consumers Union, Mt. Vernon, N. Y. Reprinted with permission.

384

some accidents, but, generally speaking, such circumstances appear to be of minor significance compared with the mental and physical condition of the driver. And recent research indicates that the driver's physical condition is of less importance than his personality and his emotional state. Many, if not most, accidents, this research suggests, are the result of wayward impulses and motivations, of faulty judgments and attitudes, of poorly controlled aggressiveness and competitiveness. Further study of personality and emotions in relation to driving probably would contribute much to the understanding and prevention of accidents.

4. Nearly two-thirds of the drivers involved in fatal accidents in 1954 were speeding, driving while under the influence of alcohol, disregarding stop lights or signs, or otherwise violating the law, according to the Safety Council. The pertinent question is *why* do people drive too fast, drive after drinking, take risks in passing, or, in general, commit dangerous, careless, illegal, impulsive, or unfriendly acts when they get behind the wheel?

5. A small beginning has been made toward finding answers to this question. Several studies comprehensively described by Dr. Ross McFarland and his associates at Harvard's School of Public Health have probed the personality and emotional characteristics of so-called accident-prone drivers and discovered such traits as emotional instability, impulsiveness, suggest-

ibility, excitability, lack of a proper sense of social responsibility, aggressiveness, and intolerance of authority. Although fault may be found with the quality of this research in terms of controls and other safeguards, it may prove provocative enough to lead to sounder efforts.

6. "A man drives as he lives," say Drs. Tillman and Hobbs in an article in the *American Journal of Psychiatry*. "If his personal life is marked by caution, tolerance, foresight, considerations for others, then he will drive in the same way. If his personal life is devoid of these desirable characteristics, then his driving will be characterized by aggressiveness, and over a long period of time, he will have a higher accident rate than his more stable companions."

7. The trouble with the first part of this statement is that no human being is, at all times, cautious, tolerant, foresighted, and considerate of others. Even though we may be exemplary persons most of the time, there are certain moments, or longer periods, in the lives of all of us when we become temporarily impulsive, aggressive, or otherwise emotionally off balance. If we happen to be driving during one of these episodes—and if external circumstances favor an accident—then an accident is likely to occur.

8. As Dr. Edward Press, of the University of Illinois, puts it: "Just as almost all of us will respond with a neurosis or other nervous disorder

385

to a sufficiently strong or repeated stress, so most average people under certain combinations of circumstances that occur frequently in our current civilization can become temporarily accident prone." Excessive fatigue, fear, worry, sleeplessness, irritability, preoccupation, headache, too much alcohol or other drugs—all may have this effect.

9. While the study of behavior and conscious mental activities by way of aptitude, intelligence, and psychologic tests and by clinical scrutiny of life histories and attitudes will increase our understanding of accident causes, our knowledge will be incomplete without more information about the unconscious and its influence on drivers. More than 40 years ago, Freud said, "Psychoanalysis has concluded from a study of dreams and mental slips of normal people as well as from the symptoms of neurotics, that . . . primitive [and] savage . . . impulses of mankind have not vanished in any individual, but continue their existence, although in a repressed state in the unconscious, and that they wait for opportunities to display their activity." For many people, the automobile apparently provides some of the most irresistible of such opportunities—especially with the current glorification of the high-speed car with its formidable horsepower, and fast-starting and quick-passing ability.

10. While, admittedly, the evidence for the great importance of psychological factors in auto accidents rests on a fragile statistical framework, the same is true of the evidence on physical defects of drivers responsible for auto accidents. The National Safety Council says that "only one out of 14 drivers involved in fatal accidents had a physical condition that could have been a contributing factor in the accident." Such statistics mean very little unless we know what is meant by a "physical condition"; and psychosomatic medicine has taught us that even major "physical" disorders often have important emotional components.

11. Some test of visual acuity is a standard device in almost all states for helping to determine the fitness of drivers. Such a test is of value in detecting impairment of ability to see far objects, and it undoubtedly deprives the near-blind of the freedom of killing themselves and others on the road. However, Dr. Leon Brody, of New York University, has been stressing for years the scant relationship between a driver's visual fitness, as measured by a conventional driver's license test, and his safety record.

12. To be more meaningful, tests of driver vision should include peripheral vision, or ability to see objects on the sides while looking straight ahead; dark adaptation, or night vision; glare recovery; and ability to "accommodate," or shift from a far focus to a near focus (such as on a speedometer) and back. Color-blindness tests are of little importance, since even a person color-blind to red and green can readily learn to distinguish be-

tween red and green lights. Dark adaptation and glare recovery are particularly important in view of the fact that the fatal-accident rate per mile of travel is three times as high during the night as during the day. Dark adaptation is impaired by alcohol, carbon monoxide and lack of vitamin A or oxygen. After age 45 or 50, there is a gradual decline in all visual functions, but what effect this decline has on auto-accident rates is unknown. Probably most older drivers compensate for it by more conservative driving practices.

13. Hearing acuteness also declines with age, but, again, there are no statistics to suggest a connection between hearing defects and auto accidents. Obviously, though, a deaf driver—or a driver with normal hearing who keeps his radio on full blast—has one less physical sense on guard to warn him of danger.

14. Driving skill by itself does not insure safety in driving, according to a study made by Dr. Brody in 1941. Many drivers repeatedly involved in accidents are skilled drivers, as determined by controlled driving tests. Some of these may get into trouble because they are convinced that they can safely take more risks than less-skilled drivers.

15. Although people with an organic disease or disability—epilepsy, heart disease, or high blood pressure, for example—may be more prone to disabling symptoms while driving than healthy persons, this very fact may act as an incentive to more cautious driving on their part. At any rate, statistical evidence of a connection between such disorders and a high rate of auto accidents is lacking. Certainly, the emotional stresses associated with contemporary auto driving are not likely to be beneficial for a person with coronary artery disease or high blood pressure. No one knows how many heart attacks in innocent pedestrians and drivers have been caused by the foolish behavior of "healthy" drivers.

16. "Carotid sinus syncope" is a disorder caused by oversensitivity of certain nerve tissue in the carotid arteries of the neck. A tight collar could conceivably produce faintness, dizziness, or even loss of consciousness in a driver suffering from this condition.

17. Other organic ailments—such as uncontrolled diabetes, kidney trouble, and neurological disorders —also can cause impairment of driving fitness. Undoubtedly, more study of this problem is needed, and other states might well follow the lead of New York in requiring a doctor's certification of the fitness of persons with mental and certain physical disorders to receive a license to drive. At the same time, physicians should warn their patients with such disorders of the potential danger to themselves and others in driving.

18. Safe driving does not require hard muscular effort, but it does call for skill and mental concentration, both of which involve faculties that are subject to fatigue after several hours at the wheel. Visual

387

fatigue also may be of considerable importance as an accident factor. It is good driving practice to take a rest or brief exercise after two hours or so at the wheel. This can also help to relieve road monotony and prevent the driver's falling asleep at the wheel—two frequently cited causes of auto accidents. Heavy meals, which dispose to sleepiness and fatigue, should be avoided by drivers.

19. The exhaust gas from auto engines contains carbon monoxide in percentages ranging from about 1% to 7%, and a car idling in a closed garage can produce enough of the gas in a few minutes to render the atmosphere deadly. Tests of passenger cars on the road have shown that carbon monoxide concentrations within the car can reach dangerous levels. The gas can come from leaks in the car's own exhaust system—such as blown-out gaskets, loose manifold and exhaust pipe connections, and holes in mufflers and exhaust pipes—and, in heavy traffic, from the exhaust of other cars. In streets where traffic is heavy, the concentration of carbon monoxide rises to about a hundred parts per million parts of air, enough to cause headaches, dizziness, faintness, weakness, and other toxic symptoms in many persons after an exposure of several hours.

20. Carbon monoxide also is one of the important toxic ingredients of tobacco smoke, and a person who smokes 20 to 30 cigarettes a day has from 4% to 8% of his hemoglobin blocked by this gas. There is little doubt that the carbon monoxide from other cars, your car, and smoking can combine to interfere seriously with driving efficiency.

21. Not long ago, Dr. Frank Dutra, the chief medical examiner for Cincinnati, urged that the carbon monoxide concentration in the blood of any driver involved in an accident be measured, predicting that such tests would pinpoint carbon monoxide as the cause of some otherwise unexplained fatal accidents.

22. Widely used sedatives, tranquilizers, stimulants, hormones (such as ACTH and cortisone) and antihistamine drugs may cause disturbing side effects that impair driving skill, judgment, and attention. The disabling effects of some of these drugs were brought out at the last highway safety research conference sponsored by the National Academy of Science and the National Research Council in 1954. Even ordinary doses of sedatives or stimulant drugs can evoke hostile and aggressive practices. Such barbiturate drugs as phenobarbital, *Nembutal*, and *Seconal*, when taken by order of a physician, are valuable for relieving nervous tension and promoting sleep, but taken at the wrong time or in uncontrolled amounts, they can cause physical and mental symptoms that interfere with driving ability.

23. The stimulants—*Benzedrine*, *Dexedrine*, and similar amphetamine drugs—are frequently misused by drivers who do not realize that there is no substitute for rest

388

and adequate sleep to assure effective exercise of their faculties. If misused, these drugs may cause irritability, excitement, and impairment of timing, coordination, and judgment. Abuse of the newer tranquilizing drugs, such as *Miltown, Noludar, Thorazine,* and reserpine, now frequently prescribed for common nervous disorders, can have equally harmful effects. The caffeine in cola drinks, coffee, and tea has a mild stimulant action which may improve driving alertness, but in excess or in sensitive persons, can impair muscular coordination and timing.

24. Since some antihistamine drugs are freely available without a doctor's prescription, many people take them indiscriminately for colds, grippe, coughs, and other acute respiratory infections. Other antihistamine drugs (*Dramamine* and *Boramine,* for example) are taken to control motion sickness. Among the more important possible side effects of these drugs are dizziness, difficulty in focusing the eyes, sleepiness, impaired reflex and reaction time, and disturbance of coordination and judgment—any of which obviously would be dangerous in a driver.

25. In the whole array of drugs capable of seriously interfering with driving skill and judgment, alcohol undoubtedly is the outstanding culprit. From the viewpoint of auto safety, the most important aspect of alcohol is its effect on the central nervous system. It is not a stimulant, as many people believe, but a depressant of the nervous system, sharing the characteristic actions of the general anesthetics. In small amounts, alcohol may improve mood and sociability, but, as Drs. Goodman and Gilman say in "The Pharmacological Basis of Therapeutics": "Carefully controlled experiments have shown that alcohol increases neither mental nor physical ability; although the individual estimates his own performance as greatly improved, in reality, actual measurements show it to be inferior."

26. To a certain extent, man can use his intelligence to overcome his physical and emotional shortcomings as a driver and the other threats to his safety on the road. He can make cars and roads safer, enforce traffic laws more rigorously, improve driving education, encourage training of visual and other skills useful in driving, and, probably most important, apply psychiatric, psychologic, and psychoanalytic research to the auto-accident problem. While Colorado has made a good start in this latter direction by requiring a psychiatric examination for persistent violators of driving laws, it obviously would be impractical to make such an examination a routine part of driver's-license tests.

27. Until we find a way to screen out potentially dangerous drivers or to get more people to practice common sense and consideration for others on the road, it would be wise for each of us to assume that other drivers will behave discourteously, carelessly, aggressively, illegally, or stupidly—and to try to maintain a

389

safety margin adequate to compensate for such behavior.

RECORD HERE THE TIME REQUIRED
ON THIS SELECTION: _____ MIN.
_____ SEC.

←**End timing**

Test Your Comprehension

Which one of the following statements best summarizes the total and final meaning of this selection?

1. If we ever hope to prevent or reduce automobile accidents, we must set up machinery to investigate the exact causes of accidents.
2. Most accidents are caused by bad weather, poor road conditions, and car defects, but the mental and physical condition of the driver is often a contributing factor.
3. Human beings must learn to be more cautious, tolerant, and considerate when they drive if we are going to reduce the toll of lives taken by automobile accidents.
4. Only those people who are physically and mentally fit—possessed of good vision and hearing, free of organic disease, well-balanced in personality—and who are really skillful at the wheel, should be licensed to drive.
5. Most important single cause of most automobile accidents is the driver himself, i.e., his mental and physical condition and his personality type and emotional state.

Compute Your Rate

(*Approximate number of words: 2400*)

TIME	W.P.M.	TIME	W.P.M.
3 min., 15 sec.	740	6 min.	400
3 min., 30 sec.	685	6 min., 30 sec.	370
3 min., 45 sec.	640	7 min.	345
4 min.	600	7 min., 30 sec.	320
4 min., 15 sec.	565	8 min.	300
4 min., 30 sec.	535	8 min., 30 sec.	280
4 min., 45 sec.	510	9 min.	270
5 min.	480	10 min.	240
5 min., 30 sec.	440		

YOUR RATE ON SELECTION 22: _____W.P.M.
(*Record this statistic on the chart and graph on page 395.*)

Discussion of the Selection

This piece, a model of clear organization, divides neatly into three parts. Let us look at the material together.

PART 1—STATEMENT OF CENTRAL THEME

Paragraphs 1–3: Direct answer to the question in the title and a statement of the central theme—*most important single cause of most accidents is the driver himself,* according to estimates of the National Safety Council. Bad weather, road conditions, and car defects cause some accidents, but the important thing is *the mental and physical condition of the driver, especially his personality type and emotional state.*

PART 2—DEVELOPMENT OF CENTRAL THEME

Paragraphs 4–9: How the personality and the emotional state of the driver cause accidents.

Paragraphs 10–18: Physical condition of the driver as a cause of accidents—vision, hearing, disease, fatigue, disabilities, etc.

Paragraphs 19–21: Carbon monoxide as a deterrent to driving efficiency and a reducer of physical fitness.

Paragraphs 22–25: The wide use of drugs, sedatives, alcohol, etc., as a cause of reducing mental and physical fitness and efficiency.

PART 3—RECAPITULATION

Paragraphs 26–27: How to reduce accidents—a kind of recapitulation of the central theme. The causes have been stated and explained, and obviously the best solution is to remove the causes.

Correct choice on the comprehension test is statement 5.

All right. That does it. Now copy, as usual, the statistics on your rates from the chart for this chapter.

SELECTION 20 (CENSORSHIP): _____W.P.M.

SELECTION 21 (PSYCHOS): _____W.P.M.

SELECTION 22 (ACCIDENTS): _____W.P.M.

Add these figures, divide by 3 to find your average rate in this chapter, and record the result here:

AVERAGE RATE IN CHAPTER 12: _____W.P.M.

Now let us construct a final chart that will depict your total progress throughout your training. Fill in the lines below by referring to the indicated pages.

A CHART OF YOUR TOTAL PROGRESS

1. INITIAL RATE (SEE PAGE 11): _____W.P.M.
2. AVERAGE RATE, CHAPTER 2 (SEE PAGE 392): _____W.P.M.
3. AVERAGE RATE, CHAPTER 7 (SEE PAGE 393): _____W.P.M.

4. AVERAGE RATE, CHAPTER 10 (SEE PAGE 394): _____W.P.M.
5. AVERAGE RATE, CHAPTER 12 (SEE PAGE 395): _____W.P.M.
6. AVERAGE GAIN: (SUBTRACT LINE 1 FROM 5) _____W.P.M.
7. PERCENTAGE GAIN: _____%

(Divide the figure in line 6 by that in line 1, and carry to two decimal places.)

IMPROVEMENT CHART—PHASE 1

(Chapters 1–2)

SELECTION 1: _____W.P.M. SELECTION 4: _____W.P.M.
SELECTION 2: _____W.P.M. SELECTION 5: _____W.P.M.
SELECTION 3: _____W.P.M. SELECTION 6: _____W.P.M.

AVERAGE RATE SELECTIONS 3–6: _____W.P.M.
PERCENTAGE GAIN OVER SELECTION 1: _____%

IMPROVEMENT GRAPH—*PHASE 1*

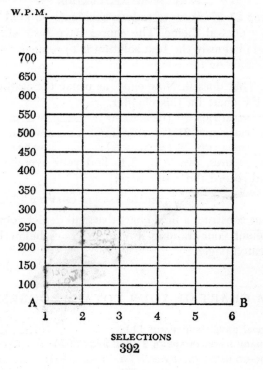

SELECTIONS

392

IMPROVEMENT CHART—PHASE 2

(Chapter 7)

SELECTION 7: _____W.P.M.   SELECTION 12: _____W.P.M.
SELECTION 8: _____W.P.M.   SELECTION 13: _____W.P.M.
SELECTION 9: _____W.P.M.   SELECTION 14: _____W.P.M.
SELECTION 10: _____W.P.M.   SELECTION 15: _____W.P.M.
SELECTION 11: _____W.P.M.

AVERAGE RATE, SELECTIONS 7–15:   _____W.P.M.
AVERAGE GAIN OVER SELECTION 1:   _____W.P.M.
PERCENTAGE GAIN OVER SELECTION 1: _____%

IMPROVEMENT GRAPH – *PHASE 2*

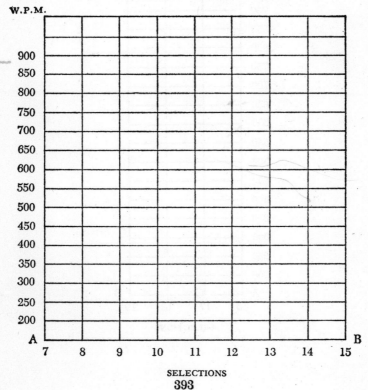

W.P.M.

900
850
800
750
700
650
600
550
500
450
400
350
300
250
200

A

7   8   9   10   11   12   13   14   15

B

SELECTIONS

393

IMPROVEMENT CHART—PHASE 3

(Chapter 10)

SELECTION 16: _____W.P.M.   SELECTION 18: _____W.P.M.
SELECTION 17: _____W.P.M.   SELECTION 19: _____W.P.M.

AVERAGE RATE SELECTIONS 16–19:   _____W.P.M.
AVERAGE GAIN OVER SELECTION 1:   _____W.P.M.
PERCENTAGE GAIN OVER SELECTION 1: _____%

IMPROVEMENT GRAPH – *PHASE 3*

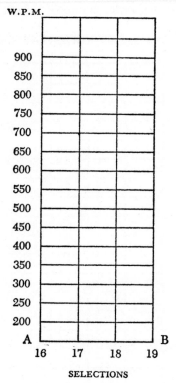

W.P.M.

900
850
800
750
700
650
600
550
500
450
400
350
300
250
200

A   B
  16   17   18   19

SELECTIONS

IMPROVEMENT CHART—PHASE 4

(Chapter 12)

SELECTION 20: _____W.P.M.
SELECTION 21: _____W.P.M.
SELECTION 22: _____W.P.M.

AVERAGE RATE, SELECTIONS 20–22: _____W.P.M.
AVERAGE GAIN OVER SELECTION 1: _____W.P.M.
PERCENTAGE GAIN OVER SELECTION 1: _____%

IMPROVEMENT GRAPH – *PHASE 4*

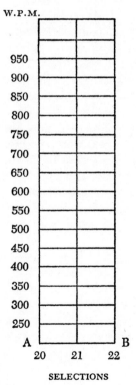

W.P.M.

950
900
850
800
750
700
650
600
550
500
450
400
350
300
250

A · · · B

20 · · 21 · · 22

SELECTIONS

LAST WORDS—A PLAN FOR THE FUTURE

I should like to suggest that this is not necessarily the end of your training, even though you have faithfully covered every page in the book, have worked hard for weeks or months, and have noted a comfortable increase in your general reading speed of anywhere from 25 to 100 per cent or more.

What you have learned, and what you have accomplished so far, should represent for you no more than a broad base, a strong foundation on which to continue building. This was *basic* training, this provided you with a good initial push, a fast start, and excellent momentum.

Now you can, and should, go on by yourself—for, as I have said in the past, *learning to read is a continuous, never-ending process.*

Books and magazines are, of course, published faster than you or anyone else can ever hope to read them. To say nothing of the vast output of the past with which you might want to catch up.

If you read twenty-four hours a day, seven days a week, for the rest of your life, you will scarcely make a dent in the volume of material that is available for reading—I grant that.

But put your training to use. With the increased skill and speed you now possess, you can do almost twice the reading you used to do in any given period of time. You can do this, that is, if you form the *habit* of reading—if you make reading of magazines, novels, and books of nonfiction as much a regular part of your life as eating, or sleeping, or going to the movies, or visiting your friends, or watching television.

Set yourself the kind of goal I have suggested—let no week go by in which you haven't read at least one book, of whatever nature. And if you can manage to make it two or three books some weeks, so much the better.

You will make no dent in the available reading material. But what a change you will effect in your own intellectual equipment, in your store of knowledge and ideas, in your alertness to what is going on in the world!

Or I can give you a far more potent and convincing reason—*you'll enjoy it, you'll have a wonderful time.* Reading, you will discover (you have probably already made this discovery), is one of the great and satisfying pleasures of human living.

Continue building your reading vocabulary. During your training program you have studied somewhat over 150 words (these are the starred entries in the list on pages 138–142), and you have learned some valuable techniques in doing research with a dictionary. Use those techniques to acquire the remaining words on the list that are wholly or partially unfamiliar—go through methodically, covering ten to twenty at a time.

And, as additional help, get yourself a good vocabulary-building manual. Here are a number of the top-notch aids in the field, listed alphabetically:

1. *English Vocabulary Builder*, by Johnson O'Connor
2. *How to Build a Better Vocabulary*, by Maxwell Nurnberg and W. T. Rhodes
3. *How to Double Your Vocabulary*, by S. Stephenson Smith
4. *New Way to Vocabulary Power and Culture*, by Wilfred Funk
5. *Six Weeks to Words of Power*, by Wilfred Funk (Also available in a 35¢ paper-covered edition.)
6. *Thirty Days to a More Powerful Vocabulary*, by Wilfred Funk and Norman Lewis (Also available in a 25¢ paper-covered edition.)
7. *Word Power Made Easy*, by Norman Lewis (Also available in a 35¢ paper-covered edition.)

Continue, also, the kind of practice that will further increase your digit recognition-span. You have mastered the technique of accurately perceiving up to six digits in split-second fixations—with added effort you can eventually conquer numbers of seven and eight digits. (A few of my unusual students have reached ten, and the army training program has records of occasional athletes who have gone as high as fifteen.) Have someone prepare several hundred numbers containing seven and eight digits, typed out with four spaces between the lines; using the Flashmeter card, practice on these at the rate of fifty to one hundred at a time. (You cannot type these numbers yourself, for your resulting familiarity with them, slight as it may be, will invalidate your score.)

And continue, in your everyday reading, your practice in occasional or partial skimming, or even in total skimming if the material and the circumstances warrant it. Continue sharpening your comprehension skill by keeping alert to the broad structure of whatever you read, by finding and following central themes, and by occasionally writing out, in your own words, the gist of what you have just read.

Continue pushing yourself quickly through material. Read with the feeling that you are comprehending fast, that you are thinking along with the author, that you are reacting critically to what he says.

Continue training your peripheral vision by every now and then sweeping down a narrow newspaper column as fast as comprehension permits and making, as far as possible, only one fixation to the line.

And test yourself periodically. Take a magazine article or a chapter in a book and time your reading. Count or estimate the number of words, and compute your rate. You may be surprised and gratified to discover that you can increase your present speed by as much as 10 or 20 per cent within the next six months if you keep up your training.

All these suggestions, as you realize, only ask you to continue on your own the kind of practice this book has provided.

The dividends of increased speed, understanding, and satisfaction that you have received from your formal training program have been in direct proportion to the amount of time and creative effort that you have invested in your work. *Continue your investment and the dividends will continue to build up.*

THE PEOPLES OF THE
ARCTIC

Senior Consulting Editor

Senator Daniel Patrick Moynihan

Consulting Editors

Ann Orlov
Managing Editor, Harvard
Encyclopedia of American
Ethnic Groups

M. Mark Stolarik
*President, The Balch Institute
for Ethnic Studies, Philadelphia*

David M. Reimers
*Professor of History,
New York University*

James F. Watts
*Chairman, History Department,
City College of New York*

The Peoples of North America

THE **A** PEOPLES OF THE
ARCTIC

Kevin Osborn

CHELSEA HOUSE PUBLISHERS
New York   Philadelphia

On the cover: Inuit children in northern Canada in the late 1980s.

CHELSEA HOUSE PUBLISHERS

Editor-in-Chief: Nancy Toff
Executive Editor: Remmel T. Nunn
Managing Editor: Karyn Gullen Browne
Copy Chief: Juliann Barbato
Picture Editor: Adrian G. Allen
Art Director: Maria Epes
Manufacturing Manager: Gerald Levine
Systems Manager: Rachel Vigier

The Peoples of North America

Senior Editor: Sean Dolan

Staff for THE PEOPLES OF THE ARCTIC

Copy Editor: Michael Goodman
Deputy Copy Chief: Mark Rifkin
Editorial Assistant: Gregory Rodríguez
Picture Research: PAR/NYC
Assistant Art Director: Loraine Machlin
Senior Designer: Noreen M. Lamb
Production Manager: Joseph Romano
Production Coordinator: Marie Claire Cebrián
Cover Illustration: Paul Biniasz
Banner Design: Hrana Janto

Library of Congress Cataloging-in-Publication Data

Osborn, Kevin
  The Peoples of the Arctic
  (The Peoples of North America)
  Includes bibliographical references.
  Summary: Discusses the history, culture, and religion of the Inuit and the Aleuts, their place in American society, and the problems they face as an ethnic group in North America.
  1. Eskimos. 2. Aleuts. [1. Eskimos. 2. Aleuts. 3. Indians of North America] I. Title. II. Series.
E99.E7077 1990
305.8'971 90-1362
ISBN 0-87754-876-5
      0-7910-0301-9 (pbk.)

CONTENTS

THE PEOPLES OF NORTH AMERICA

CHELSEA HOUSE PUBLISHERS

A NATION
OF NATIONS

Daniel Patrick Moynihan

The Constitution of the United States begins: "We the People of the United States . . . " Yet, as we know, the United States is not made up of a single group of people. It is made up of many peoples. Immigrants from Europe, Asia, Africa, and Central and South America settled in North America seeking a new life filled with opportunities unavailable in their homeland. Coming from many nations, they forged one nation and made it their own. More than 100 years ago, Walt Whitman expressed this perception of America as a melting pot: "Here is not merely a nation, but a teeming Nation of nations."

Although the ingenuity and acts of courage of these immigrants, our ancestors, shaped the North American way of life, we sometimes take their contributions for granted. This fine series, *The Peoples of North America*, examines the experiences and contributions of the immigrants and how these contributions determined the future of the United States and Canada.

Immigrants did not abandon their ethnic traditions when they reached the shores of North America. Each ethnic group had its own customs and traditions, and each brought different experiences, accomplishments, skills, values, styles of dress, and tastes in food that lingered long after its arrival. Yet this profusion of differences created a singularity, or bond, among the immigrants.

The United States and Canada are unusual in this respect. Whereas religious and ethnic differences have sparked intolerance throughout the rest of the world—from the 17th-century religious wars to the 19th-century nationalist movements in Europe to the near extermination of the Jewish people under Nazi Germany—North Americans have struggled to learn how to respect each other's differences and live in harmony.

Millions of immigrants from scores of homelands brought diversity to our continent. In a mass migration, some 12 million immigrants passed through the waiting rooms of New York's Ellis Island; thousands more came to the West Coast. At first, these immigrants were welcomed because labor was needed to meet the demands of the Industrial Age. Soon, however, the new immigrants faced the prejudice of earlier immigrants who saw them as a burden on the economy. Legislation was passed to limit immigration. The Chinese Exclusion Act of 1882 was among the first laws closing the doors to the promise of America. The Japanese were also effectively excluded by this law. In 1924, Congress set immigration quotas on a country-by-country basis.

Such prejudices might have triggered war, as they did in Europe, but North Americans chose negotiation and compromise instead. This determination to resolve differences peacefully has been the hallmark of the peoples of North America.

The remarkable ability of Americans to live together as one people was seriously threatened by the issue of slavery. It was a symptom of growing intolerance in the world. Thousands of settlers from the British Isles had arrived in the colonies as indentured servants, agreeing to work for a specified number of years on farms or as apprentices in return for passage to America and room and board. When the first Africans arrived in the then-British colonies during the 17th century, some colonists thought that they too should be treated as indentured servants. Eventually, the question of whether the Africans should be viewed as indentured, like the English, or as slaves who could be owned for life, was considered in a Maryland court. The court's calamitous decree held that blacks were slaves bound to lifelong servitude, and so were their children. America went through a time of moral examination and civil war before it finally freed African slaves and their descendants. The principle that all people are created equal had faced its greatest challenge and survived.

Yet the court ruling that set blacks apart from other races fanned flames of discrimination that burned long after slavery was abolished—and that still flicker today. The concept of racism had existed for centuries in countries throughout the world. For instance, when the Manchus conquered China in the 13th century, they decreed that Chinese and Manchus could not intermarry. To impress their superiority on the conquered Chinese, the Manchus ordered all Chinese men to wear their hair in a long braid called a queue.

By the 19th century, some intellectuals took up the banner of racism, citing Charles Darwin. Darwin's scientific studies hypothesized that highly evolved animals were dominant over other animals. Some advocates of this theory applied it to humans, asserting that certain races were more highly evolved than others and thus were superior.

This philosophy served as the basis for a new form of discrimination, not only against nonwhite people but also against various ethnic groups. Asians faced harsh discrimination and were depicted by popular 19th-century newspaper cartoonists as depraved, degenerate, and deficient in intelligence. When the Irish flooded American cities to escape the famine in Ireland, the cartoonists caricatured the typical "Paddy" (a common term for Irish immigrants) as an apelike creature with jutting jaw and sloping forehead.

By the 20th century, racism and ethnic prejudice had given rise to virulent theories of a Northern European master race. When Adolf Hitler came to power in Germany in 1933, he popularized the notion of Aryan supremacy. *Aryan*, a term referring to the Indo-European races, was applied to so-called superior physical characteristics such as blond hair, blue eyes, and delicate facial features. Anyone with darker and heavier features was considered inferior.

Buttressed by these theories, the German Nazi state from 1933 to 1945 set out to destroy European Jews, along with Poles, Russians, and other groups considered inferior. It nearly succeeded. Millions of these people were exterminated.

The tragedies brought on by ethnic and racial intolerance throughout the world demonstrate the importance of North America's efforts to create a society free of prejudice and inequality.

A relatively recent example of the New World's desire to resolve ethnic friction nonviolently is the solution the Canadians found to a conflict between two ethnic groups. A long-standing dispute as to whether Canadian culture was properly English or French resurfaced in the mid-1960s, dividing the peoples of the French-speaking Quebec Province from those of the English-speaking provinces. Relations grew tense, then bitter, then violent. The Royal Commission on Bilingualism and Biculturalism was established to study the growing crisis and to propose measures to ease the tensions. As a result of the commission's recommendations, all official documents and statements from the national government's capital at Ottawa are now issued in both French and English, and bilingual education is encouraged.

The year 1980 marked a coming of age for the United States's ethnic heritage. For the first time, the U.S. Census asked people about their ethnic background. Americans chose from more than 100 groups, including French Basque, Spanish Basque, French Canadian, Afro-American, Peruvian, Armenian, Chinese, and Japanese. The ethnic group with the largest response was English (49.6 million). More than 100 million Americans claimed ancestors from the British Isles, which includes England, Ireland, Wales, and Scotland. There were almost as many Germans (49.2 million) as English. The Irish-American population (40.2 million) was third, but the next largest ethnic group, the Afro-Americans, was a distant fourth (21 million). There was a sizable group of French ancestry (13 million), as well as of Italian (12 million). Poles, Dutch, Swedes, Norwegians, and Russians followed. These groups, and other smaller ones, represent the wondrous profusion of ethnic influences in North America.

Canada, too, has learned more about the diversity of its population. Studies conducted during the French/English conflict showed that Canadians were descended from Ukrainians, Germans, Italians, Chinese, Japanese, native Indians, and Eskimos, among others. Canada found it had no ethnic majority, although nearly half of its immigrant population had come from the British Isles. Canada, like the United States, is a land of immigrants for whom mutual tolerance is a matter of reason as well as principle.

The people of North America are the descendants of one of the greatest migrations in history. And that migration is not over. Koreans, Vietnamese, Nicaraguans, Cubans, and many others are heading for the shores of North America in large numbers. This mix of cultures shapes every aspect of our lives. To understand ourselves, we must know something about our diverse ethnic ancestry. Nothing so defines the North American nations as the motto on the Great Seal of the United States: *E Pluribus Unum*—Out of Many, One.

THE PEOPLES OF THE NORTH

The peoples of the North American Arctic—the Eskimos (now generally called Inuit after the 1977 Inuit Circumpolar Conference officially adopted Inuit as the designation for all Eskimos, regardless of local usage), the Aleuts, and the Arctic Indians—are truly Native Americans and Canadians, peoples who lived in harmony with the land for 3,000 years before the first European explorers and entrepreneurs arrived on the shores of the New World.

All Arctic peoples, from those in Siberia in the Soviet Union to those in Greenland, have certain linguistic, cultural, and physical similarities, although they are not a single, homogeneous race of people. The distinctions among the Arctic peoples are perhaps best demonstrated in the variety of their languages and dialects. The Eskimo-Aleut linguistic family consists of two distantly related branches, the Eskimo and the Aleut, which probably separated over 2,000 years ago and which developed independently from a remote common ancestor, Proto-Eskimo Aleut. The Eskimo branch has two distinct subgroups, the Yupik and the Inuit-Inupiaq. Aleut is represented by a single language spoken on the Aleutian Islands. Modern speakers of either main branch cannot understand the speakers of the other; dialects within each main group are often quite unique. Eskimo is spoken by about 16,000 people in Greenland; 18,000 in Canada; 16,000 in Alaska; and

1,000 in Siberia. Speakers of Aleut number about 6,000 and include a few hundred people on the Soviet Pribilof Islands; the others live in American territory.

The Eskimo, or Inuit, language bears no resemblance to any Indian language. It is a complex and highly inflected tongue with a great many suffixes that can be combined in an enormous variety of ways. A single root has the potential to form thousands of words. The Inuit vocabulary is rich in terms that refer to hunting, to animals, and to the technical aspects of weapons and tools. It possesses terms for empiric notions as well as terms that refer to the mind and to the senses. The term for "the people" or "the true people" is *inuk* or *inuit*, in its plural form.

Aleut, as the designation of a people, was not originally a name of their own choosing. It is thought to have come from either the Koryak or the Chukchi Indian language (the Chukchi word for "islands" is *aliat*) and to have been bestowed upon the people of the Aleutian Islands around 1750 by visiting Russians and East Siberians. Alternately, the term *Aleut* may be a Russian version of Alut, the name of an island village.

The 1980 U.S. census reported that 50,555 United States citizens claim Inuit or Aleut ancestry, and more than three-quarters of those (38,468) named either Inuit or Aleut as their sole ancestry. In addition to these Arctic peoples in the United States, more than 25,000 Inuit, almost all of unmixed ancestry, live in Canada. In Greenland, Inuit number 40,000 and compose the majority of the country's population. Six hundred Inuit currently live in the Chukotski region of Siberia. Inuit settlements stretch from northeastern Siberia to Greenland, with extensions down the west coast of Alaska and along the shores of Hudson Bay. There are some settlements on islands of the Arctic Ocean and the Bering Sea. Unlike some North American native populations, the Arctic native population is in no danger of racial obliteration.

Seventy percent (35,496) of those Americans with Aleut or Inuit ancestry live in Alaska, where they make up almost 9 percent of the state's population. In no other state do Aleuts and Inuit form even one-tenth of one percent of the population, and only California, Washington, and Oregon have more than 1,000 citizens of Aleut or Inuit descent.

Unlike Native Americans in the lower 48 states, most contemporary Native Alaskans live on ancestral grounds rather than on government reservations. Alaska has about 100 Inuit villages, each with a population of 600 people or less. Residents elect their own village councils. Slightly more than 2,600 of the 8,090 Aleuts in Alaska live in the 12 surviving villages on the Aleutian and Pribilof islands, while 3,000 others live in rural communities in other parts of the state. Only 2,466 Aleuts live in Alaskan urban centers, with the greatest number, 1,512, residing in Anchorage. Anchorage also has a sizable Inuit community (3,500), as does Fairbanks (3,000). These urban populations are the exceptions; like the Aleuts, most Inuit make their home in rural areas.

One general condition unites all contemporary native peoples of the Arctic, overriding linguistic, technical, and physical differences. Contemporary Inuit and Aleuts are torn between the traditional and modern ways of life. Although Europeans may have first encountered Inuit over 1,000 years ago, the severity of the Arctic climate left much of the land and its people relatively untouched until the last 50 years. Since World War II, government and commercial activities in the Far North have expanded explosively, forcing widespread interaction between the people of the Arctic and those to the south. Caught between two very different worlds, contemporary Inuit and Aleuts face difficult choices as they determine how best to participate in the development and prosperity of their land without losing touch with their traditional way of life.

Greenland Inuit pose in front of their sod home in 1881. Over the centuries the Inuit developed remarkably ingenious methods of adjusting to their environment.

THE FIRST AMERICANS

The Inuit and Aleut peoples came to North America millennia ago. However, because they had no written language until the 19th century, no textual account exists of their experiences before the 1750s and the influx of Russian explorers and traders. Archaeology, the study of the physical remains of past societies, has provided most of what is known about the long period of Inuit and Aleut prehistory.

During the last two centuries, archaeologists have unearthed evidence, in the form of bone and stone artifacts such as blades, arrowheads, and tools, that points to the existence of "Paleo-Arctic" cultures in North America at least 9,000 years ago. However, artifacts alone can never yield a complete picture of the prehistory of Arctic civilizations. At best, archaeologists can develop theories and models based on what information these material objects offer.

Archaeologists have determined that Paleo-Indians predate the Paleo-Inuit in North America. Paleo-Indian peoples probably crossed to North America via a land bridge; by A.D. 1, Paleo-Inuit probably used boats to cross what is now called the Bering Strait. Remains of stone lamps have been found in Inuit sites; such finds were unknown earlier in North America but common to Eurasia since the Old Stone Age. The presence of these oil-burning lamps suggests that the Paleo-Inuit must have come originally from Eurasia.

The Ice Age and the Land Bridge

Except for Antarctica, North and South America were the last continents to be inhabited. Most archaeologists agree that the first Native Americans crossed the Arctic Ocean from Asia during the final glacial epoch, known popularly as the Ice Age. During this period, from approximately 20,000 B.C. to 10,000 B.C., almost all of Canada was buried under a sheet of ice. Ice and snow deposits in the mountains and on dry lands drew an enormous amount of water from the world's oceans. This widespread evaporation caused the sea level to drop more than 300 feet, extending by many miles the coastlines of the continents of the Northern Hemisphere.

Scientists believe that this extended coastline connected the continents of Asia and North America. At one time, archaeologists speculated that this bridge of land was to be found along a mountain range, the peaks of which now form the Aleutian Islands. But advances in depth-sounding technology have shown that the sea along this chain of islands is so deep that the land between some of the "peaks" would never have risen above even the lowest recorded sea level. This geological evidence suggests that if prehistoric tribes did first come to America on foot during the period from 11,000 B.C. to 9,000 B.C., they came across a land bridge which today is covered by the Bering Strait, a stretch of water only 50 miles wide.

Paleo-Arctic peoples most likely migrated in search of more abundant hunting grounds. A wide variety of animals lived in the Far North near the end of the Ice Age. Bison, mastodons, mammoths, bears, beavers, and especially caribou roamed the icy plains of the Yukon and Northwest territories and the grassier plains and forests of Alaska.

When the glacial epoch came to an end and the vast sheets of ice began to melt, the oceans' waters rose again, separating the two continents and isolating the Native Americans from the rest of the world. Over the next 10,000 years, with little or no outside contact, these people and their descendants continued to develop a seasonal hunting culture perfectly adapted to the changing Arctic geography and climate.

Eastward and Southward Migration

After crossing over from Eurasia, the Paleo-Arctic ancestors of today's Inuit and Aleuts continued to move farther into the interior of North America, probably following the changing migratory patterns of their prey. Over several thousand years, these peoples spread eastward through the Canadian Arctic all the way to Greenland. Others moved south and west, inhabiting the Alaska Peninsula and Aleutian Islands, while still others probably migrated ever farther south, perhaps mingling with Paleo-Indian peoples.

By 7000 B.C. to 6000 B.C., the eastern Aleutian Islands were inhabited by "Paleo-Aleuts," ancestors of the modern Aleut people. Blades discovered on a small islet off the coast of Umnak Island, dating from about 6000 B.C., suggest that these early inhabitants had already begun to live off the products of the sea. By this time in the earth's history, rising ocean waters had probably isolated Umnak and the rest of the Aleutians from the mainland and therefore also from land mammals. In order to survive, the Paleo-Aleuts became well adapted to life on the ocean.

By about 2000 B.C., after thousands of years of gradual evolution, the Aleut tradition was essentially established. Archaeological discoveries suggest that by this time the Aleuts had developed the wide variety of harpoons, fishing spears, bird darts, and skin-covered boats that would thereafter characterize their methods of hunting. From 2000 B.C. until the Russian fur hunters

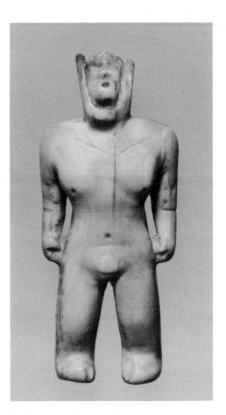

An ivory sculpture of a man wearing a high collar. Both the high collar and the type of sculpture shown here are typical of the Dorset cultural tradition, which held sway among the Inuit of the eastern Arctic to Greenland from about 1000 B.C. to A.D. 1300.

arrived in the 1740s, inhabitants of the Aleutian and Kodiak islands, as well as those of the Pacific coast of the Alaska Peninsula, maintained a remarkably stable coastal existence. Although the Aleuts continued to expand their territory westward, by 500 B.C. they had completed their migration throughout the entire Aleutian archipelago and inhabited all of the islands from Unimak to Attu.

Diffusion of Inuit Traditions

Although the Aleuts had substantially established their traditions by about 2000 B.C., the ancestors of the Inuit continued to develop their culture for another 3,000 years. Around 3000 B.C., along the northwestern coast of Alaska, ancestors of the Inuit began using flint blades to carve ivory and bone into harpoons and small tools such as arrowheads, needles, and knives. Many of these small tools have been unearthed at an important ar-chaeological site near Cape Denbigh, Alaska. These "Denbigh" hunters, with their balanced combination of ocean- and land-based hunting, formed the earliest cul-ture that can properly be called Inuit.

Over the next thousand years, the climate of the Arctic grew warmer, and the Denbigh people, perhaps in search of an easier way of life, migrated eastward. Although they continued to hunt sea creatures along the coast, the Denbigh migrants began to depend more on land animals, primarily on the caribou and musk-oxen that lived on the Arctic tundra. Over the next few centuries, the Denbigh people rapidly dispersed across the American Arctic, establishing villages and com-munities. By 2500 B.C., the Denbigh hunters inhabited the entire coast of the Arctic Ocean, all the way from Alaska to Greenland. By 2000 B.C., the Denbigh people had already established the broadly based hunting economy, balanced among land mammals, sea crea-tures, and river fish, that foreshadowed the economy of their Inuit descendants.

The Alaskan and Canadian interior became progressively colder over the next thousand years. Several species of land animals, such as the mammoth, began to die out, while others, chiefly the caribou and the musk-ox, migrated southward. Some people of the Denbigh culture followed the game in their southward migration, but many others stayed in the Arctic. The Arctic peoples who remained were forced to adapt their culture in order to survive a progressively harsher climate. From Alaska to Greenland, those who had earlier moved to the interior moved back to the northern coast of North America, where they developed specialized maritime hunting techniques.

For more than 2,000 years, from 1000 B.C. to A.D. 1300, the Arctic was dominated by the cultures of two peoples also considered ancestors of the Inuit. In Alaska and northwestern Canada, people of the Norton culture, named after Norton Sound, an important archaeological site in Alaska, established more or less permanent coastal villages. At the same time, the Dorset culture, so called because of archaeological remains first found at Cape Dorset in the eastern Arctic, spread throughout much of the rest of Canada, from the Mackenzie River in the western Northwest Territories all the way to Newfoundland and the west coast of Greenland. Together, the Norton and Dorset peoples inhabited most of the Far North, though there were small pockets of people who did not share in the traditions or technologies of either of these two cultures.

Traditional Inuit culture centers on the hunt. This ancient bow, made of ivory, is decorated with scenes depicting a caribou hunt. It was discovered on Baffin Island, the northeasternmost of Canada's Northwest Territories.

The Thule Culture

During the 10th century A.D., while the Dorset culture remained dominant throughout eastern and central Canada, the Bering Strait region of Alaska saw the emergence of the Thule people, considered the direct ancestors of today's Inuit. The Thule culture further developed the coastal hunting methods used by its ancestors, refining tools and techniques into the hunting traditions that became characteristic of the Inuit people.

As did their predecessors, the Thule established a well-balanced subsistence economy. They were especially successful in developing tools and methods for capturing sea mammals, including, for the first time, enormous whales, which they hunted from *umiaks* (skin-covered boats, similar to *kayaks* but larger, that carried 8 to 10 hunters). Archaeologists have also unearthed tools that prove that in addition to capturing whales, seals, and walrus, the Thule hunted caribou, polar bears, and birds and caught fish in the northern rivers. There is even archaeological evidence to suggest the use of dogsleds.

By the beginning of the 11th century A.D., the Thule culture had become strong enough to expand eastward,

Once provided with a wick and lit, stone lamps like this one discovered on Kodiak Island, Alaska, were used to burn sea mammal oil for light and heat. This lamp may be as many as 2,500 years old. It is ornamented with a polar bear head intended to appear as if it is floating above the pool of oil.

and it began a dramatic conquest of the entire Arctic coast of North America. The Thule people established settlements throughout northern Canada and in Greenland, following essentially the same path taken by their Denbigh predecessors almost 4,000 years earlier. In eastern Canada, the Thule took over the hunting grounds of the entrenched Dorset culture. Although the two cultures coexisted for several centuries, Dorset traditions disappeared entirely around A.D. 1400. By this time, only the Aleuts, whose culture had not substantially changed since 2000 B.C., remained uninfluenced by the Thule expansion. The powerful Thule culture had conquered or absorbed all of the other tribes of Arctic people from Alaska to Greenland.

From the 15th to the 18th century, the Arctic climate grew progressively worse. Air and water temperature plummeted, and packs of ice covered the seas for two-thirds of the year. The Thule people, with their broad-based hunting technology, were well prepared to adapt to the changing climate. Because ice had disrupted the traditional reliance on sea mammals in most areas, the Thule adopted a seasonally migratory way of life. In the summer, they lived in centralized communities, where they fished and hunted for land animals. In the winter, they returned to the coast and hunted for seals. This balanced approach to hunting, which they had begun to establish as early as the 10th century A.D., allowed the Thule to survive the climatic change and become the modern Inuit of Canada and Alaska.

To outsiders, the Arctic's dramatic landscape and unforgiving environment seems unsuited to human life.

THE ARCTIC LANDSCAPE

The sterility of the soil and the rigor of the climate no other race could survive; yet here, utterly dependent upon animal life, which is their sole source of food, live the most cheerful people in the world—the fearless, lovable, happy-go-lucky Eskimo.

—from the 1922 film documentary
Nanook of the North

Although this description of the Arctic land and its people is both romantic and stereotypical, it does emphasize two of the most obvious characteristics of Arctic life—the harshness of the land and the adaptability of its inhabitants. Over time, Arctic peoples developed the ability to survive and even to flourish in the harsh Arctic environment. Survival might mean moving on to a new area with a more plentiful food supply or establishing a seasonal migratory pattern between coastal and inland villages or conceiving of more efficient hunting tools. In each instance, Arctic peoples relied both on a finely tuned instinct for survival and on a hard-won knowledge of the Arctic land, climate, and animal life.

The Inuit of the late 20th century retain close ties to their ancestral landscape. Inuit have inhabited essentially the same vast northern territory ever since the completion of the Thule expansion 700 years ago. From east to west, they are distributed over 6,000 miles, spanning a territory that stretches from eastern Greenland, through northernmost Labrador and Quebec and the Northwest and Yukon territories in Canada, through northern Alaska, and across the Bering Strait to the northeastern coast of Siberia in the Soviet Union. Inuit live as far north as Grise Fjord, a tiny settlement on Ellesmere Island in Canada, over 2,000 miles north of Montreal and just 500 miles from the North Pole. Others live as far south as southern Baffin Island, hundreds of miles below the Arctic Circle.

The Arctic Landscape

The most rigid definition of the Arctic limits is the area north of the Arctic Circle. This boundary, located at approximately 66 ½ degrees north of the equator, was first defined in the 5th century B.C. by observation of the earth's relationship to the sun. The tilt of the earth on its axis keeps the area north of this latitude facing away from the sun throughout the winter months and facing toward the sun throughout the summer months. Elsewhere in the world, the rotation of the earth on its axis every 24 hours creates day and night, as each side of the planet first faces toward the sun, then away from it. But the land north of the Arctic Circle experiences annual periods of continuous daylight and continuous darkness. For as long as four consecutive months, from mid-October to mid-February, the entire land is plunged in darkness. During the summer, the Arctic becomes the Land of the Midnight Sun, experiencing continuous daylight for several months.

The phenomenon of prolonged days and nights is not, however, the most important defining characteristic of the Arctic. The Arctic's unique physical environment is primarily due to the relative absence of heat energy. Three definitions of the southern boundary of the Arctic have been suggested: the area that has a 10-degree mean temperature in July; the tree line; or the southernmost limit of permafrost. The extent to which the Arctic climate differs from region to region results from various factors, such as the presence of mountain barriers, the distance from open-water bodies, the surface cover of ice and snow, and the distinctive pattern of sunlight and darkness.

During the very short, cool summers of the Arctic, snows thaw, plants grow, and the midnight sun shines over most of the land. Spring and fall are almost nonexistent in the Arctic; the eight or nine months of winter arrive abruptly. Most Arctic regions experience average January temperatures ranging from 29 degrees below 0 to 14 degrees above 0 (Fahrenheit). Arctic temperatures sometimes reach deadly extremes. In January 1989, for example, the Yukon Territory and northern Alaska suffered from record low temperatures of 80 degrees below 0.

Despite these extremes of cold, there is little snowfall in the Arctic. In general, the colder air gets, the less water vapor it can carry. When the temperature falls to more than 40 degrees below 0, evaporation ceases altogether. Therefore, especially in the northernmost regions, little new snow is possible during the winter. In most areas of the Arctic, snowfall amounts to only two to three feet annually, primarily in the autumn and then again when the weather turns a little warmer in the spring and moist air masses arrive from the south. The biting Arctic winds, however, continually blow the autumn snow back and forth throughout the winter, creating enormous snowdrifts against the sides of rocks and ice floes.

The Arctic Ocean, the surrounding seas, and the rivers and lakes begin to freeze over in October or November and remain frozen until May in most areas. The frozen ocean surface extends the Arctic coastline by hundreds of miles, but this temporary coastline cannot always be traveled safely. Strong gales often drive vast floating fields of winter ice across the seas. When these islands of ice crash into fixed ice fields or into one another, they create tremendous and hazardous upheavals. Later in the year, during the sudden spring breakup of ice, quickly forming ice floes can carry off hunting parties or migrating families with little warning.

Even after the spring breakup, extremely cold water temperatures enable ice floes to remain in the sea. By May, the snows have thawed on land, and most of the ice in rivers and lakes has melted. But in bays protected from the wind, especially in the northernmost locations, sea ice remains well into summer and sometimes throughout the entire year. This drifting sea ice makes navigating a kayak or umiak through ocean waters treacherous. After only four or five months of thaw, the oceans freeze over again, reinitiating the seasonal cycle.

Thousands of years ago, the movement of enormous continental glaciers smoothed the surfaces of the Arctic landscape, creating the Arctic tundra, a series of rolling plains and rounded hills that have remained largely unchanged over the centuries. In the winter, the tundra becomes totally iced over; in the summer, long after the snows have melted, the land remains swampy due to poor drainage. The permafrost that characterizes the Arctic tundra makes it impossible for the land to absorb melting snow or rainfall.

Permafrost describes the thermal condition of the ground, not the presence or absence of water. Permafrost is a layer of permanently frozen soil and rock that lies just below the land's surface. Permafrost underlies half of the land area of Canada. Since roots cannot break through the layer of permafrost, the Arctic tundra permits little plant growth. Some colorful wildflowers, grasses, and shrubs do grow on the tundra,

The northwest coast of Greenland, 1911. In Ulli Steltzer's book Inuit, *Inuit activist Andy Carpenter says of the Inuit concept of land ownership: "In government terms we don't own this land because we have nothing in writing. Our people did not write. When they made agreements, they trusted each other. All that was needed was a handshake."*

but few trees and little deep-rooted vegetation can survive. The permafrost line is therefore almost identical
to the tree line, the northernmost point in the Arctic
where trees can grow. Most Canadian Inuit traditionally lived north of this tree line.

Certain geographic phenomena are recognizable
against the general uniformity of the land: frost heave
(the vertical displacement of ice and ground); patterned
ground (geometric patterns on the surface of permafrost
areas, often characterized by the size-ordered sorting of
stones); mass wasting (the downward movement of
soil); boulder fields and rock glaciers (evidence of shat-
tering due to the freeze-thaw cycle); and thermokarst (a
term applied to the melting of ground ice and the subsequent change in land forms—for example, the forming of lakes).

Although lacking in vegetation, the tundra is tremendously rich in mineral resources. The discovery of gold
and oil eventually brought the onslaught of treasure
seekers and corporations who introduced the Arctic
peoples to a money economy and to 20th-century technology.

The lack of environmental diversity throughout
most of the Arctic tundra north of the tree line yields a
corresponding lack of biological diversity. Permafrost,
hard soil, the absence of sunlight and warmth for much
of the year, and low rainfall makes the tundra relatively
infertile and so unable to sustain much animal life.
However, the populations of the few species that can
survive in this land are thriving.

During the winter, herds of caribou and musk-oxen
thunder over the frozen surface of the Arctic Ocean. The
solitary and ferocious polar bear also travels over the
frozen land and water. Polar bears cannot hibernate
unless they have enough food in their stomachs. Because the Arctic environment seldom provides them
with an easily available food supply, most must remain
active throughout the winter. Sharing the Arctic with
the caribou and polar bears are packs of wolves and
foxes and the occasional weasel or hare.

The Arctic supports huge colonies of birds. Millions of birds nest in the cliffs along the Arctic coast. A variety of waterfowl, such as ducks, geese, sea gulls, terns, and jaegers, migrate through the area during the spring and fall, feeding on the inexhaustible supply of fish. Several different kinds of shorebirds, including curlews, snipes, and loons, inhabit the Arctic during the summer. Predators, such as owls, eagles, and falcons, soar through the summer skies, feeding on field mice and other small rodents.

The Arctic boasts an abundance of marine life, both fish and sea mammals. The rivers and lakes of eastern and central Canada support a large population of Arctic char and Atlantic salmon. Across the Arctic, Alaska's bays and rivers are the site of massive annual runs of Pacific salmon, as many as 100 million fish in most years. In addition to the widespread salmon and char populations, Arctic waters also contain a variety of other fish of all sizes: minnows, needlefish, trout, flounder, and cod. Most important to the Inuit, an abundant population of sea mammals arrives on drifting fields of ice in the winter.

The Aleutian Islands

Eight hundred miles south of the Arctic, roughly at the same latitude as the British Isles, lies the region long inhabited by the Aleuts. The Aleut territory extends about 1,100 miles, from the westernmost tip of the Alaska Peninsula to Attu, the westernmost island of the United States. The Aleutian Islands are a chain of over 150 small volcanic islands generally considered to constitute four distinct groups: From east to west they are the Fox, Andreanof, Rat, and Near islands. For the last 200 years, Aleuts have also inhabited the Pribilof Islands, 200 miles north of the Aleutians.

Though the Aleutian Islands experience much more moderate temperatures than those of the Arctic mainland, they have their own uniquely harsh climate. Except near the Alaska Peninsula, the seas are totally free

St. Paul Island is one of the two Pribilof Islands, which lie north of the Aleutian chain. The Aleutians and the Pribilofs are rocky and inhospitable; Aleuts traditionally lived near the shores and subsisted mainly on sea mammals, fish, and the birds that nested in the cliffs.

of ocean ice throughout the winter, yet because of the milder Japan Current meeting the cold water of the Bering Sea, the climate of the islands is extremely humid. Fierce rainstorms crash down with little or no warning, and thick fog blankets the islands almost the entire year round. Summers are wet, cool, and cloudy; winters, wet, cold, and windy. Although far south of the permafrost line, the Aleutian Islands support no trees or long-rooted vegetation. The terrain consists primarily of mountains, cliffs, reefs, and rocky soil. A great variety of grasses and flowers grow on the mountainsides, but the mountains offer little else of sustenance to a human population. For this reason, the Aleuts have established their communities near the shore.

The Aleutian Islands support even fewer types of land animals than does the Arctic, but the islands do support a great abundance of bird and marine life. Enormous populations of birds, sea mammals, and fish arrive seasonally to feed in the Aleutian waters. Sea mammals, especially fur seals and sea lions, use the waters around the Aleutian Islands as their rookeries, or breeding grounds. The Aleuts, like their Inuit neighbors to the north, live on a marine diet for much of the year.

The harsh landscape of the Arctic and the Aleutian Islands profoundly shaped the character of the peoples who inhabited them. In other areas of the world, people might gain employment as tradespeople, educators, or artists. But for those who lived in such inhospitable regions, survival itself was the only occupation, demanding all time and attention. Learning survival skills was their education, and hunting became both their trade and their art.

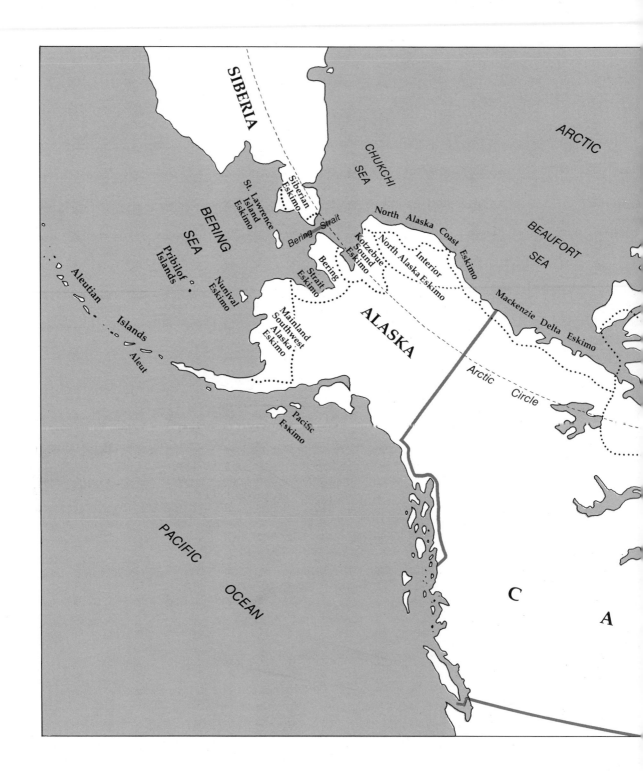

SIBERIA

ARCTIC

CHUKCHI
SEA

BEAUFORT
SEA

Siberian
Eskimo

St. Lawrence
Island
Eskimo

BERING
SEA

Bering Strait

North Alaska Coast Eskimo

North Alaska
Eskimo

Interior

Mackenzie Delta Eskimo

Pribilof
Islands

Nunival
Eskimo

Bering
Strait
Eskimo

Kotzebue
Sound
Eskimo

ALASKA

Aleutian Islands

Aleut

Mainland
Southwest
Alaska
Eskimo

Arctic Circle

Pacific
Eskimo

PACIFIC

C

A

OCEAN

This map of the Arctic delineates the native territories of various Arctic peoples—Inuit, Aleuts, and Indian groups—in relation to the North Pole and the Arctic Circle.

Homme sauuage amené des païs Septentrionaux par M. Furbisher l'an 1576

This sketch from 1576 is one of the earliest known pictures of an Inuit. The hunter, a native of Frobisher Bay in northeastern Canada, holds a kayak paddle and a bow and arrow, invaluable tools for survival.

THE TRADITIONAL HUNTING CULTURE OF THE NORTH

Each historical Arctic group adapted to its environment in a particularly appropriate way. Slight changes in climate or landscape from region to region resulted in distinct cultural traditions. Joseph Senungetuk, author of *Give or Take a Century: An Eskimo Chronicle*, stresses that the Eskimos are one race of people, but to disregard variety of custom, tradition, economy, and culture is to invite misconception, historical inaccuracy, and stereotype. The people, in their different environments, were diverse in dialect, food, clothing, shelter, and custom.

The picture of Aleut and Inuit traditional culture offered in this book is a general one. There is much more to know about the rich cultural practices of, for example, the four groups of Eskimos, or Inuit (the North Alaskan Eskimos, the Asiatic Eskimos, the Bering Sea Eskimos, and the Pacific Eskimos); the Aleuts, or Unangan, as they call themselves; and the Arctic Indians (among them the Tlingit, the Haida, the Tsimshian, and the Athapaskan) than space here allows. What this book does hope to achieve is an overview of Aleut and Inuit history and culture, both as a testimony to the fascinating and remarkable achievements of these people and

35

in the hope that it will stimulate an even greater interest on the part of the reader.

Arctic peoples recognized themselves as only one element in an interdependent environment and cultivated not only a detailed understanding of their own human abilities but also a respectful relationship with the physical and spiritual forces of their world. The control of certain aspects of life was believed to fall under the auspices of great spirits, such as the underwater goddess, Sedna. Incurring Sedna's wrath by failing to perform a ritual in honor of a sea mammal's spirit before or after killing it could result in the loss of the animal's presence in the hunting grounds. Other aspects of life were more accessible to the peoples' control. The hunter could determine his direction by carefully noting the way the wind was shaping the snow. The teaching of traditional knowledge and beliefs began with birth; even children's games reflected the more serious pursuits of adults.

Hunting

Unlike most of the world's hunting and gathering peoples, the Inuit depended almost entirely upon meat for their food supply. Sea mammals, fish, land mammals, and birds were essentially the only natural resources. Inuit understood and respected this environmental limitation. Hunters killed solely for subsistence, never for sport, and wasted no part of the game. The people or their dogs ate every edible part of an animal: meat, tendons, inner organs, and blubber.

Arctic peoples also made good use of the inedible parts of animals. Women sewed skins of land and sea mammals and birds into clothing, blankets, hunting bags, coverings for kayaks or sleds, and tents. Animal fat was a good fuel for the home and was used as lamp oil. Bones and teeth were carved into hunting and domestic tools. The Inuit shaped whalebone and caribou antlers into frames for dogsleds. Aleuts and Inuit used the flexible and lightweight inner organs,

An Inuit hunter prepares to harpoon a white whale. The meat, blubber, and oil from one whale could last 16 Inuit families an entire year.

such as the stomach, bladder, intestine casing, and esophagus, as containers or as air-filled buoys.

Arctic peoples fashioned all of their hunting tools either from captured materials, such as bone, antlers, and ivory, or from found materials. The Arctic offers few easily available metal ores, except that of copper; found materials consisted primarily of stone, shell, and, along the coast, driftwood. Knives were the single most valuable tool for all Arctic peoples. Made of walrus ivory or of stone, they were essential for skinning and carving prey. A woman's knife, or *ulu*, was made of slate and shaped like a half-moon. Winter hunters licked the blades of their knives before using them, creating a coating of ice that made the blades sharper and more efficient cutters.

The Inuit and Aleuts had no guns until Europeans introduced them in the 18th century; before this they hunted with harpoons, knives, spears, and occasionally with bows and arrows. The harpoon, used to hunt sea

*An Inuit from Coronation Gulf
in the Northwest Territories sits
before his animal-skin tent and
puts a sinew backing on a
bow. The photograph was taken
in 1911.*

mammals, is the most sophisticated of these weapons, consisting of three parts: a head made of sharpened walrus ivory or caribou antler, a six-inch ivory foreshaft, and a wood or bone main shaft, several feet long. Once the harpoon head had penetrated the animal's body, a sudden tug on the harpoon line turned the head sideways, securely anchoring it in the flesh. Hunters held on to the harpoon line themselves or tied it to an inflated sealskin bladder that acted as a drag and a buoy, marking the location of a diving whale or walrus. The harpoon's shaft was made light enough to float, and the buoys attached to the head insured its retrieval.

The hunting tools developed by the Aleuts closely resembled those of the Inuit, with two exceptions. The Aleuts fished with hooks carved from the bones of sea mammals, a technique only rarely used by the Inuit. Except on the Alaska Peninsula, the Aleuts had no access to land animals and hence no use for the bow and arrow as a hunting tool. The bow and arrow, which requires two hands to use, proved impractical for kayak hunting and was used by the Aleuts primarily as a weapon of warfare.

The kayak, employed by both Aleuts and Inuit, was built from a frame of bone or wood covered entirely with sealskin shrunk to fit the frame, creating a waterproof vessel. Although slightly longer and narrower, Aleut kayaks, called *baidarkas* by Russian traders, followed essentially the same design as those built by the Inuit. Aleuts also developed two-holed baidarkas, which allowed hunters to travel in pairs. Long, thin, and light, the kayak traveled swiftly, as much as seven miles an hour faster than the current. Because the kayak could easily be flipped over by rough ocean waves, its lightness was crucial to the survival of the pilot. A skilled paddler could right his kayak with a single motion. With only one opening, and that just as wide as the paddler's hips, the kayak's design insured that irreplaceable hunting equipment would stay aboard and remain dry whenever the kayak turned over. Although essentially a one-person boat, a kayak could transport a hunter's family, although passengers had to remain cramped in the dark, hollow core. As the main source of mobility for much of the year and the one piece of equipment essential to gathering the yearly

An Inuit man and woman share the small space of a kayak. As it is constructed without heavy planks or nails, the kayak's flexible frame yields to pressure and squeezes through narrow openings. This photo was taken off Nunivak Island, Alaska.

Alaskan Inuit in an umiak *at King Island in the Bering Strait region. A 30-foot-long umiak is light enough for two men to carry. At night it can be emptied and turned on its side to make a waterproof shelter.*

food supply, the kayak was a hunter's most valuable possession.

The Inuit developed a very light dogsled for hunting and for land travel. (The Aleuts, with little ground to cover and most of it rocky, had no need for either dogsleds or dogs.) Inuit constructed the dogsleds by stretching animal skins across a frame of bone, antlers, or wood. The harness and traces for the dogs were fashioned from seal-sinew rope or thongs made of animal skin. For the sled's runners, Inuit used almost any available material: wood, bone, ivory, frozen rolled-up musk-ox skins, and even frozen fish. Just as they did with their hunting knives, the Inuit glazed the sled's runners with ice, frozen seal blubber, or saliva, creating a glassy surface that allowed a swifter and smoother ride over the dry Arctic snow.

When traveling long distances, hunters ran alongside the sleds to keep themselves warm. Conditions were usually less than ideal—bad weather, a heavy load, too few dogs—and navigation was almost always tricky and dangerous. Inuit hunters needed to keep their dogsleds in perfect working order. To a stranded hunter equipped with nothing more than a spear or a knife, a broken sled could mean death.

Hunters' dogs also needed to be kept in good condition. It took no fewer than 8 dogs for long-distance traveling; 10 or 12 in a good team could pull an 800-pound load. Most Inuit tried to maintain about 16 dogs, in the event that 1 or 2 took ill, went lame, or died. Although adult huskies could easily withstand night temperatures, puppies were more vulnerable to the cold and were kept inside with the family. Hunters filed down the puppies' teeth, making it more difficult for them as adult dogs to chew through their sealskin harness. Because they believed the animals ran best on an empty stomach, Inuit fed their dogs every second day while traveling. Even so, it took half a ton of meat per year, or approximately seven seals or half a walrus, to feed a single dog. The dogs' feeding requirements made the success of the hunt even more critical to an Inuit family's continued survival.

For both Inuit and Aleuts, the hunting of sea mammals during the winter months provided the bulk of their yearly food supply. The Aleuts lived along the coast and so subsisted almost exclusively on marine life;

When there were not enough dogs available, Inuit men and women helped pull the sled that carried their belongings to their spring and summer camp. Dog teams were hitched to sleds in a variety of formations. In Greenland and Canada, dogs were hitched in a fan shape. In Alaska, as many as 20 dogs were hitched alternately on each side of one long trace.

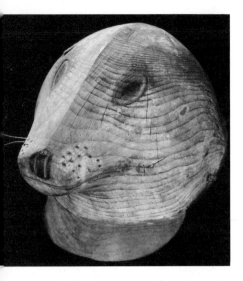

Inuit hunters sometimes donned wooden decoy helmets, such as this seal's head, in order to attract game. The hunter attached a helmet with a rawhide chin strap and lay along the shore until seals came close enough to be killed. Inuit craftsmanship created handiworks that were both beautiful and practical.

the Inuit supplemented marine hunting with fishing and the seasonal hunting of land game. Of all the Inuit, only the inland Caribou tribe in central Canada never hunted sea mammals.

Occasionally, Arctic hunters caught seals with nets set under the frozen surface of the ocean. More often, seal hunters harpooned their prey while they were still under the ocean ice. Although seals possess the ability to remain underwater for a relatively long period of time, as mammals they must breathe air at least once every 20 minutes. To do this, they maintain blowholes, or cone-shaped funnels in the ice, that allow them to breathe without having to find a break in the ice's surface. Hunters first located the seals' blowholes by searching for the small mounds of frost which form around the tiny openings when a seal's breath freezes. After probing the hole with a harpoon to discover the angle of funnel entry, the hunter then set a small piece of ivory in the hole as a warning indicator and waited with harpoon poised. When the indicator finally moved, the hunter surprised the seal coming up for air by harpooning it through the blowhole. The hunter held on to the harpoon line or tied it to his dogsled while chopping away at the ice. Most blowholes span only an inch or two in diameter; the hunter needed to carve an opening in the ice around it big enough to drag the seal's body through.

In late winter, when the ice began to thaw from the sea, the icy stretches near the water's edge offered the best opportunity for hunting walrus. The enormous walrus were combative and territorial in the water, but hunters knew that they were helpless on land, especially when asleep. After taking a sleeping group by surprise and harpooning one or two, the hunting party held on to the harpoon lines while the wounded animals dove into the water and struggled to escape. Once the animals died, the hunters towed them back to the shore or the field of ice edged up against the water. There they carved the walrus, which could weigh as much as two

Inuit hunters in search of walrus. The hunters are hoping to harpoon a walrus through the thin ice that the animal breaks through to breathe. This method entailed considerable danger, as a wounded walrus not infrequently broke through the ice directly under the hunter.

tons each, and ate some of the meat raw before returning to their families with the catch.

White and gray whales were more challenging prey; they surfaced suddenly, filled their lungs quickly, and dove once again. Nevertheless, the colossal size of whales made them well worth pursuing. A single successful hunt would make a dozen unsuccessful ones worthwhile. The meat, bones, and blubber from a single whale weighing as much as 60 tons could last 16 hunters and their families a full year.

The method of whale hunting employed by the Aleuts and the coastal Inuit in Alaska remained unchanged for 4,000 years. Native Alaskans hunted whales solely in umiaks, open-deck skin boats that held a crew of eight kneeling hunters. When the crew spotted a whale, they hurled poison-tipped spears at it. Once they had secured the whale, the Aleuts relied more on luck than on skill to bring their catch home. Hunters abandoned the dead or dying mammal, trusting it would drift ashore somewhere accessible for retrieval. This method was not particularly efficient; less than half of the whales left to drift ashore were ever recaptured.

The Inuit in eastern Canada and Greenland developed a much more efficient method of whale hunting. After first sighting a whale from shore, the hunters pursued it across open water in a fleet composed of a single umiak and several kayaks. Inuit hunters used harpoons instead of spears, which allowed them to hang on to their prey instead of waiting for it to drift ashore. This technique required more hunters than did that of the Alaskan Inuit and the Aleuts; subsequently, each hunter received a smaller share of meat, bones, and other whale products from the kill. Even so, each share was large enough to feed a hunter's family for an entire winter.

Seals, walrus, and whales were hunted by all coastal peoples of the Far North. The Aleuts also hunted sea otters. Like all sea mammals, otters need to surface regularly in order to breathe; by doing so, they expose themselves to the watchful eyes of hunters. To catch sea otters, a fleet of Aleut kayakers fanned out in a wide arc until they sighted their prey. They then formed a closed circle around the otters and threw their harpoons.

Fish provided the second greatest source of food for both Inuit and Aleuts. For the Inuit in Alaska and Canada, summer fishing centered on rivers, the sites of huge salmon runs. With the exception of the Aleuts, most Arctic peoples did not use fishhooks. Instead, they caught fish by spearing, netting, or trapping. Spears of bone and hand-held dipping nets woven from whale or seal sinew were used in shallow river waters; traps built from driftwood or bone were set in deeper waters.

In the winter, Inuit fished through the ocean ice. Fishers first tested the solidity and thickness of ice fields with long fish spears before stepping on them. After locating a good field, fishers cut a hole through the ice and built a shelter of snow blocks to protect their bodies from the icy Arctic winds. Fishers attracted their prey by jiggling a small fish-shaped lure carved from two pieces of ivory. A fish spotted through the hole was pierced with a three-pronged spear with sharp ivory tips. This method of ice fishing was very effective and especially important in areas with small populations of

sea mammals. The catch from these expeditions kept many Inuit families fed throughout the long winter.

The hunting of land animals in both winter and summer was a challenging task. The flat, barren, tree-less land made it easy for prey to spot hunters. For example, any sudden movement by the hunter when hunting caribou could scare away the entire herd. To avoid being seen by their quarry, lone hunters con-structed large snow shields in winter or hid behind rocks in summer, patiently waiting for animals to come within spear-throwing range.

Because most land animals left the Arctic for the winter, summer hunts of caribou and musk oxen had to yield extra meat for storing through the long, cold months ahead. To maximize the efficiency of the hunt, hunters often teamed up to capture large herds of caribou. One group of hunters circled around the herd and drove the animals into a lake where another group of hunters waited in kayaks. While the disoriented

An Inuit woman ice fishes on Hudson Bay in May 1905. The delicate balance between the Inuit and their environment was irrevocably altered with the arrival of Europeans and other whites.

An Inuit boy holds a bird-hunting spear and some slain Canadian geese in this 1924 photograph. As was true of all game they killed, the Inuit used virtually every part of the geese. Flesh was eaten; feathers were used to decorate clothing, artwork, and hunting decoys and in sacred rituals.

caribou thrashed about in the water, the hunters speared as many as they could. The young boys of the community dragged the bodies of the animals to land.

Summer was also the time for hunting birds and for gathering their eggs. Aleuts and Inuit alike caught birds using nets mounted on long poles. Because the Aleuts had no access to polar bears and caribou, birds and their eggs were particularly important staples in their diet. They developed a wide variety of multipronged bird darts and the *bola*, an instrument composed of weights whose lines are attached to a central knot. The bola was worn around the hunter's neck; when he spotted a bird, he threw the bola at it. The lines tangled around the bird, and the weights brought it down.

Inuit hunted polar bears in the winter and in the early spring. The Inuit believed that of all animals, only the polar bear equaled the hunter in courage and cunning. Meeting the challenge of killing a polar bear, an animal that could be as tall as 9 feet and as heavy as 1,000 pounds, reaffirmed a hunter's daring and ability. Dogs played a crucial role in the hunt, chasing the bear down, surrounding it, and barking to guide the hunter to the prey. Hunters killed the cornered bear with a spear thrown at close range; the size and fury of the animal made the battle extremely dangerous.

The only other land animal hunted by almost all northern peoples was the fox. Throughout the winter, women tended fox traps, small cages of flat stones hidden under moss and snow. A fox that pursued the bait planted inside would trip a seal-sinew wire, causing a final stone to drop into place and seal the cage. Inuit trapped foxes primarily for their skins and so hunted them only during the winter when fox furs were thick and useful for clothing. In difficult times, when the food supply dwindled or disappeared, Inuit were forced to eat the tough meat of the white fox.

The Patience to Survive

Inuit and Aleut survival was largely dependent on elements outside of their control—a rough terrain, extreme

An Inuit constructs a bow drill, which consists of a wooden shaft with a metal or nephrite drill bit, a wooden mouthpiece with a tooth grip and a shallow stone socket, and a bow made of wood, bone, or ivory with pliable rawhide stretched between the bow's ends. When the bow is moved from side to side, the shaft rotates and drives the bit into the object being drilled.

weather conditions, the seasonal movement of animals, sickness, and accident. In a land where day and night are not clearly marked by the daily rising and setting of the sun, time is considered fluid. The Inuit slept only when tired and ate only when hungry. They resigned themselves to current environmental circumstances, made few far-reaching plans, and observed no rigid schedules. Patience was a supreme virtue. Arctic peoples were capable of waiting out a fierce storm for days or for weeks, crowded but secure inside their semisubterranean dwellings; hunting and fishing invariably required silence and trust. In an uncertain universe, Arctic peoples constructed a world of relative stability in which they were masters of adjustment and accommodation.

An Inuit at Ice Cape, Alaska, in the early 1900s decapitates a walrus in order to release its spirit. By the middle of the 20th century, the majority of Inuit were nominally Christian, but they continued to interpret the universe in their traditional way.

SPIRIT AND FAMILY

Aleut and Inuit peoples did not worship gods. Rather, they acknowledged the spirits of all animate and inanimate things in their world. These spirits, many of whom were once human or potentially human, were together believed to hold the primary power of the universe. Through magic, charms, and taboos, human beings could influence both the physical and the spiritual world and so exercise some control over the universe.

As the source of all life, the land was a holy place for Arctic peoples, who saw humans and animals not as master and mastered but as humble equals who shared an icy world. Animals participated in a person's life through mutual goodwill. Arctic religious rituals established or furthered a relationship of mutual respect between hunters and hunted.

Arctic peoples believed that the success of the hunt had as much to do with proper attitude as it had to do with skill. Spirits of animals were easily offended and difficult to appease; if hunters did not treat prey with great respect, their spirits would seek revenge. An animal whose spirit was offended by a hunter's equipment, clothes, or the behavior of his family would not return to the area where it was killed and would keep all others of its species away. If a hunter properly observed all rituals and paid the animal its due respect, its spirit would be pleased and would allow itself to be killed again and again, ensuring a continued food supply for the group.

Arctic peoples practiced a variety of rituals designed to guarantee a successful hunt. For most Inuit, private rites or devotions were important, but in many Aleut and Inuit communities, public ceremonies were held to honor the spirits of prey. As a sign of hospitality, many killed animals, especially polar bears and whales, were offered a drink of fresh water by the wife of the hunting crew leader. After beheading an animal to release its spirit, hunters asked the spirit to return to the wild. Almost all northern hunters threw some part of a marine animal back into the sea, both to appease the animal's spirit and to provide a "seed" for rebirth.

The person most skilled at communicating with the supernatural became the community's *angakok*, or *shaman*, an intermediary between the human and the spirit worlds. The shaman attempted to maintain or restore order and mutual trust between humans and spirits. The rites often commenced with the beating of drums, singing, and dancing; the rhythmic sounds and movements captured the attention of the spirit of an animal, an inanimate object, or a force of nature. Carried away on the sound of the drum, the shaman rode the spirit of the animal whose skin was stretched over the drum frame. To prevent being forever carried away, the shaman was bound while in the trance. Upon return, the shaman interpreted the trance vision. Often he identified someone within the community as guilty of violating a taboo and offered advice on how to make atonement to the angry spirit. While in a trance, the shaman might meet directly with a powerful spirit to beg benefits for the group or to request the power to foretell the future, insure good weather, rescue hunters from dangers at sea, heal wounds, and cure illnesses.

Although a shaman had many charms with which to meet and influence the Arctic world, each Inuit had his or her own personal amulets. At birth, children received one or two magical objects, such as a raven's bill, a caribou's ear, or a polar bear's tooth. For as long as they carried these amulets, children were protected by the spirits of the animals from which the amulets came. Inuit children also learned individual spells and songs designed to direct or deflect malicious powers. These incantations, passed down as "property" from generation to generation, belonged solely to the individual. Although they could be sold, traded, or given away, a stolen spell always brought bad fortune to the thief.

The only other aspect of the supernatural unique to each individual was the spirit of his or her name. The Inuit believed that at least two spirits resided in every body: the unique personal soul and the name soul of an ancestor or other esteemed person. When a person's body died, his or her soul split into two parts. Although the Inuit had no definite beliefs regarding an afterlife, they did hope that the personal soul would go to a land where warmth and game were always plentiful. The name, the other part of the original soul, remained in torment on earth until called to enter the body of a newborn child. A sick child was renamed in the hope that a more fitting name would cure the child's spirit.

The union of the old name soul and the soul of the infant gave the body healthy life.

As long as an Inuit had not alienated his family, reincarnation was assured. The old and infirm, secure in the belief that they would return in a younger, healthier body and well aware of the strain they put on a mobile group's ability to survive, were known to commit suicide. Migrating families often left the dead or dying behind on the frozen tundra, a practice that was above all practical. In a world where survival was never guaranteed, even infanticide sometimes seemed a necessity. If a family faced a particularly uncertain future, its baby was killed, both to lessen the family's burden and to relieve the child from the pain of starvation. The family felt that the child's soul would understand its decision and would return at a more prosperous time.

The Aleuts preserved the bodies of their dead, mummifying the corpses of important adults and of all children. The Aleuts employed an efficient technique of embalming, which involved first removing all of the organs and fluids from a body through the pelvis or a hole in the chest and then laying the body in a cold running stream. The body was then dried and stuffed with dry grass or sphagnum moss, oiled, either dressed in a bird-skin parka or wrapped in fur skins, and finally wrapped in layers of matting or hides. The resulting mummy bundle was placed in a dry cave; often it was suspended in a kind of cradle or positioned sitting up in a crevice among the rocks. Depending on their specific relationship to the dead, Aleut family members observed a 40- to 60-day mourning period, which consisted of fasting, keeping physically and sexually clean, and lamenting.

The Aleuts believed in spirits that they classified as *Khoughkh*, the demonic spirits, and *Aglikhaiakh*, the helpful spirits. They also employed charms, amulets, and the shamanistic techniques of drumming, singing, and dancing to protect themselves, attract game, and mediate between the visible and invisible worlds. Aleuts believed that every village had a sacred place located nearby. By bringing offerings of animal skins and prayers to this sacred spot, hunters could win help for war or the hunt from spirits. The rituals of the Aleuts, like those of the Inuit, centered on obtaining the help needed to survive in a harsh environment.

Family and Community Life

The community life of Arctic peoples centered on survival. Both the Inuit and the Aleuts created societies based on the observance of immediate family ties, the establishment of a larger circle of kin, and the formation of villages primarily inhabited by relatives.

An Inuit family in the early 1900s. Children were often given the names of their deceased relatives and were seen as partial reincarnations of their ancestors. A female child could be given the name of a male ancestor; a male child could be named after a female ancestor.

Strong family bonds guaranteed individuals the utmost security in the face of misfortune. Strengthening these bonds by widening the circle of kinship through marriage, adoption, or naming a child after an unrelated person (thus creating a "familial" relationship through the soul of the namesake) provided families with even greater protection against hardship.

In Arctic societies, marriage was principally a practical arrangement in which a man and a woman joined forces against a hostile environment. Men and women had complementary roles and were indispensable to each other. Men provided their families with meat and the by-products necessary for the crafting of clothing and household goods. Women scraped and sewed skins, cooked, maintained blubber lamps, and cared for the home. Since teamwork was essential to the survival of the couple, trial marriages were encouraged among the young. No stigma was attached to divorce; when for any reason the needs of a husband and a wife became incompatible, they sought another couple with whom they could trade spouses. Polygamy, which also contributed to mutual survival, was permitted by both Aleut and Inuit cultures.

Female Inuit with a long coil of walrus gut. Women accompanied men on hunting expeditions because their domestic skills were essential to their family's survival.

In this photograph from 1928, an Inuit woman splits a female walrus hide, a trying and intricate task. The hides were sewn together to make umiak covers. An umiak was crafted during the winter in the protection of a whaling shelter.

Marriage between relatives was forbidden, primarily because it did not extend kinship ties. (The Inuit also feared that any offspring might be inhuman.) Similarly, two people who possessed the same magic amulet could not marry. The spirit of that object already protected both individuals; their marriage would not therefore augment their chances of survival.

The Inuit and Aleuts trained boys and girls in sex-specific roles from a very early age. In both societies, infants and girls were reared by the women; boys were trained by the men. Girls learned to sew, cook, and tend the lamps in the home. At the onset of menses, they learned to live away from their family once a month in order to keep their "sacred women's magic" from harming anyone. Boys played with toy harpoons, spears, and bows and arrows. To help develop stamina and strength, they were set outside naked to be toughened by the cold north wind. By age 14, Arctic children had taken great strides toward adulthood. Inuit and Aleut boys were expected to have killed their first seal, although they would not marry until several years later, when they could actually support a family with their hunting. Girls, however, were often married by the age of 14; their first pregnancy meant the end of childhood play.

In both the temporary summer settlements and the permanent winter villages, cooperation, not competition, was the basis for survival. Contributing to the survival of the group was a cultural and social virtue. Hunting parties divided the kill among themselves; for example, a polar bear skin was customarily shared by three hunters because it made three pairs of pants. More important to the survival of the village as a whole was the practice of *payudarpok*, the sharing of the kill with neighbors in the community. Inuit apportioned food and skins according to the available supply and the needs of village members. Families kept only what they could use and offered their neighbors anything extra as payudarpok.

With communal sharing a way of life, the Inuit had no notion of private property. They regarded hunting grounds as belonging to everyone and to no one. Except for their personal magic spells, amulets, and names, the only property owned by individuals was their boats. Owning one boat was a necessity and a sign of prestige; owning more than one boat was reason for ridicule.

Ridicule and public disapproval were essentially the only social controls in Inuit society. In a tightly knit community that shared virtually everything, to be laughed at or regarded as worthless or cowardly by the community was devastating. For the most terrible crimes, such as murder, the guilty could be banished from the community, a punishment in some ways worse than death.

The Inuit valued self-sufficiency, but they regarded self-assertion as antithetical to the collective goals of the community. Inuit distrusted formal leadership; they had no formal tribal structure and no chiefs, although certain individuals gained a degree of influence and esteem for their innate or acquired hunting abilities. Neither did the Inuit have subordinate classes or slaves.

(continued on page 65)

BETWEEN TWO WORLDS

Overleaf: An Inuit family enjoys American-style ice cream, a dish quite different than the Inuit variety, in a restaurant in Anchorage, Alaska. Few areas of Arctic life have been untouched by the modern world.

In recent years, Inuit rights movements have urged schools attended by Inuit children, many of which are federally funded, to provide instruction in Arctic culture as well as in European and American culture in order to instill in students a sense of pride in their native heritage. Inuit schoolchildren recreate, read, and study in much the same fashion as do their contemporaries around the world.

Traditional Inuit technology, social structure, and belief systems were perfectly designed to meet the environmental and psychological conditions of Arctic life. With the coming of Europeans and Americans, the Inuit economy and worldview began to crumble. While people still hunt walrus (below), fashion umiak keels from walrus bone (right), and go whaling (below right), hunting and fishing alone do not usually provide enough food or money for survival in modern Arctic society.

61

In the Arctic today, the native and the modern exist side by side, although not always harmoniously. At ease with modern technology, an Inuit girl (above) works as a disc jockey in Baker Lake, Canada. Skilled in traditional craftsmanship, a weaver (left) creates a basket typical of the Nunivak people. An elderly Inuit man undergoing an eye exam (top left) already benefits from up-to-date medical technology in the form of a hearing aid.

Although many Inuit inhabit government-supplied prefabricated houses, others, such as this couple in Point Hope, Alaska, prefer to live in traditional heat-efficient, semisubterranean sod homes. Still, evidence of the contemporary world abounds in their wooden furniture, Christian icons, and nonnative clothing.

(continued from page 56)

The community reached decisions through long, informal discussions that moved toward a group consensus.

To maintain harmony within the community, individuals avoided direct confrontation or violence. In difficult dealings with another person, an Inuit adopted a posture of rigid neutrality, indirection, and a smiling demeanor. For the most part, this technique of evasion helped to maintain peace. When feuds or disputes did erupt, they were most often settled through public contests of words or blows. With the group gathered, the two combatants engaged in a "song duel" (the Aleuts preferred spoken duels), exchanging insulting songs designed to sway public opinion and embarrass the opponent. The adversary who created the cleverest song won. Alternatively, the combatants might take turns striking one another until one emerged as the winner. In either case, the loser was expected to accept defeat gracefully, so that with the public determination of a winner, harmony was restored.

The Aleut population was scattered in small, relatively permanent settlements and maintained a formal group hierarchy. Each *deme*, a village composed mostly of kin, had its own chief, and a higher chief, elected from among these deme chiefs, ruled over a group of villages or an entire island. In return for a share of all catches, the village leader protected the village's hunting grounds, kept the peace by arbitrating disputes among village members, punished rare criminal behavior, organized communal activities, and commanded in the warfare that could erupt between villages as a result of insults, raids, or murders. The chief of a deme was generally the wealthiest person in the village. Aleut wealth was measured not only in furs and food but also in shells and slaves. Wealth helped determine social status, separating the population into three classes: wealthy people, common people, and slaves. Living in permanent year-round villages allowed the Aleuts to accumulate material objects, and they recognized and rewarded ownership of personal property. Men owned all of their hunting and fishing gear, their kayak, and their tools; these objects were inherited by the eldest son. Women owned the house and its contents; these were passed down to the eldest daughter.

Although they had formal leadership and a sense of personal property, Aleuts did share food and possessions according to three principles: duty, primarily to relatives; repayment of a loan of supplies or equipment; and generosity toward the less fortunate. Through this system of mutual obligations, the Aleuts protected the welfare of every village member.

Architecture

Except in the northernmost parts of central Canada, the domed snowhouse known as an igloo, or *inni*, was never used as more than a temporary shelter. Because it was quick and easy to build, requiring nothing more than snow, a knife, and subfreezing temperatures, an igloo was a handy refuge during emergencies or a convenient "disposable" home for a hunter or migrating family. When the hunters or family moved on, they left their makeshift house behind for later travelers to use.

Men and women built igloos in tandem, completing one within a few hours. Together they cut blocks of hard snow and stacked them in gradually narrowing circles

An Inuit family relaxes in its igloo at Cape Fullerton at Hudson Bay in the early 1900s. The family sits along the sleeping platform, and a blubber lamp, the only source of heat and light, burns against the back wall.

66

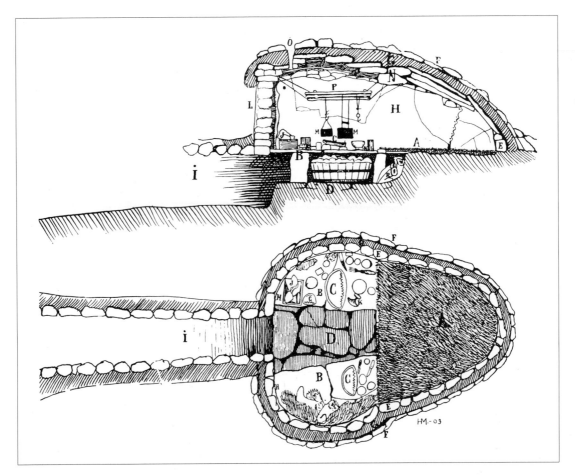

until they formed a dome. They then sealed every chink of the inni with tightly packed snow to guard against the piercing polar winds. Builders glazed the interior walls to make them more stable; they lit a fire inside, and when the walls started to melt, they extinguished the fire, quickly cooling the walls so that they froze and hardened. If the hunters or family planned to stay for more than one night in an inni, they lined the walls with animal skins for added warmth. The builders occasionally added a window made of transparent seaside ice; by constructing a small snow shield just north of the window, they reflected any available sunlight into the igloo.

In winter, Inuit lived in permanent, semisubterranean dwellings, covered with stones, clumps of sod,

An aerial and side view of an Inuit semisubterranean dwelling, showing the long entrance tunnel and the underground door.

An Inuit summer village of canvas and skin tents. On the tent in the foreground hang two inflated sealskins used as buoys or containers. Tent living allowed the Inuit mobility for the summer hunts of land animals.

and bundles of grass. These structures were additionally sealed or insulated with snow and ice, which made them extraordinarily cozy. In the summer, the Inuit abandoned their permanent houses. Tents made from the skins of caribou or other animals allowed them greater mobility for summer hunting and fishing.

Both the igloos and the sod houses of the Inuit, including the *khazghi*, or communal house, were brilliantly engineered structures, built according to the same essential design for over 5,000 years. One entered a sod house or an igloo by crawling through a long, low tunnel that emerged just under the floor of the house. This entrance tunnel, built below ground, simultaneously ventilated and insulated the dwelling. Because hot air rises, it could not escape through the entrance; instead, it remained inside the domed living space, which consisted of one large, open room, about 9 feet high and 15 feet across. Usually the only piece of furniture was a communal sleeping platform built along one of the walls. A single window of semitransparent seal intestine allowed any available light to enter the house, while a small vent near its top allowed air to circulate.

Aleut houses, like those of the Inuit, were built partially underground. An enormous structure sunk three to four feet into the ground, the Aleut house was built on a rectangular frame of driftwood logs or whalebones. Rafters of crisscrossing logs and pieces of wood supported a roof of dry grass and sod. The roof held two openings: one that allowed light to enter the house and another that served as the entrance. Like the sod houses of the Inuit, the houses of the Aleuts consisted of a single room, but on some of the islands, these Aleut structures housed from 10 to 40 families, up to 150 individuals. Dozens of stall-like living spaces lined all four walls of the common space.

Food

With little fruit and no vegetables or grains available, meat and fish constituted virtually all of the Inuit diet. Although such a diet was strictly limited, variety was created where possible. *Muktuk*, the inner layer of whale skin, was eaten raw. *Ush shak* was made by fermenting the flippers of seals or walrus. *Mattak*, a delicacy made of flakes of narwhal skin, was fermented for several years, so that the outer skin became hard and crusty while the blubber turned green.

Inuit carved lamps from soft, easily sculpted soapstone. With oil and blubber from sea mammals as fuel and with moss for wicking, they used these stone lamps for cooking meat. Chunks of seal meat cooked over the lamp for half of the day, suspended in a type of

The interior of an Aleut house on Unalaska Island. The drawing was made by John Webber in 1778. The sleeping area lies around the periphery of the house. The roof is made of driftwood timbers overlaid with dry grass and sod.

69

An early-20th-century Inuit woman chews on a piece of sealskin to break its fiber. The skins had to be softened in this way before being sewn into boots. Alaskan Inuit used the soft, thick, and oily skin of the beluga whale for the soles of their sealskin boots.

soapstone roasting pan hung from a rack by strips of baleen (whale-mouth cartilage). Seal oil was added to almost every dish. Inuit ate fish boiled as well as raw, dried, or frozen; seal and walrus meat was also eaten raw, frozen, or partially cooked.

Inuit cured or stored any surplus food. Arctic ice was a handy refrigerator for keeping fresh-killed game frozen through the winter. A catch could be stored by covering it with stones and pouring water over it. The new ice blanket not only preserved meat but also locked the stones in place against raids of wandering animals. Unlike the Inuit, Aleuts stored very little food. Damp weather on the islands made it difficult to dry food, and with animal resources available year-round, the need to preserve food was less urgent for the Aleuts. The only food stored was that reserved for special celebrations and festivals.

The Aleuts and the Inuit who lived south of the Arctic Circle had a little more variety in their diet than did the Arctic Inuit. Aleuts combined fish or the meat of sea mammals with a wide assortment of edible plants that grew along the shores: cow parsnip, wild parsnip, kelp, and a variety of other greens. Aleuts and the Inuit who lived on the Alaska Peninsula gathered many types of berries: blueberries, cranberries, blackberries, and sal-monberries.

Clothing

Sealskins, caribou skins, fox furs, and bearskins provided the material for most clothing. Since tight clothing caused perspiration that ultimately froze garments stiff, Inuit wore several layers of loosely fitting clothing that allowed air warmed by the body to circulate. Overclothes, such as hooded parkas that reached down to the knees or hips and loose trousers, were usually made of animal fur. Lighter clothes of bird skins and feathers, worn next to the body, allowed air to move under the heavy fur parkas. Inner garments of fur were worn fur-to-body, outer garments, fur-to-air; this created an air pocket for warmth. The Aleuts also wore parkas, made either of fur or bird skins. Unlike the parkas of the Inuit, these had a standing collar rather than a hood. Aleut parkas reached to the ankles, were straight around the bottom, and were seldom worn with any clothing underneath. The women's parkas lacked a pouch for a baby; babies were carried in a cradle.

Aleuts often wore nothing on their feet. Most Inuit wore *kamiks* (also called *mukluks*), sealskin boots that rose to the knees or thighs. Kamiks were worn over animal-skin stockings; a layer of dried grass was worn between the two skin garments to provide extra warmth. Every morning, women chewed on the family's kamiks, which had stiffened overnight, to make them softer and more comfortable. Because the extremities developed frostbite first, women changed the layer of grass inside the kamiks daily, ensuring maximum warmth.

Meticulous care was necessary with all items of clothing, particularly fur clothing. Women cut hides, sewed them together using a thread made of seal or walrus sinew, and cared for the clothes after making them. Clothes allowed to become damp, for example, became

Two Aleut hunters in September 1928, each dressed in a gutskin kamleika ornamented with appliqué designs and hair embroidery and a traditional decorated visor. Aleut men honored the spirits of sea mammals by wearing elaborate hunting costumes.

71

heavy and quickly froze the next time worn. After each wearing, women beat the clothes with a bone or wood stick to ensure that all snow crystals fell off the clothing in the home's entrance tunnel. Then the family removed all of their clothes and hung them up over a seal-oil lamp to dry. Nakedness, required to air out the body and to dry out the clothes, was common practice in the cozy warmth of an Inuit home.

The carefully constructed Arctic clothing was eminently practical; the Inuit employed little ornamental decoration. The Aleuts, with their milder climate, allowed themselves some flourishes. This was most apparent in the wooden hats and visors worn by baidarka hunters. On these visors, thin pieces of wood shaped like inverted garden trowels, Aleuts painted abstract shapes and animal designs in bright colors. Elaborate ornaments such as carved ivory figurines, sea lion whiskers, feathers, beads, and shells added to the impressiveness of these sun shields. Eventually, decorated headgear became a status symbol, with full hats worn only by the wealthiest hunters.

Art and Crafts

Other than the ornamental hats of the Aleuts, Arctic peoples had few purely decorative arts. Neither the Aleuts nor the Inuit had much leisure time, and both peoples were equally limited by available materials. The Aleuts had almost no ivory, and the little wood available went into the construction of homes. They did use the abundance of available dune grass to create tightly woven, intricately designed baskets. They also wove sleeping mats, baidarka seats, burial shrouds, and cradles. By interweaving feathers and other materials with the grass, artisans formed decorative patterns such as crosshatches, zigzags, circles, and human or animal figures.

The Inuit, who had even less time for artwork than did the Aleuts, did create ivory, stone, or bone carvings of birds, sea and land mammals, and imaginative

An Aleut woman weaves a basket in 1904 using a two-strand twining technique. Aleut baskets made of dune grass are both beautiful and durable.

figures of spirits. Though regarded as works of art in the 20th century, Inuit carvings, like Aleut woven goods, had essentially practical purposes. Craftspeople carved figures of animals in the hope that these figures would somehow make the animal manifest. Figures of the spirits of the weather, the sea, or the ice were carved in the hope of appeasing the spirits and avoiding evil.

Communal Celebrations, Music, and Dance

Inuit and Aleuts celebrated important seasonal events. Celebrations often extolled the hunt; songs were sung to express thanks for a large catch and to praise the seasonal return of sea mammals. Inuit song makers sent their original songs by messenger to colleagues in far-off villages; the entire village then gathered to learn the new song. Ceremonial dances were performed; men might execute vigorous and comical solo dances, while women might dance with finger masks.

In midwinter, many groups held a trading feast to which people from a local village were invited. Guests informed the host village of their feasting requirements, and the host village was bound to provide them. Hosts could expect to have the favor returned—or the feast traded. Groups also held feasts for the dead, who were believed to reside either in the sky-land or somewhere in the underworld. The dead were called by a special song to a clubhouse, where they were entertained. Any person with the same name as one of the celebrated dead was honored. At a final feast several years after a person's death, the namesake was given a fresh suit of clothes and a blessing; the dead person's spirit was laid to rest.

Both the Inuit and Aleuts used a drum as an accompaniment to their songs and shamanistic dance rituals. The Inuit *ayayut*, a flat, one-sided drum, consisted of the intestine of a walrus or other sea mammal stretched over a wood or bone frame. The Inuit beat the frame, rather than the skin, with a wand of bone or ivory. Each drum was designed for a specific individual, taking into account the musician's hand size and decorated with the drummer's personal amulet.

In winter and spring, when the Inuit had settled in permanent communities, they delighted in communal games and competitions. Some of the games, such as

A sculpture in stealite of a beluga. Inuit traditionally carved small figures of animals for use as amulets. An animal amulet might insure its wearer good hunting or grant him the animal's particular strengths.

sky tossing, were largely for fun. Members of the community grabbed hold of the edge of an animal skin.
When everyone pulled at once, the center snapped up,
propelling the person who sat or stood in the center of
the skin into the air, just as if he or she were on a
trampoline. The leader of the most successful whaling
crew was often rewarded with the place on the skin;
it was then a matter of pride to remain standing
throughout the vigorous tossing. Most games were
designed to sharpen the domestic abilities of the women
or the skill and agility of the men. Even in recreation,
the rigors of Arctic life could not be forgotten.

An Inuit sled on display at the St. Louis Exposition in 1904.

CONTACT WITH OUTSIDERS

The Inuit first made contact with outsiders in the 10th century A.D. From 982 to 985, Erik the Red, a Norwegian, explored Greenland; in 986, he returned to establish a colony. By the year 1000, Erik's son Leif had probably sailed farther westward, landing in Labrador and Newfoundland. From the beginning, the relationship between the resident Inuit and the immigrant Norsemen was problematic. In 1003, Norse colonist Thorfinn Karlsefni described the "evil-looking men" he encountered in Labrador. The first extended testimony of Norse contact with the Eskimos is found in the *Historia Norvegiae*, written at the end of the 12th century. Here, too, the mention is hostile, and the Eskimos are presented as some sort of magical creature.

> On the other side of Greenland, toward the North, hunters have found some little people whom they call Skraellings; their situation is that when they are hurt by weapons their sores become white without bleeding, but when they are mortally wounded their blood will hardly stop running. They have no iron at all; they use missiles made of walrus tusks and sharp stones for knives.

Most evidence of contact between the Norse and the Inuit is unreliable; for each group it takes the form of written and oral legend, with each tradition claiming ascendancy. Inuit legends, unwritten until the 19th century, all boast of Inuit extermination of the Norse, but to date no definitive explanation for the disappearance of these first European colonists of the New World has been settled on by historians. Whatever occurred, there is no record of the Norse population after the late 15th century.

Encountering Early Explorers

The Inuit did not have any further significant contact with European visitors for more than a century. They may have had minor dealings with John Cabot, an Englishman who in 1497 and 1498 made voyages in search of a Northwest Passage to the Orient. In 1576, 1577, and 1578, Englishman Martin Frobisher led expeditions to Baffin Island, where his crew encountered "men in small boates made of leather" who proved fascinating to the adventurous Europeans.

During Frobisher's first visit, the Native Americans traded with the English until the expedition crew kidnapped a native and his kayak. On their second expedition, Frobisher's crew again captured natives, this time a man, woman, and child. The British brought these Arctic people, as they had the man captured on the first voyage, back to England as "specimens" of Arctic life. All four prisoners died of pneumonia, a disease they had never been exposed to.

The English search for the Northwest Passage continued. In 1610, Henry Hudson, employed by English merchants, captained a ship up the strait and into the bay that would both someday bear his name. Ice made it impossible for Hudson's ship to return to open sea; after a difficult winter spent anchored in the bay, Hudson's crew mutinied and set him adrift in a small boat. Hudson and a few loyal crewmen were thus left to starve. Despite the failure of Hudson's expedition, for the next 250 years, a steady stream of British explorers came into contact with the Canadian Inuit. In

1670, the Hudson's Bay Company—still in existence today—was established by royal charter, giving British traders a firm foothold in Inuit lands. By the end of the 17th century, the British had established trading posts and religious missions there. The missionaries brought to the Inuit the previously unknown concepts of sin and damnation; the merchants introduced them to greed and aggression.

The Russian Era in Alaska

On the northwest coast of North America, no significant contact between natives and outsiders occurred until the middle of the 18th century. In 1648, a party of Cossacks, traders, and hunters under the leadership of Semyon Dezhnyov sailed eastward from the Kolyma River, in northeastern Russia, around the Cukotski Peninsula to the mouth of the Anadyr River. Dezhnyov and his crew thus became the first Europeans to sail through the strait dividing Asia from North America. Their success inspired Czar Peter the Great of Russia in 1725 to commission the Danish navigator Vitus Bering to discover whether or not North America and Siberia were connected by land. Bering's last voyage for that purpose was the most significant; in 1741, he sighted Mount Saint Elias in southeastern Alaska and charted the location of the Aleutians. When scurvy wracked his crew, Bering was forced to land and winter on what would later be called Bering Island, 100 miles east of the Kamchatka Peninsula. His ship, the *St. Peter*, was destroyed in the process; Bering himself perished on the island from the combined effects of scurvy, exhaustion, and exposure. His crew built a new ship from the wreckage of the old, and with Alexei Chirikov, the captain of the expedition's second ship, returned to Russia laden with $30,000 worth of sea otter skins.

Spurred by the wealth of furs brought home by the surviving crew of the Bering expedition, Russian traders undertook regular expeditions to North America; by the end of the 18th century they had made over

Two woodcuts by Greenlander Aron of Kangeq illustrating Inuit legends of conflict with Norse settlers. At top, Norsemen kill Inuit women and children; at bottom, Inuit retaliate by burning the Norse house at Ameralik and killing all but the Norse chief, Uunngortoq.

English explorer Martin Frobisher, one of the first Europeans to make contact with the peoples of the Arctic. Queen Elizabeth I invested in his expeditions and appointed him "High Admiral of England in Cathay."

80 trips. While amassing great wealth for themselves, the Russian traders robbed the Aleuts of their food and clothing sources by decimating the local populations of fur seals, sea otters, and foxes. In the mid-18th century, before the large-scale intrusion of foreigners, as many as 25,000 Aleuts lived in hundreds of villages throughout the Aleutian Islands, making the region one of the most densely populated in the world. But this did not prevent greedy traders from exploiting the Aleuts. The pirating fur traders raped and beat the native women, enslaved thousands, and murdered thousands more. Villages were systematically destroyed, and entire populations were transferred from their homes to unfamiliar places like the Pribilof Islands, breeding grounds for the fur seals and therefore more profitable for the traders. By 1766, between 70 and 90 percent of the Aleut population had been murdered or had died of starvation, unfamiliar diseases, or mistreatment. The few thousand who survived were employed as forced labor in the Russian fur trade.

International competition for the lucrative fur trade, centered on the islands as well as on the mainland, began to grow. In 1774 and 1775, the Spanish sent expeditions along the southwestern coast of Alaska. In 1778, British captain James Cook made extensive surveys of the Arctic coast. In 1786, the French sent an expedition under Jean François de Galaup, comte de la Pérouse. England, the newly formed United States, and China hastened to form Alaskan trading companies. Despite international competition, the Russians continued to dominate the Arctic trade. In 1781, the Shelekhov Company was founded by Grigory Shelekhov, an Irkutsk merchant who in 1784 established a small colony at Three Saints Bay, near the southwestern end of Kodiak Island. In 1799, the Shelekhov Company became the Russian American Company, in an attempt by the Russian government to regulate what had hitherto been a completely arbitrary exploitation of the fur resources. The Russian American Company was granted a monopoly on all trade and hunting; its first manager, Aleksandr Baranov, guided the company through 20 years of systematic and often brutal exploitation. By the turn of the century, the Russian American Company had established the first missionary school on Kodiak Island, and the Russians had begun baptizing Aleuts into the Russian Orthodox religion.

The fur trade expanded rapidly throughout mainland Alaska and the Yukon Territory. Because Russian traders on the vast mainland were a distinct minority with no easy means of retreat, they were forced to use more restraint in dealing with the Inuit than they had shown on the Aleutian Islands. A company representative would identify a native community leader and appoint him a *toion*, or chief. These leaders were given a silver medal that announced their special status as economic intermediaries. Toions encouraged the villagers to provide the Russian traders with furs; they collected and distributed any money and goods that were received from the trade, such as tobacco and pipes, a variety of dry goods, knives and needles, kettles and cooking pots, mirrors and combs, beads and jewelry, and "southern" clothing and blankets. The Inuit were encouraged to become indebted to and dependent on the Russian American Company. The Inuit of Alaska and northwestern Canada yielded not to violence, as had the Aleuts, but to the demand for European goods.

The Russian American Company encouraged Russian Orthodox missionary activity. In southwestern Alaska, the missionaries followed the paths of the traders; by midcentury, all Inuit, with the possible exception of those in Yukon Delta communities, had at least an acquaintance with the Russian Orthodox religion. In northwestern Alaska, Inuit remained largely unacquainted with Christianity until the late 19th century, when missionaries from the Episcopal, Moravian, Congregational, and Presbyterian churches made contact. These missionaries made a strong initial impact on the clustered Inuit villages of the Northwest by establishing schools and by providing medical services. Inuit children were educated in the Russian cul-

A hand-colored woodcut printed in 1567 showing an Inuit woman and child kidnapped by French sailors, probably from Labrador, in 1566. This handbill was printed in Nuremberg, Germany, to advertise their exhibition in Europe.

ture, a policy that created the opportunity for persistent and lasting Russian influence.

Commercial whaling in both the western (Russian) and eastern (British) seas of the Arctic increased rapidly in the 1840s and 1850s. The Inuit regularly traded with the whalers, exchanging baleen, used as a strong thread or for weaving into buckets, for a variety of products, including for the first time firearms and alcohol in addition to the usual tobacco and dry goods. Whalers also brought diseases such as smallpox, pneumonia, tuberculosis, measles, and influenza, destroying the health and the lives of a large part of the Inuit population. Even when these diseases did not prove fatal, they weakened the Inuit's ability to hunt and maintain their traditional economy.

U.S. and Canadian Commerce Come North

By the mid-19th century, Russian control of the Arctic was weakening, due both to continued resistance from natives (for example, the Tlingit revolted against Baranov in 1802) and to the encroachment of the British Hudson's Bay Company. In 1839, Russia leased all of southeastern Alaska to the Hudson's Bay Company, an agreement that may have reduced Russia's power in the Arctic fur trade but also reduced its problems with trade regulation and safety. Not quite 30 years later, Edouard de Stoeckl, Russian minister to Washington, approached Secretary of State William H. Seward with an offer he could not refuse. On March 30, 1867, the treaty of purchase was signed; on May 28, President Andrew Johnson signed his name to the deal; and on October 18, 1867, the formal transfer of Alaska from Russia to the United States was completed. The United States bought the Alaskan territory for only $7.2 million, a now famous bargain that at the time was met with ridicule. Envisioning Alaska as a land barren of all resources but snow, scoffers nicknamed the sale Seward's Folly and the land Seward's Icebox and Johnson's Polar Bear Garden. The sale and purchase of Alaska was arranged with no thought either to compensating or consulting the 35,000 native Alaskans; consequently, the Indians, Inuit, and Aleuts suffered the most from the transfer. According to the terms of the treaty, settled inhabitants were given the option of returning to Russia. If they chose to remain in Alaska, however, "with the exception of uncivilized native tribes, [they] shall be admitted to the enjoyment of all the rights, advantages, and immunities of citizens of the United States." The Arctic peoples were considered unfit for U.S. citizenship.

During the latter half of the 19th century, Canada began to assert its sovereignty over the vast but thinly populated Arctic territories north of its provinces. In 1870, the Canadian parliament laid claim to the Arctic mainland north of North America. In 1880, Great Britain officially ceded to Canada the Arctic islands it had previously claimed. The North American Arctic now officially belonged to just two countries: Canada and the United States.

This change of governing power radically altered the economic situation of many northern communities. The United States's Alaska Commercial Company, which had bought the assets of the Russian American Company, abandoned the paternalism of its predecessor. The Alaska Commercial Company halted credit and called in all loans, actions that further plunged the Inuit into debt. Half of the payment for their furs was automatically applied to their debts, leaving them very little money with which to buy the goods they had grown to depend on.

In the 1880s, commercial fishing became an important industry in the Arctic, and within 60 years it had supplanted fur trading as the region's primary large-scale business. It was also the first business to offer true wage employment to the many Inuit and Aleuts who had been abused by fur traders and who were no longer able to support themselves through subsistence hunting. The jobs open to the Native Americans, however, were almost exclusively menial labor. As the fishing

Young Inuit girls of the Catholic mission at Akulurak in the Yukon at their first communion. Newcomers to the North had little if any respect for the spiritual beliefs and practices of the native inhabitants.

industry grew, codfish-salting and salmon-packing plants, first founded on the Alaska Peninsula and the Shumagin Islands, were also established farther east. Like the native subsistence fishing that had preceded it, the large-scale fishing industry was a seasonal one. During the summer, workers migrated to Alaskan and Canadian harbors for jobs in commercial fishing; during the winter, they turned to traditional hunting and trapping.

In 1880, gold was discovered near present-day Juneau, Alaska; in 1896, gold strikes in the Klondike region of Canada led to a rush to the region. Eighteen ninety-nine saw the Nome rush; 1903, the rush near Fairbanks of the "sourdough" miners (so named because of a bread they baked). These rushes in Canada's Yukon Territory and in Alaska brought a flood of southerners and mining jobs to the Far North, but the boom of mining jobs was brief, and the huge increase in population only resulted in the need for more adequate government, including a criminal and civil code. The seasonal fishing and whaling industries continued to provide virtually all employment in Alaska and northern Canada. Because commercial whalers had drastically reduced the population of all sea mammals, further damaging the native population's chances of independent survival, the governments of the United

States and Canada decided to establish a new industry tailored to the native peoples of the Arctic.

Sheldon Jackson, Alaska's first superintendent of education and a former general secretary of the Presbyterian missions, conceived the idea of saving the native Arctic population from starvation by introducing reindeer herds from Siberia. Although Jackson's motives may have been pure, his plan was a prime example of the kind of assimilationism that had governed the United States's policies concerning all Native Americans. In 1887, Congress had passed the Dawes Severalty Act, which was designed to encourage Native Americans to engage in farming, "thus civilizing him and ridding our nation of the burden and blight of the Indian problem." Because farming was not an option for the Arctic peoples, in 1892 the U.S. government brought a herd of 1,280 reindeer from Siberia to northern Alaska and the easternmost Aleutians. Chukchi herdsmen were brought from Siberia to train the Inuit in herding; later, Lapp herders replaced the unsuccessful Chukchi. At first, most herds were owned by non-Inuit, but by 1918, Inuit owned 69 percent of the herds. After 1918, however, the reindeer industry rapidly became dominated by non-Inuit companies such as Loman Brothers. Not until the Reindeer Act of 1937 were holdings of reindeer by non-Inuit prohibited, but by that time the reindeer industry had already declined in importance.

The forced installation of Aleuts and Inuit as captains of the reindeer industry was meant to make them independent capitalists, but the scheme was ill conceived. Arctic peoples had never been stationary farmers or herders. They well understood migratory hunting and had established successful economies until the arrival of Europeans destroyed their traditional way of life. In addition to the Inuit being unfit for close herding, the reindeer themselves proved a problem. They were subject to parasites; many were killed by wolves. Some tended to wander off and join caribou herds. Left unattended by inexperienced Inuit herders, they overgrazed large areas of land. Although a privately owned herd of 13,000 reindeer exists today in central Canada, the animals had almost entirely disappeared from the Arctic by the 1950s.

By the early 20th century, the diminishing whale population had made subsistence whaling almost impossible, and commercial whaling had grown so unprofitable that the industry had all but died. In the second decade of the 20th century, the preparation and sale of fox furs replaced commercial whaling as the strongest industry in the Arctic, providing the bulk of Inuit and Aleut income in the years before World War II. The Hudson's Bay Company, long the dominant power in the economy of the Canadian Arctic, monopolized the white fox fur trade. From 1909 to 1929, by moving the Inuit off land it wanted, the Hudson's Bay Company expanded its profitable fox fur industry from Quebec throughout the Canadian Arctic.

In 1933, Alaskan natives rejected a proposal by the commissioner of Indian affairs, John Collier, to set aside 2 million acres of land as native reservations. In May 1884, Congress had passed the Organic Act, declaring Alaska a civil and judicial district and guaranteeing natives the right to possess and occupy lands "actually

An Aleut killing gang, led by Americans, slaughter a pod of seals on St. Paul Island. Russian, American, and English exploitation of the region's natural resources destroyed the Arctic's native economy.

in their use." Nevertheless, Alaskan natives had never had land officially set aside for their exclusive use; unlike the Native Americans in the lower 48 states, they had never signed a treaty with the United States. Their land claims were routinely ignored by the government, as evidenced by its 1933 proposal for the establishment of Alaskan reservations, in spite of the fact that the land was privately "in use." Not until the land claims and native rights movements of the 1970s would the desires of the Alaskan Inuit and Aleuts be considered.

Alaskan Inuit with their sled reindeer near the Kuzitrin River on the Seward Peninsula in the 1920s. The U.S. government's introduction of reindeer herding to the Inuit was ill conceived.

The Push Northward

Despite the powerful fishing industry in coastal Alaska and the lure of a wealth of natural resources, the isolation and harsh climate of the Arctic limited contact between the Inuit and southerners until World War II. Vast stretches of the Arctic, particularly the Alaskan interior and the northernmost regions of Canada's Northwest and Yukon territories, remained largely untouched by southern influence and were still able to support the traditional Inuit economy. However, during the Second World War and the years that followed, an increasing military and industrial presence largely reshaped what remained of the traditional Arctic way of life.

In June 1942, Japanese amphibious forces landed on the westernmost Aleutian islands of Attu and Kiska, taking 39 Aleuts and 2 non-Aleut schoolteachers prisoner. In an effort to protect the rest of the Aleut population from further Japanese aggression and to facilitate the construction of military installations on the Aleutian Islands, the United States government forcibly relocated 863 Aleuts, more than half of them from the Pribilof Islands, to villages in southeastern Alaska.

After the war, those who had survived the displacement were moved back to the Pribilof and Aleutian Islands, but the construction of airstrips and military barracks and the results of Japanese machine-gun strafing and years of neglect had made the islands almost unrecognizable. In 1988, the Aleuts who had suffered forcible displacement were offered an official apology by the United States government and given $12,000 each in damages.

The increased U.S. military presence during World War II transformed even the most isolated regions of the Arctic. From 1941 to 1943, for example, the United States Air Force erected first a weather station and then an air base for refueling military supply planes at Iqaluit (at that time called Frobisher Bay by non-Inuit) in Canada's Northwest Territories. Control of this airfield was turned over to the Royal Canadian Air Force in 1946, but the American military continued to build. From 1955 to 1957, during the cold war between the United States and the Soviet Union, the U.S. military constructed the Distant Early Warning (DEW) line, a series of radar stations designed for detection of Soviet bomber attacks, spanning territory from Alaska to eastern Canada. To complete this project, the military bulldozed, dismantled, or moved individual sod houses and entire villages. The Inuit, many of whom spoke no English, and some of whom relied on the temporary government construction jobs, issued no formal protest.

During the 1950s, the Canadian federal government, which until then had largely ignored its Arctic lands, began to assert its sovereignty. The herding of nomadic Inuit into fixed settlements, a process that had begun with the construction of military installations during the war, became commonplace. To make relocation easier to monitor, the Canadian sovereignty program routinely assigned the Inuit numbers that took the place of their names as their official designations. The settlement at Grise Fjord, Canada's northernmost community, is typical of the relocation program; it was established in 1953 with three Inuit families transported from northern Quebec by the Royal Canadian Mounted Police. The fish and game bird population in northern Quebec had almost disappeared; at first, the Inuit families gladly accepted the government's offer to move them to an area rich in walrus, seals, and polar bears. But the people had no experience in hunting these animals. "It was like landing on the moon," said John Amagoalik, one of the original settlers of nearby Resolute.

These makeshift villages marked the end of nomadic settlement patterns among almost all Inuit. The villages provided free housing, health care, schools, and other social services intended to ensure the Inuit a decent standard of living and to strengthen their ability to cope in a wage economy. In spite of these good intentions, the government's presence in the communities only served to further debilitate the native population. Once southerners had depended on the natives for survival in the Arctic, but with the rise of the fur and fishing industries, European capitalists had perverted their dependent relationship to the Inuit through economic and personal chicanery. By the mid-20th century, when natives agreed to live a government-designed life-style, the remaining vestiges of their independence were few. The Inuit left behind their self-sufficient life of hunting, fishing, and trapping and came to the government towns for jobs, services, and government-mandated education. The jobs, most of which were with the Canadian government, were usually temporary; they ended as soon as projects were completed or villages were constructed. The displaced Inuit found themselves dependent on welfare payments and other government support programs.

After military installations had established a permanent presence in northern Alaska and Canada, active exploration for oil and other natural resources began. Airstrips and new communications systems made the region much more accessible and much more profitable than it had once been. Daily airmail and freight services proliferated, facilitating the growth of trade and industry, which expanded so rapidly that by the 1970s the tiny airfield at Resolute had become the third-busiest airport in Canada. However, the oil, gas, and natural resource industries provided few jobs to the Inuit they displaced. Rather than train native workers, industries imported skilled labor from the south; as late as 1985, only 18 of the 528 jobs on the DEW line were held by natives.

Land Claims Settlements

In the 1960s and 1970s, through growing "Eskimo Power" movements, Arctic peoples in both Canada and Alaska began to assert the rights of native peoples to control their land, resources, and political destiny. The Alaska Statehood Act, passed on July 7, 1958, represented a direct threat to the survival of native claims. While the state disclaimed any right to land and property held by Alaskan natives or held in trust for them by the United States, it was granted the right to select more than 104 million acres from the pubic domain that were "vacant, unappropriated or unreserved" at the time of selection. Naturally, the state selected the best land, much of which natives considered their own. In October 1966, eight regional native associations that had formed to protect land rights joined to become the Alaska Federation of Natives (AFN). By April 1967, the AFN had submitted title claims to 370 million of Alaska's 375 million acres. The federal government halted disposal of the Alaskan public lands subject to native claims; a court order halted all oil drilling until the land claims were settled. Competing regional interests, unique languages, and age-old distrust among Inuit, Aleuts, and Indians temporarily hindered communication within the AFN. Nevertheless, on December 18, 1971, the U.S. government approved passage of the Alaska Native Claims Settlement Act (ANCSA).

ANCSA provided that 44 million acres of land be made available for selection by Alaskan natives for their ownership and exclusive use. Cash payments totaling $462.5 million were to be made over an 11-year period,

An Inuit family listens to a large Zenith radio in 1926. The mass media has played a major role in the disintegration of native culture.

and an additional $500 million was to be paid in revenues from oil and mineral resource lands controlled by the state or federal government. The money and the title to the land were conveyed through 13 regional and 220 village corporations created by the act. All shares in the corporations were to be owned exclusively by Alaskan natives for 20 years. Regional corporations were assigned four main responsibilities: to receive all cash payments made under the act and to invest or distribute the money to village corporations or individuals; to become owners of surface estate of some land and owners of subsurface estate of all land selected by ANCSA; to supervise the creation of village corporations and aid them in making land selections and in operating businesses; and to operate one or more businesses for profit.

By 1974, 76,500 Inuit, Aleuts, and Alaskan Indians had enrolled in the regional corporations. Since then, some native corporations have done well by diversifying their holdings in enterprises ranging from timber and fish to mining and telecommunications. But many corporations, placed in the hands of people inexperienced in the business world, made poor investments; drastic reductions in oil, timber, and mineral prices in the 1970s and 1980s severely damaged others.

In 1986, 3 native corporations filed for bankruptcy, and in 1987, Alaskan state officials reported that 18 Inuit villages were in critical financial condition.

In February 1988, Congress amended ANCSA to help native Alaskans maintain control of their holdings. The most important provision of the amendment allows native corporations, through a majority vote of the stockholders, to ban the sale of stock to outsiders, which under ANCSA would have been permissible as of January 1, 1992. The 1988 amendment also bans taxation of undeveloped corporate lands. Undeveloped lands, reserved primarily for subsistence hunting and fishing, produce no wealth; taxation had placed an unbearable burden on the corporations and their shareholders.

Throughout the 1970s and the early 1980s, Canada reached a number of limited regional agreements, all modeled after ANCSA. In September 1988, Prime Minister Brian Mulroney signed an agreement that ceded ownership of 260,000 square miles along the Arctic

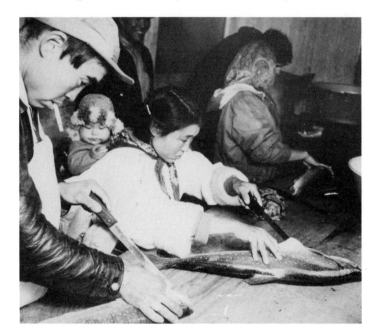

Inuit workers clean char at Port Burwell in the Canadian Arctic in 1961. Inuit often find seasonal employment at fish canneries and processing plants.

Ocean to Canada's natives and provided them with nearly $1 billion in compensation. The act also guaranteed natives a strong voice in determining the mineral development, including oil and gas exploration, of another 1 million square miles. This decision gave Canadian natives the power to determine the future of more than 30 percent of the nation's land.

This agreement may ultimately lead to the successful assimilation of native Arctic peoples into a monetary economy, but the native corporations established through earlier regional agreements in Canada and Alaska have met with uneven success. Some have come close to collapse; others, such as the Inuvialuit Development Corporation, owned by Inuit on the coast of the Beaufort Sea, have achieved great success as diversified conglomerates. The Pan-Inuit movement is relatively young; time will determine the real success of groups such as those Alaskan, Canadian, and Greenlander Inuit who in 1977 met at the Inuit Circumpolar Conference to share their experiences and to plan for the future.

The Inuit settlement at Baker Lake in northern Canada. According to Andrew Goussaert, a housing executive quoted in Inuit, *the building of Inuit housing settlements created a lot of problems: "Inuit coming from different areas were not used to living close together; they were used to spreading out in order to survive."*

*An Inuit hunter on his snow-
mobile in Igloolik, Canada. The
arrival of modern technology has
done much to dissolve traditional
Inuit cultural patterns.*

A FEEL FOR
THE CULTURE

In the last thirty years," Theo Ikummaq, an Inuit leader of Arctic expeditions, told *Maclean's* magazine in 1987, "we have gone from the Stone Age to the middle ages to the space age. Now the younger people are introduced to the school system at an early age. That is good, but they don't have a feel for the culture that my generation does. And there are going to be fewer and fewer young people who care. That is how cultures are lost."

Modern American culture has influenced every aspect of Arctic life. Motorboats, snowmobiles, and rifles have radically altered the nature of hunting. Imported foods are available in village stores. People especially welcome bread, cake, sugar, and coffee; the children's fondness for soda and candy has led to widespread dental and weight problems. Today, Arctic peoples generally wear flannel shirts and wool or cotton pants. Even traditional items of clothing such as parkas and mukluks tend to be store bought. In the 1950s and 1960s, most traditional sod-and-stone houses, tents, and igloos were replaced with government-supplied housing. Most of the new structures were imported prefab houses; they often arrived damaged or defective, and many were not equipped with plumbing. Government housing was poorly insulated against the Arctic cold; the high cost of home heating oil increased the Inuit's dependence on the government and on whatever menial jobs were locally available. The aspect of modern culture that exerts the strongest pull on the Arctic people is new technology. Just as the first Inuit to meet Europeans wanted metal knives and rifles, today's Inuit seek to acquire modern technology in the form of outboard motors, snowmobiles, sewing machines, televisions, and computers.

Of all modern conveniences introduced in the Arctic, television has had the greatest influence. Only the village of Igloolik in Canada's Northwest Territories voted against the installation of TV equipment, fearing it would destroy local traditions and values. In all communities with more than 400 people, the Northern Service of the Canadian Broadcasting Corporation supplies a steady stream of news, weather, and sports as well as programs such as "I Love Lucy," "Dallas," and "Star Trek." Television exposes Arctic peoples not only to the English language and contemporary ideas but also to the values of a consumer society.

The desire for modern technology and consumer products among Arctic peoples creates a need to join the wage economy. Even those Inuit who subsist primarily through hunting and fishing need part-time jobs to finance gasoline for snowmobiles or motorboats and to buy clothing, household goods, or food from the village store. Although it has almost replaced the traditional subsistence economy, the monetary economy has largely failed Arctic peoples. Since the middle of the 19th century, the majority of jobs that have been available to Inuit and Aleuts have been seasonal or menial. Unfortunately, many large employers, such as those in the oil and fish industries, find it more convenient to import labor from the south than to provide natives with vocational training. A lack of technical skills seriously

limits employment opportunities. The unskilled Inuit may work as a janitor, dishwasher, sweeper, or shipping clerk for an airport and may receive less than the minimum wage.

To escape from the cycle of poverty in the new monetary economy, the Inuit and Aleuts turned to the government for help. In the 1950s, Canada's newly formed Department of Northern Affairs and Natural Resources established "rehabilitation centres" for Canadian Inuit. These centers, agencies of deliberate cultural change, were intended to prepare the Inuit for productive careers in the new economy. Each Inuit was given room, board, clothing, and a cash allowance (about $50.00 a month in 1963) and was trained in semiskilled labor such as sewing, cooking, baking, carpentry, waiting tables, printmaking, office work, and sales. Although the program was designed to provide Inuit hunters and their families with technical and social skills appropriate to modern white society, its paternalistic structure only nurtured a debilitating dependency.

An Inuit family at home near Baker Lake, Canada. A television plays in the background, and posters with Christian pictures and messages line the walls. American and European culture has influenced every aspect of Inuit personal and private life.

Although adult education programs of this kind have largely failed, they have made Inuit aware of the need to educate their children in the modern culture that has firmly established itself in the Arctic. The decision to let others teach their children new and foreign ways is fraught with anxiety. "At the same time that we are pushing towards our own culture," Charlie Evalik, an Inuit of Cambridge Bay, explained to author Ulli Steltzer in 1982, "we are trying to get the kids through grade 12 and maybe even more schooling—pushing them into the mainstream of white culture. That's where the conflict is."

To increase their children's educational opportunities, Inuit have had to abandon the migratory way of life. Most high schools for Canada's Inuit are regional and serve young people scattered over hundreds of miles. When the government made school attendance mandatory, Inuit parents were forced to choose between establishing a permanent home close to a school or sending their children away from home for the duration of their schooling.

Education is a powerful agent of assimilation. While most Inuit in Canada and the Alaskan interior had little formal schooling available to them until the 1950s, 76 percent of all Aleut children were attending school by 1940. The public schools discouraged the teaching of native cultures and forbade teaching in native languages. Not until 1973 were four Aleuts trained to teach in both Aleut and English. By that time, because the Aleuts had become so assimilated into mainstream white culture, the bilingual instructors were teaching a language that was almost dead. Contemporary Inuit have experienced a similar alienation from their native culture. Only a few Inuit are certified to teach, and Inuit children are taught about their culture as if it were foreign. Joseph Senungetuk, an Inuit, wrote about the dispiriting nature of such education:

The schools which the native children attend are silent about the original cultures of the Eskimo, Indian, and Aleut. More often they teach the young Eskimo students that a "primitive" race still exists somewhere in the northernmost part of the northern hemisphere, and that this race eats raw meat and lives in ice igloos. When I read this in a sixth grade geography book . . . I hadn't the faintest idea they were talking about me.

In some form or another, racism has existed since the Arctic peoples' earliest contact with Europeans and Americans, and subtle forms of racism often pervade even well-meaning attempts at assistance by contemporary society. The name "rehabilitation centre," for example, suggests the idea that the Inuit way of life is a disease or a crime, something to cure or to atone for. Most Inuit and Aleut young people experience some form of anxiety in trying to reconcile the two disparate cultures. "We are living in two cultures," explained Kakinik Naluiyuk, a young Inuit resident of Sugluk in the Northwest Territories. "We know our own, but we don't understand what makes the television run, or the

Inuit welders work on the pipeline in northern Alaska. In 1977, 800 miles of trans-Alaska pipeline was completed. The pipeline allows 1.5 million barrels of oil a day to travel to the southern port of Valdez, but comparatively few Inuit were employed in its construction.

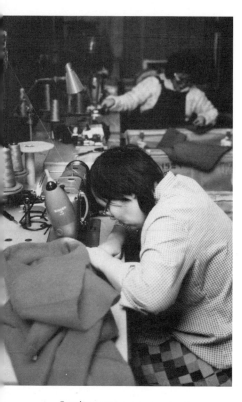

Inuit women sew coats at a cooperative. Tamusi Tulugak, general manager of Povungnituk Co-operative, sees the cooperative movement as a logical extension of the communal ways of the Inuit past: "Our forefathers supported each other. That was their way to survive. The co-operative movement, even though it was first introduced to us by some southerners, is our only chance to keep our forefathers' culture alive."

stove, or how to repair them—all the things from the south that we have and want. We are trapped without realizing how it happened."

Industrial and governmental expansion in the Arctic has forcibly pulled the native population out of their old culture; it has not, however, provided for their full welcome into the new. Most Aleut traditions, for example, have disappeared entirely. Yet even among these most thoroughly assimilated of all northern peoples, less than 25 percent of the people work full time year-round, and old ways die hard. "You think we are lonely when we are out on the land," Roger Kuptana, an Inuit from Sachs Harbour, said in 1982. "I tell you, it's the people in the city who are lonely." Those who wish to assimilate often find their opportunities restricted. The Inuit and Aleut families who moved to urban areas have found themselves confined to menial jobs and ghetto neighborhoods. Even college graduates find no profitable work when they return to their communities. The cost of living in both Alaska and the Canadian Arctic is at least 40 percent higher than it is in the rest of North America. In 1986, a head of lettuce or a loaf of bread cost up to $3.00; a dozen eggs, $4.50; and a gallon of milk, $10.00. The combination of job shortages for both the unskilled and the educated and a devastatingly high cost of living has made the Arctic peoples some of the poorest in North America.

With no sense of truly belonging to either their native or to the modern society, many Inuit have lost a secure sense of their identity as individuals and of their purpose as a group. This sense of uselessness has taken a toll on the physical and mental health of Arctic peoples. Among the Inuit, alcoholism, violence, suicide, venereal disease, and mental breakdowns have increased dramatically since World War II. From 1959 to 1974, the suicide rate among the Inuit tripled. According to one 1980 study, the alcoholism rate among the Inuit of Point Barrow, Alaska, is 72 percent; adults here drink twice as much as the average American adult. Dr. Edward

Foulks, one of the researchers of the study, reported that "drinking never really caught on before the last decade, when the values of the traditional society were minimized by the appearance of a supermarket, a dry goods store and high cash income."

To help regain a sense of identity and to combat the negative effects of assimilation, Inuit and Aleuts have worked to preserve elements of their traditional culture within the larger white culture. The Eskimo Power movements of the 1960s and 1970s inspired people to direct their ethnic consciousness toward the founding of uniquely native political and economic organizations. "We can't shut the doors to the outside world," native rights leader John Amagoalik explained in 1979. "We just want to be self-sustaining again, to have our language and traditions of equal importance, and to have more local control over decisions that affect us."

The first organizations that effectively preserved cultural traditions were economic cooperatives. The Inuit decided to make their way in the monetary economy by

Inuit children at a Point Hope school watch "Sesame Street" on closed-circuit television. Inuit parents are more aware than ever of the importance of educating their children to increase their chances of economic prosperity.

utilizing skills they had developed in the old subsistence economy. With the encouragement of Canada's Department of Northern Affairs and Natural Resources, Inuit living on the George River in northern Quebec formed the first Inuit cooperative in 1959. With $12,500 borrowed from the government, the George River Inuit bought fishing boats, freezers, and other equipment that allowed them to found their own commercial fishery.

Other cooperatives followed, each owned and operated by members of small Inuit communities. The cooperatives did not require their workers to learn English or industrial arts. Their accommodating policies inspired many Inuit to go off welfare rolls and to gain a degree of economic independence. In using traditional skills and communal attitudes to draw people together to support survival, the cooperatives roughly paralleled the Inuit way before the intrusion of Europeans and Americans and served as models for the regional and village corporations later established by both Alaskan and Canadian settlements of land claims

Anxiety about the future of the land and the culture of the Arctic has also led to the foundation of a number of ethnic political organizations. The first of these was the Alaska Native Brotherhood, founded in 1913 to prepare Aleuts, Inuit, and Alaskan Indians to exercise the rights and duties of U.S. citizenship. Later organizations, especially those formed in the 1960s and 1970s, focused not so much on easing northerners' adjustment to southern culture but on preserving northern traditions. These political groups include the Alaska Federation of Natives (AFN), founded in 1966; the Aleut League, formed in 1967 and later absorbed by the AFN; and the Committee for Original Peoples Entitlement (COPE), which led the fight for native land claims in the Northwest Territories during the 1970s and 1980s. The largest ethnic federation in the Arctic today, Inuit Tapirisat (The People Together) of Canada, attempts to negotiate political solutions to problems such as wildlife management, the preservation of environmental integrity, the restoration of self-sufficiency, and language

maintenance. The first Inuit Circumpolar Conference, in 1977, brought together Inuit from Greenland, Alaska, and Canada.

With most land claims now settled, maintaining Aleut and Inuit traditions and languages has become the foremost goal of the ethnic organizations. In many northern communities, the speaking of native languages, forbidden in public schools until the 1970s, had almost entirely disappeared. Since the 1960s, however, Arctic peoples have enlisted the mass media, the most powerful tool of acculturation, as an equally powerful tool of preservation. Anchorage's *Tundra Times*, a 12-page weekly newspaper first published in 1962, was the first mass media effort to strike a balance between preservation of the old culture and adoption of the new.

Although effective on a small scale, *Tundra Times* and magazines like *Inuit Today* have had limited success in reaching the entire Arctic population. Television, which

The Point Hope village council in session. In recent years Inuit political leaders have been very successful in safeguarding Inuit rights, particularly regarding land claims.

reaches at least 86 percent of all Inuit in the United States and Canada via satellite, has had a more widespread impact. In 1981, the Canadian government formed the Inuit Broadcasting Corporation (IBC) designed to produce programming about the Inuit in their own language. In 1985, Canadian television aired the first programs produced by the IBC. Although Inuit programming is still limited to less than 10 hours a week, most Inuit see it as an effective tool in combating the cultural and linguistic disintegration that television itself accelerated.

Programming in the Inuktitut language is just the most visible of many efforts at preserving northern traditions. In recent years, northern activists have won significant concessions from the Alaskan and Canadian governments allowing for the preservation of native languages. Since the 1970s, most public schools in Alaska and the Canadian Arctic have included instruction in Inuit or Aleut languages. The Inuit achieved another major victory in the 1980s, when the Northwest Territories' assembly began to incorporate the Inuktitut language, as well as the Slavey language of the Dene family, in its official proceedings and documents. Many place-names in Canada have recently been changed back from the English names that honored explorers and colonists to their original Inuit names, which describe features of the landscape.

Other efforts to preserve traditional culture have taken the form of recreational events. The Northern Games, held annually since 1970, bring Inuit together for three days of competition in traditional skills. Public schools often sponsor limited programs or classes in traditional hunting, trapping, and survival skills. One of the most curious programs designed to preserve traditional skills is sponsored by the Baffin Correctional Centre in Iqaluit. Believing that some Inuit who turn to crime or violence do so as a result of a loss of cultural identity, this prison program takes a group of inmates into the Arctic wilderness for two weeks and teaches them traditional hunting skills they may be able to use after their release.

Looking to the Future

The political activism of the 1960s and 1970s has guaranteed that many aspects of Inuit and Aleut culture will survive. Yet even after dramatically increasing ethnic awareness and winning landmark settlements of land claims, Arctic peoples are still fighting for control of their future. In Akiachak and other communities in Alaska, for example, Inuit village councils dissolved the local government, declaring the villages henceforth governed solely by tribal law. Many Inuit of the Northwest and Yukon territories want to see their land renamed Nunavit and granted provincial status by Canada's parliament.

For Arctic peoples, the 1990s and the 21st century promise to be a time of rapid change. Having been

Inuit hunters securing lines to a captured whale in the Chukchi Sea. "Except for the store, the post office, the washeteria, and the village government, there are no jobs in Akiachak. Without subsistence, there would be only food stamps. That is not how my forefathers intended us to live," said Inuit activist Willie Kasyulie in 1987.

Nannie Ooyahtoana and her grandson, Clyde Howarth, a city councilman from Point Hope, Alaska. Heirs to a rich cultural tradition, many young Inuit are the possessors of a reawakened sense of ethnic pride, but the challenge of defining themselves in terms of the modern society of which they are a part, however reluctantly, remains a great one.

forced from a state of independence to a state of almost complete dependence on the government, Inuit and Aleuts have been working on the difficult transition back to self-sufficiency. A complete transition will take some time. As recently as 1980, for example, there were no full-blooded Inuit doctors or lawyers. Today, an increasing number of Inuit and Aleuts are attending college and preparing to become doctors, lawyers, business executives, engineers, and teachers. Still, in 1985, less than four percent of native Alaskan adults had graduated from college. Until their educational and professional experience can bear fruit, the money, resources, and land provided in land claims settlements will help Arctic peoples in their struggle for economic independence.

Through cooperatives and native corporations, Arctic natives are hoping to find a balance between the traditional skills of the past and the economy of the present. Unfortunately, traditional skills are becoming more difficult to practice because increased industry and development have irreversibly altered the Arctic environment. Within the next 25 years, environmental pollution may make it impossible to practice the time-honored ways, even on a recreational basis. Traces of toxic polychlorinated biphenyls (PCBs), used as a coolant in now dismantled DEW line stations, have already been found in the tissues of polar bears, seals, and fish near Iqaluit. Old outboard motors, broken dogsleds, and parts of snowmobiles litter the backyards of Inuit villages. In March 1989, the worst oil spill in United States history emptied 240,000 barrels of oil into Prince William Sound on the southern coast of Alaska, killing thousands of birds, seals, and other animals in the area. Inuit and Aleut leaders have cautioned against the further destruction of their land through haphazard, unregulated development, but whether these warnings will be heeded and steps taken to prevent the destruction of the Arctic wilderness and what remains of its traditional culture, only time will tell.

FURTHER READING

Aigner, Jean S. *The Inuit*. New York: Chelsea House, 1990.

Damas, David, ed. *Handbook of North American Indians, Vol. 5, Arctic*. William C. Sturtevant, series editor. Washington, DC: Smithsonian Institution Press, 1984.

Duffy, R. Quinn. *The Road to Nunavut: The Progress of the Eastern Arctic Inuit Since the Second World War*. Kingston, Ontario: McGill-Queen's University Press, 1988.

Fitzburgh, William F., and Aron Cromwell. *Crossroads of Continents—Cultures of Siberia and Alaska*. Washington, DC: Smithsonian Institution Press, 1988.

Garfield, Viola E., and Linn A. Forrest. *The Wolf and the Raven: Totem Poles of Southeastern Alaska*. Seattle: University of Washington Press, 1973.

Miller, Polly, and Leon Gordon Miller. *Lost Heritage of Alaska: The Adventures and Art of the Alaskan Coastal Indians*. New York: Bonanza Books, 1967.

Oswalt, Wendell H. *Alaskan Eskimos*. San Francisco: Chandler, 1967.

———. *Eskimos and Explorers*. Novato, CA: Chandler & Sharp, 1979.

———. *This Land Was Theirs: A Study of North American Indians*. New York: Wiley, 1978.

Pitseolak, Peter, and Dorothy Eber. *People from Our Side: An Eskimo Life Story in Words and Photographs*. Bloomington: Indiana University Press, 1975.

Steltzer, Ulli. *Inuit: The North in Transition*. Chicago: University of Chicago Press, 1985.

INDEX

Loman Brothers, 85

Mackenzie River, 21
Maclean's magazine, 95
Montreal, Quebec, 26
Mount Saint Elias, 79
Mulroney, Brian, 92

Naluiyuk, Kakinik, 99
Nanook of the North, 25
Near Island, 30
Newfoundland, 21, 77
North Alaskan Eskimos, 35
Northwest Territories, Canada,
    18, 21, 25, 87, 88, 96, 99, 102,
    105
Northwest Territories Assembly,
    104
Norton culture, 21
Norton Sound, 21

Oregon, 15
Organic Act, 86

Pacific Eskimos, 35
Peter the Great, 79
Point Barrow, Alaska, 100
Pribilof Islands, 14, 15, 30, 80, 87–
    88
Prince William Sound, 107

Quebec, Canada, 25, 89, 10

Rat Island, 30
Reindeer Act of 1937, 85
Royal Canadian Air Force, 88

Royal Canadian Mounted Police,
    89
Russia, 79–82, 83
Russian American Company,
    80–81, 83

Sachs Harbour, 100
St. Peter, 79
Senungetuk, Joseph, 35, 98
Seward, William H., 82
Shelekhov, Grigory, 80
Shelekhov Company. *See* Rus-
    sian American Company
Shumagin Islands, 84
Siberia, 13, 14, 26, 85
Soviet Union, 13, 26, 88
Steltzer, Ulli, 98
Stoeckl, Edouard de, 82
Sugluk, Northern Territories, 99

Three Saints Bay, 80
Thule culture, 22–23, 25
Tlingit, 35, 82
Tsimshian, 35
Tundra Times, 103

Umnak Island, 19, 20
U.S. Air Force, 88
Unangan. *See* Aleuts

Washington, 15
World War II, 15, 86, 87–88, 100

Yukon Territory, Canada, 18, 25,
    27, 81, 84, 87, 105
Yupik Eskimo, 13

PICTURE CREDITS

KEVIN OSBORN is a free-lance writer and editor who has coauthored several volumes in the American Heritage *History of the United States* series. The author of many other books for children and adults, he helped create the characters for the young-adult fiction series *Not Quite Human*, which was the basis for a Disney Productions television movie of the same name. He is also the author of *The Ukrainian Americans*, published by Chelsea House.

DANIEL PATRICK MOYNIHAN is the senior United States senator from New York. He is also the only person in American history to serve in the cabinets or subcabinets of four successive presidents—Kennedy, Johnson, Nixon, and Ford. Formerly a professor of government at Harvard University, he has written and edited many books, including *Beyond the Melting Pot*, *Ethnicity: Theory and Experience* (both with Nathan Glazer), *Loyalties*, and *Family and Nation*.